JAMES N. ROWE
FIVE YEARS TO FREEDOM

BALLANTINE BOOKS • NEW YORK

Library of Congress Catalog Card Number: 70-128357

ISBN 0-345-31460-3

Printed in Canada

First Ballantine Books Edition: June 1984
Thirteenth Printing: June 1991

To Rocky
   so that others may know.
And to Jim, Tad and Joe.

Was here the one thing needful to distil
   From life's alembic, through this holier fate,
The man's essential soul, the hero will?
   We ask; and wait.
         —LORD CREWE,
            "A HARROW GRAVE IN FLANDERS"

Acknowledgments

To write this book, it had to be lived. For giving me the love, guidance and background, the foundation that formed the inner strength so essential to my survival, I humbly thank my wonderful mother and dad.

I would be remiss to exclude the individuals directly responsible for the experience upon which this book is based, even though I offer them no thanks. Mafia, Major Bay, Ong Sau, Dai Uy Muoi and the system they represent created the nightmare. To them, I offer that which they never expected, "the truth of the situation."

J.N.R.

I wrote this poem in 1961 after a dream sequence oc-curred three nights in succession depicting my capture almost exactly as it happened on 29 October 1963, two and a half years later. I had not yet been assigned to Special Forces nor was there any thought of my going to Vietnam.

Aching, shuddering, violent void
    Rending the sheltering velvet;
For flesh is weak,
    too weak for this,

  Hide, screaming incomprehension
of the inevitable;
For it is inevitable
        and it is coming.

I

TWO HU1— HELICOPTERS PUSHED NORTHWARD, TWO thousand feet above the swamp and rice paddy domain of the Mekong Delta's Vietcong legions, their blades beating a steady rhythm against the air. One of them, the unarmed "slick," carried Capt. Humbert "Rock" Versace, intelligence adviser with the Military Assistance and Advisory Group at Camau. The other chopper, flying slightly to their right front, was an armed helicopter, its landing skids heavy with rocket tubes and machine guns. Their destination was a small Special Forces camp twenty-six kilometers north of the provincial capital and in the center of a Vietcong-controlled zone.

Rocky was a trimly built, twenty-six-year-old West Point graduate who had volunteered for a six-month extension after completing one year as an adviser. His slightly outthrust jaw and penetrating eyes were indications of his personality, but his close-cut, black-flecked, steel-gray hair looked as if it belonged on someone much older.

He had recently been assigned as MAAG intelligence adviser in Camau and had witnessed some hard combat as the Vietnamese units his detachment was advising stood toe to toe with the best the Vietcong had to offer. The battles were typical of that period: Vietcong nighttime assaults; chance daylight encounters with an elusive enemy and the seeming impossibility of pinning him down; bloody ambushes; lack of adequate air support and artillery even though our pilots were flying the

2

wings off of the available T–28's; the frustration that went with the "old war" before the arrival of jets, artillery support, and American combat units. This was the war known to the American advisers, to the isolated U.S. Special Forces detachments in their efforts to combat the Vietcong in their own territory. This was Vietnam, 1963.

Small groups of huts, clustered along canal banks bordered by coconut palms and banana trees, passed below the open doors of the choppers. The countryside was deceptively peaceful. To shatter the illusion all one had to do was drop down into range of the weapons which were, no doubt, pointed skyward at that very moment, hidden by the foliage of the trees. Farmers worked thigh-deep in water, tending their rice paddies, their conical hats reflecting the sunlight. Water buffalo wallowed in the mud, oblivious to all around them. A graceful "spirit bird" hung motionless in the sky, "suspended high in a rising air thermal," its lonely world undisturbed by the passing helicopters.

Ahead, now visible at the intersection of two larger canals, was Versace's destination, Tan Phu. A streamer of green smoke billowed up from the landing zone, a small rectangular area cleared for chopper landing. At Tan Phu there was only one way in or out—by chopper—and it wasn't safe that way either. The terrain one kilometer away from camp for 360 degrees belonged to Charlie. It was an isolated fortress manned by an American Special Forces A-Detachment, their Vietnamese Special Forces (LLDB) counterpart team, and four companies—about 380 men on an average day—of the Civilian Irregular Defense Group. These were the Vietnamese and Cambodians from that area who had been recruited, equipped, and trained to resist the Vietcong in their home villages. It was a lonely spot for the Americans.

The armed Huey made its first pass over the camp, a cluster of brown thatched huts surrounded by a mud wall, narrow moat, and several distinct barbed wire barriers. Large machine-gun bunkers on the corners and scattered rifle positions along the wall marred the otherwise smooth rectangular layout of the camp's main defense. Mortar positions within the perimeter, a watchtower, a masonry and tile dispensary, and a large concrete cube completed the major interior parts of this barrier to complete Vietcong domination of the area.

The large concrete structure was being used as an ammunition bunker now that it had been strengthened and sandbagged. It was the only survivor of a militia post that had been overrun by the VC in 1962. The last of the soldiers then manning the post had been trapped inside the building as they made a final stand. The Vietcong had jammed the muzzles of their weapons into the firing ports and riddled the inside of the building, then hurled grenades into the ports and wiped out the remaining defenders. The inside walls of the building still bore the scars of that last stand.

The choppers settled onto the sheets of perforated steel matting which prevented them from sinking over their skids in the soft muck of this delta swampland. Rocky jumped to the matting, clutching a small bag in one hand and a portable Thermofax machine under his other arm. His baseball cap was canted to one side of his head and his carbine had slipped from his shoulder to the crook of his arm.

"Welcome to the end of the world! I didn't expect you so soon." Ducking against the powerful downdraft of the blades and holding my beret on with one hand, I greeted him. Members of the American team took his gear as I introduced him to Al Penneult, the crew-cut, bull-necked ex-football player—our detachment commander.

Rocky's grin was one of the nicest things about him and his greeting made it seem as if we'd known each other for years. Actually, it had been only a few weeks since I'd met him. I had been en route to Tan Phu from Saigon after picking up funds and supplies for the camp. Rocky had been just another face in the vehicle that took us from the Catinat Hotel to Tan Son Nhut Airfield and I had said no more than "Good morning" when I first saw him. It wasn't until we found ourselves sitting side by side on the same Caribou flight to Can Tho that we began to talk and introduced ourselves. Before we landed at Can Tho, we had gone through the whole problem of exchange of vital information that existed in our operational area and had hatched a plan to establish communication between our posts. We received permission at my B-Detachment to put in voice commo between Tan Phu and Camau. It was to be strictly for exchange of information and not used as a command net. With that guidance, we went to work and in three days had installed an AN/GRC 9 radio at Tan Phu and linked the two groups of

4

Americans, the Special Forces and MAAG. I had spent two days at Camau, coordinating the setup and requisitioning the radio which I subsequently took back to Tan Phu to be installed. Rocky had planned to come up to Tan Phu for a visit to check out what we had and coordinate further exchanges.

This visit had been prompted by a briefing we had given his senior adviser earlier the same day on the situation at Tan Phu. He had questioned whether or not Rocky had been up to coordinate yet and after my negative reply had decided to send the choppers for him. It hadn't been more than a couple of hours after the Colonel's departure that Rocky arrived.

Rocky, Al, and I walked through the gate into the main camp, saluting the stern-faced striker on guard as he snapped to present arms with his carbine. We passed a clothesline, sagging under the weight of dripping fatigue shirts and trousers. "Big Boy," our Vietnamese laundryman, was attempting to dry the freshly washed uniforms before the humid rainy-season climate induced mold to form. The intervals of sunlight were short and it took no time at all for the clothes to develop a broad velvety covering of either light green or dull orange.

Pluto, the team's canine mascot, lay in the middle of the path, luxuriating in the warmth of a patch of sunlight while one of the Vietnamese chickens pecked intently at some delicacy it had discovered on Pluto's tail. Neither seemed to disturb the other.

Inside the team hut, Rocky met the other members of the team and stowed his bag and weapon on the bunk Al indicated. The dirt floors and thatch construction of our buildings contrasted sharply with the masonry structures, cement floors, and screened windows at Camau, thus prompting Rocky's first comment: "Why don't you fix this place up a little?" He indicated the sacks of portland cement stacked high along the wall. "You've got plenty of cement, why not put in a floor and walls?"

The questions caused heads to turn in his direction as the team members scrutinized the visitor who had immediately begun to criticize our hootches. I felt compelled to answer, since he was my guest and I knew no one else would reply.

"We have a priority on construction, Rocky. The cement is for civil affairs projects with our Vietnamese and we can't use it to make our quarters more comfortable until we finish the sanitation and construction in the villages."

Rocky nodded. Once he understood why something was done, he would accept it. That is, if he agreed with the reasoning. I had, in the short time I'd known him, noticed a dynamic, outspoken frankness. He had an eagerness and disregard for danger that would blend well with Al's similar traits, but perhaps not so well with the older team members' outlook. It was a matter of liking Rocky a hell of a lot or disliking him intensely. He was too positive a personality to allow any other reactions and his unreserved observations could be quite abrasive.

Supper that evening was a festive occasion as our Vietnamese cooks, Hai and Sha (the grinning, bucktoothed, local con artist), outdid themselves. Barbecued pork, French fried potatoes, and green beans were steaming in serving bowls on the long tables, with French rolls and butter. Fruit cocktail topped off the meal and we were all in a relaxed mood as we sat outside the hootch, sipping coffee or beer and watching the spectacular Vietnamese sunset.

These moments of quiet were ones I think all of us will remember about Vietnam. Tan Phu was a beautiful place in the evening. The wide rice paddy, graceful coconut palms, the glorious burst of oranges and reds fanning up from the western horizon and reflecting from the masses of clouds created a feeling of harmony and peace. The village children playing and laughing along the canal banks and the birds high above, quiet and graceful, returning to their nests dispelled any thoughts of the war that began when darkness fell. The mosquitoes were the first sign that night was coming and soon after their arrival, our moments of peace ended. Darkness came and with it came the VC.

That night there was a minor probe along the outpost line across the canal. We fired a few illumination and high explosive mortar rounds. The troops on the line exchanged shots with the attackers and then it was quiet again. The team had become accustomed to these harassing attacks and paid little attention unless required to support the strikers. We slept in our fatigue trousers, with boots and loaded weapons in reach of our bunks in case something big came up. Also that night, Rocky met our mobile rattrap, a seven-and-a-half-foot python, who proved to be an affable companion to his very few friends. The strikers

6

eyed him as a substantial meal, but refrained from tangling with him for reasons other than his belonging to the American team.

The next morning, after a breakfast of Hai's two-ton pancakes, which were a good ten inches in diameter and as thick as the palm of my hand, we began to go through the intelligence gathered at Tan Phu. Captain Versace proved to be extremely efficient in extracting the pertinent facts from agents' reports and classifying it according to the information he already had. At the same time, he was filling our intelligence sergeant and me in on information that clarified our picture.

I briefed Rocky on the enemy situation, mentioning the new reports we had been getting on a buildup of VC regional force units, hard-core types with the latest Communist-bloc equipment. The day before, the Colonel had mentioned during the briefing that there were large units moving northward from the rest areas deep in the mangrove swamps south of Camau and they had disappeared after reaching this area. All indications pointed to our old troublemaker, the VC 306th Battalion, roaming around somewhere near the fringe of the U Minh Forest. We had clobbered them in an all-night battle on 30 July. They disappeared, licking their wounds and swearing revenge. They were now back with replacements and new equipment. It was a developing picture of enemy strength increasing radically, with no obvious reason to sit idle once they massed their forces. We could expect some rough nights ahead.

Rocky met Lieutenant Tinh, the Vietnamese Special Forces detachment commander, a quiet, sleepy-eyed, young second lieutenant, who had been assigned to Tan Phu for his first command position. Then he met Sergeant Canh, the Vietnamese team sergeant, a veteran of the French conflict who had served at Tan Phu from the time it was reestablished some seven months earlier. He had been team sergeant under Major Phong, the first camp commander, and was wise in the ways of staying alive at Tan Phu. Aspirant Dai was the second in command to Lieutenant Tinh and was a pleasant young man in a position where he balanced survival against fulfilling the requirements in this tour of duty for his promotion to second lieutenant. Tan Phu was a rough place to learn how to be an officer.

The days passed rapidly and on the morning of the twenty-

7

eighth, Captain Versace asked if he could pay a visit to the district chief at Thoi Binh, some eight kilometers down the canal. Since Rocky was attached to MAAG, he was in an advisory and staff role for the district chief. He wanted to check in with him. Captain Penneult arranged with Lieutenant Tinh to take three assault boats and a squad of strikers for security. They departed at midmorning.

The group returned at about 1500 hours with the word that we'd be going on an operation early the next morning. There was the immediate feeling of excitement as we waited to hear the details. Al said that Lieutenant Tinh would be over after supper to go through the complete briefing with us, but the general plan was for a three-company operation to Le Coeur, a small hamlet about eight kilometers to our northwest. I walked into the operations hut to check the map for an exact location.

Le Coeur was located in a Vietcong-dominated area on one of the main canals leading into the dreaded U Minh Forest. We had never ventured into that area before and the close proximity of the legendary forest sanctuary of the Vietcong made this a cinch for a damn good fire fight.

I was joined at the map by Master Sergeant Dennis Lima and Sergeant First Class Jim Browning, our team sergeant and intelligence sergeant respectively. Lima and Browning both had replaced original members of the team who had been wounded. We measured the distances from camp to the hamlet and from the hamlet to the edge of the forest. Browning was leafing through a recent intelligence summary he had taken from the files. "I wonder whose idea this was?" Lima asked no one in particular as he studied the map. I was busy measuring maximum range for our 81mm mortars and the 155 mm howitzers at Thoi Binh. We would need all the fire support we could get in case we got caught out there by something more than we could handle.

Al and Rocky came in discussing possible courses of action for the operation. The district chief had gotten information, Al told us, that a small enemy unit had moved into Le Coeur and was establishing a command post there. The possibility that it would be used to direct attacks against us existed and we were going to hit the village, driving out or killing the VC. We would be taking two of our striker companies and one of the militia companies from Thoi Binh.

8

I went to work on calculations for fire support while Browning checked the map for possible routes to and from the objective. The terrain was easy to analyze—rice paddies with scattered banana and coconut groves and scattered hamlets. The Vietnamese would select the final route, but this analysis would give us a rough idea to check with their plan. We had no intelligence on the possible units in that specific area and would rely on Lieutenant Tinh for that. We would require no special equipment and the Vietnamese already had sufficient ammunition. Radios and batteries would be required, so I made a note for Leigh Wade, one of our team commo men.

Al and Rocky were talking over plans and alternates with Lima. The basic plan was to hit the hamlet with one company, while the other two formed an ambush between the hamlet and the forest. If the VC escaped the assault and ran for the forest, they would be cut up by the ambush. The two companies would also have sufficient strength to fight off VC reinforcements coming from the forest. The problem of fire support was crucial, since the objective and ambush site were well out of range of our camp mortars and the 155's were less effective for close support.

I was thinking that this plan would be relatively sound if we could hit with surprise, do our job, and get the hell out of there before anyone could react. We would be deep in Charlie's territory and with the reports we had received about his troop concentrations around us, there was no telling exactly how many men were out there. It wouldn't be too smart to roam around for any great length of time after they knew we were in their territory. I imagine the same thoughts had occurred to others.

We went in for chow at about 1730, taking our time to eat and avoiding shoptalk during the meal. Afterward I went to my desk in the operations hut and began a letter to Lorene, my fiancée. Three discarded attempts later I decided to put it off until after the excitement. I would feel more like writing then.

It was already dark when Lieutenant Tinh entered the mess hut, a map and several sheets of paper in his hand. We went into the op hut where he spread out his map and began to explain the detailed plan. There was complete silence among the gathered Americans. We would leave the camp in two

9

increments. The two ambush companies would depart at 2400 hours, since they had a greater distance to travel and would have to be in position before the assault began on the hamlet. The assault company would leave at 0200 hours, traveling almost in a straight line along canal number one to the objective. We would attack at day-break, catching the VC as they awoke. First Company, with Sergeant Canh, would go with the Militia Company to the ambush site. Third Company, with Lieutenant Tinh, would assault.

"What about fire support, Lieutenant Tinh?" Lima asked.

"We will take the mortars from camp and place them here." He pointed to the map. "They can fire for the operation from there." I checked the location he indicated. It was within three thousand meters of both sites, giving adequate coverage.

"What about return routes?" Captain Penneult asked.

"We will return along canal number three and canal five," Tinh answered. "First Company will join us after the attack." The return routes were out of range of the mortars.

"Lieutenant Tinh," I offered, "I'd suggest leaving at least one tube in camp to support us on the way back. We'll be out of range on canal five, and most of canal three." Al and Rocky checked the map and nodded in agreement. Tinh accepted the idea, making notations on his papers.

"Sir, who's going to be firing the mortars tomorrow?" Big John Lowe, team heavy-weapons man, asked Captain Penneult.

"I don't know, Sergeant Lowe. What about it, Lieutenant Tinh?"

"I will have two crews to go with the mortars on the operation," Tinh replied.

"Sir, what about me and Ponce going along just to keep an eye on things? After all, those are the crews we trained," Big John volunteered. Al thought for a moment.

"*Ti-Uy,*" he addressed Tinh by the Vietnamese term for second lieutenant, "what type of security will be with the mortars?"

"I am sending one platoon for security," came the answer.

"Will it be all right for Lowe and Navarro to go with the mortars?"

Tinh nodded an affirmative.

"Lieutenant Tinh, what about the 155's?" I asked, still concerned over the fire support. "Will they screen our north flank on the way back?" Canals eight through fifteen had been a problem in the past and Charlie tended to congregate out there. It would be nasty to have that side open.

"The district chief has said he will provide artillery for the hamlet, but I do not know about when we come back," Tinh confessed.

"Can you check with him and make certain we're covered out there?" I pursued the point. Tinh replied that he'd contact the district chief, but there was a nagging doubt in my mind about that flank's being open.

The discussion went to the departure times and whether or not the assault company had sufficient time to reach the objective. Contingencies were covered and as the plan unfolded in detail, there were weaknesses. Timing was critical and surprise essential. We would be moving, most of the time, through VC-controlled areas and would be forced to pass either near or through a number of hamlets, any one of which could give warning to the enemy. Our mortars would be separate from the three companies and protected by one platoon. They were vulnerable. The lack of adequate coverage on the return was yet another problem. I began to have doubts about the operation. More than usual.

The plan was finally worked out, imperfectly, but the best that could be done under the circumstances. Tinh bid us goodnight and left to complete his preparations. He was damn good for a lieutenant, but I wished we had Major Phong back with us. Lima was shaking his head. Good, bad, or indifferent as far as plans went, the Special Forces advisers would go along and tomorrow was my turn to go on the operation.

Rocky announced that he would be going and drew surprised glances from the team. MAAG advisers weren't allowed to accompany Special Forces operations, and Al brought this to Rocky's attention. The probability of making contact with Charlie and provoking action, coupled with the chance of picking up good intelligence in the previously untouched village, were enough reason for Rocky. We talked it over for a while, with Rocky insisting that the district chief's initiation of the operation and militia participation made it a joint operation and he was going as an adviser to the militia. There was no way around his determination and it was decided that Rocky and I would go with Lieutenant Tinh and the assault company.

11

"Who else do you want with you, Nick?" Al asked, regarding the other team member who would go along.

I glanced into the mess hut where Dan Pitzer, the team medical supervisor, was sitting, munching at a bowl of cereal. "You want to take the walk tomorrow, Dan?"

Dan looked up. "Doesn't matter to me. Might as well." He went back to his cereal.

I stood by the doorway studying the map I'd carry with me. "I don't like this one, sir," I commented to Al, who was standing beside me.

His eyes flared for a moment. "If you don't like it, stay home. I'll take the walk!"

I stood shocked for a second at the idea, then thought that perhaps because I'd been here a little longer, I might be a little more cautious than necessary. "No sweat," I replied. "It's my turn, I'll go." If for no other reason, because Rocky was going.

"All right," Al replied, calming a bit. "Those who are going on the operation tomorrow go ahead and sack out. Get some rest before you leave."

I nodded and entered the commo bunker to find Rocky Versace speaking angrily into the handset.

"Who refused the request? I want a name! Over."

We apparently weren't going to get that L–19 for some reason. We'd never had one before in Tan Phu, although some units never went out without the reliable "bird dog" overhead to spot the enemy and call in airstrikes. It would be nice to have one, particularly for this operation. I tapped Rocky on the arm and gave him the palms-up shoulder shrug indicating "What's happening?" Rocky's face answered my question before he said a word.

"Someone down there won't approve an L–19 for the operation tomorrow, damn it! They've got them. Why won't they let us have one?"

"Al said to go ahead and get some sleep before the op in the morning. Whoever is pulling guard will wake us up in time to grab a cup of coffee before we go. See you in a couple of hours." Rocky nodded as he continued his conversation with Camau.

I walked around to the positions and told the others to grab a little sack time before we left in the morning. After a last look at the map of the area we were going into, I walked through

12

the mess hall and into the team sleeping hut. Big John was pulling off his boots as he sat on the edge of his bunk. Ponce Navarro was already inside his mosquito net and well on the way to sleep. It took a lot to shake him up and we had yet to come up against anything that really bothered him.

"See you tomorrow, John. Have those tubes ready when you hear me calling 'shoot 'em.'" John was a good man to have on your side—particularly with the mortars, which he handled with deadly accuracy.

"You call for 'em, Lieutenant Rowe, and me and Ponce will put 'em there."

I left my tiger suit on and climbed under the mosquito net. Time to log a few Z's before morning. I was glad that unit at Le Coeur was supposed to be small. I closed my eyes and thought about Lorene. As her face came into my mind, everything was quiet. I drifted thousands of miles from this Asiatic Fort Laramie and sleep came quickly.

"Lieutenant Rowe! Lieutenant Rowe. It's 0100 hours, sir."

"Thanks, Van." Roger VandeBerg, the team medical assistant, was standing beside my bed. "Are the others up yet?" I asked.

"Yes, sir, I just got them up. Coffee's on in the tavern."

VandeBerg walked back through the doorway and into the mess hall. He had another hour to pull on guard and this had been a long night.

I pushed the mosquito net aside, shivering slightly in the cool, damp night air. I mentally checked my gear. Boots, harness, canteen. Check. Grenades, knife. Check. Rifle—and I need about three more bandoleers of ammo. I can get them in the mess hall. Compass into my jacket pocket. Now where in the hell is my hat? Damn it, I had it last night. Where in hell did I leave it? Not on the shelf, nope. Not on the chests. Maybe in the commo bunker. I'll check while I'm getting coffee.

Slinging the harness over one shoulder and carrying the M–1 in my right hand, I walked into the mess hall where the others were already standing around drinking cups of the strong, black brew. A carbine with two "banana" magazines taped together lay on the table. A shotgun-like M–79, Pitzer's weapon, hung by its sling from the back of one of the chairs. Harnesses, bandoleers of ammo, grenades; gear was laid on the tabletop, on the chairs; and there, on the table, was my hat where I'd left it after the briefing the evening before.

VandeBerg poured a cup of coffee for me. "It's hot, sir. That's about all I can guarantee." The others stood, drinking in silence, still trying to shake the grip of those brief hours of sleep.

The steaming liquid seared my tongue as I took my first sip. I was suddenly wide awake and aware of the thatch walls of the hut; the lantern burning on the table; the small, screen-enclosed shelved rack with the moldy boxes of Post Tens cereal and cans of Mother's Oats, some of which were left over from the first team that had been here; the table and chairs where our team had shared so many meals. I thought of the long hours ahead, the rice paddies, the mud, the impossible-to-cross, single-pole monkey bridges, and the inevitable plunge into the small canals as I slipped off the bridges. Somehow, in the light of what was to come, this mud-floored thatched hut seemed like the ultimate in comfort and convenience. Perhaps this was a reason for the Vietnamese farmer's love for his hut, no matter how poor—it was all relative. If what was around the hut was less desirable, less comfortable, less convenient, then it would seem better, and often the next step down from such a place was no hut at all.

It was odd. Coming from America, with all the conveniences and comfort I had known, even in the BOQ's at Fort Bragg that we never ceased to curse while we were there, I had looked on our huts at Tan Phu with dismay. Dirt floors, thatch walls and roofs (which leaked no matter how many repairs were made), a kerosene refrigerator which never quite got anything really cold; yet here I was looking at all this with a fondness, regarding it as more than adequate, compared to what I would be wading around in very shortly.

"Lieutenant Rowe," Wade jarred me loose. "Do you want to check out the radios now?"

"Right," I answered. "John and Ponce will have one PRC/ 10 with them and I'll be using Lieutenant Tinh's.

"Let's go over call signs and frequencies again right now," I interjected. "The call sign will be 'Rattlesnake.' Wade, Tan Phu will be Rattlesnake nest.' I will be Rattlesnake one.' John and Ponce will be 'Rattlesnake two.' Our primary frequency will be 50.1. Alternate will be 49.5. Emergency frequency will be 38.1." Each of the men repeated the call signs and frequencies, which had already been committed to memory. Pitzer and Rocky Versace took note of the frequencies and call signs. We didn't know who might have to make contact.

"Will the Vietnamese be using this base set also?" Rocky asked.

"Negative, sir," Wade answered. "They have one of their own."

"Why is there a shortage of radios?" Rocky continued.

"The problem is with maintenance, Rocky," I replied. "We started out with what looked like enough sets, but it seems like the strikers do 'em in faster than we can send them for repairs, and replacement radios don't exist. I suppose other camps are having the same problem and there just aren't enough '10's to go around. It's something we have yet to straighten out. As far as sharing one base set, which is what you might be thinking of, we've already tried that. We've found that it's best to have two separate nets. Particularly in this case, since we'll be handling a resupply drop tomorrow as well as the op. LLDB will have to continuously monitor their radio during the op and if worst comes to worst, they'll call Wade over and we can use their frequencies."

At this point, Lieutenant Tinh came into the mess hut, his prized American bush hat pushed back on his head, carbine slung over one shoulder, and a map in one hand. He still looked sleepy, but then, he always looked a little sleepy.

"Morning, *Ti-Uy*." "Good morning, Lieutenant Tinh." "Time to go back to bed, *Ti-Uy*," he was greeted as he entered.

Turning to Rocky and me he said, "We will leave in twenty minutes. Third Company prepares now. We will go to the village."

"What about the other companies?" I asked.

"First Company has already gone. They will be in position by 4:30."

VandeBerg set Tinh's coffee on the table and pushed the can of milk and the sugar bowl over to him. Tinh continued, as he poured generous amounts of milk and sugar into the coffee to produce a mixture which all the Vietnamese seemed to favor—half coffee, half milk, and a lot of sugar—"We will attack at daylight. We must travel through the rice fields because the canals have many grenade traps."

Wade, in the meantime, had checked all the radios. Pitzer

laid out his harness and examined it. I found myself again checking off the equipment I was carrying. The extra ammo! I walked over to the boxes of .30 cal. bandoleers kept in the mess hut and took out three. That gave me a total of five and should be enough for just about anything we might run into.

We finished our coffee and began putting on our equipment—slipping harness straps over our shoulders, adjusting the belt, making sure the rubber band which held the grenade handle to the base was secure so the grenade wouldn't drop off the ring on the harness shoulder strap through which the handle had been slipped.

The plastic jungle canteens were filled with water and after a final look at my M–1, I opened the bolt and pushed a clip of ammo in and let the bolt slide forward. Pushing the safety on, I reached for my cap, put it on, and took a last look around to see if there was anything left to do.

Rocky and Dan Pitzer were ready. "Van, John, Ponce, we'll see you all later." I followed Lieutenant Tinh out of the hut and into the darkness outside. The night was cloudy, though stars shone through breaks in the passing cloud formations. Faint, pale moonlight gave promise of at least a little help in navigating the soggy-bottomed, water-filled rice paddies. Lieutenant Tinh made his way toward the camp gate, his flashlight throwing a yellowish oval on the ground.

We walked across the bridge and into the village, where we immediately encountered activity. Strikers, wearing the black-and-green-slashed tiger suits, carrying so much ammunition I wondered how they were able to move, hurried down the packed mud main street toward the assembly area. The Cambod machine gunner from Third Company came by, grinning as he carried his .30 cal. weapon and a full belt of link ammo draped around his shoulders like a necklace of huge shark teeth. As it turned out, quite a few VC that day felt the bite of those "teeth" before the young Cambod died.

As we approached the village chief's house, which seemed to be the meeting place for all the honchos on this operation, the street became jammed with our strikers. Talking in low voices, the various groups seemed to be segments of a vast disorder and I wondered how anyone could create a company out of this shadowy-bodied mass. It was apparent that the company commander and platoon leaders were in control of the situation, for as Lieutenant Tinh approached, certain voices stood out and there was a brief milling around prior to an orderly double file forming from the group of strikers nearest me and, no doubt, extending throughout the company.

Lieutenant Tinh stepped into the dimly lit house, where he spoke briefly with the village chief and "Ho Chi Minh," ex-Vietminh company commander of Third Company.

Rocky was suddenly by my side. I hadn't even noticed him as he came out of the darkness. "How much longer before we move out?"

"Shouldn't be more than five or ten minutes. Tinh is getting the final poop now and we'll move out as soon as he finishes."

Rocky smiled. "It's a lot better when you get started on one of these things. I hate the waiting."

"I don't mind waiting if there's a place to get a little sleep," Pitzer retorted with a grin.

Lieutenant Tinh walked out on the narrow porch and spoke briefly with one of the local Vietnamese intelligence agents, who were always around the village chief's house before an op. The strikers were beginning to shuffle and finger their equipment. An air of tension was settling as we neared time to move out. I shut my mind to those long, slushy, thigh-deep rice paddies that lay ahead and fixed my thoughts on that tall, cold glass of iced tea that Sha would have waiting when we returned, even though iced tea didn't seem too desirable right then. I would have settled for another cup of coffee at the moment.

Lieutenant Tinh walked over to us. "It is good. They are in Le Coeur and do not expect us. We will go now." He turned and spoke one word to the company commander: *"Di"*—Go.

Slowly at first, the double column of serious-faced young Vietnamese, old soldiers scarred by battles long past, and the carefree Cambods began to move forward down the street to canal one, which cut across the land to the northwest, to Le Coeur.

We joined the middle of the column as it began to move faster, the strikers grinning at us as we stepped in with them. We walked past quiet, darkened huts. Pigs grunted sleepily as the columns of troops strode along the packed mud walkway bordering the canal inside the village. We passed the inner

17

barbed wire fence, which meant the head of the column should be even with the outpost line. Soon we'd be clear of the defenses and in no-man's-land, and soon after that we would be in Charlie's territory.

The column began to slow as we turned right, into the first paddy. As I stepped from the firm surface of the path there was a short second of fighting for balance when my jungle boot sank into the soft muck. The water slipped up around my legs as I walked forward. Damn, it's cold, I thought, as my trousers became soaked and clung to my legs. Christ, I hate to walk through this crap. Then my thoughts turned to keeping my position in the column. These little Vietnamese troops walked through a paddy as if they had webbed feet.

Clumps of reeds separated us from the canal as we moved along. We became a single column, plodding as quietly as possible through the thigh-deep water. The moon broke through the clouds for a brief moment. Silhouetted coconut palms on a distant canal were standing like a row of sentinels over the sleeping land, deceptively peaceful. A dog barked in the distance.

Hours passed as we made our way toward the unsuspecting Le Coeur. Walking became automatic. No longer did I notice the water or the slippery mud beneath. The column had stopped several times as the Vietnamese conferred in low voices, checked the route, and then moved out once again.

The column halted short of a northeast-southwest canal that intersected our path. I could see the dark shapes of huts in among the coconut and banana palms. Lieutenant Tinh walked forward to meet the company commander. They spoke softly for a few minutes as the company commander pointed toward the huts and then to the west of them where our canal and the village canal crossed. Lieutenant Tinh waited as the column began to move, this time bearing to the left, toward the village canal. Stepping in beside me, he said quietly, "VC in the hamlet. We must go into the canal and go around them. This will be difficult. There are *dap loi* and grenades here. Be very careful."

After repeating Tinh's message to Rocky and Dan, who were behind me, we made sure we had a Vietnamese between each of us. In case one of us blundered onto a booby trap the other would have a chance of not being injured. We slid down an incline on our asses and went up to our waists in the canal. Carrying my M–1 across my shoulders, my bandoleers of ammo high on my chest, I followed the Vietnamese in front of me by about five meters, watching his every movement. On the bank to my right I could see a spiked fence made of brush and sharpened bamboo stakes. Behind it was a mound of packed mud about five feet high used as a firing position by the VC. Coconut palms bent gracefully over the canal, but this time their beauty was not appreciated. They created shadows and we needed all the illumination we could get from available moonlight.

The striker to my front moved off to his left and I followed. There was a portion of fence extending into the canal. He turned and indicated for me to give it wide berth, which I was quite willing to do. I turned and passed the signal on to the man behind me. Some distance later we climbed up onto the canal bank and proceeded down the hard-packed path paralleling the canal. We had passed the semidefensive line found on the perimeter of what Charlie considered his territory and were now traveling along the same routes he used. I checked my watch: 0425. A little over an hour and we'd be hitting Le Coeur.

We passed more darkened huts. Dogs barked and followed us, the first ones to bark alerting others that seemed to come from every hut, determined to defend their masters against these strangers. At one point we halted briefly near a dimly lit, relatively large hut with a broad front porch and wooden plank front. I could see Ho Chi and one of his squad leaders standing in the shadows to the right of the open door talking with a slightly built, elderly Vietnamese. They finished talking, bowed, and walked back toward the column standing silent in the darkness. The old man stayed in the doorway for a moment, peering into the night that had enveloped his two visitors, then turned and reentered his home. In a couple of minutes, Lieutenant Tinh appeared, grinning. "We tell the old man," he said, making one of his infrequent English slips, "we are VC and asked if he has seen any Government troops here. He told us the Government forces did not dare to come here. Then we asked if any of our brothers had passed recently. He said a large unit passed early yesterday morning, but he did not know more."

I grinned back at him, unenthusiastically. I was wondering where that "large unit" was going and just how large it was.

Was it one of the units normally around here, or a new one? I hoped the old man hadn't bothered to look out again, and perhaps see the tiger-suit-clad strikers, not exactly a "brother unit."

We passed beyond the huts and came to a smaller canal, bordered on both sides by banana groves. Thank God the dogs had quieted down. They were enough to wake up General Giap.

Lieutenant Tinh, "Dih Dah," the LLDB radioman, and the Strike Force leaders gathered at the head of the column. I looked at my watch: 0515. We should be just about ready. Daylight would be breaking in about half an hour. I walked up to the group and listened. Dih Dah was holding his hand cupped over the mouthpiece of the PRC/10 handset and speaking softly. All I could hear was a series of numbers, which evidently meant something to Lieutenant Tinh, for he nodded seriously as Dih Dah repeated the message: *"Hai, nam, ba, nam, chinh, bon."* I looked questioningly at Tinh.

"First Company is in position. We are one and a half kilometers from Le Coeur and will reach there shortly after daybreak. This is not good."

"We'd best get on the road then, *Ti-Uy*," I said. Our assault would be across nearly 750 meters of open rice paddy, and to cross in broad daylight could be costly, particularly if the VC decided to fight instead of run.

I noticed the strikers checking their weapons as we moved out. Ammunition was carefully checked, grenadiers fingered the rifle grenades hanging around their waists, faces were all serious now. We passed through the banana groves and into a field of twisted scrub brush, reeds, and skeletons of dead trees. The reeds were high enough to cover our movement as the column began to fan out to the left and right.

By 0540 first light was showing to the east. It wouldn't take long for the sun to come up. In the mornings it seemed to hang back for so long and then suddenly rocket into the sky, making the transition from night to day a short one. I checked my own weapon, ammo, and grenades and took my hat off and pushed it under the murky brown water, letting it sop up the wetness. Later on when the sun was up it was going to be hot. Rocky and Dan were back beside me, their eyes intent as they watched the strikers fan out. We walked together now as the reeds began to thin out. The paddy should be just ahead. The sun was now on the horizon to our right, robbing us of the invisibility we

20

had enjoyed. I could see the line of soldiers to my left and right walking steadily forward through the scattered clumps of reeds, their squad leaders working to keep the line straight. There was about a meter or so between each man. Bazooka teams were slightly to the rear of the rifle squads, their ungainly launching tubes already on their shoulders, muzzles aimed upward at a slight angle. The ammunition bearers, close beside the gunners, carried both H.E. and white phosphorus rounds, the latter being more desirable as an antipersonnel round. The H.E., because of its shaped-charge effect and general lack of fragmentation, was principally to destroy any fortifications we came across.

We walked at an angle to the right and joined Lieutenant Tinh and the command group as they moved forward. "Lieutenant Tinh, I'll make contact with the mortars now and make sure we're netted in," I said as I stepped in beside the striker carrying the radio, which was almost as broad as his back. Lieutenant Tinh nodded. He was concentrating on something else.

I took the handset from the little Vietnamese and reached to set the frequency on the dial. This was tricky, particularly if you were walking through a semi-swamp while you were doing it. On the upper portion of the set there is a dial with the frequencies and a small round knob beside it which is used to adjust and select the desired frequency. Next to this is a multi-position switch which is the off-on, mike, or remote selection and calibration switch. The latter is spring-loaded and must be held in the calibrate position while the frequency is tuned. This requires one hand for the selection dial, one hand to hold the calibrate switch, and a third hand to hold the handset to your ear as you listen for the "zero beat," the sound of exact calibration. Thanks to Rocky's lending that extra hand I set 50.1 on the dial, got a zero beat, and began the transmission. I never failed to think dark thoughts about whoever designed that damn thing.

"Rattlesnake two, this is Rattlesnake one, over." I released the press-to-talk switch on the side of the handset and listened to the rush of static in the earpiece. Nothing.

"Rattlesnake two, this is Rattlesnake one, over," I repeated. Again the rush of static; then, loud and clear:

"Rattlesnake one, this is Rattlesnake two. How do you read me? Over."

21

"This is Rattlesnake one. Read you five by. How me? Over."

"This is Rattlesnake two. Read you five by. Over." We had good communication with the mortars.

"This is Rattlesnake one, in position, moving out, wait." Ponce would know we were about to begin the assault and a fire mission for the mortars would be coming soon, if needed. He'd keep the frequency open and be standing by to receive.

"This is Rattlesnake two. Roger. Over."

"The mortars are ready," I said to Lieutenant Tinh as I handed the handset back to Dih Dah, who began to readjust the frequency to the Vietnamese net.

Rocky grinned at me. "Now I know why you didn't object too strongly to my coming along. You needed someone to hold the handset for you while you talk to your buddies."

I glanced at my watch: 0557. Ahead, the rifle squads brought their weapons to the on-guard position. A squad leader on the left lifted his arm in a signal to the command group; they were entering the rice paddy. All down the line squad leaders' arms went up. I walked out of the sparse reeds and there, spread out in front of me, was the biggest, widest rice paddy I'd seen in my young life. That paddy seemed at least a mile across, but the distant tree line, marking the canal and village, was too distinct for that to be true. I could see the thatched walls and roofs of the huts, thin streamers of smoke rising from cooking fires, grayish-white against the dark green of the trees, fences of split bamboo behind some of the huts.

Crack! Bam! Instinctively, I dropped to a crouch. The familiar sound of a round passing nearby, then the report of a weapon was followed by two more. To our left, a sentry had spotted us and fired a warning. The village came to life. Black-clad figures tumbled out of the huts, paused to look out at the advancing troops, then dove back inside. The strikers gave out a terrifying howl, like a pack of wolves, and the line broke into a slogging run toward the village, the strikers stopping only to fire and then rejoin the line.

The black-suited VC reappeared, carrying weapons and gear. Scattered shots whistled and snapped above our heads, but the VC were running. Wait! What the hell? They were going the wrong way! The bastards were going the wrong way! Toward the canals, not the forest!

The VC had elected to retreat toward the more distant sanctuary to the northeast, ignoring the forest and leaving our am-

22

bush useless. Tinh was shouting to the company commander, while platoon leaders and squad leaders encouraged the strikers, who at this point really needed no encouragement. The VC were running; it didn't matter to the strikers that they were avoiding our carefully laid ambush and might escape. All that mattered was that the VC were running and the strikers were the hunters.

Our right flank swept ahead, trying to cut the VC off. The backblast and spray of water to my right front marked a 3.5 gunner firing a round toward the VC. Seconds later, a plume of white smoke climbed from behind the trees as the white phosphorus hit.

I turned to Rocky and Dan. "Where's Rock?" Dan was the only one with me. Dan pointed toward the advancing line of strikers and there was Rocky's tall figure among the Vietnamese, racing with them toward the village.

"Oh my gosh. What's he doing up there?" I asked the asinine question.

"As soon as the VC broke and ran, he decided to get with the program," came Dan's answer.

"Well, he can handle himself, but that's not our job up there. Let's see if Tinh will buy a few mortars to scramble 'em on about canal four."

"Can we reach 'em that far out?" Dan asked.

"It'll be close, but they'll be that far before we can get rounds on them," I replied as we joined Lieutenant Tinh and the radioman.

Dih Dah was engaged in furious conversation with someone on the ambush site, his words too fast for me to even tell one from the other. Lieutenant Tinh was carefully studying his map, his face unperturbed.

"Do you want mortar rounds put in, Lieutenant Tinh? We can hit canal three and possibly catch them. I'm not sure we can reach canal four."

Tinh looked up. "They have gone the wrong way."

Profound, I thought to myself. "Looks that way. Do you want to use the mortars to try and stop them?"

"No." He shook his head. "We will go into the village. First Company will meet us there."

"Ok, *Ti Uy.* We'll see you in the village." I turned to Dan. "Let's go catch up with Rock."

Dan smiled, pulled his cap down a little, swung the cloth

23

bandoleer of bulky M–79 rounds behind him. "OK. *Di. Di.*"

The first squads of strikers had nearly reached the tree line. Their yelling had died out as they became winded. A few shots came from the squads on our right, some of them already in the village. As we came nearer the huts, I could see chickens and ducks scattering along the canal bank as strikers swept through the closest huts and began to cross the canal to set up security on the other side.

I walked past a small garden plot beside one of the bamboo-fenced huts. Pepper bushes, spices, a fruit of some type grew in the well-tended plot. Two papaya trees and numerous coconut palms bordered the weathered palm-thatched hut, heavy-laden with fruit. The hut itself was in two sections, a larger main structure in front and, adjoining it in the rear, a lower lean-to-roofed room, which I later learned was the cooking hut. In the fenced area were a moderate-sized pig and several ducks, all of which were free to walk from their backyard domain through the hut and out to the canal.

At first glance the only people in the village seemed to be our troops. All the huts appeared to be deserted. The only sounds were the buzzing insects and a solitary dog snarling at the intruders. The strikers quickly set up a close perimeter while other squads waited along the canal bank for further orders.

Rocky, still breathing a little heavily from the long jog, waited for us, leaning against a coconut palm. "You people certainly are slow."

"That's the kind of slow we get paid for being, sir," Dan replied with more than a trace of sarcasm.

"Is Lieutenant Tinh in the village yet?" Rocky continued without noticing the remark. "We ought to make a close search and I'll bet we turn up some good information."

"Not yet," I answered. "He was about fifty meters behind Dan and me. We'll meet him here when he comes in."

The strikers on the canal bank near us were squatting and laughing among themselves, their gestures pantomiming the rapid departure of the VC. Spirits were high and grinning faces were everywhere, even though we were deep in the middle of Charlie's country and now he knew it for damn sure.

Lieutenant Tinh and Ho Chi walked up to us. "We will rest here until First Company comes from the ambush position, sir. Then we shall go to find the VC."

24

"Are you going to search the village, Lieutenant Tinh?" Rocky asked.

"Yes, sir. We will begin in a short while."

The conversation between Rocky and Tinh went on, but my attention went to the apparently deserted village. Dan was looking around also, his eyes searching the area.

"Want to take a look around, Dan?" I asked, having made up my mind to satisfy my curiosity.

"Why not?" came the reply.

"Rocky, Dan and I are going to take a look around on the other side of the canal. Why don't you stay with *Ti-Uy* Tinh in case he needs anything. We'll be within eyesight if you need us."

"Fine. I'll be with Lieutenant Tinh when he begins the search. OK?"

"Right. See you in a little bit." Dan and I walked down the path beside the canal till we reached a bamboo bridge spanning it. The twin poles which formed the bridge and the far from substantial handrail almost discouraged me as I counted back the number of times I had slipped off of these typical walkways that the Vietnamese considered adequate. I made a promise to myself that the next big civil affairs project from our camp would be to replace all of the monkey bridges with plank bridges that I could navigate easily.

On the other side I found my attention drawn to the lush banana groves that stretched behind the village. The tree trunks and foliage were so thick that it was impossible to see into the grove. I wondered what was possibly in, or perhaps behind, that mass of trees. I could see some of our people between the village and the grove, but it was doubtful that any of them had gone in to check it out. Maybe all the VC did make it down the canal. But I wondered where the people went. Passing one of the open huts, I glanced inside. There on the floor was a crumpled black shirt. I could see a cuff and button on the sleeve; generally speaking, one didn't find cuffs on the average farmer's shirts. I reached inside the door and picked it up, looking at the shoulders. Epaulets. Funny that guerrillas would be wearing this type of shirt. It was well cut and tailored. I hung it on the outside of the doorway since this hut obviously had housed VC and would require a thorough search.

As I turned away from the hut, Pitzer handed me an object

he had picked up off the ground, making no comment.

"Hm—7.62. This is a Mossin-Nagant round, Dan," I said, looking at the cartridge he had given me. The bullet had a painted silver tip, making it appear like a soft-nose shell. Lieutenant Tinh might be interested in this, I thought as I put it in my pocket.

Behind us First Company came up the path into the village from the southwest. There was almost a festive air as Third Company's victors greeted the disappointed ambush force, welcoming them to the village. Dan and I recrossed the shaky bridge and joined the company commanders and LLDB, who were in deep conversation. Sergeant Canh, the LLDB team sergeant leading First Company, was talking with Lieutenant Tinh and Ho Chi while Dih Dah and "Pee Hole Bandit," whom I hadn't seen until now, were talking with someone over the radio.

We walked up, unnoticed, and stood with Rocky, who was fluent in Vietnamese and was able to determine what was being planned. "It sounds as if we're going to pursue," he said. "Sergeant Canh will follow us with his company and we'll sweep two different canals on the way back to the main one."

Pee Hole finished what he was doing with the radio and came over to us, his face split by an enormous grin. He was probably the most likable, as well as the most competent, of the LLDB team and a favorite among the Americans.

"Trung-Uy, Bac-si, VC di, di, huh!" he chuckled, calling Pitzer by the title he had earned being the team medic. He was doing his best to communicate with us in a language he knew we barely understood.

Pitzer laughed and playfully jabbed at Pee Hole's arm. Pee Hole immediately took on an exaggerated fighting stance and all of us began to chuckle as he went through a two-step shuffle and tapped Pitzer gently on the brim of his cap. The two beer-drinking buddies began conversing in their own English-Vietnamese dialect as Lieutenant Tinh came over to where Rocky and I were standing. A partial search of the huts had begun and now that First Company was there a more thorough one would be conducted. After that, Third Company would proceed down the canal in the direction the retreating VC had gone and try to make contact. First Company would follow and when it was decided to halt the pursuit (which, by this time, would not amount to much if the VC had really intended on breaking contact) the two companies would sweep separate parallel canals en route to the canal Kinh Song Trem and back to camp. As usual, the advisers' role in a tactical situation was minimal and it became a matter of tagging along until something happened, hoping it wouldn't.

The search revealed terrified families hiding in the protective packed mud bunkers built under the flat wooden sleeping rack in the huts. The soldiers either coaxed or dragged the villagers out of their hiding places, checked identification cards, searched the people and their huts, and questioned them about the VC who had run from the village. Apparently that particular unit as well as others had spent quite a bit of time here as many of the villagers carried photographs of Vietcong and letters from members of various VC units operating in the area, and most of the huts produced at least one red-and-blue flag with the yellow star in the center. As on other operations, the Americans were presented with a flag, or flags, as a souvenir of the operation. I got mine. Hot damn.

Lieutenant Tinh wasn't at all disturbed by the obviously pro-VC sentiment in the village. He explained a short time later that this village was in an area controlled first by the Vietminh and then the Vietcong. Those who had disagreed with them or opposed them were executed as "fascist traitors" and "enemies of the people," so those who remained were either sympathetic to the VC, or did not dare oppose them. The value of this particular village lay in the fact that the canal running through the village was a freshwater canal, unlike the canals nearer the main Kinh Song Trem which was a noticeably saline tidal canal. Even during the long dry season, this canal would provide potable water.

Lieutenant Tinh stated that in the near future Tan Phu would establish an outpost in, or in the vicinity of, Le Coeur, so that the area could be returned to government protection. From what I had seen, that was going to take some doing, and would require more than one company. We'd have to do some more recruiting and training to fill the requirement for troops to do the job.

I noticed that the strikers were thorough yet polite in their searches, even when they found evidence of a family's being connected with the VC. Such treatment was particularly im-

27

portant here because this was the first contact some of these people had had with Government troops in a long time. Any mistreatment would only substantiate what the VC had no doubt told them would result from an operation's hitting the village. On the basis of several past performances I expected the worst, but was very happy to see Lieutenant Tinh in complete control of a relatively effective search that was free from any mistreatment of the people, other than physically lifting some hesitant individuals from their hiding places.

The search was continuing as Tinh and I stood beside the canal talking. I remembered the Mossin-Nagant cartridge and dug in my pocket, fishing it out and handing it to Lieutenant Tinh. "Pitzer found this on the other bank. One of the VC no doubt dropped it as he was running."

Tinh turned the round in his fingers for a moment, then put it in his pocket. "Yes," he agreed, "the VC dropped it."

Pee Hole Bandit came up to us and declared he was ready to take the lead squad in pursuit of the long-gone VC. I enjoyed being around Pee Hole and trusted this brash, grinning LLDB sergeant in a tight situation. He had been on patrols with him before and was satisfied with his competence as a soldier. This caused me to violate one of my personal rules about leaving the command group. "Tinh, how about Pitzer and I going with Pee Hole? Captain Versace will stay with you and the radioman in case you need anything and if we hit trouble I'll be in contact with you." Tinh nodded an affirmative and I turned to Rocky: "Dan and I will stick with Pee Hole for a while and give him the benefit of Dan's M–79 in case he wants to bring smoke on whoever is ahead of us. You stay with the *Ti-Uy*. We'll be back with you when we turn off on canal seven or eight and head for camp. OK?"

"Shouldn't I go with you?" Rocky asked, probably hoping to get into some action.

"It'd be better if you stayed with Tinh, Rocky. He'll need one of us with him in case he wants mortars and Dan can't go alone. Besides, you had your tour with a lead squad, coming into the village."

"OK, if you say so." Rock was disappointed. "It's your show."

"Bueno. See you shortly. Take care." Dan and I joined Pee Hole and his group of eager strikers as they started down the canal bank.

28

Walking along the path, we passed beyond the huts and trees. Now, on both sides of the canal stretched huge rice paddies; ahead were scattered huts built along the canal bank and behind them were green-topped fields of pineapple.

Snap! Bam! From ahead the report of a carbine told us that we were being checked out. The VC had security ahead to keep tabs on us and to harass. Three more shots whistled past and Pee Hole, tired of the harassment, said, *"Bac-si, bang di,"* and pointed down the path from where the shots had come. Pitzer raised the sight to maximum range and sighted, the muzzle of the weapon canted at an angle above forty-five degrees. He fired and the weapon recoiled into his shoulder as the steel-pellet-laden 40mm shell arched toward its target some three hundred meters away. The *ka-whump* sound as it exploded was surprisingly loud for the size of the shell, and the spray of pellets was extremely devastating. The enemy firing stopped and we proceeded.

After passing several canals, we came to a neat, unusually clean hut with a large pineapple field behind it. Immediately after being told to take a break, the squad called to the owner that they wanted to buy pineapples to eat. An old grandmother shuffled from the front door and stood in the bright sunlight, squinting slightly as she surveyed the soldiers standing around her. Apparently deciding the soldiers did in fact wish to buy pineapples, she told them to pick what they wanted and she would charge for what they took. Her face was thin, with deep wrinkles on her cheeks. Her hair, a lustrous graying black, was pulled back severely into a tight bun which protruded underneath the faded red-and-white-checked towel wrapped and folded about her head. As she talked in a high, sharp voice, I could see her red-stained teeth and soon, as I expected, she spat a stream of reddish-black betelnut juice, inundating an unwary resting grasshopper.

As the strikers walked through the field selecting fruit, the old woman spotted Dan and me standing with Pee Hole. Obviously curious about these "Yankee Aggressors" the Vietcong had told her about, she walked over to have a look for herself. Stopping in front of the Vietnamese sergeant, she peered at us, her sharp eyes flitting from muddy jungle boots to weapons and ammunition to our faces. Both of us were watching her, knowing we were being scrutinized, and we were smiling. Perhaps the smiles did it, but she suddenly burst into rapid-

29

fire Vietnamese, speaking to Pee Hole and gesturing toward Dan and me. I watched their two faces and tried to catch some of the words. She was now smiling a broken-toothed smile and referring to Pee Hole as *"Con"*—a Vietnamese family expression for child or son. Pee Hole was nodding; then he turned and called to one of the strikers in the field. The striker waved and came running toward us. He arrived carrying two beautiful ripe pineapples which he handed to Dan and me. As we took them the old lady stepped over to us and told us through gestures and speech that the pineapples were from her, and she wanted us to eat them immediately, gesturing toward the sun and wiping her face as if to rid it of perspiration. It was hot and she wanted us to have refreshment, fearing that the Vietnamese had not thought of sharing with us.

I thought, How can a person say "thank you" except to say the words which came out? Inadequate to repay generosity and thoughtfulness. The old lady and Pee Hole were beaming as Dan and I dug into the juicy, sweet fruit after offering each of them a portion, which they politely refused, indicating for us to enjoy it.

The strikers returned from the field carrying their fruit, and after paying the woman in soiled, crumpled, well-worn one-piaster notes, devoured the tangy, sharp pineapple. Shortly thereafter Pee Hole gave the word and the squad again moved down the canal bank. The old woman stood in the shade of her hut and watched us go.

We walked on with only occasional odd shots fired at us by snipers further up the canal bank. Once or twice Dan fired back with the M–79 and each time a respectful silence followed.

Finally, Pee Hole called the squad to a halt as we came up to one of the canals. *"Kinh tam, Trung-Uy,"* he said. *"Di ve nha."* Canal eight and we were going back to camp. I thought of that tall glass of iced tea and the cool shade of Titus Tavern. Oh, that was going to be good! We waited for the rest of the company to catch up with us. Lieutenant Tinh and Rocky came up as the lead platoon turned southeast along the canal. Pee Hole reported to Tinh and as Ho Chi arrived the three of them conferred, with Pee Hole and Ho Chi dominating the conversation. Tinh listened, asked several questions, and turned to Rocky and me: "Sergeant Tung has said that the VC do not

30

want to make contact with us because we are strong and they stay away from us. It is dangerous to go further so we will go back to camp now." This was partly true. Most of the VC had kept away and those who had been firing at us were to harass and act as bait, pulling us as deep into their territory as possible. Ho Chi, like the other leaders we had who were ex-Vietminh, was well aware of this tactic and refused to be lured on.

First Company had turned down canal five and was proceeding back toward the main canal. The long column of strikers moved at a brisk pace down the irregular bank. Along here there were no houses and the fields on both sides were uncultivated, with only reeds and dead trees scattered throughout. Clumps of moderately tall, leafy trees stood along the bank.

We had walked about twenty-five minutes when the column came to a halt and the strikers formed their version of a loose security by facing outward and squatting in place. We walked forward with Lieutenant Tinh and when we reached the lead squad, halted beside one particularly thick clump of trees, I saw a long, low, partially open-front thatch building hidden under the foliage. There were signs, written on rectangular pieces of tin, nailed to the trees: *Nguy Hiem. Min. Dung Vao.* Danger. Mines. Do Not Enter.

Heaps of scrap metal, iron fragments, and rusty lumps of metal lay to the left of the open front. What looked like a bellows and a crude forge stood inside the shadowy interior. Lieutenant Tinh walked back to where I was standing. "It is a Vietcong arms and ammunition factory. We will have to destroy it."

"What about the signs?" I asked, wondering about the possibility of their being accurate.

"The Vietcong must enter to work here. We will enter as they do," Tinh answered without hesitating.

The strikers had already begun picking their way toward the building across the ten meters of grassy ground to our front. They entered the building without mishap and began to look through it. Once again my curiosity was aroused and I found myself following their footsteps toward the hut. Several of them waved me back, but I was too near the hootch to turn back. As I entered the building, I found Dan Pitzer walking behind me. He just grinned and we checked out the arms factory.

At one end was the crude bellows and forge I had seen from

31

outside. Pieces of scrap metal, old shell casings, bomb fragments, and other pieces of unidentifiable metal lay scattered on the floor. In one corner were separate piles of charcoal and sulfur to be used in making gun-powder when combined with saltpeter. Dan picked up an L-shaped piece of light metal that looked like the stamped form for half a .45 cal. pistol, as if a toy pistol had been split down the center. He dropped it into the utility bag he was carrying and we walked into a small room at the far end of the building. On the floor was a 250-pound bomb! A closer examination disclosed that the fuse and explosive had been removed and the casing was probably scheduled to be reworked and made into a form usable against us.

As we walked out of the door back into the sunlight, the men inside were already at work preparing to destroy the building. Lieutenant Tinh joined us on the bank and the column again began to move. I looked back and saw flames soaring from the roof and eating through the walls.

We walked on, no one saying anything in particular, everyone looking forward to getting back to camp. I glanced across the field on my right in the direction of Tan Phu and on the horizon was a Caribou, the upsweep of its tail unmistakable, even at this distance.

"Look." I pointed. "Resupply going into camp." Dan and Rocky glanced in the direction I indicated, nodding. As we walked along, the Bou made another pass and suddenly the familiar shape of a T–10 parachute blossomed below it.

"Look at that!" Dan exclaimed. "It must be Martin jumping in." Bill Martin, our lanky demo man, had been on R&R to Saigon and at last report was stuck in Can Tho trying to find a ride back to camp on one of the infrequent choppers that came our way. When he heard the camp was in danger he elected to jump in and rejoin the team rather than wait for a chopper. I chuckled to myself, thinking that this was a typical stunt for Martin and feeling damn glad to have a team with men like that on it.

We watched as the Caribou came in lower and made its passes to drop the critically needed supplies. As soon as we got the wire and claymores in, Charlie could come ahead and get his nose bloodied.

Suddenly, excited shouts came from the lead squad, then from the squad behind it. All eyes snapped to the left, across a broad paddy to canal nine toward which the strikers were pointing. Black-clad figures were running along the bank, moving ahead of us one kilometer to our left. Lieutenant Tinh spoke rapidly with Ho Chi and commands were immediately shouted to the still-gesturing troops. Pee Hole again took the lead squad and Dih Dah grabbed the handset as the column lurched into an accelerated pace. Tinh stepped in behind me. "VC are running to get ahead of us. They try to cut us off. I must call Sergeant Canh and inform him," he spoke rapidly, his eyes wider than usual.

"Can you get Thoi Binh on the radio and request 155's?" I asked, referring to the two 155mm howitzers located at the district capital.

"We cannot reach Thoi Binh," he replied frowning. Then, "Sergeant Canh will contact Thoi Binh and request." His face relaxed into its normal calm as he came up with a solution.

That wasn't the ideal solution, but under the circumstances it would do. F.O.-ing through two Vietnamese radio operators was not a pleasant thought. I wished that L–19 was up there right now. Rocky spoke my thoughts: "Damn it! We need that L–19 now, Nick! We could really hurt 'em."

"Affirmative on that, Rocky. However, due to a slight miscalculation on the far turn . . ." I replied, thinking of the answer he had gotten the night before.

The column slowed abruptly; strikers bunched up. Again excited voices, this time all up and down the column. Tension gripped all of us, it was so strong. The lead squad had come to a high patch of reeds that lay on both sides of the canal and masked the path. The question, unspoken, was there. Ambush? The strikers were not going to blindly enter the sight-masking reeds. Ho Chi called to his nearest grenadiers and they immediately fitted fragmentation grenades with their stabilizing fins down over the adapters on the rifles. The sharp report of the weapons was followed shortly by explosions and puffs of dark smoke as the grenades detonated above the reeds, spraying the ground beneath with a deadly rain of steel.

Both sides of the canal were doused with steel. Ho Chi spoke to the platoon leader and the troops began to move once more, the lead squad reluctantly entering the high reeds. The attitude and previous bravado was slipping away as the company found itself the hunted, instead of the hunter. Pee Hole rejoined our command group, leaving the squad leader to handle the lead squad. A strange uneasiness began to settle in my stomach. "Lord, please let me get back to that iced tea," I asked.

The canal came to an end, meeting a larger northeast-southwest canal. Across from us was a large rice paddy to the left, extending all the way to canal nine. A narrow strip of tall reeds bordered what seemed to be a type of irrigation ditch running directly across from this canal. There were reeds between the ditch and canal nine. On the right, maybe thirty meters from the ditch, was a coconut grove, and looking further to the right, I could see a canal similar to this one continuing on in the direction we were going. It looked as if canal eight had been stopped here and shifted fifty meters to the right. Among the coconut palms I could see huts bordering the canal to my right.

The Vietnamese leaders surveyed the area, carefully scanning canal nine, a little less than eight hundred meters to our left. Their faces were concerned as Ho Chi gave the word and the company began crossing the canal and wading into the ditch, then climbing up onto the low mound of mud and clay that had been dug from the ditch. I crossed the canal and mounted the pile of mud, although walking along it was only slightly easier than walking in the water.

Suddenly the air was filled with hissing, snapping bullets. The rattle of automatic weapons shattered the morning calm. From behind us now, as I dropped into a crouch and turned toward canal nine, came the wail of ricocheting bullets spraying through the trees. Canal nine was alive with the flash of weapons.

Dropping backward off the crest and down behind the relative protection of the packed mud and clay, I looked around for Rocky and Dan. Good, both were behind the mound, their weapons ready, eyes searching for targets. This was a case where we, as advisers, could fire back because we had been fired at first.

The strikers began to fire all weapons in the direction of the distant enemy. One soldier sprang on top of the bank and, screaming in hate at the VC, emptied his Thompson SMG in one long burst, churning up water and mud as the unaimed bullets struck fifty meters to his front. The enemy rounds were all passing high overhead. The range was too great for accuracy.

Then the thought hit me, they're trying to fix us in place. Stop us long enough for that blocking force to get ahead of us and cut us off. Where's Tinh? I glanced to my right and saw him crouching about ten meters away with Ho Chi and Dih Dah. Scrambling over to him through the knee-deep water, I immediately told him to get the strikers moving. The VC firing wasn't hurting us and we couldn't effectively return fire at this range. We had to hit the blocking force before they got set or we were in for a bad show.

Lieutenant Tinh was maddeningly slow in considering what I had said. When it was translated for Ho Chi, he nodded rapid assent and Tinh then seemed to realize the impact of what was happening.

Ho Chi was shouting for the strikers to cease firing and move out, but the strikers, obsessed with the noise, the power of firing their weapons, continued to pour a useless barrage of steel into the rice paddy and over the heads of the entrenched VC.

"Dan!" I yelled. "Get them moving!" I scaled the low mound and, standing on top, looking down at the wide-eyed soldiers, yelled and waved for them to cease firing and move out. Dan was up on the other end of the mound and the firing came to a ragged halt, but not before we heard the dreaded *thunk, thunk, thunk* of mortar tubes. "Mortars!" Rocky shouted as he joined Dan and me in moving the hesitant Vietnamese from behind their muddy refuge.

The first rounds exploded in the paddy about two hundred meters away, their detonations blending with the now almost continuous sound of more rounds being fired.

Oh shit, shit, shit, I thought, almost in time with the explosions that were walking closer as the VC gunners adjusted their aim. We were in the ditch now, crouching low in the water, pushing through the dirty grayish-brown fluid that seemed to be as thick as motor oil. Damn, it was hard to move. My stomach tightened into a small compact knot as if trying to draw my whole being into its protection. Fragments whistled and cut the air around us. I instinctively crouched at the sound of tubes firing, knowing that the next round surely would be right on top of me, fighting the urge to sink down into the protection of the water and hide.

"Keep 'em moving, Tinh!" I called to him as I saw him crouch in the water after a near explosion showered him with water. He looked back at me and nodded vigorously, then moved forward again, encouraging the troops around him. Dan and Rocky were calling to the strikers, telling them to keep moving, don't waste ammo, don't stop.

The VC gunners were having difficulty finding the range. We were somewhere between the reeds and canal eight, but they didn't know exactly where. The going was miserable in the water but at least they didn't have the range.

One of our squad leaders grabbed a 60mm mortar tube from the striker who had been carrying it. Finding a firm spot on the low mound of mud, he slapped the base plate down, set the tube into the socket, and holding the tube with his hand, called for ammunition. An ammo bearer splashed up beside him and drew out three rounds from his canvas carrying case, handing them one at a time to the squad leader who dropped each, in turn, down the mouth of the 60mm mortar. He adjusted the tube slightly each time, his face confident as he pumped H.E. rounds back at the enemy.

I started to cry out but it was too late, rounds were on the way, their safety forks unpulled. The rounds would not detonate. Before the three remaining rounds were fired, I reached the blank-faced ammo bearer and grabbed them, pulling the safeties and handing them to the squad leader. Seeing the American pulling the safety wire from the rounds made him realize what had happened with the first three rounds. The squad leader's face was stricken as he dropped the final three rounds down the tube, our only answer to the VC's overwhelming superiority.

Behind me I heard strikers shouting. Turning, I saw a group of strikers break off from the column and begin slogging toward the trees and canal bank. Realizing that it would be much faster to travel along the canal bank, they had left the company and were trying to reach the canal.

Oh, no! My mind screamed silently. That's what those gunners are waiting for. They know the range to the canal! "Tinh!" I yelled, pointing to the retreating figures, "get them back! Tell them to come back!" Knowing already that it was too late, Tinh and Ho Chi called to the men who continued to run, giving no indication they had heard. There was a momentary lull as the rounds ceased to fall around us. I could see in my mind the gunners quickly turning the ranging knob on their mortars, stretching it out to reach the bank. Then it came: all the mortars firing at once. One short, murderous flight of shells, range correct, arching high above and slanting downward.

The group of strikers broke through the trees, reached the bank, and started to run down the canal. We were all watching as the whole bank suddenly exploded. Smoke, clods of earth, fragments splattering into the unprotected bodies, short screams torn from the throats of dead men. The bodies were flung down like limp rag dolls. Silence. There was no time to mourn. The mortars were firing again, this time at us.

Lieutenant Tinh pointed in toward the canal bank ahead. I could see a number of huts beyond the trees. It was a small hamlet and we were turning toward it. Ahead the reeds stopped and an open rice paddy meant certain death if we were foolish enough to try to cross it.

As we entered the shade beneath the trees I realized I was very tired. My legs were like two lead pipes that had been sunk into the ground and each step required that I pull them out, one at a time. I had to take a leak and decided to combine a rest stop with relieving myself. My mind had shut itself to the situation, as if entering the grove of palms had transported me to another world. I stopped beside a palm tree as strikers hurried past me, some of them openly staring, disbelieving that anyone would stop at a time like this. An older Vietnamese who had been a member of a militia unit before he discovered the better pay and equipment at Tan Phu, where he had been nicknamed "Crazy" by the American team, slouched by, carrying his BAR across his shoulder. He broke into a jagged grin and called out, *"Trung-Uy,* you'd better put that thing away before some VC shoots it off and puts it on his wall for a trophy!" The other strikers broke into grins at this unexpected jibe and their tension slipped away as fast as it had come.

I walked past a hut and turned the corner by its narrow front porch, finding myself in the midst of the command group. Tinh and Dih Dah were talking rapidly with Pee Hole. Dan was checking the huts to the right and left. Rocky and Ho Chi were nowhere to be seen. I scanned the area, searching for defensive positions or anything that would provide cover. Tinh turned to me, again his normal sleepy-eyed self. "The company commander has gone to see if we can proceed. I have contacted Sergeant Canh. First Company is already near camp, but they come to help us. Do you want anything done?"

The situation was not good, but neither was it hopeless. Since First Company was "already near camp," we were hung way out with no immediate support. We had taken casualties and inflicted none. We had over 150 rounds of ammo per man, at a rough guess, although it wouldn't last long the way the strikers were using it. Our mortar was out of ammo so there was nothing to counter the VC mortars unless we could call in 155's or get an airstrike. We had a 3.5-inch rocket launcher and somewhere were ammo bearers with at least four rounds. Commo was apparently still good. If we could push on to the main canal, not giving Charlie a chance to get set, we might make it even though everyone looked a little beat from the paddy walking. This, I thought, was a beautiful example of the old tactic of never attacking a fresh enemy: let him wear himself out, and hit him when he's tired.

I estimated the VC had at least a couple of companies against us, perhaps more than that, but he wasn't showing it yet. The mortars were an immediate threat. I could hear the explosions in the tree line as the VC gunners shifted the range and deflection, feeling for us. Soon they'd be dropping them in on the hootches.

Rocky came up from the far end of the hamlet. "This is a good defensive position, Nick," he said quietly. "If we have to stop anywhere it might as well be here. We can cover the paddy from the tree line and cut the canal from here. The other side," he pointed across the canal, "is the weakness unless we can get more troops."

"What about up ahead?" I asked. "Can we break through?"

"Didn't get that far, but there's a lot of firing and we don't have that many people up there. It must be Charlie."

Lieutenant Tinh was at my side listening to Rocky and me. After we finished he asked what we thought was the best course of action.

"Are you certain First Company is coming?" I asked. "And do we have commo to call in 155's and airstrikes?"

Ho Chi came trotting up before Tinh could answer, his face flushed. He reported. The VC blocking force was in position and had a machine gun covering the path. We couldn't get past it without heavy casualties. Lieutenant Tinh looked at me questioningly.

38

"Let's set up a perimeter here, *Ti-Uy*. We can stick it out till help comes," I said with a confidence I didn't really feel.

Tinh gave orders in short bursts to the different leaders who had gathered. Ho Chi and his platoon leaders broke off in all directions, returning to their positions. Pee Hole nodded silently as Tinh briefed him, then departed toward the grove we had passed through entering the hamlet, ordered to take charge of the perimeter segment that was to bear the weight of the heaviest assaults. Tinh and Dih Dah, followed by one of the company medics, entered the nearest hootch. Rocky, Dan, and I looked at each other without speaking and followed them inside. The sound of firing increased all around us. The mortars were a continuous threatening sound, frustrating because we had no weapon against them. The assaults were beginning as lines of VC shock troops swarmed over the rice paddy, flowing like a black-crested wave toward us.

Inside the hut I found myself in a relatively large room which no doubt served as a type of living-dining room combination. An elderly Vietnamese stood in front of a handmade cabinet, the family's meager collection of rice bowls and larger ceramic serving bowls placed on its shelves. A beautifully ornate Buddhist shrine occupied the top, its joss sticks visibly protruding from the small receptacle in front. The old man's wispy white goatee shook as he spoke with Lieutenant Tinh and he glanced fearfully at us, his eyes widening when he recognized us as Americans. Lieutenant Tinh and the others stepped into a smaller room to the right rear which served as a kitchen. The old gentleman bowed slightly and reached to a small table to his right. He took a teapot and cup that resembled a rounded shot glass and poured tea, indicating for us to drink. His eyes never left my face as I quickly sipped the lukewarm bitter liquid and murmured, *"Cam on, Ong."* He bowed again slightly, and the ritual of accepting guests into his home, invited or uninvited, being completed, he went quickly into the other room and rejoined his family in the packed clay bunker under the flat wooden sleeping rack. I wondered briefly what an American would do if this happened in his home.

Lieutenant Tinh had the radio handset and was apparently trying to contact First Company. We couldn't reach camp directly, according to Dih Dah, and had to relay through First Company. Dan took the medic aside and began preparing to

39

treat the wounded that would soon be coming in. Rocky squatted beside me as I listened to Tinh.

"Can we get mortars or artillery?"

"If I can get Ponce or John, we'll have mortars in no time. Providing they can reach us. I'm not really sure how far away we are," I confessed.

Tinh finished his transmission and handed me the set, shaking his head. "VC jam the signal, sir. I cannot talk with First Company."

"Give me coordinates of our position, Tinh, and coordinates of the VC position on canal nine," I said as I changed frequencies on the PRC/10.

"Nick, listen!" Rock exclaimed. "Aircraft!" He sprang to the small side door and looked up searching the sky.

"It's the Caribou, Nick, and he's got a loaded T–28 flying shotgun." I spun the dial to 38.1, our ground-to-air frequency at Tan Phu, working feverishly to get a zero beat.

"CV–2, CV–2, this is Tan Phu, over." I almost shouted, using the official designation for the Caribou. The rush of static was unbroken.

"CV–2, CV–2, this is Tan Phu. Can you hear me?" He was on a direct flight back to Can Tho or Soc Trang after the supply drop and if he didn't hear me soon, he'd be out of range. Lord, we could use that T–28. Come on, answer, damn it.

"CV–2, CV–2, this is Tan Phu. Can you hear me? Over."

Only the rush of static, and then, a break in the static and very faintly: "Lieutenant Rowe, Lieutenant Rowe, I can hear you."

It was someone back at camp. Tinh read the expression on my face and thrust his plastic-covered map toward me. Written in black grease pencil were two sets of coordinates one marked "VC." I read the coordinates slowly, repeating them twice and released the push-to-talk switch. The handset was filled with whistling, babbling, a jabbering *"Mot, hai, ba, bon. Mot, hai, ba, bon."* So loud it was piercing. The VC had found the frequency and were jamming. Please let the camp have gotten the coordinates, I prayed as I dialed the primary, 50.1.

"Rattlesnake two, this is Rattlesnake one, over." I tried the call sign three times with no answer. The range was too great. Then the whistling and screaming came over the handset. They had that frequency covered too.

I handed the set to Dih Dah and turned to Rocky and Lieutenant Tinh. "If they got the coordinates we'll have some help soon. They know we're in a fix and they'll be busting their ass to get something to us. It boils down to our holding here until that something arrives. I'm going outside and find a nice quiet hole where I can put this M–1 to use."

Tinh nodded and said he'd stay with the radio and run the CP. I knew that Rocky was itching to get out where things were happening and his answer confirmed it. "Let's go!" he said.

Dan was bandaging one of the strikers who had been hit a glancing blow along the cheekbone. The lower portion of his cheek hung, spouting bright blood, over his jaw. Dan looked up, nodded, indicating he had overheard the situation, and turned back to his work. I didn't envy the job he had in store that day.

As we stepped out of the door onto the packed mud porch, the sounds of battle engulfed us. It was many times louder outside and the air seemed to be filled with a continuous snap of bullets around us, over us.

Rocky tapped me on the shoulder and, crouching low, disappeared around the corner of the building. I hunched over and ran for a shallow hole I had seen earlier at the edge of the path along the canal bank. Its position gave me a straight shot down the path. I slid into the hole and peered over the edge cautiously. The path was empty. I didn't know whether to be disappointed or relieved.

Looking around, I checked the huts on the other side of the canal. All, understandably, appeared deserted. I couldn't see any of our people over there and made a mental note to tell Tinh we needed at least half a squad to cover the immediate area. Beyond the huts I could see a large open paddy and thought it odd that the VC weren't putting pressure on us from that side. Their main effort was directed at the tree line to my right, where Pee Hole was in charge. The blocking force to my rear seemed to be just that, an entrenched force cutting off our retreat to the main canal. As soon as First Company hits that blocking force from the other side, I calculated, we can break loose and pin the blocking force between us, and once they're finished, the two companies can fight back to Kinh Song Trem. When we get there, it'll be a matter of calling in everything that will fly for one huge airstrike.

There was a steady stream of strikers entering the hut to report and then reappearing on the way back to their positions. The Cambods were conspicuous in their utter disregard for personal safety. They strolled around as if they were walking down the main street of Tan Phu on payday. I had learned earlier that most of them were Buddhists and had tattooed on their chests a particular design which was supposed to protect them from bodily harm. So strong was their belief in this tattoo that on an earlier patrol, one of them who had been seriously wounded blamed the tattoo artist for making a mistake in the design, thus rendering it ineffective.

Well, I thought, this isn't accomplishing anything. Wondering how Pee Hole was doing, I decided to take a look at our perimeter. Having climbed out of the relative safety of my position, I ducked and ran across the open area to the palm grove. I didn't have a tattoo, I wasn't going to stand up.

In the grove, the trees showed ragged scars of passing fragments and bullets. Shredded palm fronds littered the ground as bullets hissed overhead, slashing through the drooping branches. Ahead, where the sunlight broke through at the edge of the grove, I could see the prone figures of the second platoon, lying behind tree trunks and mounds of earth. Some of them were lying twisted in unnatural positions, no longer mindful of the struggle raging around them.

I dodged from tree to tree until I was beside Pee Hole, looking out over a field of carnage. Bodies lay scattered all over that damn paddy, some of them within ten meters of second platoon's weapons. These strikers of ours were fighting like tigers and Charlie realized by now that he had a fight on his hands. There was a surge of hope. If only the ammo holds out . . . Pee Hole looked at me. *"Dai doi mot?"* It was a question. Where was First Company?

"Dang len," I answered—"On the way."

Pee Hole grinned his gold-capped grin and called to the troops to fight on: First Company would soon be here. A full-throated cheer came from the strikers as they settled themselves to await the next assault.

I returned to the CP hut and found Lieutenant Tinh conferring with Ho Chi and a platoon leader. The VC were moving up on canal eight behind us, thus fixing us from the front and

42

attacking on two sides. Still, there was one side open in case we had to make it. That bothered me. Why would they ignore that flank? Unless they intended for it to appear as a possible avenue of escape. Tinh translated for me as I asked Ho Chi why that flank was not being exploited by the VC. The stocky company commander squatted and silently sketched a rough map of the immediate area on the dirt floor. Pointing to his work, he indicated what were tree lines on two sides of the large paddy that occupied the open flank. *"Phuc-kich,"* he said—Ambush. I nodded silently. That was it. Give us an opening to run, let us get into the middle of that open field, and cut us to pieces. So much for that question.

Tinh gave orders shifting one of the platoons slightly to meet the new threat, after which Ho Chi and the Cambodian platoon leader hurried out of the hut. This new assault was coming down the canal toward the hole I had selected, so it might be a good idea to get back outside. I asked Tinh what the latest word was from First Company and how the ammunition was holding up. First Company was still on the way, and the ammunition was down to about eighty or ninety rounds per man with redistribution of ammo taken from dead strikers. Not too bad, I thought. The big push is just beginning, though.

Dan had finished treating a badly wounded soldier and was turning the task over to the Vietnamese medic and his assistant. Men less seriously wounded than others sought to help. Some sat with their backs against the mud bunker, staring ahead, their faces gray in the dim light.

"Let's go scramble a few," Dan said, picking up the M–79 and walking toward the front door.

I told Lieutenant Tinh about my look at second platoon and gave him a brief status report. "Well, *Ti-Uy*, there isn't much I can do in here. If you need me I'll be out by the canal bank. Keep me posted on First Company."

"Yes, sir. I cannot talk with First Company yet. I have tried all frequencies." Dih Dah was trying, at that moment, to make contact.

"OK, *Ti-Uy*. I'll be outside." I left him and walked through the front room, pausing at the door. The sound of explosions was increasing as mortar rounds slammed one after the other into the trees and along the canal bank. Fragments whipped past over my head, causing me to crouch alongside Pitzer,

43

squatting near the door, studying the situation.

A Vietnamese was lying partially in a ditch to our left, unwounded but apparently unwilling to move. He had a bazooka with him and no intention of using it. Dan and I thought, and moved, at the same time. I grabbed the launcher tube while Dan looked for an ammo bearer, finding one huddled a few meters away. He had one Willy Peter round left, and Dan relieved him of it immediately.

"Range to that canal about a hundred meters?" I asked, indicating the point at which we had crossed from canal eight into the smaller ditch. The target was obscured by trees, but it was worth a chance to catch some of the VC moving toward the canal we were on.

"'Bout that," Dan replied as he loaded the rocket into the rear of the launcher. "Watch out for the branches."

He tapped the top of my cap as I was aiming to avoid hitting the overhanging branches, his tap indicating the weapon was loaded and he was clear of the backblast area. I pressed the trigger and with a *whoosh* the round was heading toward the oncoming VC.

"That ought to frost their balls," Dan chuckled as I handed the weapon back to the striker and pointed toward the hut, motioning him to take it inside. No sense in having him ditch it out there.

Short, rattling bursts of fire came from the canal bank, our SMG's easily distinguishable from the *"burrr-ip"* of the Communists' K–50's. I dove for the hole, this time sliding the last three or four meters on my stomach as bullets zipped and hissed all around me. No longer was the canal bank empty. I looked over the edge of the hole at what appeared to be a solid wall of bodies, floppy bush hats, and muzzle blasts. My weapon was recoiling into my shoulder. The ping as the empty clip ejected brought my mind back into focus. I don't know if I even aimed those eight rounds. Get organized! The two words slammed through my mind. *Get organized!* I fumbled another clip out of the cloth bandoleer, cursing my clumsiness, jammed it into the M–1, letting the bolt slide forward. OK, now, Rowe, cool it, take it slow, aim, squeeze. The rifle jerked back. Through the peepsight I saw a black shirt and green cartridge belt stop and crumple over. It was replaced by another. Aim, squeeze the trigger, recoil. The black shirt jerked upright, then

44

dropped. Another, then another. The second clip flew out of the weapon. I could hear the shouting, distorted faces hurling their bodies forward. *"Tien len! Tien len!"* the leaders screamed to their men, *"Mau len, Dong Chi! Mau len!"*—Attack! Rapidly, comrades! Attack!

I emptied one bandoleer, setting the clips down just below the lip of the hole, and pushed a new clip into the M–1. The tree growing to the right front of my position must have been catching hell; it was snowing bits of leaves and shattered bark. Geysers of water spouted from the canal, an arm's length to my left.

The Vietcong found themselves in a crossfire, losing men rapidly, their dead and wounded sprawled along the bank. One of their leaders blew a shrill blast on a whistle and the VC began to withdraw, back along the way they had come, some of them continuing to fire while others could be seen dragging bodies of their fallen comrades by an arm or by the cartridge belt.

I fired another clip of ammunition at them as they withdrew, this time painfully conscious that each time I squeezed the trigger, a man fell. I found myself picking among the crouching figures. "You die! Piss on you! You die!" One firing at our strikers. Die! One with a small triangular red-and-blue flag. One struggling to drag a body away: Pass; you've got enough trouble.

They disappeared into the trees farther down the canal. Now I felt the perspiration dripping. My mouth was dry, sweat stung my eyes. I pulled off my cap and wiped the moisture from my face. Boy, I'm glad they're gone. I slouched lower in the protective depth of the hole, finding it suddenly hard to catch my breath. I felt as if I had just finished a mile run. OK, I told myself, relax, there's more to come and you've got no place to go, so cool it and enjoy the break. I checked my ammo. What the hell is this? I already had clips from the second bandoleer laid out. When did I do that? I had gone through all but one clip from the first bandoleer, and, at some point, had taken clips out of the second. Gotta hang loose on that stuff. I must have been pumping shots like a runaway striker.

"I wonder where . . ." Bullets tore the air just over my head, bark showered down from the tree trunk. Christ! Where did that come from? I hunched lower, at the same time tossing a quick glance to my left toward a clump of trees across the canal. Movement! I rolled to my left and brought my weapon up just in time to duck as another burst sprayed into the path in front of me. I saw the flashes from the weapon. He was moving to his left as he fired. Fire, move to his left, fire, and he should stop about right, there! I snapped off three quick rounds toward a shape in the trees next to a ditch. There was silence, then a long burst from the SMG. Water erupted in the ditch as a finger closed in a death grip on the trigger. A body sagged from behind a tree and toppled into the ditch.

I searched the trees for other movement. This was going to be a little tight if they were in those trees. Damn, why didn't we have somebody over there. A body dropped in behind me! My spine turned to ice. I slashed backward with my elbow, nearly braining Lieutenant Tinh, who parried with his forearm. Relief flooded over me. His face was practically white, eyes enormous. "Damn, *Ti Uy!* Knock before you come in," I exclaimed. His face was grim, a mixture of anger and surprise. Thinking my actions had prompted it, I continued, "I'm glad you're quick. I didn't mean to swing on you."

He shook his head. His eyes dropped, his whole body sagging as we crouched in the cramped hole. An awful premonition made my stomach curl within itself.

"First Company has been ambushed. They are dead. They will not come to help us." The words out, his face once again became a stoic mask.

I heard without my mind accepting. They have to come. This can't be happening. I've been on patrols before and we've always made it back. Thoughts piled over one another in my mind, a kaleidoscopic tangle: Mom, Dad, their faces, home, my room. Then closer association: camp, the village. So damned close. The mess hall, that glass of iced tea. This can't be happening.

Stop this crap! Everything dissolved and I was back in the situation. Tinh was looking at me, his eyes questioning. It's odd you should ask me what to do, Lieutenant Tinh, I thought, chuckling sarcastically to myself, 'cause I don't have the slightest idea right now. Why didn't you ever ask me in a simple situation? I wondered. "What's our status? Troops, ammo, do we have commo with anyone?"

"There are many wounded," he replied quickly. "I do not

know of the dead. There is enough ammunition for one more assault, perhaps a little more."

"What about commo?" I prompted.

"We have lost contact."

Well, Rowe, I thought, this is what you're here for. Advise him!

"We cannot stay, sir, there is no help," Tinh added.

"Do we have enough men to try to break the blocking force?" I was thinking that if we could get beyond them it would be possible to either withdraw as a unit or split up and exfiltrate in small groups. There would be no real chance to break contact and we'd be fighting all the way to the main canal. The first thing was to get out of this cul-de-sac.

"I will find out, sir." Tinh slipped out of the hole and dashed to the hut, disappearing inside.

I looked around for Rocky and Dan. They were crouched behind one of the earthen firing positions the VC had built some time before, both of them continuing to fire as targets appeared in the trees. Dan had just fired the M-79 into the grove and was reloading. I called to them that we were going to make a break for the main canal.

Rocky yelled back, "Where's First Company?"

"Ambushed. They're not coming," I called. They fired at the VC another time and, crouching, zigzagged back to two trees near me.

Rocky asked what the story was and I repeated the situation. Dan glanced in the direction of the blocking force, then turned back, shaking his head. "Doesn't look too good," he said. We all agreed on that, but there were few options open.

Lieutenant Tinh appeared in the doorway and came running over to us. We had enough men to try to break for the main canal and could begin to withdraw now, before another assault. Tinh had already passed the word. We decided that the three of us would stay in position here, covering the strikers as they pulled back from the perimeter. After they passed our position, they would set up and cover us as we withdrew. Tinh agreed to this, and we took up firing positions.

Shortly thereafter, the strikers appeared, walking backward at an angle, their weapons pointed toward the VC. Scattered shots at first followed them, increasing in volume as the VC discovered that the strikers were pulling back.

Rocky and I began to lay down covering fire, spreading our shots over as wide an area as possible. Dan held the M-79 ready, searching for any group of VC to show so he could clean them with the 40mm. The strikers reached us and, facing ahead, began to move out. None of them stopped. I snapped a glance at the disappearing strikers. It looked like we were alone. Glancing back toward the trees, I saw more figures coming toward us and thought immediately that they were the last of second platoon. The next thing was Dan yelling, "Nick! Get out of there! Those are VC!"

Kiss my ass! The VC assault squads were pouring through our freshly vacated perimeter. I snapped a couple of quick shots off at the nearest black-clad figures and scrambled out of the hole, diving back toward the trees with Dan and Rocky. Dan popped a round into the chest of one of the oncoming VC and the man's upper body disintegrated, the explosion and flesh-tearing steel pellets stopping him cold and at the same time crumpling several of his comrades. This gave me a chance to reach the trees.

"Let's go! Make it!" We turned and ran for the next thing that would give us cover.

I tried to jump over one of the ditches running perpendicularly from the canal to the huts where the families kept their low, flat-bottomed boats. My foot stuck at the edge, and I sprawled in the water. The ditch was deeper than I thought possible, and it took a great deal of effort to pull myself out. I rolled clear and ran for a nearby hut. As I walked across the porch I saw a line of tracers flash ahead of me in the space between this hut and the next. The staccato bark of an automatic weapon sounded from my left. As I peered around the corner of the hut, searching for the telltale muzzle blast in the patch of reeds where the weapon must be located, I heard footsteps behind me. I whirled, crouching, my M–1 leveled. A frightened striker dashed onto the porch, a grenadier, the rifle grenades bouncing and swinging from his waist as he ran. I grabbed his equipment harness as he came past me, intent on continuing his retreat. Forgetting the two grenades hanging from my own harness, I released him and snatched a rifle grenade, pulling the stabilizing fin free. As soon as I released him, he bolted into the open area. "No!" I yelled, but it was too late. Again I saw the line of tracers, heard the weapon. This time they terminated in the body of the speeding grenadier. He was slammed sideways by the impact and hit the ground, his legs still churning. I stepped around the corner, pulled the pin, and tossed the grenade into the reeds, where wisps of smoke had disclosed the weapon. Ducking behind a squat cement water crock, I waited. The explosion was close, the water crock shattered, and I was drenched. What a dumb ass; I could have killed myself! I started toward the next hut.

My legs were beginning to feel like lead and it was difficult to get my breath. How long has this been going on? I wondered. I looked at my watch. The crystal was shattered, the dial scarred. The hands were gone. Lord, I'm not going to make it if I have to go through any more of those ditches. I looked toward the canal bank and path. Screw it! I don't give a rat's ass, I decided as I headed for the path. It's just as easy to get hit back here as it is out there. Leaving the line of houses, I walked rapidly to the path, too tired all of a sudden to even think about running.

As I walked down the canal bank I felt a curious detached sense of not really being a part of my body. I felt a little light-headed, and my chest was burning as I sucked huge breaths in, trying to ease the muscle cramps setting in. Bullets snapped around me, but I was only partially aware of them.

I crossed a short bridge and came to an abrupt halt. There on the bank, lying face upward, his chest pumping a bloody froth, was one of our Cambods. A sucking chest wound, one lung punctured, and death coming shortly. His pain-filled eyes fluttered, then opened as he saw me. His eyes seemed to glow for a moment, I don't think I imagined it, as if he were saying, "Ah here's one of the Americans. He'll take care of me." The strikers all had a type of faith in their American adviser friends, one we sought to develop and never betray. I knew I couldn't help him and only hoped he died before Charlie got to him. I bent down, his eyes on me all the time, and loosened his equipment harness, then took his weapon and ammo so Charlie wouldn't get them. The light died in his eyes. "May your God be merciful," I prayed. The Cambod couldn't understand me. Maybe Buddha heard me.

I rose to a crouch and moved out. I hadn't taken ten steps when I heard this horrible gasping behind me. I turned and there, staggering, stumbling, was my Cambod, trying to follow me. As I stared, he looked straight at me, then took a full load

49

from a K–50 in the back. He pitched forward as I raised my M–1 and gunned the VC. If he hadn't been there those rounds would have been for me. After that incident I turned in toward the line of houses again, continuing to move away from the perimeter we had left.

The VC were getting closer now, their firing was sharp and steady. Ahead I could see some of the strikers grouped beside one of the houses. As I neared them I noticed heads showing above a depression in the ground. It was another, larger ditch and around it, in it, were the survivors of what had been proud Third Company, Tan Phu Strike Force.

Huddling in the reddish-brown water, seeking protection from the hail of bullets zipping overhead, along with dead and wounded, were Lieutenant Tinh and Dih Dah. Pee Hole stood knee-deep in the small ditch that drained from this into the adjacent rice paddy. He had discarded his distinctive camouflage uniform which marked him as a member of the elite LLDB, realizing what would happen if he fell into VC hands. He wore a pair of trousers taken from a dead striker and clutched a fragmentation grenade to his chest. He was no longer the brash, grinning Pee Hole I had known. He looked up as I approached and, seeing me, shook his head, then glanced at the mass of disorganized soldiers, *"Het Trung-Uy,"* he rasped, his breath coming in jerks. *"Het roi"*—Finished, Lieutenant, it's all finished.

"Nick!" I heard Dan's voice and looked to the end of the ditch. Unlike most of the Vietnamese, Dan and Rocky still had their weapons. Rocky had lost his glasses and couldn't see to fire. They climbed up on the bank, and we surveyed the remnants of our force. Strikers not in the ditch were lying prone behind trees and sprawled out on the side of the hut. Wounded lay glassy-eyed, their blood flowing from unbandaged holes. The Vietnamese medic wasn't with us. Only a few strikers held onto their weapons; most were demoralized and merely trying to avoid the death that was whistling all around us. This company would never fight again, even though they had extracted a horrible price from the attacking Vietcong in exchange.

The single possibility for escape was a large field of reeds growing at the edge of the rice paddy to our left front. If we could get into them, it would be possible to evade the enemy and at least some of the people could hide until dark and make it back to camp. Lieutenant Tinh had joined us as we hurriedly discussed the plan. I gave Tinh no options as I told him to get his people moving and get into the dense reeds. He immediately called to the men, and they began hesitantly to inch out of the ditch. He called again and the exodus was under way. Soon only the dead and a couple of terrified strikers remained in the bloodstained water. There wasn't time to coax them. The VC were closing in and we'd all buy the farm if we didn't clear out.

As the last of the troops stumbled toward the reeds, ten or fifteen meters away, across a U-shaped patch of clear water, Dan, Rocky, and I followed. A striker, partially hidden in high grass on the edge of the paddy, refusing to go, reached out and handed me his M–1 as I passed, his eyes on mine, frightened but intent. I took his weapon, slung it over my left shoulder, and pushed on after Dan and Rocky who were almost into the reeds.

Shouts came from my left and, whirling instinctively, I was confronted by a group of VC, not more than thirty meters away as they turned into this clear space from the other side of reeds separating us from the main paddy. The one in front wore a camouflaged bush hat, its floppy brim pulled down all the way around, and in his left hand carried a triangular red-and-blue flag, edges ruffled with gold cord. A squad leader! He carried a K–50 in his other hand.

I jerked the M–1 to my shoulder and fired two hasty rounds toward his stomach. Back at Bragg, someone had told me that there is a tendency to fire high in combat. This flashed through my racing mind as I saw the back of his head burst with the impact of the round.

I lined up the man next to him as he raised his carbine. I jerked the trigger and got a round off; then the awful *ping* as the empty clip ejected. I knelt quickly, raising the M–1 into a vertical position, cramming a fresh clip in. Zipping bullets passed by me and my M–1 was knocked out of my hands. I dove backward, following the weapon, grabbing in the muddied water. My chest and stomach tensed, expecting the next rounds to be hits.

My groping fingers closed on the stock. Pulling the weapon out of the water and scrambling to my feet, I made a headlong dive for the reeds. Rocky grabbed me as I crashed into the thick growth. He sprayed the VC, depending more on sound and vague shadow than clear sight. I looked at the weapon.

Rounds had struck the gas piston and upper handguard, making it impossible to open the bolt. I heaved the useless M-1 into the brush and unslung the striker's rifle, rejoicing that I had taken it.

Dan was ahead of us. There was a narrow path of broken and bent reeds where the Vietnamese had preceded us. We walked rapidly along, trying to move as quietly as possible yet sacrificing no speed. Tinh was suddenly in front of me. He pointed to a bloody mess on the side of his head where a bullet had grazed him. I patted him on the shoulder as I glanced at his wound. It was not of any real importance to me at that moment. The objective now was to put as much distance as possible between us and the pursuing VC. I motioned for him to continue, telling him to keep his people moving until they could hide and escape.

He disappeared into the reeds and Rocky stepped ahead of me, taking the lead for our tiny group of Americans. He hadn't gone more than five or ten meters when an automatic weapon fired from our right, and Rocky sagged, then dropped with a low moan. Oh shit, no! Not now! I started toward Rocky's crumpled shape and started to kneel. A muffled *whump* to my front, a spray of stinging hot water, and a huge fist slamming me backward. I sat there, up to my waist in water, the smell of burned black powder in my nostrils, my eyes refusing to focus. Everything was a multicolored haze. Sounds were coming from the end of a long, long tunnel, everything was so far away. I'm dead. The thought stood out in the gray fog that was my mind. I'm dead.

Slowly the haze began to clear, things roared into focus as I squinted, then slid back into a confusing mass when I relaxed. I'm not dead. This thought was as positive as my first evaluation. I began to think again as my vision became clearer. I could see Rocky now. He hadn't moved. Check yourself out, I ordered mentally. "Yes, sir," I replied.

No gaping holes in the tiger-suit jacket, no particular pain. I sat up and got to my knees. The world did a quick 360-degree rotation and I sat down again briefly, then tried again. This time I could examine my thighs and upper knees. When did this happen? I wondered, looking at a graze wound on my right leg. Small-arms round, not deep, easy Purple Heart, but who the hell wants a Purple Heart?

Now get to Rocky. I crawled on hands and knees to where Rocky lay, one leg out of the water, his knee drooling bright scarlet blood.

"Nick, I'm hit," Rocky gasped.

"Yeah, I know." This was all part of an awful replay of a drama I remembered from somewhere. Somewhere, before.

"Take it easy, Rock. I'm going to drag you off the path and then get that bleeding stopped. Hang with me for a second." I looked around for Dan. I was afraid to call out. I couldn't see him. Rocky helped me as I dragged him off the path and into a thick clump of reeds, after which we broke reeds over the entrance to camouflage our position.

"How many rounds have you got left?" he asked as I tore open a compress bandage. I checked my bandoleers.

"Three clips," I answered reading the instructions on the compress for which side toward the wound. I had, without thinking, picked up my acquired M–1 when I got up and had it with me.

"We can take on some of them if they get to us. We're not through yet!" Rocky declared, wincing with pain as I tied the first bandage around the most serious of the three wounds. I paused to put a clip in the rifle, thinking, Rocky, you better not count on this "not through yet" stuff until I get that bleeding stopped. What was this? I pushed back on the bolt handle, forcing, then slamming it with the heel of my palm. It was jammed! That damned striker, that son of a bitch! Rocky watched as I struggled with the bolt.

"It's jammed. Ditch it," he said. I pushed the muzzle into the soft mud to my rear and pushed until the butt plate disappeared below the surface of the water.

"I've got about eight rounds left," Rocky whispered as voices, calling in Vietnamese, came from the edge of the reeds. I nodded and began to bandage the other wounds: two small holes neatly drilled so that one compress adequately covered both. My head was beginning to throb. I wondered if I'd be around to ever drink another glass of iced tea.

"Nick, are you Catholic?"

"No, Rock. I'm Episcopalian."

I was making the final turn with the bandage. The reeds rustled behind me.

"Do tay len!" came the sharp command.

53

I tied the bandage and slowly turned my head. There was the muzzle of an American carbine and behind it, the Vietcong. I stood up, the two VC pulled my equipment harness from my shoulders, grabbed my arms, and quickly tied them behind me, once at the elbows, once at the wrists.

"God bless you, Nick."

"God bless you, too, Rocky."

"Di!" They threw me down the path.

2

FORT SILL, OKLAHOMA, WAS STILL SWEPT BY THE ICY winter winds in February 1961 when the personnel officer informed our Artillery officers' class that eighteen Airborne-qualified Artillery second lieutenants were needed for assignment to Special Forces. We were members of Artillery Officers' Basic Course, Class 2, a mixture of West Pointers and ROTC Distinguished Military Graduates, all of us new second lieutenants ready to graduate in two months and go to our first assignments in Artillery units. The thought of Special Forces immediately appealed to a number of the bachelors; our married classmates declined. Forty volunteered and I was one of the eighteen selected.

We had completed Ranger and Airborne training before coming to the Artillery School, which gave us an advantage over our ROTC classmates, in that they would have to attend Airborne School before reporting to Fort Bragg. We were ready to go immediately after graduation.

The available literature concerning Special Forces contained a broad picture of the mission and capabilities of the organization, then in the beginning of its tremendous expansion. Images of Rogers's Rangers, Francis Marion the "Swamp Fox," and Merrill's Marauders were clearly on our minds as we traveled to Fort Bragg, North Carolina, where we would join the 7th Special Forces Group.

I arrived in the early afternoon and, after parking my TR-

3 behind the long, wooden, two-story headquarters building, entered the adjutant's office to report. The captain was seated behind his desk, busily writing as I entered the room. I stood in front of him and announced, "Sir, Lieutenant Rowe reporting as directed." Without looking up, he returned my salute and held out his hand.

"Let me have your records, Lieutenant Rowe." I handed him the brown folder while remaining in the position of attention. He opened the folder, then looked back at the identification tab. Only then did he look up, his eyes going to the insignia on my shoulders. Unbelieving, he asked, "Are those second lieutenant's bars on your shoulders?"

I answered in the affirmative, wondering what was the matter with my bars. I glanced out of the side of my eye to insure they were properly placed. They were, so that wasn't it. He stood.

"At ease, Lieutenant Rowe." With that he disappeared quickly through the door.

"I don't give a good goddamn what the orders say! Get that second lieutenant the hell out of here!" The voice echoed down the hallway, leaving no doubt in my mind that either I, or second lieutenants in general, were unpopular here. The adjutant came hurriedly back into the room and sat down, looking slightly flustered.

"Where were these orders cut, Lieutenant Rowe?"

I answered that as far as I knew they had been cut at Fort Sill.

"There will be seventeen more second lieutenants in, sir, if I'm the first," I offered. His face was stricken. He stared at the orders assigning me to 7th Group as if he expected them to explode at any second.

"Call D.A.!" That voice roared down the hall again. "Find out what the fuck is happening!" The adjutant picked up the phone, then paused, turning back to face me.

"Lieutenant Rowe, go. Come back and check with me at about 1600 hours."

"Yes, sir." I saluted, picked up my records, and left. Outside I reread my orders, checking the sign in front of the building. Yep, 7th Special Forces Group, Airborne. According to the orders, I was in the right place even though they disagreed inside.

I drove to the 82nd Airborne Division open mess for a beer.

What a way to arrive at your first unit, I thought. I began thinking about the assignment with the 82nd Division Artillery that I had given up in order to go Special Forces, only to find they obviously didn't want me. My car was loaded with luggage and I had to get quarters for whatever length of time I'd be here, so that was the next task. The others of our group began to appear at the 82nd Club as the afternoon wore on. The reaction had been the same for all of them. Someone had failed to tell 7th Group that their new officers were second lieutenants. We discovered during the course of conversation that there were no second lieutenants in Special Forces, nor did anyone want them in Special Forces.

We went back to the adjutant together, somewhat discouraged at the reception, but primarily rebelling at the thought that we were unwanted. The general opinion was, "Screw them. If they don't want us, we can find another home!"

The adjutant met us as we walked in the door.

"Gentlemen, I can't give you any reading on this situation yet, but I'll have definite word in the morning." He seemed anxious to get us out of the building and suggested that we go to the BOQ's to get our rooms and report back in the morning. We were more than ready to leave and as we walked to our cars we heard him respond to a piercing order to "get your ass in gear and get those lieutenants out of my unit!"

That night we talked with some of the captains we knew who were in the 7th Group, expressing our disappointment at being rejected without so much as an opportunity to prove ourselves. We were certain that reassignment to another unit would be no problem, but this was a challenge. They listened and introduced us to three majors sitting at another table. The majors were deeply tanned and as tough-looking as unsheathed bayonets. They listened without expression as one of the captains explained, after which they talked with us for a short period. They departed and we went back to the BOQ's.

The next morning, there was a different atmosphere—one of resignation. The adjutant informed us that we'd be briefed at 0900 hours by the principal staff officers and the deputy group commander. We would then be assigned to a detachment and given duties. Apparently D.A. had refused to alter the orders and for better or worse, we were in 7th Special Forces Group, Airborne.

The briefing was an experience in itself. Two of the majors

we had met the night before turned out to be on the staff. Their briefings were as if they'd never seen us before, but they covered every point that we needed to know about their portion of the operation. They seemed so coldly professional that I wondered if they actually breathed like the rest of us. They had to have been second lieutenants sometime during their careers.

We sat for a few minutes after they'd finished, waiting for the next briefing, when the announcement "Gentlemen, the Deputy Group Commander!" brought us to our feet, ramrod-straight. We had no sooner hit the position of attention when that voice cracked out over us, "Sit down!" It was the same voice that had caromed through the halls in the headquarters.

A hulking figure squared off in front of us, massive arms folded across the chest. From an unsmiling face I heard the voice say, "I should have been here sooner, but I had more important things to do. You people have probably heard that I don't like second lieutenants!" We sank a little deeper into our chairs. "Well," he continued, "to clear up any misconceptions which might have arisen, it's true!" That was our introduction to Lieutenant Colonel "Rusty" Riggs, who took it upon himself to either drive us out, or make us "the best fucking lieutenants in the whole goddamn army."

That morning he disclosed his philosophy to us.

"We don't have room in Special Forces for an officer who makes mistakes. A second lieutenant, by definition, makes mistakes, so you should have been sent somewhere else first to make all your mistakes before coming here." We were then told, "A second lieutenant needs some son of a bitch on his ass thirty-six hours a day just to keep him straight. You're in my unit, you belong to me, so I'm going to be that son of a bitch, and from the time you leave this room until you get out of Special Forces, when you move out, I don't want to see your shirttail hit your ass!"

From that day on, we "belonged" to Lieutenant Colonel Riggs and found ourselves taking a one-block detour walking from classes to our cars, just to avoid crossing the parade ground where we were sure to be seen from his office window and reprimanded by an unseen stentorian voice for being alive.

We were assigned to the Training Group as platoon leaders for groups of NCO's taking the required preparation for joining a team. Our duties included conducting the physical training program and attending the same classes as the men. The days began at 0300 hours when we got up to conduct P.T. at 0330 and usually ended about 2300 hours after we completed all the day's tasks and prepared for the next day. It was a grueling pace and the periods of frustration and discouragement far outnumbered any satisfaction we might have derived. We were learning that no mistake went unnoticed. It was a lot easier if we just didn't make them.

The classes we attended were training the NCO's in their particular specialties: weapons, demolitions, communications, medical, or operations and intelligence. These are the skills found among the ten NCO's on one of the twelve-man A-Detachments and we, as lieutenants, were learning right along with them. The weapons class, for instance, trained us in the use of forty-eight foreign weapons and U.S. weapons practically back to the bow and arrow. The men could disassemble and assemble all of the weapons, repair and exchange parts between weapons, fabricating parts that were not obtainable. The other specialties provided equally intensive training.

In the familiarization firing phase, we spent days on the rifle range taking our turns firing each of the weapons we had studied in the classroom. To us, they were tools of a trade and it was essential that we be as skilled in their use as a mechanic with a wrench.

The days passed rapidly and we found ourselves toughening up physically and mentally. The senior NCO's provided a real challenge to us and it required maximum effort to perform the duties assigned. The whole program was designed to create, out of the raw material, the type of officer desired in Special Forces, combining technical and tactical proficiency with mature judgment. Had we not been determined, the program would have driven us out.

Lieutenant Colonel Riggs kept a close watch on our progress and never let us forget that we were "his" second lieutenants, joining the constant pressure to excel with unending commentary on the obvious lack of any military talent in a second lieutenant. We began to see a new facet of this hardened field commander during a brief incident in the Smoke Bomb Hill Officers' Club Annex one evening. The officers from the Special Forces would gather after work for a drink in the annex and we were included in this select gathering. This particular evening, three of us were matching out with dice to see who would buy the next round of drinks. Lieutenant Colonel Riggs always joined any of our number who happened to be in the club and would expound at great length for the benefit of all present on just how incompetent and hopeless were his second lieutenants. The Special Forces officers present took it in good humor, realizing the effort we were putting in and the progress we were making. As Lieutenant Colonel Riggs completed one extremely blistering tirade on the multitude of unforgivable mistakes committed by his second lieutenants, a short, slightly built captain at the corner of the bar spoke up.

"You sure are right, sir!" he agreed. "Those damn second lieutenants could screw up a free lunch. I bet you wish you could get rid of 'em."

Rusty Riggs fixed the captain with an icy glare.

"Who do you belong to, Captain?" His voice snapped across the bar. "Are you one of my people?"

"No, sir," the captain managed, taken by surprise. "I'm in 50th Signal Battalion."

Lieutenant Colonel Riggs pointed a thick forefinger at the captain, his voice cut, "Well you just shut the fuck up! Nobody talks about *my* second lieutenants!" There was silence in the club, and suddenly it began to feel good to be Rusty Riggs's second lieutenants.

The training cycle continued as we began the "cross training" phase. In this portion, the members of the Special Forces teams are trained in the skills of the other men of the detachment in order for them to be able to aid, or take the place of, other members during actual operations. This provides a detachment with the ability to continue to function even though it might lose men as combat casualties or from their being assigned special missions. Thus a demolition specialist might also be trained as a medic or radio operator. A well-trained team would have each man capable of performing two other jobs in addition to his basic skill. The cross training, though more abbreviated than the primary skill training, was comprehensive and added greatly to the overall abilities of the men.

Interspersed throughout the days and nights of training were the frequent training jumps from every conceivable type of aircraft. Since parachuting was a major means of infiltrating an area, there was great stress placed on parachuting proficiency. Day jumps, night jumps, jumps with combat equipment, "Hollywood jumps" with only a helmet and cartridge belt, jumps from the standard C–123's, C–130's, C–124's, and C–119's, jumps from helicopters and light aircraft, jumps from the World War II C-46 and C-47, the tight exits out of the tiny door of an air-sea rescue SA–16 (which was not designed for jumping). It seemed as if the only requirement for an aircraft to be a jump ship was that it had wings, an engine, and some sort of opening that a man could squeeze out of with a parachute on his back. I was extremely happy on numerous occasions that I was only five feet eight inches tall instead of six feet like some of the others, particularly when the SA-16 drops came around.

After the training phase was completed, our platoons began preparing for schooling at the major Army schools for their primary MOS. My medical platoon was scheduled to go to Brooke Army Medical Center, where they would receive special training equipping them to act not only as combat medics, but to perform minor surgery when required by operational contingencies. The radiomen would go to Fort Jackson, South Carolina, for communications training and radio repair. Each MOS had a particular school which would enhance the knowledge already possessed by the men. The second lieutenants were assigned to detachments and prepared for the Unconventional Warfare School, which was a requirement for all officers.

I was surprised to learn that I was one of eight lieutenants designated to attend the Army Language School in Monterey, California. The shock came when I discovered I was being sent to study Mandarin Chinese! The idea of spending a year in the Monterey-Carmel area dispelled my apprehension about the difficulty involved in mastering a language like Chinese. Within three weeks I was enrolled in the course, living in Pacific Grove and enjoying one of the best assignments the Army offers.

The language school was highly efficient in presenting its course of instruction during a six-hour day, five days per week. The various language departments were staffed by instructors teaching their native languages, and it would have taken effort not to learn. I nearly provided that effort, as I found the lure of Carmel, Big Sur, and all associated activities cut deeply into my initial study time and my Texas accent didn't lend itself well to being molded into the melodic Mandarin dialect. This handicap was overcome in time, and I found myself absorbing the instruction.

The idea of sky-diving came up in a conversation one day and I decided to try it on an odd weekend basis, using the Fort Ord Parachute Club equipment in order to keep expenditures of time and money at a minimum. Within the days it took to make my five qualifying static line jumps, I was hooked on the sport and found myself jumping every weekend and during the week when possible. I had somehow acquired three parachute rigs of my own and became a member of the Fort Ord Command Parachute Team before the year was finished.

The next year, with a reasonable command of the Chinese language and growing love for their history and culture, a dark suntan from the beach at Carmel, three parachutes, a parachutist's B license, and a dead-center, slam-landing cast on my right ankle, I departed for Fort Bragg to rejoin my unit.

While at Language School we had been promoted to first lieutenants and the albatross was removed from around our necks. I was reassigned to the newly formed 5th Special Forces Group and looked forward to taking my place in an operational detachment.

En route to Fort Bragg, I stopped at home to see my family before reporting in. My hometown, McAllen, Texas, is a growing city of about forty thousand in the tropical Lower Rio Grande Valley. Citrus groves and palm trees cover the fertile irrigated farmland surrounding the "City of Palms." I was born in McAllen, and grew up there, going to McAllen schools before attending the Military Academy at West Point. I suppose my academic standing in high school would have been higher had I not devoted three seasons a year to football, basketball, and baseball. Football and baseball were my favorites, and basketball was a challenge because of my height. It became a matter of eating more jump shots than I got off because of taller opponents slamming them back down my throat. Working in a Boy Scout troop and the Order of DeMolay filled in much of my spare time. Perhaps the first time I gained a knowledge of the wonders of nature was in the Scouting program, never realizing how I would draw on that early experience.

There was the average amount of trouble to get into, and I stayed far enough in to enjoy participating, yet far enough out to avoid serious damage (my nose not included). It was a satisfactory balance as far as I was concerned, but at times concentration was required to determine just where the balance point was. I learned in my early years that extremes in anything rarely are beneficial and learned to gauge the limits I considered acceptable. There were periods of accepting being alone rather than going along with group decisions, but I found nothing wrong with that and rather enjoyed solitude at times.

There are a multitude of ways for parents to be exceptional, depending entirely upon who evaluates them. From a son's standpoint, I am among the most fortunate of sons. My mother, born in the Ukraine and raised in Poland, experienced as a young girl the upheaval of the First World War and the Bolshevik Revolution. Her education included not only formal schooling at a private girls' school, but harsh confrontation with devastation and hardship. The tempering of mind and spirit in the furnace of war developed her love and respect for mankind, a bond of unshakable faith in God, and the ability to accept and deal with the world around her. Her spirit is one of steel encased in the warm tenderness of wisdom and love. My dad was born in the small town of Devers, Texas. The strict moral ethics of his Northern Methodist parents and the intellectual environment at his home created a deep love for books and literature. The three-thousand-volume library in our present home is a result of his collecting, and always provided for me an entire world within the space of our house. He graduated from Ellsworth College in Iowa Falls, Iowa, and served in the First World War. He was uncompromising in his beliefs, once having established the framework of Christian ethics by which he fashioned his life. One of the most beautiful aspects of my dad is his tolerance for the beliefs of others and the quiet dignity with which he demands respect for his beliefs.

Mom and Dad met in Poland after the First World War when both of them were serving in the American Red Cross. They were married there and came to the United States a short time later. Mom always says she's "Polish by birth, American by marriage, and Texan by choice."

They moved to McAllen in 1921, joining my grandfather in the real estate and insurance business. After Grandfather died, Dad took over the business and still maintains his office behind our home.

Heartache and loss challenged their faith with the accidental death of my sister, whom I never saw, in 1936. My brother Richard shared their grief in her passing and their joy which greeted my birth in 1938. Six short years later, Richard died just before his graduation from West Point. Their depth of understanding and faith, twice tested, was conveyed in part to their remaining son. We went to West Point for the graduation of my brother's class at the invitation of his classmates and there, surrounded by the spirit of the Academy he had loved, I made the decision that I would complete the task he had begun.

During my years of growth and development, my parents were not always able to provide me with the material things a young boy desires, but they gave me something far more valuable. They gave of themselves unselfishly and unceasingly to provide for me the inner knowledge and strength that no amount of ill fortune can destroy, as it can the fleeting benefits of material possessions.

It was like a holiday whenever I could take leave and visit the folks. The days passed too rapidly, with family talks continuing into the early morning hours and covering every possible subject. I had to display my newly acquired ability with the Chinese language and was geared to ad lib when I felt the need, only to discover that a friend of Mom and Dad's that they invited one evening turned out to be a native Chinese who was a professor of English literature at a nearby college. It was just like them to keep me straight. My departure time came and I continued to Fort Bragg.

As I drove on post, I could feel the excitement building inside me. The anticipation of joining the new unit almost cost me a speeding ticket as one of the alert M.P.'s spotted my TR-3 cruising at about ten over the limit toward 5th Group headquarters. He stopped me, but when I told him I was just reporting in to the 5th Group he asked to see my identification card and noting the first lieutenant rank, smiled condescendingly and gave me a warning. I almost felt like telling him to give me a D.R. There had to be a difference between first and second lieutenant.

I reported in and was happy to learn that this time I was expected. My first assignment was as executive officer of a nonoperational, half-filled A team, with a primary function of providing guerrilla elements for field problems and supporting demonstrations. It wasn't exactly what I had in mind, but the opportunity to take advantage of extra training was perfect and I managed to get my name on various training cycles. The desire to get as much extracurricular training as possible was still strong and I broadened my base of knowledge while time allowed.

The field problems were more of a game for us as we devised methods of harassing the A-Detachments pitted against us when we were the aggressors or tried to make their advisory problems as realistic as possible when we played the role of villagers. The A teams were serious in their work and even we felt the imperative undercurrent of necessity to perfect the teams since the next guerrillas they met would be the real thing. Life for that period of time consisted of weeks in the field, cross training, special skill training, demonstrations, and the decreasing thrill of jumping. The last is so commonplace in Special Forces that for some it's just like stepping out of any door, even though this one is a thousand feet up. Jumping began to fit into its proper place—as a means of infiltrating an area—and just as a commuter takes a train to work, the Special Forces trooper takes a plane and gets out halfway through the ride.

My routine was altered radically when I received assignment as assistant group adjutant. This job requires more paperwork than I care to remember and my initial thought on the first day was: How do I get out of here and back to a company? I feel no attachment for a desk job and this was exactly that: 0730 to 1600 hours daily, shuffling papers from my In box to the Hold box, waiting one day and putting them in the Out box. It usually resulted in the admin sergeant's giving me profuse instructions concerning the disposition of the multitude of forms and papers that went across my desk.

I changed my attitude slightly and got the paperwork in order, deciding to keep the poopsheets flowing while I was there, but never ceasing to look for that opportunity to return to an operational company. My chance came as the adjutant was preparing to leave his post for a new assignment. In the mild confusion of his departure, I was signing the orders normally handled through his office. This created the exact situation I had been looking for and I typed out a set of orders transferring myself back to an operational company and assigning a second lieutenant as assistant adjutant. Once the personnel officer had processed the orders, I signed them, picked up my things, and joined B Company.

Once in B Company, I was assigned to detachment A-23, one of the twelve A-Detachments found in a Special Forces company. The organization is unique to Special Forces. The company is commanded by a lieutenant colonel and has as its component parts a C-Detachment, three B-Detachments and twelve A-Detachments. The C-Detachment provides for command of uncommitted B-, and A-Detachments or, when committed to an operational mission itself, can control and support two or more operational detachments within its zone. The B-Detachments, consisting of twenty-three men each and commanded by a major, control and support the subordinate A-Detachments operating in their zones. The basic working detachment in a company is the A team. This is a twelve-man team, normally assigned with four A teams per B-Detachment. The detachment commander is a captain, with a lieutenant for his executive officer. Ten NCO's fill out the team, two in each of the basic skills required: operations and intelligence, medical, communications, demolitions, and weapons. These twelve-man teams are assigned a primary mission in counterinsurgency of "acting as advisors to indigenous special forces, provincial authorities, and tribal leaders in the recruitment, organization, equipping, training and operational employment of host country tribal elements or ethnic minority groups," as the field manual puts it.

The requirements of maturity, tactical and technical proficiency, ingenuity, and physical conditioning, coupled with a deep sense of dedication, are essential in a good team. The rapid expansion of Special Forces had attracted many young men seeking either fast promotions or the excitement of the recruiting-poster version of Special Forces. Within this group, some made outstanding team members while others found the actual duty sometimes repetitious, the classes sometimes boring, and the thrills minimal. The "ash and trash" police detail conducted every day was not the new soldier's idea of what Special Forces should be, but even our NCO's pulled that detail. It wasn't garrison duty that exemplified Special Forces, it was the field operations.

Training was conducted under the direction of group headquarters and teams preparing for deployment to Vietnam were given primary consideration, with the nonmission teams supporting the training effort. I attended the Unconventional Warfare School during our period of training support, rejoining the team in time for a series of field problems. One of the proudest moments I experienced was upon completion of the UW School when I became qualified to wear the white-bordered, black 5th Special Forces background insignia on my beret. The small cloth patch, worn behind the insignia of rank for officers and crest for NCO's, was a symbol of having served a required period of time in the unit, completed required schooling, and been on a required number of field problems with a detachment. This was another step in my development. Prior to that, I had worn the "black weenie," a quarter-inch-high section of the background, below my lieutenant's bar, indicating that I belonged to the unit, but wasn't completely qualified.

Being a bachelor, I looked forward to the field problems as relief from the routine of garrison duties. There was so much to be learned and the various situations arising in the field exercises were challenging, whereas a normal day in garrison consisted of avoiding as many bad deals as possible. The constant need for teams to put on demonstrations, escort duty for visitors, inspections, and the multitude of administrative details made garrison duty a real pain.

My detachment, A–23, began to develop even though our detachment C.O. was pulled away to replace a commander killed in Vietnam. The NCO slots were slowly being filled. Team Sergeant Tom Kemmer, a short, compactly built underwater demolitions expert, with primary qualification in operations and intelligence, kept the team functioning and gave me my first long look at the relationship that exists between officers and NCO's in the close-knit fabric of this extraordinary organization. There was the rapport required by the mission, the constant close association. In the field we found ourselves cooking over the same small fire, working side by side, seeking protection from a rainstorm under the same poncho; back at Bragg we tipped a lot of off-duty beer together, yet the sharing and friendliness did not breed familiarity. The differentiation between officer and NCO existed, each with its privileges, each with its responsibilities. Each respected the other for who he was and for the abilities he possessed. It was an essential lesson for me.

Norman Hardy took over as intelligence sergeant, John Lowe

as heavy-weapons man, Sidney Cross as radio operator supervisor, and Bill Martin as combat demolitions specialist. Ken Carey was attending an engineering course at Fort Belvoir prior to joining the team. That left us with openings for two medics, a radio operator, a weapons man, and, of extreme importance, a detachment commander.

In the next weeks we began to receive filler personnel and the rumor circulated that our B-Detachment would be the next to replace outbound teams in Vietnam. This was early 1963, and the Special Forces effort in Vietnam was being shared by 1st Group on Okinawa, 7th Group and 5th Group at Fort Bragg. The 5th Group wasn't at full strength, but three operational companies were taking responsibility for the counter insurgency program in the Mekong Delta and providing a C-Detachment for the Special Forces Operational Base in Nha Trang, headquarters for all Special Forces operations in country.

There was a definite need to conduct intensive detachment training, but the expansion was creating problems that our manpower sources couldn't fulfill. The public relations push to sell Special Forces to the nation took valuable detachment time to put on demonstrations. Training for inductees was doubled and the need for qualified instructors doubled correspondingly. The men applying for Special Forces were coming in under relaxed qualification criteria, thus increasing the washout rate, and the UW School had so many non-Special Forces students that a Special Forces officer found it difficult to be included in the overflowing classes. This was compounded by the "housekeeping" duties required on a post like Fort Bragg and we met ourselves coming and going in an attempt to fill the commitments. Only the rapport among the four A-Detachments in B–7, our controlling B-Detachment, enabled us to complete all tasks and slip in a little cross training on the side.

Team Sergeant Kemmer, who normally obtained the word on anything of importance several days before I got it through official channels, told me that our new team leader was due to arrive in a couple of days. I checked with the orderly room and discovered that several officers from the graduating UW class would be assigned to the company, but definite assignments hadn't been made. Kemmer assured me that ours would be in that group, and within two days we met Bob Leites, an ex-first sergeant and now a captain. Bob was a stocky, muscular individual with a Yul Brynner pate, which earned him the nickname "Mr. Clean." Captain Leites impacted like an exploding 105mm shell and left no doubt in anyone's mind that as a first sergeant he had been hell on wheels. As a detachment commander he was still hell on wheels.

Leigh Wade joined Cross as our radio operator and Carey came in fresh from the bridge and construction course at Belvoir. We needed a weapons man badly and the best man available was Robert Navarro, who had returned from an interrupted tour in Vietnam and was looking for a return trip. Bob Leites overcame the opposition from headquarters to Navarro's quick reassignment to Vietnam and picked up our medics as well. Dan Pitzer and Roger VandeBerg found themselves members of the A–23 clan. We were finally at full strength and working toward a mission assignment.

The official announcement that our controlling B-Detachment, B–7, would be bypassed for the next mission came as a shock. The mission was to be filled by Charlie Company and we'd have to wait for at least another six months. The teams in B–7 were at full strength and capable of going directly into mission training, whereas Charlie Company's teams would have to be brought up to strength, taking men from our detachments as fillers. Based on this, Bob and the other detachment commanders from B–7 approached the company commander, requesting that we be given the mission. It took concentrated effort to convince the powers that be that we should take the assignment, but the final decision was for three of our teams and one team from Charlie Company to go into mission training. A–21, A–22, and A–23 would go!

We began to draw the necessary items to complete our team equipment. The demo chest was filled, medical equipment and supplies added, and team communication gear brought up to the prescribed level. Individual items were checked and replaced if necessary. The team members were taken off the normal duty roster and mission training began.

I had already been through one mission training cycle in 5th Group, so it wasn't a new experience. A limited-fluency language course provided instruction in French or Vietnamese for the members of each team and, as before, was initially interesting but sagged into a series of scarcely heard monologues by an understandably discouraged instructor. Interest would periodically reawaken, but hot frame mess halls become classrooms and the monotony of repetition hampered the enthusiasm of the most determined student. Area studies presented the sociopolitical background and a broad picture of the economics, culture, history, and various other facets of the country. Teams that had been in country and returned gave briefings on specific situations they had encountered. It was a matter of attempting to sort useful, applicable information out of a lot of smoke. I had little interest in how many tons of rice were produced per hectare of cultivated rice paddy in 1962, but analyses of the underlying problems in the current Buddhist unrest were of value.

The overriding emotions involved in preparing physically for the mission carried us through the classroom work. Field problems were training vehicles used to familiarize the teams with the tactical situations which might be encountered. Again, the training fell short of its mark because there were no means of creating the specific environment in which each team would find itself. North Carolina would never be like the Mekong Delta. We did learn the important lesson of discarding any thought of fighting a timetable war. The men acting as guerrillas had recently returned from a tour and put to use on us the lessons they had learned in combat. Ambushes, surprise night attacks, hit-and-run raids, the variety of tactics employed by the enemy we were to meet tested our ability on those field problems. We discovered how much we didn't know, if nothing else.

The lighter side centered around the team parties instigated by Bob Leites and Tom Kemmer. The opportunities for families to meet and party together created in A–23 a feeling of understanding and mutual support. The wives formed a close sorority which was indispensable in the months to come.

I took a short leave to go home prior to departure for Vietnam. I sensed the concern for my safety in Mom and Dad's mood, but their support for my independence of decision was as strong as during my years at home. I failed to grasp the full significance of their concern as they watched their only surviving child prepare to undertake a task which could, if fate were cruel, bring a final tragedy into their lives. They masked their emotions and made the visit as happy as the ones in the past. I wasn't preoccupied about the mission, but I took off my West Point ring and left it at home when I returned to Fort Bragg. It was the first time I had left my ring and I did it automatically, without thinking.

On 10 July 1963, we departed on the first leg of the flight to Hawaii. I said goodbye to Lorene that morning in front of the orderly room where the teams waited with their individual equipment. She looked so damned pretty in her crisply starched nurse's uniform and her quiet smile reflected the multitude of undefinable qualities that had so strongly drawn me to her. I was already thinking about plans for the future and saying goodbye was made easier only by the shouts to get aboard our vehicles for the ride to Pope Field where the aircraft waited.

The giant C–135 was parked on the ramp, and as we formed in ranks prior to boarding, several jeeps drew up alongside and the group commander and his staff stepped down. They bid each of us goodbye and wished us luck as we walked up the steps into the cabin door. We took our places in the rearward-facing seats and the door was clamped shut.

I discovered after takeoff that there were two windows in the entire passenger cabin, neither of which was adjacent to a seat. It was an unusual feeling to be flying backward and not have any means of seeing what was going on outside. Not that there would have been anything exciting, but as far as I knew, we might still be parked on the ramp with the engines running. Leave it to the Air Force, I thought.

The stop in Honolulu gave us an opportunity to wander around Waikiki, seeing what partying could be engaged in on short notice. The aircraft crew must have done better than we did because the next morning we learned there would be a layover due to illness. The navigator was sick. From the hangovers among those of our group who had indulged with comparative moderation, I could imagine what the navigator's head must have felt like. The second night was a wipe-out in Don the Beachcomber's cocktail lounge and the next morning when we climbed aboard the C–135, pale, slightly green-tinged faces with dark sunglasses shutting out some of the piercing sunlight seemed to be the style. Between takeoff from Honolulu and landing at Tan Son Nhut there was only the sound of the engines and a few snores.

I had barely awakened before the crew chief opened the cabin door, allowing the muted Vietnamese sunlight to break up the dimness inside the aircraft. We gathered our personal gear and stepped down onto the concrete runway. Rain-heavy clouds hung above us, with narrow breaks between them through which lances of silvery sunlight spotlighted the ground. I saw the familiar banana shapes of H–21 helicopters parked in rows across the taxiway. A pair of lumbering T–28 fighters were taking off, their engines straining to pull the bomb-laden wings into the air. The balcony circling the second floor of the large terminal building was lined with people waving hands and a multihued splash of color. There were other Green Berets standing in the open-portico lower floor of the building, talking with groups of camouflage-fatigue-clad Vietnamese soldiers and young, attractive Vietnamese women. Most of the Americans wore the .45-caliber automatic pistol on their hips and held several clothing bags in addition to their personal equipment bags. It looked as if the Chinese tailors in Cholon had done a booming business.

As our team equipment was lifted out of the cargo compartment by a forklift, a long flatbed truck rolled up beside the C–135 with a new load of team lockers and equipment. There were teams going home on the same aircraft we had come in on. We stacked our team footlockers near a small tin-roofed, wooden building where we received our first briefing. A harassed American civilian official in a short-sleeved white shirt, who had expected us yesterday, covered the regulations applying to our status in country, checked our passports and international driver's licenses, and told us to wait for the C–123 transport aircraft that would arrive shortly to take us to our headquarters in Nha Trang.

Outside again, we sat beside our baggage, keeping an eye on the clouds overhead and hoping that the rain would hold off until we were gone. The day dragged on and no C–123's arrived. We talked with the departing teams before watching them begin their return to the United States. It was a strange sensation of being left behind as my eyes followed the plane, climbing and then banking, disappearing in the clouds on its way home.

An hour or so later, two squatty C–123's, their bodies a dull camouflage green and brown, taxied up near our stacks of equipment and slumbering figures. As soon as the engines shut down, we began loading. Footlockers, steel-banded equip-

72

ment boxes, and duffle bags were carried on board in a minimum amount of time. The teams filed into the aircraft and as the rear loading ramp raised to the locked position, the engines were sputtering to raucous life.

It was a short flight to Nha Trang and after landing we were taken to our billets for the night. We drew our weapons and went to a rifle range near the city to zero them for battle sighting. Briefings on our operational areas and general ground rules for our missions were given, expanding the skimpy detailed knowledge we already had but leaving many questions unanswered. The next day we were scheduled to fly to Can Tho, where we would meet members of the teams we were replacing for a more complete briefing.

The morning of 14 July, we flew to Can Tho, the largest city in the Mekong Delta, where our controlling B-Detachment was located. We landed at the airstrip adjacent to the Beau Geste fortress-type compound occupied by the Special Forces. It was a concrete square with open courtyard and gun embrasures at each of the cylindrical corner turrets. A thatched roof covered the partitioned rooms in the hollow square. We were greeted by members of the B-Detachment and taken to the mess hall where we met the other team members. After getting our gear put away and receiving operational briefings on the areas we would be going into, we paired off with the men from the outgoing detachments and pumped them for all the information they could give us about the camps.

That evening we sat around in the Alamo Lounge, a reasonably comfortable combination of cocktail lounge, recreation room, and movie theater that had been included as a place to relax during off-duty hours. It became late and some of the men went into the team quarters located next to the lounge while others remained talking. There was a feeling of anticipation as we all thought about the next day, when we'd see our camps for the first time. The night was quite dark and only the hum of the mosquitos outside the wire-screened sleeping area and the sound of soft snoring broke into the muted sound of music coming from the lounge. Men were indistinct shapes under gray blankets as I walked to my cot and prepared to join the sleeping group. I put my carbine beside my boots, took off my fatigue shirt, and lay back, pulling the clammy blanket up around my shoulders. My thoughts revolved rapidly for a few

73

moments, then slowed as sleep took its hold.

A vague dream of combat crashed into sharp reality as I awoke suddenly to the sound of explosions all around us! Instinctively, I rolled off my cot onto the floor, grabbing for my weapon. The room was lit by a flash, followed by an explosion that left my ears ringing. Fragments pinged into the wall above me, ricocheting with a whine. From the darkness which settled immediately came voices: "Shit, I'm hit!" "Get your weapons!" "Medic!" Someone was groaning loudly. The darkness added confusion.

Outside, staccato bursts from automatic weapons added their clamor to the continuing detonations. I pulled my boots on and was lacing them up while assessing the situation as best I could. Someone lit a cigarette lighter. Six voices shouted for the man to put it out. I could hear John Lowe calling to Dan Pitzer that he was hit. Tom Kemmer's voice commanded the men to get their weapons and get near a firing position. Someone in the courtyard screamed, "They're coming through the gate!" John Colby, exec for A–21, and I scrambled through the partitioned area, past the wounded, toward the door where we could fire into the courtyard. Flares hung in the sky now, casting a faint yellowish light over the compound.

There were no VC coming through the gate, so we turned back to help the wounded. With the meager light I could see bunks overturned, men crouched by the wall, peering out, their weapons at the ready. Tom Kemmer, holding his shattered wrist, directed the men in seeking out the wounded. "Hook" Schrieber, outgoing team sergeant from Tan Phu, lay crumpled on the floor, blood oozing from his fatigue jacket. The medics worked quickly, checking the wounded, finding those who were seriously hit, while others bandaged themselves. Bob Leites and Doug Horne, detachment commanders, scrambled through the door, their faces taut. A rapid report showed we had fourteen men wounded, two very seriously, and Kemmer with his hand dangling limply from a fragment-torn wrist.

The firing dropped off to scattered shots in the distance. Men appeared in the compound in all states of dress and undress. Flashlights aided in assessing the damage as control was reestablished. The B-Detachment personnel immediately wheeled two jeeps up in front of the gate and the wounded were loaded aboard for a breakneck-speed ride to the hospital in the city proper. Another machine-gun jeep with armed Strike Force soldiers led the small convoy. It would be close if the seriously wounded were to be saved and the American surgical team at the hospital was the answer.

I went back into quarters to help in case another assault came. Inside, we discovered that a mortar round had detonated in the roof above the sleeping men and its fragments had inflicted all the wounds. Kemmer and Schreiber had been in the Alamo Lounge when the firing began and had dashed out of there, scrambling back into the team quarters to get their weapons. As they dove in the door the mortar shell had gone off just over their heads. Hook caught a large fragment in the back, which glanced off of his rib cage, collapsed a lung and lodged in his chest. Tom's wrist was nearly severed by a razor-sharp chunk of metal.

Reports were coming in from the Vietnamese units around the compound. There had been an assault force approaching the airfield, which was the apparent target of the attack. One of the Strike Force sentries had spotted them and emptied his weapon into the advancing enemy, giving the alarm and continuing to fire until he was cut to pieces. The mortars had been fired primarily to damage the airstrip, but the Special Forces compound, located so near the target, had received numerous hits, including the unlucky round that hit the roof.

The jeeps came back with word that blood was needed desperately at the hospital. Both Hook and our other seriously wounded men were undergoing surgery and blood supplies at the hospital were insufficient. John Colby and I climbed aboard one of the jeeps and with men hanging onto the sides we sped over the mile or so to the hospital. The doctor was placing drain tubes from Hook's chest into a one-gallon bottle. From the tubes dripped a pinkish fluid, the level in the bottle rising with surprising rapidity. Hook was lying on the table, talking quietly with the doctor while he worked. Pain showed on his face, but he was unflinching.

After giving blood, I checked with the other members of A–23 who had been hit. They were sitting on the tile floor in the sparsely equipped room that was serving as an operating room, waiting to be examined. Cross had a deep wound in his thigh and John Lowe had caught a number of small fragments in the leg. Carey and Pitzer had been checked and Tom Kemmer proved to be the badly wounded member of our team. He sat, cradling his wrist, his face ashen, but still in control of himself. The wound had been bandaged, but still showed blood seeping through the gauze. I found a strip of wire mesh and fashioned a brace to support the wrist, hoping it would relieve the pain somewhat. All of the wounded were to be flown to the Eighth Field Army Hospital in Nha Trang as soon as the surgery was completed. This was our welcome to the Delta, and we'd be going into Tan Phu without a full team. The biggest question was whether Tom would be able to recover in time to rejoin us.

The next morning, John and I walked around the compound surveying the shell holes and damage from the night before. The tower at the airfield bore the spider-web shatter holes of machine-gun fire in its large windows; fragment holes were everywhere. It had been an effective attack, although the damage to the runways was superficial and repairs were easily made. It was effective because one mortar round, unwittingly placed on the roof of our hut, had put fourteen men out of action.

Later, the team loaded the equipment aboard the waiting helicopters and, after saying goodbye to the other detachments, climbed aboard for the flight to Tan Phu.

Tan Phu had originally been a militia post built at the intersection of the main canal, Kinh Song Trem, and the Cho Hoi canal, which were major routes of communication in Thoi Binh district. It controlled and protected travel along the canals in conjunction with other smaller posts scattered along the length of the waterways. In August 1962, the VC had attacked and overrun the post to open the canals for use by various VC units. In early 1963, plans were developed to reopen the road from Camau to Can Tho, a winding dirt-topped trail that had been cut in many places during the war against the French and abandoned. The road ran from Cho Hoi through Tan Phu northeast to Kien Long and further to Can Tho. It was decided to reestablish the post with a stronger force to secure the area for the road as well as shutting off canal travel for the VC. An American Special Forces team was assigned to advise the Vietnamese team which would reoccupy Tan Phu. The team we were relieving had gone into the village after weeks of clearing operations to push the Vietcong away and allow enough time to build adequate defensive positions. They had built, organized, and advised for three months before we arrived, giving us the foothold required so we could assist in expanding the protection of the area and training the Strike Force.

The camp was far from secure and quite vulnerable to attack, as we learned later on; however, the construction which had been completed gave us adequate quarters for the troops, team quarters for ourselves, and the required security for immediate protection. One of our tasks would be to improve the fortifications and add to the facilities of the camp in general.

After our arrival and the two days spent with the old team before they departed, we went to work. Training schedules were worked out with the Vietnamese team, logistics necessary to support our training and operations were planned and requested from our headquarters, and we began the civil affairs and medical programs so essential to bringing relief to the people.

Pitzer and VandeBerg got together with the Vietnamese team medic, who had been dubbed "APC," to carry out the multipurpose training program for nurses, company medics, village health workers, and midwives. Estimates of the health and sanitation requirements were staggering; the people lived with almost primitive sanitary conditions. The sick calls held in the village for treatment of civilian patients brought an overwhelming response as most of the people received modern medical treatment for the first time in their lives. Medical patrols were taken into VC-controlled areas to treat people who for some reason would not or could not come to our village. It was physical proof that our presence was not going to be so entirely detrimental as the VC had claimed.

Van went further in his efforts as he began teaching English in the village to some of the schoolteachers. We found that the four Vietnamese nurses who had been trained earlier and were working and studying in our dispensary could diagnose and prescribe medication for a variety of common ailments, thus requiring us to provide only supervisory control over the sick calls. Serious illnesses or wounds were treated by Pitzer, Van, or APC. However, the emphasis was placed on training the student medics and nurses as well as APC to handle all the patients.

We were engaged in combat of varying intensity almost

from the first day in camp. Whether it was a mortar attack, probing attack, sniper, or one of the patrols we initiated, the level of excitement at Tan Phu was never low. It was difficult to make contact with the VC unless they wanted to fight, and even though our units surprised them on several occasions, it was a rare case when we forced them to engage on our terms. The constant threat of booby traps set by the guerrillas made us wary when traveling through VC-controlled areas. *Punji* pits, the camouflaged holes lined with sharpened stakes that could pierce a man's legs, groin, and stomach should he step into the trap. *Dap loi*, the expended .50-caliber shell case from one of our aircraft's machine guns, with a new primer, filled with black powder and topped with chunks of metal and sealed with wax. Placed in a bamboo cylinder with a nail point in the bottom and then buried in a path so only the wax top is above ground, when a passerby steps down on it, the shell case is pushed down onto the nail point, detonating the primer and blowing the scrap upward into his foot. These and many more kept us alert whether we were engaging the enemy or just seeking him out.

Having been trained as an Artillery officer, I established a fire direction system for the 81mm mortars which were our camp's main heavy weapons. Big John and Ponce took charge of one mortar apiece and after observing the results we achieved on several fire missions, Major Phong, the Vietnamese camp commander, began to call on us for most of the supporting fire. The system before had been a sort of "estimate the distance, point the tube, and drop the round" type of action, which obtained less than desirable results. The Vietnamese Special Forces gunner still fired H.E. support for camp support while each company had 60mm mortars for their individual areas of responsibility. Classes were begun for mortar crews and the forward observers who would accompany the patrols to direct the supporting fire with greater accuracy. It was difficult to advise the veteran commanders like Major Phong, who had fought with the Vietminh, on matters of tactics, since he had been fighting this war since 1946, and we were relative newcomers. We could, however, advise on better employment of the weapons we made available for his use and train his troops to use them more effectively.

The constant problem was the recurring assurance we received from our counterparts that all of our strikers were "old soldiers" and completely versed in the use of weapons. While testing the men on marksmanship, we found the evaluation to be false and instituted a training program designed to qualify the men in the use of the weapons. It was difficult for a five-foot-one Vietnamese who weighed, perhaps, 105 pounds with combat equipment, to effectively fire the M–1 Garand rifle, which was designed for a huskier American, so we turned to the lighter, smaller carbine whenever possible. The only automatic weapons we had to issue were World War II Thompson submachine guns, a heavy, sophisticated weapon that normally ended up with its stock removed to lighten it, thus making it less accurate than it already was, and the M–3 "grease gun," a submachine gun of simpler design, more reliable, but still inaccurate and heavy for our average striker. Big John and Ponce worked unceasingly to overcome our handicap, but progress was slow.

There was the lighter side of our activities when we showed American movies, which were immediate hits with the soldiers and villagers alike. It was the first time most of them had ever seen films and when word went around that we were going to show a movie in the village, there was almost certain inactivity by the VC. I would still swear that somewhere in the laughing, jovial village crowd cheering the Indians in a Western or gasping at travelogue films showing automobiles, planes, and various modern conveniences in America were most of the VC.

There was a sense of accomplishment when we completed the first set of houses for Strike Force families and the new village dispensary. The marketplace was renovated with a new cement floor and dock for the canal boats; a new bridge was built across the canal between the camp and village; and a cement drain system was put in for the village streets. These contributions helped offset the frustrations and disappointments that were part of being an adviser.

The days passed and the team worked well even with the changes in personnel. Tom Kemmer was shipped back to the States for treatment and Dennis Lima came in. Bob Leites was transferred after a conflict with the Vietnamese camp commander and weeks later Al Penneult arrived. Norman Hardy was wounded, shipped to the Philippines for treatment, and Jim Browning took his place. In the Vietnamese team, Major

Phong developed a liver ailment shortly after a major battle on 30 July and was transferred to Saigon for a rest, being replaced by Lieutenant Tinh.

We had planned, built, trained, and developed to the point we could actually see progress being made. Then came 29 October 1963.

I wrote this poem in Nam Can Region in 1964 when the attacks of dysentery were severe and a fungus infection had set in. I dreamed it one night, woke up, and wrote it down. I believed it.

When all outside and round about,
is crushing, pushing, crowding down;
The air itself is filthy, dirty,
the outer shell corrupt, unclean.

From deep within, a voice rings through:
"Be calm, be still and carry on;
For I am untouched by all mundane,
and so forever shall I be.

For I am God's and thy shell is God's;
Together, we form thee;
Thy shell is clay and will be dust,
but I am all eternal.

You and I, we travel far; through birth and life,
through mortal death and life hereafter;
What happens now, in time will pass,
and memory, like your shell itself, cannot last.

So look up ahead at times to come,
despair is not for us;
We have a world and more to see,
while this remains behind."

3

THE STOCKY VC PULLED ME AWAY FROM ROCKY, BACK onto the narrow path made by our fleeing soldiers, and shoved me violently in the direction from which we had come. I stumbled, almost fell. My arms were tied at the wrists and at the elbows, and this prevented me from balancing as I slipped and struggled in the muddy water. Another of the VC prodded me with the long spike bayonet on his Mossin-Nagant carbine. *"Mau di!"* he commanded—Go fast! They were anxious to get me to the rear as soon as possible. I stumbled into one of the deep irrigation trenches that bordered the rice paddy, and found myself underwater with no means of pulling myself out. Instinctively, I began to tread water, trying to get my face out of the murky fluid. I was strangling. Panic sent flashes into my brain as I kicked more violently, trying to reach the air. The sides of the ditch were slick and offered no foothold. Then I felt something solid under my right foot and pushed down, propelling my head upward, and broke the surface, gasping a deep breath of air before going under again. I heard a harsh chuckle from one of the VC before the water closed over me.

A hand grasped the band of cloth binding my elbows and pulled me upward, pushing my face into the mud on the opposite side. I managed to kick one leg onto the bank and as the hand held my body against the side, I rolled over onto dry land. Immediately the VC pulled me to my feet and pushed me toward the path along the canal bank where a short time before we had been fighting. I was exhausted, my breath came in short, painful gasps, my lungs were two dense lumps of burning pain.

Through the whirling haze in front of my eyes I saw crumpled, sprawled bodies strewn across the packed mud front yards of the huts we had so recently left. Many of the bodies were stripped. A few still wore the black-and-green-slashed camouflage uniform of the Strike Force. I found myself stepping over and around some of our dead strikers. Each had a gaping hole in the front of his head, his face unrecognizable after the explosive exit of the bullet.

My captors kept pushing and prodding with their weapons, trying to make me run, but I was too tired to manage more than a shambling walk. Finally, one of them attached a length of rope to my left biceps and began to drag me along at a faster pace.

The bank was lined with a constant flow of well-armed soldiers. Thin strands of black telephone wire ran along the path, indicating they had landline communication with the assault elements. There were khaki uniforms mixed with the black-clad troops. A tiny portion of my conscious mind, still functioning, began to add up what I was seeing. These were not the guerrillas we had expected. The faces were not the young faces of the irregular units we had encountered in the past. These were hard faces, older faces, the faces of men who had seen long months or perhaps years of combat.

I saw Mossin-Nagants and the K–50 submachine guns in the hands of most of the men. Then it hit me! None of the guerrilla units carried the Mossin-Nagant. Only Main Force units were equipped with those weapons and it should have been immediately obvious that we were up against a lot more than we had counted on. One lousy screw-up like that and we're over our heads in shit! I cursed the district chief who had set up this operation.

Just then there was a commotion behind me and Dan came shuffling past at a slow jog, two VC trotting along behind him. I caught only a glimpse as he went past, but he looked OK. "I'm sorry, Nick," I heard him say as he passed. I wondered what had happened to Rocky. The creeping fear of being killed was stronger now that I was recovering my senses. I prayed that they hadn't killed Rocky just because he was wounded.

The thought of dying was suddenly terrifying and death was very real.

A shouted command caused my guards to halt momentarily beside a small clump of coconut palms on the edge of the path. I stood with my head hanging, trying to get my breath and wishing that my head would stop throbbing when I saw a pair of tire-tread-sandaled feet in front of me. *"My, khong?"* came the rasping voice from above the knobby feet—Is it an American? *"Da, phai, Dai-Uy!"* snapped one of my guards—Yes, Captain. I looked up in time to see the huge fist coming straight at me. It took what seemed like hours to land, but I was too tired to even roll with it. My head snapped back, pain shooting across my face, and then blackness.

I found myself lying on my side, with one of the guards tugging at the tow rope and kicking me in the back. The kicks didn't hurt and were apparently to get me on my feet. I could feel wetness on my face and I couldn't breathe through my nose. The guards pulled me to a sitting position where I shook my head gently, even then sending waves of nausea from the violent throbbing in my temples and above my eyes. I was pulled to my feet and led, more slowly this time, down the canal bank.

Somewhere I had picked up a third guard and had two behind me and the new one in front, pulling me along. The banks were still crowded with soldiers and at this point, occasional civilians. I asked one of the guards for a drink of water. My throat was raw and the salty taste of my own blood was making me sick as hell. He shook his head, no, and we continued.

After crossing a larger canal, I was halted and ordered to sit down. A group of soldiers gathered around as one of my guards stripped my boots from my feet. My socks went next and there was a rapid discussion among the group as to who would get them. Someone grabbed my camouflage hat which had survived up to this point. It was no sooner snatched from my head than someone else replaced it. It was taken again, this time for good. I asked again for water and one of the soldiers called out for someone to *lay nuoc*. A wiry, wrinkled old man approached with a tin cup of water and held it to my lips as I swallowed rapidly. The cool liquid settled the waves of nausea which had threatened to engulf me. I wished I could have washed the blood off of my face, but that would have been pushing the point. I was placed in the bottom of a long, narrow boat, and shortly after we moved away from the bank, I passed out.

I awoke blindfolded with one of the guards wiping my face, using a wet rag dipped in the canal water. He swabbed my mouth and nose almost gently, for which I was grateful, and the refreshing chill of the water brought me fully awake. As we came alongside a bank, I was pulled out of the boat by a group of khaki-clad soldiers who began to adjust the blindfold. Before they had finished, I heard a voice asking me in French if I could speak French. Simultaneously I got a sniff through my distorted nose of an almost overpowering fragrance. I looked under the loosened cloth and got as far as a pair of cheap oxfords, gray trousers and a blue shirt before the tightened blindfold cut my sight. I think he was wearing a sun helmet, but the face was indistinct. I didn't acknowledge his question and the guards led me down the path.

I could see about a quarter-inch of light under the bottom edge of the cloth around my eyes. It disappeared as I was pushed into a hut and forced to lie down on the dirt floor. Low voices came from all around me and I could see along my body toward the door, thus aiding me in orienting myself somewhat. A woman's voice spoke next to my ear, *"Anh nguoi My, khong?"*—Are you an American? Another voice answered that I was, indeed, an American. Fingers felt my arms, squeezing the biceps and forearm, almost as if I were a piece of beef. A hand and fingers rubbed the hair on my forearm. Someone touched the stubble of a beard on my face. Comments in rapid Vietnamese words flew back and forth across the room. I listened for other voices, any indication of where Rocky and Dan were. I thought I heard Rocky's voice asking if there was a doctor available. I couldn't be certain and the feeling of utter loneliness crept over me. I didn't know how much of an enemy I was to these people, and even though they had displayed only curiosity thus far, I had no idea what might happen next. The desire to stay alive was strong and growing stronger.

One of the women was idly running her toes over my foot. She stopped when a voice from the door told someone in the room to bring me outside. I didn't want to go. I felt that the people in the room were nonantagonistic enough that I could have safely stayed longer with them.

Outside, the blindfold was untied and removed. Several of the members of the Militia Company from Thoi Binh squatted near me, their arms tied as mine were. Neither Dan nor Rocky was anywhere in sight.

A young boy placed a large pot of steaming rice in the middle of our group of prisoners and one of the guards untied the militiamen's hands, giving them, at the same time, small ceramic bowls and chopsticks. One of the other guards caught my attention and pantomimed scooping rice from a bowl into his mouth, indicating the pot and making his question, whether or not I wanted to eat, quite clear. I discovered I was extremely hungry and nodded an affirmative. He spoke to one of the militiamen who in turn scooped rice into a bowl and fed me.

I ate two bowls before thirst prevented me from continuing. I asked for a drink of water and was given a cup of yellowish water, tasting strongly of the thatch roofing. It satisfied my thirst and I sat back taking advantage of not being blindfolded to scan the area. Soldiers and civilians squatted around pots of rice similar to the one now being devoured by the prisoners. The others were also eating from plates of a brownish substance. My eyes refused to focus for extended periods of time so I couldn't stare. Still no sign of Dan and Rocky.

Artillery sounds slammed into the tree line about one kilometer away and I watched the columns of mud rise with each detonation. No one else seemed interested until the rounds began to fall in the rice paddy across from us. I was pushed into a prone position as were the other prisoners. The people around me squatted and continued talking and eating. I wished that artillery had been used a little earlier. Seeing the rounds go off in the middle of an empty rice paddy when we could have put them to such effective use only a short time ago made them appear doubly futile.

The artillery stopped just before sunset and I was led along with the Vietnamese prisoners to join another group. Dan was standing in front of the second group of dejected-looking militiamen while a skinny, sharp-faced VC lectured them, using eloquent gestures to support his tirade. I was exuberant that Dan was still OK and felt a surge in my confidence that I'd be all right.

I was placed beside Dan and became the object of the speaker's comments. The little man stepped close to me, his bright, rodent-like eyes searching my face. *"Anh noi tieng Viet, khong?"* His voice was sharply questioning if I spoke Vietnamese.

"It lam," I answered, indicating I spoke very little, wondering what he intended. He turned to the other prisoners and rattled off a burst of Vietnamese accompanied by wild gesturing toward the field where the shells had landed, then turned back to me and snapped, *"Phai khong?"* asking me if what he had said was correct. I shrugged my shoulders, not having understood more than one or two words. This seemed to infuriate him and he stepped back, shaking his forefinger at me and blurting phrases in Vietnamese about "American aggressors." He next asked if I had not been granted my life rather than being killed in combat. "Yeah, yeah," I answered, wishing he'd go back to haranguing the Vietnamese. I was becoming uneasy, feeling that I could adversely influence the whole situation by unwittingly aggravating this rice-paddy orator.

He snapped several other questions at me in which I caught the word *"Dai-Uy,"* indicating Rocky might still be alive. I answered "yeah" to several of the questions, trying to understand or make out what he was saying about Rocky, the "yeah's" an unconscious acknowledgment that I had understood one or more of his phrases. He stopped abruptly when two other individuals in peasant clothing stepped up to the group. They spoke for a moment, and I took that opportunity to look around.

Dan was standing as if favoring his left ankle. His face was tired, but his glance said: "It's a shitty situation, but let's see what we can make of it." He was standing near a group of villagers who had gathered near the captives. The guards stood between him and the muttering civilians, their weapons held in front of their chests. The sound of their voices carried a pronounced threatening tone which had been growing as the little speaker had lectured the militiamen. Dan and I became the target of several older women and men, who shook their gnarled fists at us, speaking in cutting, high-pitched voices. As Dan and I were moved farther down the canal bank by one of the newcomers in black peasant garb, I heard a screech and turned my head to see an old crone lunging toward me from the crowd. In her upraised hand was a wicked-looking chopping knife. Her face was twisted into a grimace of hatred. I could do nothing but stand and watch. My arms were securely bound and I felt my fingernails dig into my palms as terror hit me.

One of the guards stepped quickly between the old lady and me, grabbing her arm with one hand while holding his weapon between himself and the struggling woman. The black-clad man with Dan and me walked over to the woman and took the knife, speaking in low, soothing tones. She quieted somewhat, though continuing to glare at me. I could feel the sweat in my palms, and my knees were suddenly much weaker. The second new man took Dan and me away from the crowd, leading us along the canal bank until we stood at the edge of the small hamlet.

I noticed at this time that Dan was limping. The first opportunity we had to stand next to each other, I asked what was wrong. Dan told me that he thought his ankle was broken. In the dimming light, I could see pain lines in his face. We were told by one of the accompanying guards not to talk and stood silent, waiting to see what was to happen next.

I had no idea where we were or how far it was to anything friendly. I recalled the chapter in the pamphlet on "Escape and Evasion" that had said, "One should attempt to escape as soon after capture as possible, before the enemy can move you to a secure area." I wished the author had included at least one paragraph on how to do it! I was beginning to feel rotten, but the situation was not as bad as I had anticipated because we were still alive. My head was one horrible throbbing mass, with a sharp pain running between my eyes. The expenditure of energy during the operation and fire fight, the full flow and now ebb of adrenalin in my system had left me feeling like a stuffed doll with all of the sawdust running out. My body ached, but there wasn't any one particular place that stood out. I was drawn with an overwhelming thirst which left my mouth feeling like I'd eaten hot sand.

The guards and two leaders motioned for Dan and me to begin walking along the canal bank. There was a tiny path along the uneven ground which ended a short distance later, forcing Dan to traverse the difficult terrain with a bad ankle and bound arms. I had problems merely because of exhaustion and inability to balance without using my hands. I slipped while attempting to cross a single-pole bamboo bridge and found myself hanging upside down with my legs locked around the pole and my head and shoulders underwater. Fortunately, I was pulled out quickly, and we continued along the bank.

It became dark rapidly and moonrise occurred a short time later, casting its soft glow across the landscape. The situation as well as the terrain became unreal in the moonlight. I found my mind wandering, settling on scenes at camp or at home and then jolting back to reality. I thought about that glass of iced tea that was waiting for me and thought how unfair it was that I wouldn't be able to drink it. I kept waiting to wake up and find all of this just a bad dream.

We walked until the moon was almost overhead when the dim glow of a lighted window appeared ahead. One of the guards went ahead of us, and when we arrived at the squalid hut set back from the canal, he met us and indicated a spot beside the hut where Dan and I were told to sit. One of the other guards squatted a short distance from us while the others went inside.

My wet fatigues and total exhaustion combined to thoroughly chill me in the cool night air. I moved my arms up and down as far as my bonds would allow, trying to get circulation back into my forearms and hands, but without success. The place we were sitting was muddy, and this added to the discomfort. I found a partially chopped log that the owner here was apparently using for firewood and leaned back against it, letting myself relax for the first time. I awoke when one of the leaders shook me by the shoulder, sending tingling shocks down my arms which were nearly numb.

We stooped slightly to enter the low doorway and stepped into a dimly lit room, smelling of woodsmoke and the rotten stench of *nuoc mam*, the salty fish sauce. The leader pointed to a figure lying on the floor and smiled when I recognized Rocky Versace. There was obvious pain from his wounds, which were still covered by the compresses I had applied earlier, but the bleeding had ceased and most important, Rocky was alive.

"How's it going, Rocky?" I asked quietly. His head jerked toward me and our eyes met. There was an immediate light in them and his mouth curved into a trace of his old grin.

"Nick! Am I glad you're alive! I thought they'd shot you after we left the village." The leaders let us talk for a moment while I asked Rocky about his wounds and learned that he had been transported in a boat from the site of capture to here and although his leg was giving him a lot of trouble, he was better

89

off than he had counted on being. He asked about Dan, who stepped into the light and talked with him for a moment before the guards herded Dan and me back into the yard. The leader followed us and squatted near us, speaking in slow Vietnamese, with frequent gestures, to let us know that the three of us would not be killed and were not to worry.

I lay shivering for a long time, dozing periodically with my mind transporting me back to the warmth of my bunk at Tan Phu, only to reawaken in the cold. The guard got Dan and me to our feet, directing us to the canal bank where we were seated in another of the long, narrow boats. One of the leaders sat behind us and a guard stood in the rear, poling the boat down the canal.

We traveled blindfolded once again and I lost all sense of direction during the ride. We had to get out several times while the boat was lifted across earthen dikes, after which we would take our seats again. When we finally stopped and the blindfolds were removed I could see low, thick-leaved trees, ferns and reeds on all sides of our boat. We seemed to be stopped in a wide place in the reeds and high grass with only the trail left by the boats through the grass as an indication of any course of travel. The guards stepped into the knee-deep water and pulled me from the boat. The bottom was relatively firm and I followed the guard until he was greeted by another, younger-looking boy wearing a torn black shirt and black shorts. The new one carried a tiny kerosene lamp and indicated for me to follow him. I did so and after passing through clumps of reeds and into a grove of trees, I found myself in front of a cage-like structure with a low thatched roof and floor made of ir-regularly shaped poles laid side by side across the six-foot width. The walls, front and rear, were made of similar poles spaced about six inches apart both vertically and horizontally. I was standing on two larger poles which served as a walkway above the water to a second hut not far away. The second hut had an open front for its entire length and a longer overhanging roof on the near side.

Rocky was already inside at the back of the six- to eight-foot-long enclosure. I stooped to pass through the opening at the front and walked to the rear, sitting down beside Rocky. Dan followed and as soon as both of us were in, the young serious boy and a second guard, Thanh, with very pleasant features entered and untied our arms. The relief as I was once again able to move my arms was a beautiful sensation. I rubbed my wrists where the split-bamboo thong had cut, enjoying the surge of blood back through my hands and fingers. The skin was wrinkled and withered-looking from the wetness and lack of circulation. I wasn't certain about what we could or could not do, but decided to find out. Turning to Rocky, I asked him how his wound was. He replied that it was giving him a lot of trouble and he suspected that a bone was broken or his kneecap was fractured. Dan offered to check it for him and we began to assess our condition. The guards stood by silent and watching.

More of the poorly clothed new group of guards crowded by the door, staring at us as we talked in low tones. There were seven of them sitting and standing in the front of the cage when another new man pushed his way through and deposited two mosquito nets and two sleeping mats on the floor. He said a few words to the others and two of them arranged to sleep in a larger, double net. I asked for a drink of water and the latest arrival, apparently the local leader, told the younger boy to get a cup of water. He was gone only a short time and returned, handing me a rice cup of water. In the semi-dark interior of the hut I couldn't see the contents and drank greedily. Too late, I felt the slimy moss in my mouth. The water had been scooped up from right outside the hut and was stagnant-tasting. I was too tired to think any more about it and returned the cup, thanking him for the water.

We climbed under the mosquito nets and the group of guards walked back down the logs, leaving one man sitting outside the cage with a submachine gun.

The sun was above the trees when I awoke. Dan and Rocky were already awake, but none of us really wanted to admit to ourselves that we were awake and yesterday had actually happened. I sat up and flinched as the effects of the ordeal sent pain shooting through sore and stiffened muscles. My head continued to throb, as it would do for the next six days. I discovered that I was unconsciously breathing through my mouth because my nose was entirely stopped up. I gingerly felt the bridge and was rewarded with a sharp pain that creased my forehead, causing my eyes to water. Clotted blood blocked both nostrils, and accepting the continuing pain I cleared one

91

nostril, allowing me to breathe normally. Rocky was in severe pain and his knee had begun to swell. Dan and I lifted our net and slipped over beside Rocky. Dan loosened the compresses which had stuck to the now-dried blood, giving Rocky a little relief, but medical care was a necessity.

Dan examined the three red-rimmed holes in Rocky's leg, determining that there was, luckily, no fracture involved. Swelling had bloated the kneecap slightly and there was obvious pain. Rocky had a graze wound on his back which offered no problem if it could be disinfected and kept clean. Rocky called to the guard and got him to understand through gestures that we needed medical treatment.

While waiting, Rocky asked if we thought he should let the guards know he spoke Vietnamese. Since there was a requirement to communicate our needs and no English speakers were in evidence among the guards, we decided he would use the minimum vocabulary possible to request the necessities. Rocky's command of both French and Vietnamese would allow him to monitor their conversations, if overheard, providing they were not aware of his capability. We were not convinced that our lives were not immediately threatened, although the guards had said several times that we had nothing to fear. There appeared to be an urgency in their attempts to dispel our fear of being killed.

Rocky explained to Nam, the guards' leader, that his wounds were very painful and he needed to have some sort of treatment before they got worse. Nam had satisfied himself that all of us did indeed understand some Vietnamese and, after assuring Rocky that an *"y-ta"* or medic would check his wounds, began to tell us that we were fortunate to have been captured rather than dying in the battle. He restated the pledge that we would not be killed since we were now prisoners. It was all too sudden for me and I retained my doubts, thinking that we were being lulled into a false sense of security. Nam seemed sincere and I was amazed at his lack of animosity after our experiences yesterday. It was as if someone had thrown a lighting switch, changing the complexion of this drama.

We lay down, having nothing else to do at the moment, and slept until the arrival of a delicate-featured, slightly built boy carrying a canvas bag. The remaining guards once again gathered around the front of the cage, peering in at the attraction.

"Intern," as he became known, was the local medic and was studying to become a physician. At present, he was qualified only to roll bandages and wash syringes, as far as we could tell by his examination of Rocky's wound. He apparently had a great deal of studying yet to do, but was the best they had to offer. We received a couple of bottles of *thuoc do*, a water-base merthiolate which acted as a mild antiseptic, and two rolled lengths of cotton cloth to rebandage the knee. He promised that Rocky would be moved to a hospital where his wound would be treated. After assuring us that there was nothing to fear, he walked out and was followed by the others. We received boiled water and some soap, which enabled us to cleanse the wound, and Dan rebandaged it.

The rice was a little more difficult to eat this morning since the terrible hunger had worn off. I wondered how long I could go without some sort of real food. I was still thinking in terms of American rations. Before I finished my meal, made doubly difficult by the persistent feeling of nausea, I experienced wrenching stomach cramps followed by an immediate urge to crap. The guard responded to my frantic gesturing by pointing toward a shaky, thin single-pole walk that ran away from the cage into the brush. I barely made it to the small platform nailed between two trees above the water before my intestines voided themselves of a diarrhetic flood. The guard stood about fifteen feet from me with his head turned as I went through the spasming pain of oncoming dysentery. Within two days, I was spending more time running between the cage and latrine than anything else.

Back at the cage Nam had brought an unexpected bowl of warm sweetened milk. Several days ago, I wouldn't have thought it any more than it was, but here it had become a rare delicacy. We took turns sipping the sweetness, wondering what had prompted our captors to give it to us. One of the guards who had been silent before, squatted smiling as we drank and told us it was given by the "Mat Trang," the Front. It was the first time I had heard reference made to the Liberation Front, known to us as the Vietcong. The guard glanced at Nam, who gave no indication of having heard, and proceeded to tell Rocky that the Mat Trang would care for his wounds and repeated the familiar phrase about not fearing death. Rocky, who had been able to understand more of the conversations, turned to me, his face alight, and said softly, "Aren't these wonderful people!"

The immediate fear of the unknown, of death, was being dispelled, and the actions of these guards, in contrast to the animosity we had experienced initially from the combatants and some of the people, created a sense of gratitude. Rocky, who had come to love the Vietnamese people he had known before capture, was fitting our present captors into his overall frame of reference. Dan was more cynical than either Rocky or me regarding these guards, but all of us were taken by surprise with the mild treatment we were receiving.

Rocky engaged in an animated conversation with Nam, forgetting his leg for a short time as he probed into Nam's reasons for being a member of the Vietcong. I was amazed, from what I understood of the conversation, at Rocky's ability to converse at length in Vietnamese, using simple phrases, but getting his points across. Nam accepted Rocky's statements supporting his role as an adviser to the Government forces and questioning Nam's reasons for being a revolutionary. There was a quiet assurance and maturity about the young man which made me wish he had been on our side. I discovered later that Nam's answers were not ones that revealed his thoughts, but only served to draw Rocky further out in explaining his beliefs and to cause Rocky to display more fluency with the language than he had originally intended.

The days passed slowly. Helicopters and T–28's flew near us as they crossed above the forest going to what must have been Tan Phu to our southwest. The thought of friendly forces being within our sight and hearing, yet so far from physical contact, was frustrating. Rocky was moved out of the cage after a couple of days, supposedly to be taken to a hospital. Dan had cleaned the wound well enough to prevent serious immediate trouble, but it would require debridement and antibiotics.

The third day, while bathing in the clear standing rainwater a short distance from the cage, I was astonished to find small puncture wounds in my legs and chest. I picked and scraped tiny chunks of metal from the festering cuts. At some time during the battle I had been hit by fragmentation without even realizing it. The continuing splitting headache and general exhaustion had masked the pain from these wounds, which turned

94

out to be more of a nuisance than a hindrance. The graze wound on my thigh was open, but clean, for which I was thankful. I hoped that Rocky's would clear up without complications. Dan had caught fragments in the shoulder and had cleaned his wounds up so that he and I were quickly healing. My increasing problem with mucus and blood in the watery stools I frequently passed caused me concern.

Almost a week and a half after we arrived in the camp, Thanh came to the cage and got Dan and me, telling us that the "representatives of the Mat Trang" wished to see us. We followed him to the guard hut and saw three older men sitting crosslegged on a mat which had been placed across the pole floor. One was dressed in the black trousers and shirt we had seen so often, the second in black trousers and a blue shirt. The third was wearing a khaki shirt and trousers. All were barefoot, just like the guards.

Dan and I sat on the edge of the mat while the three cadre studied us. The blue-shirted one spoke in slow, careful English, "We are representatives of the Liberation Front and come to see to your needs. Do you have any demands of the Front?" The only thing I could think of was asking to get out of here. Dan asked about medical treatment for Captain Versace. "Blue Shirt" assured us that Rocky was being treated for his wounds and was all right.

The older one spoke rapidly in a whining, high-pitched voice, his eyes never leaving our faces. Blue Shirt listened intently, then said in the same careful English, "The representative of the Front wishes to know if you have heard the results of the battle in which you were captured." I replied that we had no way of knowing what the final outcome was, since we had been captured. My answer was translated in one word, *"Khong"*—No. The older one spoke directly to me even though I couldn't understand what he was saying. Blue Shirt translated after he finished, "The Liberation Armed Forces dealt a heavy blow to your post and the puppet soldiers. You are fortunate to be alive and well treated by the Liberation Front. We care for your wounds and see that you receive sufficient food for your daily ration." It was almost as if he were reading a prepared script, and as he went on, I began to wonder what was in store for us. It wasn't anything I had been prepared for.

Back in the cage Dan and I tried to determine what was

going on. The thought of attempting to escape, complicated when Rocky was moved, slipped into the background as we optimistically discussed our apparent good fortune and hopes for an early release. Before Rocky had been separated from us he had talked about another American who had been captured some time before and released after six months. We had speculated that we would be held for anywhere between two weeks and six months, with the latter as an outside limit. Our hope was for a negotiated release and the problem we immediately faced was staying alive until that could be accomplished.

Two days later, we were told that we were to be taken to another part of the camp. Thanh, Frank Lloyd and Nam escorted us along a twenty-five-meter walk through the water and grass to another low-roofed hut, much like the guard hut. There, sitting on the porch with a fresh bandage on his leg, was Rocky! I was overjoyed to see Rocky looking better and his face lit up when he saw us walking toward him. The guards let us talk for a few minutes before a short, almost dwarfed individual appeared, his ugly features twisted into a leering smile that tended to pull his oversized eyes out of shape. He was carrying a 35mm camera and immediately began instructing the guards to place us for a photograph. Dan was seated on one side of Rocky, I on the other, and the little man snapped several quick photos. After that, Dan and I were led to a boat, blindfolded, tied at the elbows and made to lie down in the bottom. I had no idea what was happening and ideas from execution to release poured through my mind. We traveled along a narrow canal with high banks. The freshly turned earth on the banks that I could see from under the blindfold indicated it had been recently dug. I thought about a report we had received about a month earlier at Tan Phu about a new canal the VC had dug near the U Minh to improve their communications. I wondered if this might not be that canal.

The boat pulled up beside a lower bank and I was led over what seemed like plowed ground to a clump of trees and pushed to a sitting position. Dan sat down beside me and when we heard the guard's voice fade in the distance we tried to determine what was happening. Optimism made us think of release and our spirits soared. I could picture an exchange or outright release and wished the negotiators would hurry.

"Squeaks," the soprano-voiced guard, returned and pulled me to my feet, leading me back to the plowed ground. My blindfold was stripped away and I found myself standing beside a large pineapple field. The older cadre of the three who had visited was talking with the photographer as they stood in the shade of one of the trees bordering the field. Most of our guards were standing around with their weapons, which were either old French MAS 36 rifles or French MAT 49 submachine guns. I saw one American Thompson submachine gun and a carbine. The cadre spoke to the guards and I was led over to him and the photographer. He gestured, indicating for me to lie down. I recoiled, thinking I was to be shot! I shook my head no; I wasn't going to die that way. He repeated the gestures, this time speaking sharply in his high tenor voice. I still refused and he became obviously angry. He snapped a command to the guards and I was led back to the trees and blindfolded again. I could feel my knees shaking as the façade of optimism came crashing down.

Minutes later I was pulled to my feet and led to the field once again. After the blindfold was pulled away and my arms untied, I was told to put my hands over my head. I saw the photographer with his camera poised and decided to comply. As I started to raise my hands, the smallest of the guards stepped up behind me holding a rifle that was almost as long as he was tall. I dropped my arms, but heard the shutter click. The older cadre yelled for me to put my arms back in the air. By this time I was weighing the advantages and disadvantages of pushing them in a dispute over a photo of me with my hands up. I placed my hands on my head and stood while the photographer snapped several shots.

The older cadre was not satisfied and tried for different poses of a captured American. I refused to do more than stand with my hands on top of my head and in a burst of anger he grabbed one of the MAS 36's and jabbed it into my stomach, threatening to pull the trigger. There was more than a moment of indecision in my mind, wondering whether or not he'd actually do it. The photographer saved the situation by calling to the cadre and pointing to a second group of guards who were gesturing for us to come to them. With a snort and several sniffles, the cadre withdrew the muzzle from my stomach and gave the rifle back to the guard. I was pushed toward the tree line where the guards waited.

I found Dan standing beside a small portable table on which were a bottle of La Rue beer and soda pop. Seated behind the low table was a new man in a freshly creased khaki uniform with a 9mm automatic pistol prominently displayed on his belt. We were seated in front of the table and offered the beer and soda. Before we could accept or reject the offer, the photographer began snapping pictures. In less than a minute, we were back on our feet, blindfolded, tied and being led back to the waiting boat. Within an hour we were back in the cage, trying to fit the new pieces of this jigsaw puzzle into place. Optimism was fading.

On the evening of 13 November, Dan and I were told to fold up our net and mat in preparation for a trip to another, better camp. Blue Shirt was back with us and explained that we would be traveling for several days and precautions would have to be taken during the trip to guarantee our security. We would be moving through several dangerous areas and our cooperation was a necessity. He spoke as if we were already a part of this organization and our cooperation was to be expected.

After we walked to the boats and I was seated, I found that the guards, at least, didn't take chances. I was blindfolded, my arms were tied securely, and I was placed in the bottom of the boat on the wooden flooring racks. "Moon," an older guard so named by us because of his round, full-moon face, was sitting in the boat with me. He checked to see that I was reasonably comfortable and covered my feet to protect them against the clouds of mosquitoes which surrounded us. This gesture was reassuring and I relaxed as much as possible, trying to ignore the stinging mosquito bites, though my feet were tender after a lifetime of wearing footgear.

The routine of the four-day trip was basically the same. Travel from sundown until just before sunup, arms tied during travel. After the second night, I was allowed to sit up when there were no other boats near us. The blindfold was used only the first night. We stopped one day in a lean-to shed behind a modest thatched hut belonging to a village cadre. Dan and I were placed in the hut while it was still dark and spread our mat on the mud floor, putting up our net rapidly and dropping into a quick sleep. I awoke at daylight and started to go back to sleep when I noticed blood on my arm. I sat up and stared in horror. My arms were covered with small, shiny, grayish-black leeches! I woke Dan and we checked each other out, our disgust mounting as we found ourselves bleeding from numerous completed bites and many more of the slimy creatures still sucking. Luckily a guard was nearby and we first borrowed his cigarette to burn the leeches, forcing them to release their suction and drop off, and afterward used a candle to remove those remaining. It was nasty business trying to get rid of them and the thought of more of them having a shot at our blood was definitely unappealing. We slept poorly the rest of the day.

The early morning hours of 18 November marked our entry into our first formal prison camp, and it wasn't that much. The vegetation had changed gradually as we moved southward from the Thoi Binh area. From the broad rice paddies and lush groves of coconut and banana palms we entered the mangrove swamps of the southern Camau peninsula. The water was salty and was controlled by the tidal flow from the Gulf of Siam, thus restricting vegetation to that which could survive without fresh water. Nipa palms and broadleaf ferns abounded throughout the area, mixing with the broad mangrove trees and dense clumps of *cay duoc*, a straight-trunked tree highly valued for use in construction. During the hours of low tide I saw mud flats emerge, littered with trunks of dead and rotting trees.

The camp was more elaborate than the temporary setup we had left. A log dock extended a quarter of the way into the entry canal with a log walk beginning at its rear edge. To the right of the walkway was a small hut serving as a kitchen and mess hall. Just behind it was a storage hut which became Rocky's first home. Further down the walk, under the spreading leaves of a thicker clump of trees, were a series of four long, relatively narrow huts, built, as were all the huts, on posts, raising them above the water level. One, for the guards, was beside the walk and the other three were facing it on the other side of a crosswalk. The middle one of these was slightly higher than its companions and had open sides. The two other huts had barred walls and were obviously for prisoners. To the left of the walk, midway between the kitchen and first guard hut, was a single square hut with thatched walls as well as roof. It was of better construction and housed the cadre.

Dan and I were placed in the second cage during the first days in the camp. Rocky was in the storage hut, next to the kitchen, and we weren't allowed to communicate with him. It was becoming clear that the separation was not based on his wound or the "hospitalization" he had never received. Rocky had assailed the revolutionary movement from his first encounter with Nam and had been marked as a definite reactionary. Dan and I, because we couldn't speak Vietnamese, were unknown quantities.

We had been issued a pair of gray pajamas and an aluminum cup, plate and spoon apiece. Blue Shirt, we came to learn, was Mr. Ba; the older cadre was Mr. Muoi; and the uniformed cadre was indeed military—Major Hai. The camp was commanded by Major Hai with Mr. Muoi as the political representative. Mr. Ba was the interpreter who would deal primarily with Dan and me. Rocky had apparently divulged his ability to speak French and was receiving lectures from Major Hai and Mr. Muoi as well as entering into discussions with Nam and "Alvin," an obnoxious, chipmunk-cheeked guard. The initial period when Rocky had talked with Nam was used to form a picture of Rocky's beliefs and attitudes which enabled the cadre to begin to cut away at them.

The second day in camp, I was given one of the hand-towel-and-scarf cloths carried by the guards and told to put on my new gray pajamas. Mr. Ba told me I was to be treated for my wounds and dysentery in the storage hut, which had been transformed into a dispensary. Thanh led me down the walk and into the hut. The inside had been altered from a crudely built pole-and-thatch hut into a dispensary by lining the walls with white muslin cloth. Mats were placed on the floor, covering the irregular flooring and a colored cloth and plastic-covered table supported a display of surgical instruments, syringes, needles, and trays of antibiotics. Two men and a woman stood at the side of the room, waiting as Mr. Ba instructed me to lie down on the mat and place my new towel under my head. I learned that the two men were doctors and the woman, a nurse. I noted that all of them were capped, gowned and masked, as if prepared for surgery. I happened to glance at floor level and smiled when I saw three more pair of bare feet. The woman was pregnant under the loose-fitting gown and had difficulty in bending over to arrange the towel behind my head.

At a word from Mr. Ba, the three squatted around me and one of the "doctors" began to check my heartbeat with a patched stethoscope. I lay there, not really comprehending what he was looking for since there was no problem with my vital signs. It was a case of the runs and a couple of infected fragment wounds. The next thing I knew, there was a young man standing in the doorway with a Canon 35mm camera, snapping away. It took him only a minute or so to catch the medical team in various poses, treating an American prisoner. After he departed, Mr. Ba mentioned offhand that it was routine to photograph American prisoners in order to satisfy requirements of the Front. The nurse then prepared a syringe and as treatment for my runs and infection I received a 100 mg injection of Vitamin B_1! I left the hut totally discouraged and only hoping I wouldn't get anything more because of an unsterile needle.

On the morning of 21 November, Dan and I were given a small can of sweetened condensed milk which made the day seem like Christmas. We opened it at the urging of Mr. Muoi and Major Hai, who appeared anxious for us to drink and enjoy it. As soon as the can was opened, the photographer was standing in front of us. He took several shots of us with the milk, one with me scooping the delicious liquid out of my cup while Dan scowled. It was a long time before we saw another can of milk.

That evening, as Dan and I were sitting before our cage waiting for the rice to be brought to us, there was a commotion by the kitchen. Excited shouts from the guards, Nam, Frank Lloyd and Alvin scrambling to get their weapons and dashing back along the walkway toward the kitchen. We stood and tried to determine what was happening, but it was outside the camp. I could see the guards disappearing into the trees by the canal, wading in mud up to their thighs, rifles held over their heads. Shouting continued further from camp as the guards spread into a line, sweeping the palms and fern thickets. Mr. Muoi walked up to our cage carrying a long iron rod with a loop on one end. In his other hand he carried two U-shaped iron rods with loops on the ends. We were ordered back into the cage and put into leg irons. The long rod was the stationary iron on which the U-shaped anklets were slipped, fastening the individual's leg to the long rod. We questioned the reason for this action, wondering what was up.

Muoi was visibly incensed and snapped that "Versace was very bad" and had attempted to leave the camp. Rocky, with a wounded leg, surrounded by deep mud terrain and a camp full of guards, had tried to escape. He had more guts than brains to try it at this point, and he was caught, pulling himself through the oozing slime toward the canal. I learned later from him that he was attempting to reach the canal where he could swim and possibly make it northward to a friendly outpost.

Before, the cadre had assumed from Rocky's opinions that they had a hard case on their hands. Now they knew it.

Mr. Ba spent the afternoons, or parts of them, at the cage with Dan and me. He gently probed our ideas about the United States and our involvement in Vietnam. There was no effort to contradict anything we said, primarily because we did more listening than talking. He resolved the impasse by showing us a copy of an "Open Letter to President Kennedy," signed by sixty-three or sixty-four American "intellectuals," calling for our disengagement from Vietnam. An assortment of propaganda leaflets stressing the losses we were suffering in an "unjust and dirty war" followed. (I couldn't recall any war that I would have considered "clean" and the question of "just" and "unjust" depended on which side you viewed the war from). The central theme was the generosity and leniency of the Front toward prisoners.

Rocky was moved into the front portion of the guard hootch across the walk from Dan and me. We'd been shifted into the slightly smaller cage a couple of days before when preparations were begun for the arrival of additional prisoners. The guards constructed a tiny cubicle wide enough for a mosquito net and barely high enough to fully raise the three-foot height. The sides and top were covered with thatching, blocking out light and any flow of air. With his wounded leg in the restriction of irons and forced to stay in the cramped, hot cell, Rocky continued to duel verbally with the cadre in French, Vietnamese and English, depending on who was trying to lecture him. He received his meals at the same time as Dan and I, and we kept a close check to insure he wasn't cut back on the meager amounts of food we received. The cadre seemed to be experimenting with Rocky and letting Dan and me watch him. It did nothing to enhance Mr. Ba's claims about leniency.

The next incident that came up was the push for a letter to our families stating that we were in good health and being well treated, and thanking the NLF for its lenient treatment. After Mr. Ba came up with the requirement, Dan and I talked it over, weighing the possibility of getting word out that we were alive against possible use of our signatures on forged "confessions" as had occurred in Korea. When we talked, Rocky could hear us and we worked out a song reply where he would sing a melody and insert words to answer. We decided to write a single letter to the International Red Cross informing them that we were alive and asking them to notify our families. When Mr. Ba heard my solution to the requirement he immediately vetoed it, saying the letters must be individually written and addressed to our families. One paragraph would state that we were alive and in good health and that we thanked the National Liberation Front for its kindness. All I had to do was look across the walk at Rocky's predicament, or wait a few minutes for my next virtually uncontrollable burst of mucus, blood and excrement at the latrine, to know that I wasn't going to thank anyone for anything yet. I wrote a short note to the International Red Cross giving them my name, rank, serial number and date of capture and requesting them to inform my family that I was alive and in reasonably good health and was receiving adequate food to keep me alive. I felt I might be stretching the last point, but I wanted the message to stand a chance of going through. Dan copied the format, supplying his data, and we handed them to Mr. Ba. A week or so later, he informed us that the Front could not get the messages through, but would try again.

Three South Vietnamese ARVN prisoners were moved into the cage that Dan and I had vacated. One of them was a medic and was assigned to treat Rocky's wound. Alvin had taken a particular dislike to Rocky and lost no opportunity to make his difficult situation more miserable. The only time Rocky displayed a burst of temper was one day when Alvin was unlocking the leg irons in order for Rocky to go to the latrine. He was anything but gentle with the iron, and jerked it so it pulled Rocky's injured leg abruptly from the mat. Rocky cried out in pain, knocking the iron out of Alvin's hand and shouting in English, "What are you trying to do? Kill me?" Alvin had recoiled at first, but immediately reached back in, grabbed the iron with Rocky's leg still secured to it, and shook it until I could feel the pain in my own leg. Dan and I jumped to our feet, heading for the door of our cage, bent on reducing the now shouting, redfaced guard to bloody pulp. Thanh and several other guards tumbled out of the hut beside ours, blocking our way with outthrust rifles. Muoi and Major Hai arrived at the hut almost simultaneously. Rocky was on his back groaning in utter misery. Alvin was shouting threats at the prone figure and had to be led away by Squeaks and Intern. Muoi quickly assessed the situation and called for the ARVN medic, who hurried over to assist Rocky. Dan and I were ordered back into our cage and our leg irons were put on for the rest of the day

Shortly thereafter, a separate cage was built in the area behind the guard hut for Rocky and it became virtually impossible for Dan and me to communicate with him. The young ARVN medic changed his bandages and kept the wound clean, having permission to visit Rocky's cage once every two days. He was the only person to talk with Rocky aside from the cadre and the guards.

A fourth ARVN prisoner joined the original three and all four began a political school, conducted by a slick-looking cadre who also gave the political indoctrination for the guards. I felt that the drill was put on for Dan's and my benefit, allowing us to watch the response and how the ARVN prisoners functioned within the camp.

In addition to the guards from our first camp, there were members of a second squad with them here. The squad was newly formed and its young members, most of them in their late teens and early twenties, were undergoing political indoctrination. These guards treated us with curiosity and controlled disdain, probably resulting from the violently anti-American lectures they received from the cadre.

Mr. Ba came down one day with a piece of paper he said would have to be filled out as a matter of processing. I read the title, "Red Cross Index Data Card," and the information required. Beneath the heading were: Name, Rank, Serial Number, Date of Birth—all as prescribed by the Geneva Convention. Under these items was a subheading: "Information required to allow the International Red Cross to notify your loved ones of your safety." The following list of questions astounded me. "Unit stationed with in USA. Military training. Military schools attended. Unit assigned to enroute to SVN. Date of arrival in SVN. Method of travel. Unit assigned to in SVN and location of unit." I read further with a sinking feeling in my stomach: "Previous service, wounds, decorations, punishments. Names of mother, father, wife, children, any relatives living in, or near, SVN. Religious belief, educational background, political background, club and organizational affiliations, hobbies," and a "short biographical story" with several sheets of paper to write it on. Mr. Ba was watching as I read the paper and as I finished it, he said in a matter-of-fact tone, "You may complete your declaration and give it to me after." He treated this form as if it was something to be filled out without question, like a credit card application.

"Mr. Ba." I was quietly sincere. "We are not required nor allowed to give you more than our name, rank, serial number and date of birth. This form contains both military and personal questions which we cannot answer."

He looked surprised that I would refuse. "But you must answer the questions! It is a requirement of the Liberation Front for all prisoners." Then his voice became conciliatory. "All the Front wishes to do is to notify your family that you are not killed on the battlefield. You do not want them to be concerned for your safety."

"We wrote letters to the Red Cross," I reminded him. "They will have sufficient information to notify our families that we are alive."

"No!" His answer was emphatic. "The Red Cross is a tool of the imperialist aggressors and the Front does not recognize them." There was a contradiction which he had overlooked, but I didn't bring it to his attention, saving it for later when I might need it. "You do not wish to fill out the form?" He made it a question, assuming that we wouldn't. Dan and I shook our heads, no.

"We will give you our essential data as required by the Geneva Convention, Mr. Ba, but we are prevented from giving more." He picked up the form and turned to walk away.

"Consider your decision carefully. Do not concern yourself with the Geneva Convention. Think only of the Front which has given you your lives. I will come again later."

I was still attempting to determine several things: First, what was their purpose in taking us prisoner rather than killing us? Second, what requirements would be placed upon us that we could not fulfill and finally, to what lengths would they go to insure fulfillment? The thought of ultimate release was still strong in my mind and I found myself clinging to that hope, tending to ignore or dismiss anything that would breed pessimism.

My dysentery, which had grown progressively worse, was now accompanied by fever and nausea. There was a continuing inability to eat sufficient rice.

We were allowed to take a bath in the canal once a week, and wash our clothes. I was happy I still had my tiger suit because of its durability. The gray pajamas didn't seem as though they would last very long, although I was hoping I'd be out long before they wore thin. Soap was a luxury and only when Mr. Ba or Major Hai let us borrow some of theirs did we enjoy a good scrub. Dan asked repeatedly for toothbrushes so we could begin caring for our teeth. We recalled the extreme problem the POW's in Korea experienced because of lack of dental care, and wanted to avoid it if at all possible. Mr. Ba told us we would soon be issued the necessary items and later reassured us it would be only a little longer.

The probing of our thoughts continued, with Mr. Ba spending from thirty minutes to two hours at our hut during a day, explaining the lenient treatment we were receiving and highlighting cases of Americans who had been released after a period of captivity. He concentrated on whether or not we believed we could be released, encouraging us to strive to return to our families. The other side of the talks was the illegality of American intervention in Vietnam, based on the Front's interpretation of the 1954 Geneva Accords. With little success he sought to draw our comments on the war, and our parts in it. We had adopted a sit-and-listen attitude, feeling that the more we said, the worse off we'd be.

Rocky, on the other hand, was engaging all comers. I could hear Mr. Muoi's voice climb an octave from its already high pitch as Rock would contradict something Muoi had said. Major Hai alternated with Muoi and Ba in attempting to sway the steadfast Versace. Major Hai spoke fluent French, and I could picture Rocky's complete absorption in debating each of these men in a different language, using the problems of expressing a logical argument in a foreign language as a method of occupying his mind. Ba would completely lose his composure, yelling, "No! No! No!" when Rocky maneuvered him into a contradiction, using Ba's lack of familiarity with English to trip him up. After a while, the cadre stayed primarily with French and English to prevent the guards from understanding Rocky's counterarguments which might have adversely influenced the indoctrination they were receiving.

In late December, air activity increased in our area. We were taken out of the camp on several occasions while T-28's or twin-engined B-26's struck at targets near us. It was extremely disturbing to be on the receiving end of our weapons, and I found myself dreading the sound of the L-10 spotter air craft as it sought targets. Even more disturbing was the VC disregard for the tiny unarmed plane. They felt that its lack of armament made it harmless, apparently failing to realize that it was the one that called in the big boys. Only when they heard the sound of approaching fighters would they head for the palm thickets, away from camp. We could only hope our move out would be rapid enough to escape detection in case this camp was spotted.

There was an effective airplane alarm in the camp in the form of Mr. Muoi. We learned that he had had an unpleasant experience in an airstrike in the past, and I would have sworn he could detect the T-28's as they were taking off seventy-five miles away. Long before anyone else heard the roar of the engines his tenor screech, "*May bay! May bay!*"—Airplane! Airplane!—would cause the hair on the back of my neck to crawl. This trait earned him the nickname "May bay Muoi."

In January 1964, after two months, the guards from our first camp disappeared along with Major Hai. Mr. Ba and Muoi were in and out periodically. On one of these visits, Muoi was squatting in the guard hut next to our cage as Dan and I sat on the small porch in front.

"Do you know that Kennedy was killed?" he asked in slow, careful Vietnamese. I looked at Dan, wondering if I had understood. Muoi repeated the question, emphasizing the words for killed. I didn't understand "*bi am sat,*" which means "assassinated," and couldn't picture the President dead.

Muoi asked if I was sorry President Kennedy was dead. Thinking he was trying to shake us up, I replied, "Is President Kennedy sorry we are prisoners?" Muoi thought the answer was extremely funny and walked off repeating it to himself, chuckling. I wasn't trying to be funny; on the contrary, we had been told earlier that Ngo Dinh Diem had been overthrown and killed and the govenment in Saigon was toppling. The possibility that these reports might contain some truth made me wonder what was happening on the outside. I finally dismissed the reports as false, choosing to believe that the situation was stable and, most important to us, we would not be forgotten because of chaotic repercussions from two alleged presidential killings.

The last week in January, Dan and Rocky were removed from the camp, leaving me by myself. Mr. Ba assured us we were all going to a new camp, but the idea of being split up disturbed me. There was an instant reluctance to be left alone in this camp, not knowing whether Ba was telling the truth or not. After the other two departed, I spent an anxiety-filled six days even though I was ignored for the most part by the members of the new squad and their cadre. On the first of February, I was taken on an evening trip to the new camp by Nam and "Short Sleeves," a minor cadre who seemed to be in charge of logistics. As before, I was tied at the elbows and placed in the bottom of a boat with a rice-straw mat covering me. In less than two hours I was untied and led from the boat to my new home.

In the semidarkness, broken only by the flickering light of a kerosene-filled toothpowder-bottle lamp, I made my way along a shaky log walk, through a large hut which would house the guards, and onto a series of single logs that seemed to extend back into the darkness for half the length of a football field. I balanced precariously, with my meager belongings under one arm and reaching with the other hand for trees and branches with which to steady myself. Finally, at the end of the logs, I came to a small, partially completed hut.

In the morning I awoke, and after I was unlocked, I washed out the filth from several nightime crap runs. After this, I took my first look at the camp. Construction was still going on, but the guard hut and a kitchen between it and the canal had been completed. Ferns and thick-trunked mangrove trees with their spreading aerial roots prevented me from seeing more than the beginnings of walkways which probably led to other huts. I estimated there were at least two or three more huts. Cut poles lay in the water, ready for use, and palm branches were piled on a portion of walkway prior to being laid on the hootches for roofing. It was obvious that the location for my cage had been selected to limit my range of vision and create the feeling of isolation even here in the forest. I could see the latrine to the north, and on the south perhaps fifteen meters of scattered ferns and trees before vegetation blocked my view. Behind my cage was a wall of palms, ferns and tree trunks. My only area of open vision was to the east, directly along the twenty-five- or thirty-meter-long log walk extending to the guard hut.

Thanh came down to get my plate and cup for breakfast and asked if I thought my new quarters were *dep*—beautiful. I assured him they were more than I had expected, then asked him if Dan and Rocky had similarly comfortable accommodations, trying to determine if they were in the camp. Thanh either didn't understand or chose not to understand as he took my utensils and retraced his steps without answering. I was again tormented by the thought of being in the camp alone. The fear of immediate death was stilled, but the unknown was a greater burden. I couldn't imagine myself holding out for an extended period of time on the diet of rice and minute amounts of fish—when we had any at all. The hope for release was my source of strength, but I still had no idea what requirements other than the "index data card" would be made. I knew I couldn't comply with what they had already demanded and wondered how long I could go, obeying the Code of Conduct, and at the same time come out alive.

Later in the morning Mr. Ba came down to visit me, nearly slipping off the log walk as he wasn't accustomed to this type of living. I learned from him in later discussions that he was a journalist by trade, and had joined the revolution because his paper had been closed down for subversive editorial policy. His knowledge of English had gotten him this assignment even though he was not trained in dealing with POW's. A tendency of his to philosophize was the reason for his nickname, "Plato."

He explained the camp regulations to me which were much like the ones Muoi had read to Dan and me at the last camp. Permission was to be requested from a guard anytime I wished to go anywhere; I was responsible for keeping my belongings and hut in order; guards' orders were to be obeyed and, specifically for this camp, I would not be allowed to leave my cage except to go to the latrine or places designated by a cadre. He commented on the amount of work the guards had gone through to provide me with adequate shelter. He pointed to the long log walk with pride. "We have constructed a street so you do not have to walk in the mud. It is the policy of the Front that you will not be mistreated, tortured or put to shame."

"It's a shame," I mused, "that I'm not allowed to use that 'street.'"

After a few comments about the release of another American a short time before, he drew from the side pocket of his blue shirt the index data card, which had been slightly revised. It was now entitled "My Declaration" and the questions pertaining to military and family background had been amplified. "The Front has a simple requirement which must be completed. We ask nothing which will endanger your status. It is merely so the Front may know you better and evaluate your case and release you." The thought of release was overpowering and I wanted to believe that I could get out of this predicament alive.

109

I repeated my argument that I was allowed to give only the information required by the Geneva Convention and couldn't complete the form.

Mr. Ba had prepared for this. "You are a prisoner of war only if the Front declares you such. Soon you will attend a school which will show you the truth of the situation in Vietnam so you may know clearly the just and unjust cause. When you have completed the requirements of the Front and can recognize your mistakes, you can be released to rejoin your loved ones. You must complete the information to show your sincerity vis-à-vis the Front."

My next question was one of vital importance, since the means to resist were greatly influenced by the methods of extracting information. "Mr. Ba, what if I refuse to give you the information on the questionnaire? You said your policy was not to mistreat, torture or put to shame. How do you expect to obtain information if a person won't give it and you can't force him?" The thoughts of physical torture were flashing through my mind, making me cringe, wondering how much I'd be able to take.

"Ah, do not fear torture." Plato's voice was reassuring. "We are not barbarians who rely on physical torture to gain information." His next statement was an explanation of a theory I was to learn in the following years. "If you take an individual and control his physical, you do not necessarily control the man; but, if you can control his mind, you also control the physical and the whole." He explained that it was his duty in the following days to explain the situation in Vietnam to me and help me to realize the mistakes I had made in coming to Vietnam. The ultimate goal, he said, was to help me to correct my errors and become a better person.

I had asked for and had been allowed to keep the "declaration" in order to read its contents carefully. I knew I wasn't the bravest person around and decided it would be better to say "I don't know" rather than "I won't tell you." There was a greater chance of holding out if I could convince them I knew little or nothing. For that reason, I had to determine what they wanted to know and then devise some story which would hide my knowledge of the subject. In the new form were questions concerning Special Forces, its composition, commanders, training and capabilities in Vietnam. It went into my family's places of birth, education and religious beliefs. Ages, names of other relatives in the United States and the professions of all family members were included in this form. Name, rank, serial number and date of birth wouldn't cover what these people were after.

As I sat thinking, I looked up in time to see Dan crossing the long walk down by the guard hut. He grinned and managed a wave without the guards noticing. One of the guards sat at the end of their hut nearest my cage, watching me during the day, and it was difficult to do anything unobserved. I waited until Dan reached the latrine, squatting on the narrow pole platform. My spirits immediately went up even though our huts were separated and communication was limited. I asked him how he was doing and what the score was in the camp. He told me he was having trouble getting the rice down, and because the guards were involved in construction, they had little time to catch enough fish for themselves as well as feeding us, hence the *nuoc mam* and "no food" for the Americans. Before we could say anything else, my cage was filled with guards, all talking rapidly, pushing me into the locked portion and ordering me to be quiet. It was clear that the isolation of individuals was to be more than just physical separation. Plato came scurrying down the walkway and seemed very upset that I would try to talk with Dan. He told me that for reasons of camp security, we were not allowed to talk with each other and any repetition on my part would be a violation of camp regulations with appropriate punishment following.

That evening, after a day of watching the guards at work building the other huts and finishing the roof over my porch, I discovered where Rocky was. The sound of voices was difficult to hear as far from the other huts as I was, but Muoi's outraged voice echoed through the woods immediately after I heard Rocky's resolute pronouncement, "*Cong San!*"—Communist. Shortly after that I saw Muoi walk rapidly toward the kitchen, hands clasped behind his back, skinny shoulders hunched forward, his discomposure very evident. Rock wasn't easing up one bit.

I was told to bathe in the water around my cage during high tide, which brought two to three feet of clear salt water throughout the area. To rinse off, one of the guards would fill my drinking cup with rainwater from one of the 300-liter storage drums. I never quite got clean, but it was refreshing to splash cold water over myself. There was the thought that all of this would come to an end soon and I could get back to soap and a hot shower. I was given a pair of pajamas made from old rice sacks, dyed with black dye that ran the first three or four times I washed them. At the same time I was forced to give up my tiger suit, something I didn't want to do.

The first week in camp I met a short, chunky young man who was introduced as the "camp physician." "Ben," named for Ben Casey, proved to be a life saver for me. I had received, shortly before departure from the last camp, several packets of powder marked "Entimine" from Short Sleeves which were to cure the dysentery. Their effect was only to increase my nausea for about thirty minutes after I took them. Ben had been informed of the extreme problem I had with "*ia chay*," which covers the entire spectrum of "runny bowel movements." So, equipped with a stethoscope, symbol of a medical practitioner among the VC, he proceeded to check my heart and lungs. After assuring himself that I was breathing, he used the finger-pressure method to probe my abdomen along the bottom of my rib cage, seeking points of tenderness, and found them with no difficulty. He asked about the duration of pain and content of my stools. I answered, mentioning the frequency and the fluid loss, which was my primary concern. Dehydration and further imbalance of my system under these conditions could be fatal and I was doing all I could to avoid that. Plato and Muoi listened as Ben questioned me, Plato translating questions and answers. It was the first time I had experienced genuine concern for countering the illness, and after a couple of days I received a series of tablets, sulfaguanidine, which tended to slow the stools for a period of time, but failed to stop the blood and mucus.

Ben paid daily visits after that, checking on frequency and amounts of blood and mucus. Plato became more concerned when the frequency again increased and I continued to drop weight. From my 165 pounds at capture, I estimated I had dropped to 140 or 145 pounds, and I found the bouts with fever increasing as my body weakened. I was assured that the Front would provide medication to cure me, and after three weeks of unsuccessful administration of sulfaguanidine and sulfa-thiazole, Ben gave me two injections of streptomycin. I was fortunate that I had no toxic reaction to the antibiotic because there was no antihistamine available and dosage seemed to be based on available supply rather than approved clinical treatment. The main effort, as in all subsequent attempts to treat illness among the Americans, was to eliminate the symptoms, not necessarily cure the disease.

Immediately after administrations of any medication came the question "*Bot chua*?"—Is it better yet?—as if instantaneous results were to be expected. Any elimination or treatment was normally given before an admiring audience of guards who seemed to regard Ben's medical ability as some sort of magic. Plato or Muoi added a dose of gratitude-inspiring propaganda, insuring I realized the magnanimity of the Front in giving medication to a prisoner. I would have been thankful to receive anything that would end the intestinal problem, but nothing had worked.

In the meanwhile, plans for the school we were to attend progressed rapidly. The building south of my hut, it turned out, was to be the schoolhouse and a great deal of additional work went into its construction. Plato, in one of his visits, said that the Front was dispatching two high-ranking cadre to conduct the classes and I would be expected to apply myself to learning the lessons well since the question of my release hinged on my attitude and behavior.

Dan and I established a "dead drop" at a point on one of the walks we both had access to. One of us, whenever the mood seized him, would leave a note, written on the paper unwittingly supplied by Plato for us to write the declaration, and the other would pick it up when he passed. We began to exchange information on the procedures and questions we were getting from Muoi and Plato, thus breaking their attempts to play one of us against the other. I learned that Rocky had been put in both leg and arm irons upon arrival at this camp and kept in them day and night. The increased restraints had only served to strengthen his determination, and even though he was unable to leave his cage except to go to a separate latrine, he managed to look in better physical condition than either Dan or me.

Plato had kept coming back with the requirement for the declaration, and I was now telling him that because of the concept of family and military honor, I could not betray the trust that had been placed in me—that his questions would cause me to disgrace myself, which I was certain he could understand and sympathize with. Plato found it difficult to counter this, as his stated policy had been not to put me to shame and by answering the questions I would be put to shame. I bought several days of no pressure except for the probing on political thoughts and the war's origin and course. I learned through the discussions with him that there was a total lack of understanding of the American soldier since we were the first Americans captured by these forces. They were feeling us out, determining what methods would be most effective in obtaining what they wanted, yet not alienating us from their political doctrine. Plato commented in an offhand manner one day, "To apply physical pressure thoughtlessly often defeats its purpose. Once inflicted, it can eliminate the individual from our instruction and when ceased, there is immediate relief. On the other hand, we can apply pressure on the mind which is multiplied by the individual and is continuous. It is more efficient."

I asked what happened if an individual refused to cooperate. "He may rest here for a long time," Plato answered calmly. "If we are unsuccessful in our instruction the first time, we must recommence." The patience of these people contrasted sharply with the inherent American impatience. I had set my survival timer for six months and was counting on going home at the end of that time. There was still no indication beyond the declaration of what price I'd have to pay for the release.

The thought of an exchange or release arranged by the government was my constant dream, and unbeknownst to me at that time, there was a strong attempt being made by the Vietnamese and American officials in Vietnam to secure our freedom. Our captors were responding to that attempt, but because we had no way of knowing about this activity, we could only draw from what was happening around us in an attempt to evaluate our position.

On 15 February, the concern about my continued loss of weight and problem with diarrhea was at an all-time high. A sense of urgency prevailed as Ben administered more sulfaguanidine in conjunction with doses of a dark brew, "*thuoc nam*," native herb medicine which was supposed to act as an antidiarrheal and, in effect, plug me up. I began to suspect that the forthcoming school and arrival of "high-ranking cadre" might have something to do with the crash program to get me presentable. We had been receiving pieces of an indigenous "dogfish" with our rice and the addition to our meals was of noticeable benefit. Dan was having definite problems consuming the rice and his health was dropping even without serious illness.

The cadre arrived on the night of the sixteenth and spent a day in conference with our three cadre. I was given a type-written lesson to "study" before my first attendance. Plato came to my hut with a rather unkempt young man, wearing Western-style trousers and shirt, who was the typist and apprentice interpreter. His attitude immediately caused me to dislike and distrust him. He was brash and arrogant, using a few phrases in English to thrust himself upon the carefully structured relationship I had established with Plato.

Over a period of weeks, I discovered that Charlie's store of English was as limited as his personal hygiene and manners. He would begin a conversation with a burst of carefully re-hearsed English, then stare with incomprehension when I re-plied. It was frustrating to be limited by language, to understand and be unable to answer in kind.

The school began on the eighteenth and Thanh, dressed in new blacks, wearing an ammo belt and carrying a carefully cleaned weapon, came to my cage and marched me along the log walk to the school hut. The inside of the thatch-walled hut had been decorated with slogans, painstakingly printed in En-glish, "Welcome the lenient policy of the Front toward POW's," "Do not die for the profit of Capitalist-Imperialist," "Oppose the dirty, undeclared war." A large Vietcong flag hung on the front wall above a poncho-covered desk. Two khaki-uniformed Vietnamese sat behind the desk watching me as I slid onto a bench on the right side of the room. A table of pole construc-tion, legs embedded in the mud below the hut, was in front of me. Plato sat to the right of the two cadre and Muoi was across from me on a pole bench similar to mine. Thanh had reported formally to the group when I entered that the American prisoner was present for instruction. He then took a position near the door, standing at parade rest with his rifle canted away from his feet, in drillbook perfection.

The older of the two men, appearing quite intellectual with his hornrimmed glasses and receding hairline, began to lecture in a slow, precise voice. Plato translated into English as the cadre spoke: "The National Liberation Front has dispatched us to present to you the truth of the situation in Vietnam. In the coming days you will learn of the just cause of the revolution, and the certainty of final victory. You will learn of the lenient and humane policy of the Front toward captured alien soldiers and of your duty toward the Front. Your release, sooner or later, will depend upon your good attitude and repentance of your past misdeeds, so I encourage you to have a good attitude, be well disposed toward this instruction." There was no expression on any of the faces as he spoke. My mind was fixed on the phrase "good attitude and repentance of your past misdeeds," and I barely heard Plato begin translating the first lesson: "*Vietnam la mot*"—Vietnam is one country."

I was returned to my hut after the lesson, my stomach revolting, and nauseated as if someone had poured warm barf down my throat. Suddenly, the long hours of debate with Plato, the delays, minor verbal victories I had counted, the evasiveness and refusals came crashing down around me. There was a wall in front of me and they held the key which would open the door to freedom. The price for that key was more than I could pay, but I didn't want to die. My mind began searching for some way over, around or under that wall; there had to be a solution!

Midway in the next morning, as I sat hunched in a corner of the cage, staring, without seeing, at a clump of fern, I heard a commotion and loud, commanding voices by Rocky's cage. Minutes later, I watched Rock hobble across the crosswalk by the guard hut on his way to the school. Alvin and "Shithead," named quite fittingly for his disposition, followed close behind, bayonets fixed on the MAS 36 rifles they carried. From the angry expressions on their faces, I could tell that Rocky had not gone willingly. There was an immediate jolt as I realized I had considered my position extremely bad without thinking of Rocky! He was in a hell of a lot worse shape than I was and wasn't showing an outward sign of submission, even though his bent and twisted drinking cup I had seen in the last camp bore mute testimony to the terrible strain he was experiencing. During the long hours of lying in the hot, cramped cell, he had mashed the aluminum cup, twisting it out of shape, probably as a relief to keep from crying out.

I listened as Rocky entered the school hut, hearing, shortly after Alvin's report, the words that made my back straighten and my face grow warm with a feeling of pride: "I'm an officer in the United States Army. You can force me to come here, you can make me sit and listen, but I don't believe a damn word of what you say!"

"Rocky," I prayed, "Bless you. You're a hard-core son of a bitch!"

I began to reevaluate my position, realizing strongly that I was also an officer in the United States Army and had the same responsibilities as Rocky. The purpose for separating us was quite evident, as the individual becomes a single animal fighting for survival, losing the ability to identify or associate with anything other than himself and basing his actions on his immediate needs.

The school continued through 24 March and covered a sketchy history of the revolution against the French, the Geneva Accords of 1954, Ngo Dinh Diem's accession to the presidency in South Vietnam and the suffering which was occurring because of Diem and the intervention of the United States. The role of the NLF as a savior of the people was stressed and the unquestionable final victory of the Vietnamese people in their fight against foreign aggression was asserted. I found the illogic overwhelming and the blatant omission of facts which tended to invalidate primary assumptions of the cadre gave me the impression that these lessons were geared for individuals of a low educational or semi-illiterate status. Some of the terminology, particularly "U.S. aggressor," "puppet government," "imperialist warmonger," and "neocolonialism" sounded harsh in terms of what I had known of our involvement, and rather than believe what was said, I found myself picking holes in the pattern of instruction.

When Plato came for my lessons, I handed him a printed sheet with the major points covered by the lesson outline neatly numbered as they had come from the study sheet. He was disturbed when I refused to sign the paper and wouldn't write the lesson out longhand, but he became immediately involved in the multitude of contradictions and errors I had detected in the day's lesson. He would spend the major portion of his visit attempting to correct my "misconceptions" on the spot, taking notes on the ones he had to discuss with the other cadre. My knowledge, limited as it was, of the 1954 Geneva Agreements and the I.C.C. special report on Communist infiltration, as well as having read numerous works on Vietnam including *People's War, People's Army* by General Vo Nguyen Giap, provided me with enough material to adequately confuse the issue and reduce Plato's concrete points to a fraction of what he began with.

Plato became less inclined to debate after he failed to clarify his original presentations, but the problem was resolved when

117

he declared, "You have heard the truth of the situation and can judge now the just and unjust cause. If you can know the just cause of the revolution and realize your past crimes against the Vietnamese people, the Front can release you. If you persist in your bad attitude, we must let you rest here a long time until you can correct your bad thoughts." He said that I could write a letter to the Central Committee of the NLF, requesting my release, stating what I now believed about the situation in Vietnam after being exposed to the "truth" and expressing repentance for my crimes. If they examined my case and determined that I was qualified, I could be released. The declaration, he added, would also have to be completed in order for the Central Committee to "better know me."

While the visiting cadre were in the camp, Ben came by with two redcoated tablets which he said were Aureomycin and in conjunction with more sulfaguanidine would clear up my diarrhea. He added an injection on the first day of a five-day period which I discovered later was emetine, a toxic drug capable of producing a number of extremely unpleasant side effects if I had reacted. Fortunately for me, the shotgun cure was effective and I found myself suddenly constipated.

After the school, Rocky's treatment changed radically. He was released from the irons during the day and allowed to read Vietnamese newspapers printed by the NLF. Muoi and Major Hai stayed clear of him. Plato would stop by to chat on occasion, but there was no more open confrontation. The cadre at the school, probably in a position to pass judgment on POW attitudes, had something in store for Rocky, but it wasn't evident just what. There was strict decision-making control at higher echelons and the cadre at our level merely repeated the words of their superiors. There was an amazing subjugation of personal feelings on the part of the cadre in dealing with us. To further the cause of the revolution, to aid in achieving a particular goal with respect to an American, the cadre would disregard personal animosity or perhaps friendliness and assume any attitude required of him. Initially, I couldn't determine reasons for almost radical changes in the attitudes of the cadre and guards with regard to myself. I analyzed my actions prior to the sudden change from tolerance to hatred, or from apparent interest to complete disinterest, and became confused when no pattern emerged. Only when I included the immediate demands placed on me by the cadre, and my response to those demands, did a glimmer of comprehension dawn. The entire response pattern centered around influencing me to respond to the demands of the Front and whatever actions and attitudes were deemed commensurate with accomplishment of their goal would be used.

Plato came by one day with a requirement for the names of the U.S. Special Forces team at Tan Phu and a map of the camp. As with the declaration, he made the requirement sound like an insignificant bit of inprocessing which would be of little value other than "displaying my sincerity vis-à-vis the Front." When I refused, Plato opened a new verbal offensive with "my duty to the Front" and what I was required to do to repay the NLF for its lenient treatment.

"You are no longer a soldier," he stated flatly. "You are a prisoner and under our control. Because you have committed crimes against the South Vietnamese people, the South Vietnam National Liberation Front, which is the only true representative of the fourteen million South Vietnamese people, can judge you according to your crimes. We can kill you, we can torture you, but no, we choose to show you the truth of the situation and create conditions so you may return to your families. Is it not correct for you to also strive to return to your loved ones and not die a useless death tens of thousands of miles from your homeland?"

I told Plato that my fondest dream was to return to my home and I didn't care at all for the idea of dying in a prison camp; however, prisoner or not, I was still a soldier and bound by my code. The code stumped him although he had argued that I should only consider the honor of the Front, disregarding the entities of family and government which couldn't secure my release. After my return to the United States, he said, I could again consider personal honor, but here it was useless. He left without the information he desired, having only presented another side of the mask and given me a little more insight.

During one of his visits, he told me that Rocky, because of his attitude, could not be released and I would join him if I did not alter my "bad attitude toward the Front." I learned from Dan, in a message drop, that Plato had used the same line on him. We knew we had to hold out for a minimum of six months, no matter what was done to us to extract military information. It would require at least six months for the new team at Tan Phu to alter and improve the camp defenses so that the information we had would be useless. All personnel on our team would be gone and the standard operating procedures changed. It surprised me that there hadn't been more pressure to obtain the information we did possess. Plato had assured me that they could find out anything they wanted to know about the camp from other prisoners and the intelligence agents paid by the VC to keep the camp under surveillance. Any details we gave, he said, would only be used to check our truthfulness and "sincerity."

The evening of 8 April, I was visited shortly after dark by a group of old guards, along with some of a new squad which had come into camp. Squeaks, Ben and one we had named "Hot" because of the phonetics of his Vietnamese name, Hat, led the curious new guards to my cage and began a conversation. In the guard hut another group was nosily playing a guitar, mandolin and violin, the discordant renditions of revolutionary songs giving ample proof of enthusiasm which far exceeded any evidence of talent.

I noticed Ben tossing glances in the direction of Rocky's cage and found my attention focusing there also. I barely heard Muoi's voice yelling, *"Di!"* Rocky's voice slightly hesitant, was fainter, but clear, *"Tat ca* or just me?"—All or just me? They were moving Rocky out! I strained to see into the guard hut and beyond into the darkness where Rock would be taken. Squeaks and Ben immediately blocked my view and began to talk rapidly, attempting to draw my attention. It was a tense few minutes until the noise in the guard hut ceased abruptly and voices called for these guards to return. They arose without a word to me and made their way back to join the others.

I fell into a fitful sleep later that night, tormented by new indecision and concern for Rocky. His fate was directly linked to mine, and the two-pronged thorn of fear for his safety and hope that I would escape a similar experience dug deeply into my mind. The morning was something I wished would never come.

Shithead came down to my cage to unlock me and after I made an urgent run to the latrine, breaking loose with diarrhea once again, he ordered me to bring my plate to the kitchen to pick up my rice. It was the first time since I had entered the camp that I was allowed to leave my cage and walk to the kitchen for rice. I was surprised, but unaware of what lay in store other than the experience of leaving the confines of my small world. Walking through the dim interior of the guard hut, I noted the sleeping racks built along the two walls and the packs, weapons and other equipment neatly arranged on them. The guards sat crosslegged, staring silently as I walked between them. Outside again, on the small porch area behind the hut, I walked toward the logs leading to the kitchen. A pile of rags and crushed, twisted pieces of aluminum caught my eye, but I was past them before the image became fixed on my brain. As I entered the smaller kitchen hut with its packed-mud fireplace, I realized what I had seen. The rags were Rocky's gray pajamas, torn into shreds. The twisted pieces of aluminum were his eating pan and cup, crushed completely out of shape; the tin cover for the lamp in his cage was smashed and tossed on the heap. There was an agonizing, deep sense of loss as the scene from last night spread itself across my vision. Rocky was dead! The impossibility of the act of murder having been committed clashed violently with the reality of what was left of his belongings. Dazedly I accepted the portion of rice and saucer of dried eel and turned to go back to my cage, forcing myself to look toward Rocky's cage.

Wreckage was there also. The bars had been ripped from the sides of the cage and either hung crazily from the tangle of poles, or were strewn in the mud about the cage. The scene was one of violence and reinforced the impact of seeing Rocky's belongings. I walked back past the clothing, controlling my urge to strike out, to hurl myself at one of the cadre who had done this. There was blood on the clothing. I could see the dark red stains splashed on the gray material and related them immediately to the excution my imagination had created.

Plato visited my cage later in the day, his mood unusually somber. He told me that it was unfortunate that the Front had been forced to take drastic action with Rocky, but they had been left no other choice. Rocky's attitude, he continued, was unrepentant and the Front couldn't continue to extend its lenient treatment to one who refused to realize his crimes. He said he hoped my attitude would improve in order for the Front to be able to release me. He confided that he had given a good report to the Central Committee on Dan and me, even though we had not helped him in carrying out his duty of obtaining required information. He had been angered by Rocky, who had shouted at him and questioned his instruction, Plato went on, and because Rocky had opposed the Front, he had paid.

I sat, containing the boiling anger, hating my hypocrisy for listening as if undisturbed by what had happened to Rocky, whatever it might have been. The one thought of not striking back until I could hurt them was predominant. It would have been useless to batter my head against a wall and only lose what slight freedom to act I had now. I began to formulate ideas with the ultimate goal of gaining my total freedom without compromising my beliefs or harming my country and its efforts.

After Plato left, I reviewed a cover story I had devised, checking for loopholes and possible points I might be tripped up on. The old "KISS" formula, "Keep it simple, stupid," served as my guide as I built the biography which would allow me to deny knowledge of the areas they had displayed an interest in. Since they were seeking information concerning Special Forces and Artillery, I became an Engineer, with no knowledge of tactics or the highly specialized workings of the military. I was a citizen-soldier, intellectually inclined, doing my three-year commitment and planning for a career as a civil engineer. Bridges, roads, houses I could discuss, world literature (which I actually like), the works of Shakespeare and a few Chinese literary figures, but beyond these subjects, I was virtually useless. Of major importance later was my professed lack of knowledge of, and interest in, politics. It was obvious that they held the advantage in dealing with us and the hope for release could be a very effective lever when a prisoner was reduced to a level of total struggle for survival. I was going to avoid giving them the impression of open opposition since this allowed them to bring whatever pressure they chose to bear and I wasn't certain I could hold as Rocky had done, particularly when the pressure could be maintained for as long as they chose.

I thought, oddly enough, of Mahatma Gandhi and the concept of passive resistance which could be more effective than overt struggle. The dangers of attempting to lie to my captors were something I'd been warned about at Fort Bragg, in a class on resistance to interrogation, but the theory of holding out no matter what was done to you suddenly became the scenes from the training film and not the reality facing me.

For the next month I related for Plato the details of my education as an Engineer, relating the numerous technical seminars I had attended at civilian universities around the nation from 1961 through 1963, conveniently covering the period of time after I had "graduated from the United States Armed Forces Institute in Washington and attended the Engineer School at Fort Belvoir."

I avoided the subjects of commanders and units by being assigned to the Adjutant General in Washington, D.C. My studies were on the order of the engineering subjects I had at West Point, the universities were ones with which I was familiar and the dates of attendance on convenient three-or six-month intervals. I was able to probe the inexperienced Plato's knowledge to determine what actual information he already had about me through other sources and found, as I expected, that the team at Tan Phu was fairly well known. The VC in the Strike Force and agents around the village had given a reasonably accurate, though superficial picture of us.

He came down one day with a list of the team members, telling me to verify it. I noted that it contained Kemmer, Hardy, and Leites, which immediately indicated that it wasn't current, possibly one copy of our original team lists that had fallen into their hands. I told him it contained names with which I was familiar, but I had not been closely associated with the team except at meals because of my duties outside the camp taking charge of the civil affairs projects. Rather than compromise the rest of my story by lying here, I told him it looked accurate. He left satisfied and that evening Nam and Alvin came down to the cage to talk about how "joyful it would be for me to return to my family after I was released."

Plato brought a completed map of Tan Phu post for me to "verify" after I had told him I couldn't draw it for him. I had said that I wouldn't give him information which would result in injury or death to other Americans as drawing the camp at Tan Phu would do. The map was almost perfect, even to location of generators, although I knew that one of them had been ruined by a mortar round prior to my capture.

As I looked at the map, an idea developed and I decided to try it. I retracted my previous refusal to help with the map and told him it was so accurate that anything I could do wouldn't prevent a successful attack, but there were a few omissions. His immediate attention and visible joy at my cooperation gave me new hope that I might screw them up a little. I carefully added a nonexistent minefield, telling him the barrier had been put in by the Americans without the Vietnamese knowing. Electronic early warning devices and command-detonated mines went in the rice paddy southeast of camp and the groves of trees to the southwest. Any assault against the camp would utilize these avenues of approach and my additions could effectively scramble an attacking unit if it hit them unaware. For a second time he left enthusiastic over the results he was achieving.

Reviewing my two gambits, I felt the first was sound because our team had left Tan Phu in December and was back in the United States. The second suddenly became a nightmare as I realized that the new team might have placed barriers in the exact places I had indicated. This made me swear not to pull anything like that again. I was learning. The lessons were to stay with me for the entire period of capture.

The cadre had become suspicious of Dan and me because the results of our communication nullified the activity to play one against the other. Dan was able to observe the activity at the front of the camp and kept me up to date on arrivals and departures, an indication of pressure if any wheels arrived and periods of absolute boredom when Plato and Muoi left. We had kept each other abreast of the line Plato was putting out, allowing us to catch him in contradictions and sometimes ruin an entire indoctrination period. To remove any possibility of communication, Dan was ordered to use Rocky's old latrine, thus preventing him from coming near my cage, and this ended our dead drop.

In one of the last messages, I had proposed an escape to Dan, only to learn that his strength was so depleted by ill health that he was unable to try. I had noticed that he was extremely skinny, but was unaware of the extent of his weakness. It was discouraging to realize that if I had to try an escape, it would be alone. The thought was like a door closing and I found myself still looking toward our exchange or release.

In May, I wrote a letter to the Front, asking for my release, but omitting the requirement for admission of guilt to crimes against Vietnamese people. Plato returned it immediately and said it was inadequate because I'd have to "repent" before the Central Committee would even consider it. I questioned him about admission to guilt that didn't exist and, for that, received a second rehash of the "crimes of the U.S. aggressors" perpetrated through assisting the Vietnamese government. I wrote that I was "sorry if any innocent Vietnamese civilian had suffered from any act I had committed during my tour in the country, but happy that I had the opportunity to aid them by bringing medical programs, schools and technical advances into areas where little, or none, had existed before." He attempted to influence the "repentance," making it "more sincere," but finally left after several days to submit what he had. There was still an air of preparation as if we were being processed to fill certain specified requirements before they let us go. The thought of a six-month period of captivity was past, but I had considered eight months as a tolerable period.

Outside, American efforts to obtain our release were continuing in conjunction with the Vietnamese, but there had been few results because the Vietcong made demands of both the negotiators and the prisoners. Reports of our status seem to have been sketchy and some doubt existed as to whether we were still alive.

One afternoon when some of the guards were at my cage listening to one of their group talk to me about the lessons he had learned in political classes and, particularly the good treatment given to POW's, I questioned the policy, saying that the POW's never knew when one of them would be executed, thinking of Rocky. The young guard, in defense of his statements, blurted out, *"Khong ay chet!"*—No one is dead! I was immediately alert, but couldn't show my excitement. One of the others cautioned him to be quiet and they went back to the original spiel. When they left, I heard a comment about the scene with Rocky's torn clothing and *"mau luon."* I wasn't familiar with the two words other than *mau*, which in one of its intonations means blood.

Several days later, I asked Ben, in an unrelated conversation, the possible meanings for *mau luon*. I repeated the words as close to the tones I had heard as possible. The only definition he came up with was "eel blood." I almost jumped up and shouted! If it were true that they had used eel blood on the clothing, then it was purely deception, even though it had been effective in weakening our resistance. The knowledge that Rocky was still alive was overpoweringly wonderful! I held my urge to jump up until Ben left, then stepped out on the porch, jumped as high as I could, and rammed my arm up to the elbow through the thatch roofing bringing a shower of leaves and shreds of palm leaf with me as I dropped back to the porch. I felt like whistling, or singing, or shouting.

The days passed with the hope of returning home making

125

them bearable. The diarrhea returned and became so bad that the guards, rather than come to my cage five and six times a night to let me go to the latrine, brought a *nuoc mam* crock with the top broken off so that it resembled a large flowerpot and told me to use that during the night, emptying it in the morning.

I had developed a fungus infection which began like ringworm, spreading rapidly until the circular, raised red areas linked up and became one large irregular patch extending from just below my knees, around my crotch where it had begun, up to my chest and arms, threatening to envelop my neck and face. There was a constant itching which became almost unbearable if I perspired. Scratching to relieve the itching proved to worsen things considerably, as the broken surface of the fungus exuded a clear, sticky fluid which dried on the black pajamas, causing them to adhere to the damaged areas of infected skin. Pulling the cloth free seemed to excite the nerve endings, doubling the itching sensation and generating new aggravation.

I also noticed a tendency toward extreme fatigue and pains beginning in my lower legs, but dismissed them as being due to a vitamin deficiency which I couldn't correct. I had begun to fill out again although there had been no change in our diet: rice twice a day with *nuoc mam* and a minimal amount of fish. The fish served to add enough flavor so that I could get the rice down, but on a generous day wouldn't have made more than one large mouthful by itself. I couldn't understand the increase in weight, although I was happy it was occurring.

Ben provided a small ¾-ounce bottle of a clear liquid, labeled *"Thuoc Ong Gia,"* for *lac*, the Vietnamese name for the fungus. It turned out to be something like medicinal Clorox mixed with ammonia, and when it came in contact with the infected skin, there was an immediate whitening and nearly unbearable burning sensation as it oxidized the tissue. I found it particularly unpleasant when I tried to kill the areas covering my testicles and had to decide whether or not the pain was worth the temporary cure. The major problem here was that the bottle would serve to treat only several square inches effectively and I was dealing with square feet of fungus.

The efforts by Plato to "fulfill the requirements of the Front" continued through June. My letter came back from the Central Committee with the comment "incomplete." Knowledge that

Rocky was still alive caused my decision to let Plato hang with what he had. I didn't want to leave Rocky in here alone and I wasn't going to give them any more than they had. It was a source of revitalization to me to feel that perhaps I could pull some of the pressure off of Rocky, even at this late date.

Plato had been pushing for a complete declaration and explanation of military subjects I had studied, hoping to get information which might be used to counter the efforts of the American advisers and Special Forces team. A non-English-speaking intelligence officer gave him questions to ask on a sheet of paper. After writing anything I might say, including opposition to the questions, Plato would return to the cadre hut across the canal and, with his Vietnamese-English dictionary, would translate word for word what I had given him. He would then give it to the intelligence officer for evaluation. I noted that this gave the intelligence officer complete freedom to deal with a number of Americans, since Plato did the legwork for him. I decided to try to foul them up, and on Plato's next visit I told him I was ready to talk. His reaction was like a young child after he has been told that it's time to open his Christmas presents. He prepared to write, fidgeting with his ball-point pen as I decided how to begin. I gave him four pages on the theory of laminar flow to include my interpretation of its applications, actual or nonexistent, to airfoils, weirs, storm sewers, dams and drainpipes. I had a bit of difficulty passing the course in mechanics of fluids at West Point, so I had to fill with formulas in order to cover my actual lack of knowledge on the theme of this dissertation. When he finished, his scribbled and misspelled notes reflected the scrapings of my memory on fluids, differential calculus, kinetics and a hell of a lot of distortion.

He left my hut, scurrying along the logs, smiling and talking to himself. For the next five days he laboriously translated what I had given him, checking with me on the formulas he didn't understand (all of them). On the fifth day, having had no time to deal with other prisoners because of his translation work, Plato presented the completed document to the S–2, no doubt quite pleased with his accomplishment. I heard the S–2's outraged cry all the way out to my cage. It took him only a second to scan the pages and determine that Plato had absolutely nothing but five days of practice looking up English words in his dictionary.

I met the S–2 that afternoon after he had regained his composure and Plato had recovered from shock. For the next four or five days, the S–2 would sit and ask questions which Plato would translate for me, then do the same with any answer I gave. I found that my cover story, and the ability to say "I don't know" under its protective distortion of fact, allowed me to give him absolutely nothing. The S–2 was quite perceptive and I'm certain he doubted my truthfulness, but was prevented from taking measures to force me to talk.

Plato tried to cover his inefficiency and protect his future with this group, conveniently covering me with his explanations of the great difficulty in communicating using English and how misunderstandings often occurred. I couldn't understand the restraint the S–2 showed, because his attitude was one of constantly seething anger when he got an "I don't know." I felt that one "I won't tell you" would have touched him off on a violent rampage. It was startling to discover that the political importance of a prisoner could take precedence over his military value.

Our new complement of guards was now in full control of the operation of the camp, and most of the original guards had departed. I began assigning names to the newcomers, as I had done with the old ones, based on some trait, appearance or duty in the camp. "Kildare" was an effeminate nineteen-year-old in training to become a medic, "Clem" was the Vietnamese version of a Tennessee plowboy, "Abortion" looked like a salvaged placenta, "Yes Yes" knew one word in English and repeated it twice everytime he said it, and "Buck's boy" was the gimp-legged boatman and bodyguard for a buck-toothed cadre who visited the camp. The ability to apply an English name to the guards, adding a trace of levity to the situation, made their less pleasant side more tolerable.

Probably the greatest morale factor I had was a small tree shrew that spent his days policing up bits of rice and fish bones around the cage. His physical characteristics were enough to cause a good laugh even under these conditions, but his antics made him a one-animal circus. He had an extremely long snout, tipped with a dark brown nose and alert dark eyes. His big nose inspired me to name him for one of my favorite characters, Cyrano de Bergerac. His body was the size of a medium gray squirrel's and ended in a long scraggly tail, of which he was extremely proud, spending long hours grooming it by pulling it over the sharp needle-like teeth in his lower jaw. He was quite uncoordinated and had difficulty grasping his tail with his front paws as he sat on a limb, but he would sit attentively watching the ragged tail as it waved near his paws. When it appeared close enough, he would grab wildly, paws scissoring over and around the tail. After losing his balance and scrambling to keep from falling off of the limb, he would resettle himself and try again and again, until finally the elusive tail would be firmly clasped between the paws. Then he would proceed to draw it carefully across his lower teeth, his eyes half closed in blissful enjoyment.

Dan and I had questioned Plato frequently about the separation of POW's, asking if the Front was afraid to allow Americans to converse freely. Initially his replies centered around the security of the camp and preclusion of unwise attempts to escape, but constant reference to the interrogations and indoctrination made him request permission from the higher cadre for Dan and me to visit each other for a short period of time once a week. This, he explained, would dispel our misconceptions about the isolation serving to aid them in obtaining information and indoctrinating us. The major "requirements" had been taken care of, he said, and there was only the security of the camp to consider.

A note on the security. A series of *punji* had been dug around the camp, filled with sharpened stakes. Plato had stated that these were built to keep the angry peasants from coming into the camp at night to kill Dan and me. The guards were present to protect our lives, and escape would only endanger us as the civilians wouldn't hesitate to kill us. I noticed that the sharpened stakes all pointed inward toward the camp; effective in preventing anyone from going out, but hardly placed to deny entrance. As with everything else, I took his comments with a grain of salt.

In our first meeting, held at my cage with Plato sitting in to monitor the conversation, I was shocked at Dan's emaciated appearance. His pronounced cheekbones and deep-set eyes gave an idea of what the rest of him must have looked like. On his bony wrists were a series of infected cuts, running around the entire joint. I asked how he was, indicating the cuts. Plato interjected immediately that they were infected mosquito bites. Dan sat quietly, listening to Plato, then commented briefly in German: "*Nein.*" I nodded, wondering what had actually happened. Dan remarked how healthy I looked, and I could see the difference in our arms. I had known that I was putting on weight, but didn't realize the relative difference. I almost felt guilty. The short period of time passed too quickly and Plato declared it was time to go. Before Dan left, I passed him a note I had written, telling about Rocky still being around and giving a short outline of what had transpired at my cage. I knew that Dan would have a reply ready on the next meeting and we could communicate even with Plato present. After they left, I almost laughed out loud when I discovered a note Dan had slipped under my sleeping mat. We were operating again!

During the next meeting Plato had us listen to a broadcast over Radio Hanoi by Robert Williams, who had left the U.S. and was in Cuba, and Anna Louise Strong who praised a solidarity conference they had attended in Hanoi and condemned the U.S. for its intervention in Vietnam. I listened, wondering who these people were and thinking how unfair it seemed for them to be able to condemn our country and then return to enjoy the benefits it offered them while POW's had to sit in a rotten swamp forest and listen to them spout off. Dan slipped me a note and back at my cage I read the story of the infected cuts, shocked at a coincidence I hadn't expected. Dan having suffered partially because of one of my unwiser reactions to the frustration.

Charlie had been down at my cage one afternoon, giving me an unwanted lecture on the power of the Front to deal with those who opposed it. This was in conjunction with my "bad" attitude and was designed to give me an "unofficial" idea of what lay in store for unrepentant Americans. I was in the midst of a violent bout with diarrhea and felt feverish, a splitting headache adding to my misery. I was in no mood to listen, but there was no way to get him to leave. In the course of frightening me he began to use Rocky as an example, saying that he, personally, would bring Rocky to his knees, no matter what it took. I felt a rage building, but held it in check. The thought of this repulsive outcast from any society with his overinflated ego and sadistic nature having the ability to touch Rocky when Rocky was unable to resist was too much! Rocky could break him in half physically or mentally, but here Charlie had the advantage. I grabbed Charlie by his shirt and with strength I didn't know I possessed, pulled him to his feet, shoving him onto the porch and telling him in as level a voice as I could manage to get the fuck out of here before I broke his skinny neck. His eyes were tremendous and terrified as he clung to the railing along the walk, struggling to keep from falling into the mud below. He regained his feet and dashed away toward the guard hut. I had barely turned back to the cage, breathing heavily and feeling my arms trembling, when I felt the shaking of the log walk as feet ran toward my cage. I was grasped sharply by the shoulder and whirled around, then slammed back against the bars of the cage. Shithead, his face contorted in anger, was in front of me. Charlie stood about five meters back, still on the logs, shouting gibberish at Shithead.

It must have been a combination of frustration, built over months of captivity, and the utter desolation of the illness that made me react. As I hit the cage with my back, my mind turned into a glowing red fireball. Shithead's left arm was up as if to strike downward. I stepped to the left, jabbed four stiff fingers into his solar plexus, and slashed a backhand upward toward his exposed throat. The knife edge of the palm, still hardened from long hours of workouts at Fort Bragg, was aimed for the windpipe. He doubled from the first jab and dropped his chin in time to catch the full weight of the blow along the jawbone, snapping his head over. He sagged and Charlie began to scream.

The next minutes were a blur. Guards piled onto the porch, someone slammed me in the chest, and I was thrown into the cage, landing in a heap. I was trembling all over, my head felt like a hot axe had split between my eyes. Nausea swept over me as I felt the hot wet filth spread in my pajama bottoms; I couldn't stop the diarrhea. If someone had shot me I would have welcomed it as relief. My ankles were thrust into the leg irons and jerked into an extended position. I lay with my eyes closed, accepting whatever was going to happen. I could hear Muoi's voice, its tenor pitch going up an octave with excitement and anger.

Then there was quiet as I felt the logs shaking. They were leaving, but I didn't really care. After a few moments, I began to realize what I had done and the trembling began again. Hot and cold flashes went through my body like electric shocks, nausea rose and ebbed. "You stupid son of a bitch. Stupid, stupid, stupid," I cursed myself. I had promised myself I wouldn't physically assault one of them when it wouldn't accomplish anything.

Later, Muoi and Plato came down to the cage; Muoi obviously angry, Plato controlling himself, but also angry. I could understand why and waited to see what was to happen. Muoi stood outside the bars, looking down at me, his hands clasped behind his back. Plato squatted outside the cage by my head, watching my face. I let him know how I felt by rolling on my side, to the rear of the cage and throwing up, the spasming dry heaves that followed curling my body.

When I finished, Muoi began in rapid Vietnamese, snapping the words out. Plato translated, but I'm sure he softened Muoi's words. Even then, the impact of what I had done was reiterated and the possible punishments that I could have incurred, including being shot. I agreed silently that it was an idiotic thing to have done, but wished they'd get on with what would result from it. Plato told me that the Front still maintained its policy and would administer just punishment. I saw Hot coming down the walk with another leg iron which was used to fasten my arms after my shirt and trousers were removed, the filthy pajama bottoms being dropped gingerly in the mud beside my cage. I was allowed to tie my towel around my waist, before being locked up, to cover myself. Muoi directed the guard to remove my mosquito net and other belongings, leaving me stretched on the bare floor, extended between two sets of irons. Plato squatted beside my head before they left and encouraged me to "use this lesson to correct my thoughts." That night I lay bare-skinned among the swarming mosquitoes, unable to stop the seeming thousands of stingers that probed every inch of body surface. The diarrhea, nausea and fever competed with the mosquitoes for top misery award. I was in a semi-stupor, which reduced the effect of the bites, and sometime before morning I drifted into delirium, the fever providing my escape mechanism.

Several weeks later, after the incident had become past history and the program of instruction had been renewed, Shithead, who had nearly recovered from the dislocated jaw, was at Dan's cage, harassing and threatening him about the leg irons, which were preventing Dan from getting any sleep at night. As Shithead tried to physically force him to put them on, Dan's now bony fist lanced out between the bars, knocking Shithead stumbling off the porch, into the mud. It was too much for Muoi, who had experienced belligerence from the Americans too often, even more for Shithead, who was tearfully holding his redislocated jaw. Dan was strung up, spread-eagled outside his cage, his wrists and ankles bound with wire that had cut so deeply that it left the scars I had seen. Plato, after the incident, had told Dan that he should refer to them as "infected mosquito bites." It was a lesson in the futility of trying to match muscles with the guards. As long as they had the ability to tie your arms behind you, they could, over a period of time, beat you to death with one hand, and open resistance just gave them a bigger lever to use on you.

The incidents were superficially forgotten by the cadre and guards as soon as the punishment was completed. They were in the midst of indoctrinating us and grooming us for possible release, hence the proper atmosphere had to be reestablished. This mood of preparation reached its high point in June when Dan reported that Plato had informed him he would be released in a couple of weeks. I heard the news from Dan and assumed I would be included, hoping at the same time that Rocky would go also. The days passed with frequent trips out made by Plato and Muoi. Different cadre visited the camp, indicating higher-level interest in us. I found my morale rising as the thought of leaving this environment developed. The most important thing was to get out before illness either incapacitated or killed us.

The date for Plato's "release" passed without so much as having fish for the evening meal. I sat, contemplating the small saucer of rotten-smelling *nuoc mam* and wondering if there would ever be an opportunity to drink iced tea again.

After that the activity and interest sagged. Plato was absent from the camp for long periods of time and when he did visit he tried to avoid Dan, who never missed an opportunity to question him about the unkept promise. Plato was visibly embarrassed and had only the answer that "the Americans" had not "met the requirements of the Front," indicating lack of blame shouldered by the Front. The days were even longer now and I turned to the study of the Vietnamese language I had begun earlier as a time-killer and an essential skill to be developed. For recreation, in addition to mild stretching and bending exercises when possible, to maintain muscle tone, I used my aluminum cup to devise a baseball game. Using a nail, I cut lines across the circular bottom of the cup, dividing it like a pie into a number of segments. Each was marked as a particular play: "1B," single; "2B," double; "SAC," sacrifice fly; "SO," strike out; "W," walk; and so on. Using a spinner I had devised from a piece of wood, I played two entire seasons

133

with the National League, devising my own team rosters, since I couldn't remember all the major leaguers' names, and moving tiny pieces of wood as runners around a baseball diamond I had drawn with a piece of charcoal on the floor of the cage. I would choose an American League team to face my National Champs in the World Series. Unfortunately my Mets never got past third place, but again, this was 1964.

Dan's health took a sharp decline after the aborted release. I saw him on the log walk between his cage and the guard hut as he went to get his rice one evening. Our meetings had been curtailed since Plato was rarely around to monitor them and I was stunned to see Dan's pipestem-thin legs sticking out of a pair of baggy shorts he had been given. There seemed to be nothing but bone and I thought of pictures I had seen of Dachau. His condition became so serious that a new cadre, a second "Mr. Ba," later named "Won Hung," came into the camp, dispatched by the higher headquarters to provide a better diet for the Americans since it had been observed that present conditions were not conducive to keeping them alive. I met him shortly after his arrival in camp and found him sincerely concerned about the lack of food for the American prisoners. In a short time, chunks of pumpkin had been added to our soup.

In September, I received a bigger surprise when I was told to move in with Dan in his cage. It was larger than mine and would accommodate two people. On the second of September, I joined him in the front of the camp, extremely happy to have this change in scenery and particularly to be able to communicate freely again. The thought of escaping began to grow as I hoped Dan's health would improve enough to try it. It was an outside chance that he could regain enough strength, but there was hope. We went through a period of adjustment as each of us was forced to readapt our schedules and habits, designed for isolation, to a joint effort. Won Hung seemed pleased with the arrangement, although Muoi was not too happy having two Americans together. One of the reasons Won Hung gave in a brief conversation one day was that he wanted us to aid each other in maintaining our health. This was one of the gestures by Won Hung that set him apart from the other cadre in my estimation. His efforts to improve our health were not brief ones motivated by a need to make us presentable for inspection by higher-ranking officials, or to make us more receptive to the indoctrinations, but strictly to keep us alive, and for this I will remain grateful. He was unique among all the cadre I encountered.

A second reason for the move was revealed on the night of September ninth, when a new POW was moved into the camp and placed in my old cage which had been worked on after my departure.

The first day we had no chance to see the new man although we heard him asking the guards and Muoi for his boots. We wondered how long he had been in captivity, remembering how fast we had lost our boots after capture and realizing that it had never occurred to us to ask for their return. Muoi, after visiting the cage, would wander back along the log walk muttering what sounded like "yeah, yeah, yeah," and shaking his head. It didn't occur to me until later that the Vietnamese word for "yes" is "da," pronounced like "ya" and our saying "yeah" was taken for the polite "da."

The thought of receiving some word of the outside was enough to make us begin plotting to establish communication. I made one of my trips to the latrine and was greeted by a wide-eyed, unbelieving stare which broke into an expansive smile when I spoke softly in English, telling our fellow prisoner, a powerfully built Negro, that there were two more Americans with him and we'd get word to him soon. He waved in reply, stopped from speaking by the appearance of Yes Yes and "J. Fred Muggs," our Neanderthal reject, near the cage. I went back to the hut, happy to have seen another American and particularly so because he looked so damn healthy. Muoi came immediately over to me and ordered me not to attempt to try to talk to the "da den—(black skin). He then spent nearly an hour asking about American Negroes and how one determined just what an American was; his estimate being that a yellow skin was an Asian, white skin an American or European, brown skin a Latin American, and black skin, "appropriately," an African. The concept of a multiracial nation of varying colors of skins was completely foreign to him.

A note of concern crept in when Dan and I considered the possibility of the new POW being a "plant." During the revolution against the French, a large number of Moroccans had been captured by the Vietminh and had chosen to remain in Vietnam, intermarrying with Vietnamese women. There was a slight possibility that this man was one of these individuals, sympathetic to the VC, being employed to gain our confidence as a fraudulent POW. I decided to go ahead with the message drop, not willing to risk the chance to fill the new man in on what to expect and perhaps help him at the price of having a dead drop compromised if he proved to be VC. We compiled a list of questions about the United States and various activities in the U.S. that would be virtually impossible for an outsider to answer, planning to check him out before exposing ourselves with regard to the VC.

The first message gave our names, ranks and date of capture to acquaint him briefly with the authors of the note. I felt that our appearances would substantiate the period of captivity. Questions for him, concerning sports, music, cars, food and specific facts about New York City, San Francisco, Atlanta, and Washington, D.C., were crammed into the small scrap of paper. Assuming he had no writing instrument, I also left a cut-down piece of ball-point pen filler to which a point had been attached. We were saving the pens Plato had given us during the indoctrination phase, writing as little as possible to conserve ink. Dan had begun drawing pictures for the guards for their homemade decks of cards, gaining the use of their pens, but that source could be stopped at any time.

Dan made the pickup several days later and we scanned the answers, analyzing them and soaking up the information like a dry sponge does water. In the hastily scrawled print were not only answers to what had been asked, but extensions and promise of more in the next drop. It would have been impossible for someone not acquainted with the United States as an American to have answered the way Edward Johnson, Master Sergeant E-7, had done.

We continued the drops, learning that President Kennedy really had been assassinated, which came as a distinct shock, the new situation in Vietnam after the assassination of Ngo Dinh Diem, the new baseball franchises, new cars and mention of a new rock group, the Beatles. John, as we found he was nicknamed, declared broad knowledge of current events and invited any questions which we might have. Dan's interest waned, but I continued pumping for the latest word on practically every subject imaginable. John's fund of knowledge was limited, it seemed, only by the amount of paper and ink available. It was like a breeze of fresh air to discover all the changes that had occurred in the months I had been away and to contemplate what it would be like to go back to them.

Year number one passed on 29 October 1964, and as I evaluated our situation with Rocky separated from us, John added to the camp, Dan in still dangerous physical condition and myself weakening daily because of the constant diarrhea, the only bright spot was that we were still alive.

T HE NEW YEAR BEGAN WITH A FRIGHTENING EXPLANA-
tion for my relative lack of weight loss while eating the same
food as Dan. The "healthy" weight became an obvious abnor-
mal swelling in my legs and abdomen. I had practically ceased
to urinate, and when this was brought to Ben's attention, he
examined the swelling, poking at the flesh, watching his finger-
mark remain indented for several seconds before the surface
rounded out again. Short Sleeves was called over and they
pronounced the swelling a result of "thung." I had beri-beri
and was bloated with stored fluid.

It was not that much of a surprise after I considered the diet
we'd been on and the constant diarrhea that prevented absorption of what little nutrients were available. Thiamine deficiency
as well as protein deficiency were well within the realm of
possibility and the problem lay with the damage they could do
to my system. The central nervous system and heart could be
affected, depending on the severity of deprivation.

The next night I received the first of several injections of
strychnine sulfate. When Ben showed me the vial, I looked
quizzically at Dan, thinking of strychnine in the category with
arsenic and cyanides and wondering what an injection would
do. Dan studied the vial and asked Ben if this was for the
thung. Ben nodded an affirmative and Dan shrugged. "Might
as well try it. Can't be worse than the disease." I had my
doubts, but let Ben inject 2 cc of the clear liquid. Within three

hours I was experiencing the most intense pain in my legs, far beyond any of the rolling cramps associated with the diarrhea. It was fortunate that, prior to Johnson's arrival, we had been taken out of leg irons because I began urinating shortly after dark and continued through the night, passing roughly a gallon of fluid. As the swelling decreased, the sharp stinging ache built in my legs and before daylight I was barely able to hobble to the edge of the porch to relieve myself. It was like having the muscle and flesh, from ankle to thigh, razor-slashed down to bone and then having raw alcohol poured into the wounds.

The next morning Ben appeared with another injection; he seemed pleased with the results. I was losing my weight rapidly and bones were showing, clearly defined through the sinking flesh. I discovered he was buffering the strychnine with injectible Vitamin B_1 which gave me new hope that he knew what he was doing. After another day of strychnine and B_1 I was given three more injections of B_1 without strychnine. The result was a second emaciated American. I stared at my skinny arms and legs in horror, the rapid transition making my physical condition even more evident. It took several days for me to adjust to my condition and determine that I'd have to make a maximum effort to gain my strength using whatever food was available, primarily rice and the pumpkins while they lasted.

Our little friend Cyrano the tree shrew gave us the only real opportunities to laugh. He had become enamored of a delightful young female of the species and when not busy cleaning up the remains of one of our meals, combing his tail, or attempting to commit adultery with a female chipmunk whose nest was in the roof, he was out bounding along the log walks, sniffing the trail the young lady would leave by dragging her bottom on the logs at various intervals. Once he discovered her scent he would begin a series of frantic dashes, attempting to track down the source of the maddening aroma. I watched her one day, scampering daintily along the logs, apparently out to run our budding Lothario a wild chase. She chose the intersection of two log walks and carefully applied the necessary scent to all four possible exits, after which she climbed several of the mangrove roots in the vicinity, repeating the process. She went up the side of one tree, across a limb to another tree and down that tree, making certain she left an adequate trail. All complete, she bounced unconcernedly away through the ferns.

I watched with increasing interest as Cyrano came on the scene minutes later. He came to the overhead bars of the cage, scrutinizing Dan, who was sleeping, and me sitting on the porch. Assured that his meal tickets were still in place, he proceeded down the walk. His tail shot straight up in the air when he caught the first whiff. Down to the intersection, nose pressed to the logs! Hook a sharp left, almost losing balance and skidding off of the logs in the turn. Whoops, end of scent. Back to the intersection, check the next walk. Dead end, back to the intersection. By this time he was frantic. His little legs were churning so fast he couldn't keep track of them, and he tripped while traveling full speed toward the intersection. He missed the turn and splatted into the mud below, then picked up the scent on the tree root as he pulled himself out of the slimy mud. He didn't bother to clean himself off, but dashed madly up the root, switched to the next root, then up the tree, chattering in helpless frustration.

Cyrano perched on the high limb, finally realizing he'd been had, and he was looking so forlorn and bedraggled that I had to feel sorry for him even though my sides were aching with laughter. That night I gave him some fish bones with meat still on them, knowing he'd have to keep his strength up if he was ever going to catch that female. He was a lot like a human being.

The guards had gotten a pig to be fattened up for their celebration of Tet, the Lunar New Year in early 1965. We immediately named it Ho Chi Pig in honor of our host. Another new animal in the camp was a black dog, which we christened Mao Tse Dog. (All their animals, particularly dogs, seemed to have black coats. Perhaps a uniform requirement for a VC dog.) Clem was assigned as pig keeper and managed to let the pig die by early December, a little more than a month before its scheduled demise. I'm certain there was greater mourning for the passing of Ho Chi than if one of the Americans had gone instead.

A new cage was under construction on 15 December, causing speculation about an incoming prisoner. This camp was beginning to take on the appearance of a long-term prison. There was a log platform built as a P.T. area between the guard hut and the kitchen, an arched bridge built from the guard hut to the kitchen instead of the original two logs, and now a new cage near the guard hut along thw walkway to John's cage.

The evening of 18 December, the new American prisoner arrived, escorted by Nam, whom we hadn't seen since early in the year. The man was obviously wounded and was taken to the guard hut where Ben tried to examine him. Over in our hut, I could hear his refusals to let Ben touch the wounds. It occurred to me that it would be good if Dan could check him out and at the same time get word to him about the situation in the camp. Muoi came to our cage a short time later with Ben to check on English words for "Do not worry," "I will help you," and "What is your name?" They tried unsuccessfully to repeat "Desist in your perturbation" and didn't even bother with the next two phrases I gave them.

I suggested that Dan go over and check the man out since he was a medic. Muoi thought for a moment and refused, returning to the hut with Ben. Minutes later he retraced his steps to our cage and told me to write the three phrases on a slip of paper. I argued with him, insisting that the three phrases would be insufficient to convey the idea and suggested that either Dan or I be allowed to assist in getting the man treated. Muoi finally consented and told me to follow him.

The dim interior of the long guard hut, lit by two kerosene lamps, revealed the guards grouped around a husky, deeply tanned individual. His straight black hair and broad-faced features made him look like a beach boy straight from Waikiki. I walked up beside him, noticing the small puckering wounds scattered along the insides of both thighs and several on his arms.

"I'm Lieutenant Rowe," I told him, "captured in October 1963." He was staring at me, taking in my gray pajamas and stubble of a beard. "Muoi here," I nodded toward the cadre hovering near my right shoulder, "agreed to let me talk with you to try and get your wounds straightened out."

"Are you an American?" he asked.

"Sure am," I replied, smiling. It was odd to think that anyone would wonder whether or not I was an American. "There are three of us in the camp already." Muoi was leaning over my shoulder, peering at the wounded man and demanding to know what we were saying. "His wounds are very painful and I'm finding out about them," I told him. He leaned back and ordered me to find out the man's name. "He wants to know your name,"

141

I translated, adding, "It's authorized to give him name and rank, serial number and date of birth, stuff like the Code calls for, but make him ask."

"My name is Davila," he replied. I repeated it to Muoi and turned my attention to the wounds.

"How many times you hit?"

"Got about six small ones on the legs, one larger one up high on the left leg. I think they were from a mortar round."

"Mieng, sung coi sau muoi ly," I told Ben, who was standing patiently by—fragments from a 60mm mortar. Muoi was urging me to find out Davila's rank and unit, upset because he couldn't understand what we were saying. I told Muoi that I was trying to help Ben and Davila work out a method of treating the wounds and couldn't do both at one time. Muoi accepted this, although he was beginning to regret having let me come over.

Davila allowed Ben to examine the wounds with me there. The fragments in most of the wounds could be scraped out with little difficulty, which Ben did after sterilizing a well-used scalpel. The larger dime sized hole in the upper thigh was a different question and I advised Davila to wait until Dan could get a look at it and then if deeper cutting had to be done, Dan could do it. There was no way to determine how deep the chunk of metal had penetrated and Ben was still an unknown quantity when it came to cutting. Ben agreed with my suggestion for immediate antibiotics and told me they'd be administered in the morning. A coating of the *thuoc da* was swabbed on all the wounds and I was ordered to return to the cage.

In between translations for Ben and Davila, I had managed to give him a brief idea of the situation here. His first question was "What's the fastest way out of here?" He related how, when I had entered, he had seen the gray pajamas, and because I was Occidental he had immediately thought I was a Russian adviser to the VC. This had prompted his first question about my nationality. I went back to the cage and gave Dan as clear a picture of the wounds as possible, hoping I could talk Muoi into letting Dan examine him.

Davila spent two nights in the guard hut while his cage was completed. He was up and walking on the second day, which indicated his wounds weren't too bad—provided infection didn't set in. Communication was stopped after the first encounter, but Ben visited the cage and Dan had an opportunity to learn more about the wounds and give a few suggestions to the medic.

On 20 December, all Americans were in their huts and Muoi came by to see Dan and me, stating that the Front would provide a Christmas meal for the POW's and wanted to know what we wanted. When he said Christmas meal, I immediately thought of Christmas suppers at home and had to drag my imagination, hand over hand, back down to the level of the prison camp. In the past, we had on infrequent occasions been given small amounts of brown sugar candy or a serving of *che*, a sweet soup made from water, sugar, peas and rice. In July, in an unprecedented move, Dan had been allowed to purchase bananas, condensed milk, sugar and cookies with five hundred piasters (500$VN = $5.00 U.S.) which had been taken from him when he was captured. The demand for keeping Dan alive, made by a higher headquarters, had prompted the local cadre to give him his money back, but his request to buy substantial food or nutrients was refused. Finally, he was able to convince them that milk and fruit could be considered "desserts." The Front, according to Muoi, provided "sufficient for our livelihood." I was quite fortunate that Dan immediately shared with me, much to the displeasure of the cadre.

Based on what Dan had been able to purchase we requested a meal, leaving the final decision up to Muoi and knowing that no matter what we asked for, he would choose what we would receive. There were no complaints from us, however; anything would be a blessing.

I noticed increasing air activity around us in the next days as Christmas neared. On the twenty-second, a couple of helicopters stayed high above the area for about half an hour and a twin-engined L–23 liaison-type craft, normally used by high-ranking commanders and staffs, flew over a couple of times. We wondered what was up.

The morning of the twenty-third, after Dan and I had finished a dish of regular rice and a "food" plate of fried rice, prepared with the grease rendered from Ho Chi's fat, we were lying on the sleeping rack trying to sleep until time for supper, thus killing a day of monotony with escape in the arms of Morpheus. The sound of low-flying helicopters brought us to a sitting position in time to cringe instinctively as the unexpected roar of machine guns and rockets firing almost directly over us shattered the morning calm. The dull *ka-whump* of exploding rockets echoes back under the staccato bursts from the machine guns and repeated salvos of rockets. We dove for the porch simultaneously. I scrambled onto the surface of the mud, sinking in as Dan piled over on top of me. The rounds were going into another camp, just to our north, where we suspected Rocky Versace was being held, but there was no telling when this camp would be hit.

An L–19 that had been circling to the northeast came directly over the camp, observing the striking rounds and adjusting fire. Dan and I crawled rapidly away from the cage into the surrounding vegetation, putting as much distance as possible between us and the buildings which would surely draw fire from the helicopters. I could hear Muoi's frantic voice yelling at the guards and shouts from the various guards, most of them under fire for the first time.

Shouts came from our freshly abandoned hut, "*Phit! Ro!*" The guards were looking for us. I continued to crawl, my mind piecing together a plan for getting to a clearing somewhere and waving a chopper in to pick us up. If we could only separate ourselves from the guards, we'd have a chance. The sound of branches snapping behind us foretold the arrival of Thanh and Squeaks, who ordered Dan and me to our feet, pointing with their weapons back toward camp. We walked ahead of them, not wanting to return to the camp, thinking of the attack that would be coming.

The helicopters were low now, flying barely above the tops of the trees, fifty to a hundred feet above the ground. Thanh gestured for us to move toward the east, skirting the edge of the camp and heading for the surrounding forest and denser vegetation. We passed within twenty yards of John's cage and I scanned the interior, wondering what had happened to him and Davila. There was no one visible in the cage and my attention was diverted as a skimming armed helicopter banked sharply around at the edge of a clearing to our front. I was looking directly into the sun-visored face of the door gunner and was certain I could have read his name tag if he'd been any closer. It was fortunate that they were flying so fast or he would have had an opportunity to fire at us. Dan and I were wearing VC-style clothing and would have been just two more targets for him. We plunged ahead after Thanh, who was now leading. Squeaks was in the rear, prodding us to hurry.

The mud became deeper and walking was very difficult. I began to realize how weakened I had become as my breath came in ragged jerks and cramps set in all through my thigh muscles. We traveled east until we were about a hundred meters away from the camp, then turned north, traveling about fifty more meters before we halted. Nam joined us, and after the initial attack on the north camp ceased, we moved west, cutting between the two camps, crossing the north-south canal that ran by the camp and entering the densely wooded area on the other side.

AD–6 attack dive-bombers had appeared and were circling lazily to the east, waiting for the L–19 to call them in. Nam had brought word of troops on the ground to the south, moving toward us. I wondered what would happen if a ground attack developed and these guards were engaged. I didn't think they'd bother trying to keep prisoners in a situation like that. It was a case of being killed; the only question remaining was by whom.

We traveled through the thick growth of straight, slender-trunked *cai duoc*, for almost an hour, slipping, struggling in the mud, cautioned numerous times by the guards not to grasp the tree trunks for support. The waving upper branches would mark our path for the aircraft and could bring a hail of machine-gun fire.

Thanh departed to join the cadre and Nam led us to a large, sparsely covered field which seemed to be almost a mile away from the center of activity. Dan and I squatted on semi-dry clumps of earth, feeling our cramped muscles grow cold and tighten even further. The forced march had drained what energy and strength I had stored. Dan had been in even weaker condition than I when this thing began, so I knew he was in real agony. Nam and Squeaks squatted a distance from us, watching the helicopters sweep over the wooded area, spraying targets below with machine guns and rockets. They were too far from us to be able to spot the four figures hunched near the clump of ferns.

The strike continued for most of the day. As the late afternoon sun threw long shadows across the field, robbing the helicopters of the ability to see targets in the deeply shadowed forest, the L–19 broke its circling pattern and droned northward. The choppers followed and silence settled over the scarred terrain. We began the long walk back to the camp, encountering the thigh- and waist-deep mud once more. "Leo," our VC version of Leo Gorcey of the Bowery Boys, took over for Nam and Squeaks, who proceeded along a shorter route to aid the others in cleaning up the damage.

We reentered the camp just before dark, noting the bullet-torn poles of our cage and shredded palm thatch littering the porch. Muoi stood on the porch of the guard hut, his trembling legs visible from our hut as he directed the guards' efforts to salvage usable items from the fragment- and bullet-marked camp. Dan and I got permission to wash the mud off in the canal before returning to our hut and while washing, saw Ben working over a prone figure in the cadre hut across the canal. Apparently there had been casualties, but we had no way of determining how many until a head count could be made of remaining guards.

Later, as the guards were frying shrimp and fish for their meal, Dan was lying on the rice straw sleeping mat, his breathing shallow and rapid. I checked his forehead, which was clammy and covered with beads of perspiration. I got a cup of water from the guards and brought it back to him, letting him sip as I propped him up. He seemed better for a while and I encouraged him to try to eat some of the rice we'd been given for supper. He almost vomited when he saw the lump of cold pork grease, our meal, causing my stomach to turn over as the same revulsion swept over me. After a few minutes he made an attempt to eat, using a tiny piece of brown sugar to aid him in putting down small mouthfuls of the dry-tasting rice. In the middle of taking a bite he began to chuckle softly. I wondered what was wrong when, suddenly, the spoon dropped from his hand and he fell back on the mat.

The malnutrition had done its work on Dan. After going beyond the normal limits of human endurance that afternoon, his body had been so drained that any expenditure of energy burned muscle tissue, and there was not enough food input to meet the demand of the system. He came to after a few moments, but the effects of this episode were to have the greatest impact days later.

During the next three days we would load into the camp boats before daylight, getting up at 0300 hours to eat a meal of rice and pork grease before moving out to a distance of two kilometers from the camp and spending the day hidden in an out-of-the-way spot by one of the canals. The boats would be pulled under the trees while the tide was still in, and as the day progressed, the tide would ebb, leaving us sitting in stranded boats. The guards had political classes, slept, or cleaned weapons during the long daylight hours while the Americans sat, separately, staring at the surroundings or dozing when fatigue overcame cramped positions. In the evening, when the tide came in, we would return to the camp for the night, eating a late meal of rice and pork grease before dropping into exhausted slumber, dreading the thought of morning coming.

The third evening the schedule changed as we were moved back to the old camp to pick up all our meager belongings, then taken nine kilometers north and one kilometer east to a temporary camp. Muoi was not with us for the short trip and the inexperienced guards failed to blindfold us. I watched the entire trip, marveling at how clear the night sky was and how clean the sparkling stars made the heavens seem. It had been months since I'd seen a night sky except for glimpses through the bars and thick canopy of leaves above my cage. Trees bordering the canals on which we were traveling left an open slash down the middle of the waterway, extending into the distance like an overhead clear stream.

As we approached the new camp, I became aware of rows of long, low thatch-roofed buildings under the trees. We passed six identical structures on the narrow entrance canal en route to ours, which was evidently built to house a large unit since each of the huts would hold a ten- or twelve-man squad easily. Muoi met us at the walk leading from the canal to several of the huts. Seeing us unblindfolded was enough to earn the guards a severe reprimand. He hadn't wanted us to know what the area contained and was certain we had checked out the widespread construction effort.

Dan and I were put in one of the long buildings and John and Davila in the other. The guards were divided between the two huts to provide security. I put up our nets near the end of the hut that consisted of a raised sleeping area along one side separated from a slightly lower walkway which ran the length of the structure. Near the entrance, at the end of the walkway, was a raised platform on which mud had been packed for use as a cooking fireplace. Old *nuoc mam* crocks and discarded pieces of clothing testified to its use in the past. It was in a state of semi-disrepair which indicated lack of recent use. That night Dan finally ran out of whatever had kept him going since the night of the attack and passed out, going into a near-coma that lasted for the next twelve days.

The next week was nightmarish as the struggle to pull Dan through was complicated by my own weakness, topped with my violent, new outburst of diarrhea. Dan would regain consciousness briefly several times during the day, then lapse back into a stupor. He had no appetite and couldn't force the rice down. The problem was compounding itself and the chances that our captors would provide the direly needed food were nil.

Dan agreed to use some of the last of the money he had saved from the 500 piasters to buy a can of condensed milk, hoping the sweetened milk would increase his appetite as well as contribute the sorely needed calories. Ben talked Muoi into consenting to the purchase, and in several days, Leo came over with the only real hope I had for Dan getting enough rice in him to pull through. As it turned out, the milk wasn't the answer, but it marked the beginning of change and Dan started to force rice. Over a period of days he succeeded in achieving enough of a balance that his body could again begin to function without destroying itself. It was as if the body had immobilized itself while the danger of burning vital tissue was acute, throwing Dan into the semi-coma. As his intake of carbohydrates increased, his level of activity also increased. Before many more days had passed, I was trying to keep Dan from over-exercising as he struggled to walk and regain his strength.

John and Dave, as we learned Davila liked to be called, were in rough shape during their initial days in the camp. Their hut was parallel to ours and about ten meters away, allowing me to see them, but restricting conversation. Because they had the only functional latrine, I had to make frequent trips through their hut en route. I got the word from them that during the attack on the camp the guards had locked them in their cages and left them. Dave had just lain back on his pole floor bed, disregarding the firing since he had been a door gunner on choppers during his first tour in Vietnam and figured the choppers were hitting someplace other than the camp! Shortly thereafter his estimate changed abruptly as one of the choppers dropped a red smoke grenade into the middle of our camp. He managed to break his door loose and was heading out of the camp when he saw John under the sleeping rack in his cage. Dave made it to John, but not before the first salvo rockets slammed into the trees and John was hit a glancing blow on the wrist by a passing fragment. Dave helped him pull the door open and they took cover from the fire pouring into the camp. When the first guards returned, Dave and John were returned to their cages. John was given some of the *thuoc da* for his deeply scraped wrist.

The days passed more slowly after Dan regained some of his strength and was able to eat enough rice to make a come-back. The sun seemed to hang in the sky, unwilling to go down. When it finally did set, the night would skim past, leaving me staring at another morning, the exact duplicate of its predecessor. There seemed to be preparations by the guards for some activity, but I couldn't determine what. Bud and "Elvis," the latter a long-haired, guitar-playing guard with a changeable disposition, were in charge of fishing for the camp. In a typical performance, at approximately 1100 hours, judging from the sun, they climbed into the low-gunwaled *xuong* with the nets. After placing their equipment in the bottom of the boat, they lay back on top of it for a snooze in the warm sunlight. By 1500 hours, four hours later, they had traveled a full six feet on their journey to catch fish and that was due to the slight current in the canal pushing the boat and sleeping guards. Constant calls from their comrades finally aroused them and they grudgingly poled the boat down the canal, returning only minutes later with the report that there were no fish.

Elvis was typical of the eighteen-to-twenty-four-year-old group we were seeing as replacements for the older guards. There were still ones in their mid-twenties to early thirties, like Thanh, Nam and Leo. They formed the core of this unit and guided the younger ones under the direction of the cadre. Ben, Old Moon and Frank Lloyd fell into the older category. I learned that a number of the older guards had a substantial combat record, having fought with guerrilla units, and some of the over-thirty group had even gotten in on the fighting against the French. I began to see a personality emerging from each of the black-clad bodies, after having regarding them as one faceless, black-clad mass during my earlier contact in combat and first days of captivity. It was revealing to discover the human characteristics and habits which made each one of them stand out in my mind as a distinct entity.

The latest group of recruits included the outgoing, "big man on the campus" type dubbed "Showboat"; chubby-faced, introverted "Porky"; intelligent and intensely dedicated "Chinh," whose entire family was involved in the revolutionary struggle; brash, loud "Cheeta," named for the monkey in *Tarzan*, who was competing with J. Fred Muggs for the "missing link between man and ape" award; and the walking inferiority complex, "Base," so named because of the cruel joke concerning the woman who responded to a question from a group of youngsters, asking if her son could come out and play baseball with them, by telling them that he was a multiple amputee and couldn't play. They replied, "We knew but we need a second base!" After a few weeks, we discovered that it wasn't an inferiority complex that Base had. He was really inferior!

Dan and I were bathing in the canal which ran in front of our hut, checking some new boats and speculating on our future, when we heard voices to the south along this same canal not more than a hundred meters away. We had determined that there were huts, similar to ours, extending for some distance down the canal and the voices were obviously coming from the next series of huts, screened from view by the thick vegetation. We listened for a few moments before I realized one of the voices was speaking English. It took only another second to identify the voice. Rocky Versace! He was still hanging in, despite anything they had done to him. We raised our voices, talking loudly, hoping he'd be able to hear us and continued until Leo and Elvis hurried over and ordered us to shut up.

On the night of 20 January 1965, we were told to prepare to leave on a five-day trip to a new camp. An unknown cadre had come into the camp several days before and would be in charge of the movement. His sleepy-eyed, slack-mouthed appearance didn't make me overestimate his ability, as he spent most of his time in a relatively somnambulant state. When all nine boats were assembled in the canal, each American was placed in a separate boat with either two or three guards who would alternate paddling the boat. We had been told by the new cadre, whom we referred to as "Useless," that during the trip we would be required to lie in the bottoms of the boats on

150

the flooring racks with camouflage over us to prevent detection while traveling. We were not to talk or move while traveling and would respond immediately to any orders given by the guards in our respective boats. With that, he produced four sheets of black-coated nylon which would be used to cover us. I had anticipated the use of our sleeping mats, which would have adequately covered us while permitting enough air to circulate so that we would be able to breathe comfortably. The poncho-like sheets of nylon would permit no air to enter and I could visualize a stifling ride.

Clem and Elvis were in the boat with me. Neither had shown any great amount of antagonism toward the Americans, which made me think, briefly, that it might not be as bad as I had assumed. That idea was squelched as soon as they began preparing me for the trip. I was placed on my back in the boat, lying on the slatted wooden rack. Clem placed the poncho directly over me, tucking it all around and laying equipment along both sides to hold it down. A sack of rice was placed squarely on my face, but I managed to move my head lower, slipping out from under the suffocating weight. I managed to bring my hands up across my chest, raising the nylon away from my nose and making a small pocket of air which was soon warmed by my exhalation. I felt a touch of panic as it became increasingly difficult to breathe. I turned my head to the side, seeking cooler, fresh air and finding none, returned to the face-up position. We hadn't even left the dock and I was having problems.

The guards were taking so damned long to get started. As they finished their preparations and got a final briefing from Useless I envied them standing in the cool night air. I could feel the perspiration beginning to drip from my forehead, running over my temples and puddling in my ears, causing a tickling sensation which became increasingly irritating as I repeatedly rolled my head from side to side, trying to unclog my ears.

A new factor was added when I heard the first mosquito humming near my head. In the blackness and with almost total restriction of movement I was helpless as the little insect darted about, selecting his point to sting. I cursed silently, thinking that fresh air couldn't reach me, but the mosquitoes homing in on me, could. The first was soon joined by others, and I lay waiting until I felt the bites on my face or neck before reaching up and trying to crush the little bloodsuckers.

The boat began to move, rocking slightly as Elvis pushed the long oar into the bank, propelling us forward. The five nights of drenching perspiration, mosquitoes and periodical near-suffocation under the shroud-like poncho that followed left me with a deeply etched case of claustrophobia. The travel was accomplished between sundown and sunrise, using the hours of darkness to conceal our journey from observation. Eight to ten hours a night I rode on my back, fighting the urge to throw off the choking cover and suck in deep breaths of cool, clean air, knowing that any movement would bring a sharp warning from Elvis or Clem, followed the second time with a blow from either the butt of a weapon or a paddle. Only the blessed cold night air finding its way under when I was able to raise the edge of the poncho slightly enabled me to keep from succumbing to panic.

The guards, pushed by Useless to paddle all night, were emotionally and physically taxed. The constant threat of ambush by Government forces or discovery by civilians loyal to the Government added to their strain. As a result, they treated their unwanted American burdens like sacks of rice, ignoring requests for a little fresh air or the chance to change position and kill some of the feeding mosquitoes. It was conceivable that through their ignorance and total disregard for the prisoners, one or more of us could have passed out and possibly suffocated.

The fourth night I was thrown into the boat with my arms tied as punishment for sitting upright and making an impulsive threat after being slammed in the groin with a paddle by Elvis the night before. We had been traveling on a narrow canal with no other traffic and I had worked the edge of the poncho up over the gunwale, forming it to work as an airscoop, funneling beautifully cool air into my nylon casket. My hand was against the gunwale, holding the nylon outward, when Clem, sitting in the bow of the boat, noticed the loose edge and jammed it back in place with the edge of his paddle, smashing my hand and fingers. I groaned loudly, pulling my hand to my chest, biting my lip in pain. Elvis snapped, "*Dung nghic!*" as I rubbed the aching hand—don't fool around.

"Fuck you, Elvis," I managed between clenched teeth. Sudden knifing pain shot all the way through my body as a well-directed blow caught me in the lower abdomen. Luckily, it missed my testicles, but the edge of the paddle felt like it had cut me in two. *"Dung nghic!"* I heard Elvis reemphasize his command. A combination of pain and sudden anger brought me to a sitting position, trying to pull the restraining nylon free. Another jabbing blow to the chest knocked me back and I felt the butt of a rifle pressing against my forehead, holding me down. Nausea hit me and I felt my body sag. All it would take would be one smash from that rifle butt and my brains would be draining onto the flooring rack. It wasn't worth it. I tried to relax, fighting the urge to vomit, knowing I'd lie in it until morning. Neither of the guards even lifted the poncho to see what damage they had done.

When getting underway the next night, I was tied before going into the boat and what I had thought was bad before became minor inconvenience compared with that night. For endless hours I lay, unable to lift the moist inner surface of the poncho away from my nose and mouth, feeling the warm, stale air fill the cavity around me, threatening to smother me. Mosquitoes fed unhampered, and only the repeated thought that there had to be enough air coming from under the flooring rack to prevent suffocation kept me from giving in to panic. I let my mind fasten on how wonderful it would be in the morning to get out from under here and breathe again.

During the next afternoon, which I spent thinking, while the guards were dozing in the shade of the reeds broken over the boat as it sat next to a bank, I caught a glimpse of another boat pulled against the bank some fifteen meters away. Normally the Americans were separated during the day so we had no chance for contact, but I could hear an American voice speaking Vietnamese. There was only one person in our group that fluent and it had to be Rocky. I reached over Clem's sleeping body and unfastened the tie rope, freeing the boat, and gently pushed it several feet closer to the other boat, staying under the shade so as not to wake the guards.

Leaning toward the bank, I could see the second boat and squatting on the bank next to it, washing his hands and talking to an unseen Vietnamesee was Rocky Versace. He was turned partially away from me, but I could see his sharply defined features and his hair. It was nearly solid white! He was deeply

153

tanned and looked much thinner, but hard. I tried to catch his attention without success by waving and rattling the reeds. I didn't want to awaken my guards, but I had to let Rocky know I was here.

Elvis awoke as I was searching in the reeds for a branch that I could break and throw in Rocky's direction. He provided a solution to my problem as I asked him in a loud voice if I could go crap, slaughtering the Vietnamese pronunciation in order to let Rocky know I was here and to confuse Elvis as to what I was asking. I saw Rocky' head whip around and he squinted trying to see me, his eyesight bad enough that he obviously couldn't focus. Elvis was still sleep-drugged and, half comprehending what was happening, asked crossly what I had said to him. I repeated the question, adding on in English, "Nick here, Rock. All of us still hanging in and pulling for you." I watched Rocky's face break into a beautiful smile as if it were the first one in a long time. I could see his throat working, but no sound came. Finally, I heard faintly: "Thank God you're here, Nick. God bless you."

Elvis came sharply awake as he realized I was speaking English and started to sit up. I quickly directed my next remarks to him, phrasing the request to go crap in careful Vietnamese, then repeating the question in English, gesturing to my ass and then to the bank as if trying to explain to him what I wanted. He comprehended and sank back on his pack, cushioning his head to return to sleep. Once settled, he grunted an affirmative "*Ua.*"

On 25 January, 1965, we arrived in the new camp of thatched huts. The guards spent a week, leaving in shifts of six with Thanh as leader, working somewhere away from camp between 0800 and 1500 hours each day, returning muddy and tired. There was no indication of what they were doing until Muoi informed Dan and me that all of us would be going to a permanent camp soon where there would be dry ground for us to exercise. I thought back to the last time I'd walked on dry land and determined it was in October 1963, immediately after capture. Since then, except for the brief stop en route up here, we had been confined to log walkways over the swamp water or mud. On 7 February, we were moved by boat down the canal blindfolded and after a very short ride arrived at a spot where logs had been dragged from the canal up onto the bank, forming a ragged clearing. More logs and poles floated in the canal, jamming its four-foot width. When the blindfold was removed, I scanned the overhanging tree branches, tangled hanging vines and dense thickets of reeds that lined both banks, thinking how dark and closed-in everything seemed. Unknown to us at this time, our journey had brought us into the Rung U Minh, the legendary "Forest of Darkness."

Our group of guards led us through the maze of reeds and vines into a clump of trees, standing ten yards back from the canal, that provided more than adequate leafy camouflage for the huts I saw scattered in the area. We were taken to a large hut capable of holding four mosquito nets and shortly we were joined by John and Dave. Muoi made a production out of the four of us being allowed to stay together and enjoy free conversation. With gestures and enthusiasm, he got the idea across that we were to be happy living in the same hut and that would enable us to get healthier. I didn't quite follow his logic, but agreed that morale would improve now that the restriction on communication was removed. The biggest boost to my morale was the lack of bars on the hut. It had four open sides, a pole floor and a thatched roof.

The next morning, we arose after having spent a good portion of the night getting acquainted. Only broken patches of sunlight shone on the layer of dead leaves covering the ground, making the shadowy camp almost dismal, but the elation at walking on the spongy earth outweighed any feeling of depression. It wasn't completely dry because of the high water table and the fact that during the rainy season, six months of the year, all of this would be underwater, but we could walk without sinking into mud. Even Dan, who remained quite weak, was out stretching his legs, trying out muscles which were long unused.

Intern returned several days after our arrival and brought a variety of medications including the badly needed penicillin for John and Dave. Dan received injections of "hemo-cyto serum," which Intern said would strengthen his blood, and "hepatana," a horse-liver extract for the liver pains. I received more sulfaguanidine to slow the diarrhea and a couple of shots of hepatana on the side. Bottles of tooth powder were provided and soap was purchased for us. It was a caustic, homemade type, but served to remove some of the accumulated dirt. I felt foolish at times, trying to bathe in cold, dirty water with poor-quality soap and feeling clean when I finished, knowing that I had just rearranged the dirt.

There was an effort by some of the guards to establish rapport with the Americans through conversation and super-ficial camaraderie. It never really got off the ground due to the simultaneous construction of a six-foot pole fence entirely around our hut, leaving a small rectangular strip of cleared earth, four feet wide, between the fence and the hut. The fence made obvious the fact that we weren't just one big family as the guards were trying to prove by their sudden amicability. We named the camp "No-K Corral" because of our private corral and let the guards ramble on while we watched certain of their number who were poorer actors than the others and gave a more accurate picture of actual attitude.

The arrival of a bandy-legged, muscular-chested Vietnam-ese during the month was an occasion for celebration among the guards. He was about five feet four inches tall and had a weathered, long craggy face which had been marked by each of his thirty-four years of age. His sun helmet, which, when covered with a plastic camouflage rain cover, became the "hard hat" we'd seen so many times on their main force or regional troops, the well-used, well-cleaned equipment and the Movado seventeen-jewel watch, probably taken from an American body, marked him as a combatant. He spent a short time conferring with Muoi before departing for a second camp which was located a short distance to our east. That must have been a special camp to require a new cadre to run it, but we had no idea why.

In mid-March 1965, John and Dave were moved out of the camp unexpectedly. The guards assured Dan and me that it was not a punishment and that we would see them again soon. On 30 March, we learned where they had gone when Leo came by the hut and told us to pack up our belongings to return to the "mosquito junction" where we had lived when we came into the U Minh only two months earlier. Our gear was placed in a boat while Dan and I had to walk. We followed Yes Yes and Leo through the fields of reeds and trees surrounding our camp, proceeding along well-worn paths until we crossed a wide canal running east-west. The field on the other side was covered with similar reeds, but with only scattered trees. Water remained standing in pools in the series of ditches that spanned the field and we crossed small mounded-dirt borders that indicated this field had, at one time, possibly been cultivated. Looking back toward No-K, I saw the grove of trees in which the camp was built and, around it, the thinning number of trees and this field of nothing but reeds and a few trees. From the air, it would look like a relatively open area, with scattered clumps of trees, but hardly enough to conceal a series of camps. The area had been well chosen. Why not? These people had been fighting a guerrilla war for a long time now.

We found ourselves back in the mosquito junction, but with improvements and reconstruction. New log walks ran throughout the area and the guard huts had been made more comfortable. The hut in which we had stayed in January had been rebuilt and was now curiously like the school hut in the mangroves, though smaller. Since it was near dark, we were told to put up a mosquito net and prepare to sleep, both of us in the school hut.

The next morning I was told to move my things to a smaller hut, built low to the standing water behind the guard hut. Dan remained in the school hut as I made myself as comfortable as possible in the decaying wood structure I had at first glance thought was abandoned. There was barely enough room to spread out my sleeping mat and I hoped the stay here wouldn't be a long one.

That afternoon I was visited by a stocky young man wearing Western-style shirt and trousers. His pleasant face was creased by an ever-present grin which brought me to call him "Smiley," an erroneous evaluation of the individual. It was a surprise to learn that he spoke English, not well, but enough to communicate. I was given a new "*cai khan*," the handtowel-sized checkered towel used for everything from a bath towel to a mosquito swatter. He asked about my health and the food I had been receiving. I based my answer on what had happened in the last month, not thinking of the year before. He left shortly after that, quite pleased with my report on the treatment I was receiving.

A young cadre whom we had seen briefly months before came down to the hut for a chat, his gold-filled mouth glistening. He spoke in general terms of a school we would attend here and our opportunity to meet a new representative of the

157

Front, Mr. Hai, who would speak to Dan and me tomorrow. It was an enjoyable afternoon as the different members of this group traveling with Mr. Hai came to sit and talk for a few minutes, keeping the conversation light and avoiding politics or the war. I began to relax, trying my Vietnamese language out on the different visitors and watching their surprise, feigned or real, at what ability I possessed. Supper that night was pineapple soup and the tangy sharp flavor, even boiled in water, was superb.

The next morning, I again had pineapple with my rice, which made the rice quite easy to eat. Leo had brought a full boatload of ripe pineapples, small but acid-sweet and a change from the salty *nuoc mam*. About midmorning, Smiley came to the hut and told me to put on my best set of pajamas for a meeting with the representatives of the Front. There wasn't much of a choice. I wore the black ones, draping my new towel around my neck in case I wanted to slap mosquitoes during the meeting. I recalled the formality that had gone with the school in the mangroves and figured it was standard practice with high-ranking cadre. Dan was waiting at the intersection of the main walk and the smaller one leading to the school hut. He had apparently been evicted while the guards and cadre prepared for this session. When a voice from inside the hut called to Leo, we were marched up to the doorway and halted. Leo stepped inside and reported that "American prisoners Phit and Ro" were prepared to enter. Another voice from the shadowy interior, this one flat and cold, ordered us in.

We were standing in front of a high desk, draped with a sheet of dark green plastic. Behind it were three men, one of them "Goldie," the citified new cadre with gold-capped teeth. The man in the middle was a balding, chunky individual, whose almost rounded almond-shaped eyes and narrow nose indicated some French ancestry. A plank of wood placed on the pole floor against the wall to our right seemed to be the obvious seat. Once seated, we were forced to look up at almost a 45-degree angle to see the cadre, psychologically giving him a position of authority. Goldie and the one on the right sat quietly studying us while the balding one glanced through a sheaf of papers on his desk in front of him. I noticed the slogans written on long sheets of paper and fastened to the walls. "The Front grants lenient and humane treatment to captured US and Alien officers and men." "Your release, sooner or later, is based on your good behavior and repentance of your past misdeeds." "Do not die for the enrichment of the Wall Street capitalists." These people really seemed to go for these things. A large VC flag hung on the wall behind the seated cadre as it had in the mangrove school. Smiley and another more slender Vietnamese with sharp features accenting his flattened nose sat on a short bench at the rear of the hut by the door. Both had note pads and ball-point pens.

The balding one finally looked up, his eyes turning the space between us frigid with his stare.

"I represent the Central Committee of the Liberation National Front and I have come to review your cases." His was the flat, cold voice we had heard and his manner indicated he was no Plato. There was a harsh air of assurance of a man completely confident of his dominance over another. "I can kill you, I can torture you," he paused, letting the words sink in. In a few words, he had let us know what relationship existed here and made the passing threat Plato had uttered many months ago become a frightening new reality. "But no." His voice softened only slightly. "I choose to allow you to enjoy the lenient policy of the Front, even though you have shown a bad attitude."

He continued, "The Front has spared your lives and gives you good treatment. It has been reported to me that you receive adequate food and medication for your maladies. In the past days you have been allowed to practice physical exercise and engage in games of cards. This is proof of the lenient policy of the Front and yet you choose to have a bad attitude." Again he paused, allowing us to consider the treatment of the past month, ignoring what had gone before. "I have come to allow you to fulfill the requirements of the Front and display your knowledge on certain questions. Your attitude can be judged by what you do in the camp here and your release to rejoin your families and loved ones can be based on your realization of your past misdeeds. It is wise for you to believe in the Front and act accordingly."

My mind was whirling, seeking some escape from this wall closing down on me. I knew what the requirements would entail and I didn't believe any of the things he wanted me to say. I knew that there was protection for a prisoner of war that forbade

159

forcing him to make statements to be used as propaganda, forbade physical or mental coercion to create an environment which was so oppressive that a man would violate his beliefs and honor to escape it. But what good was this protection when it wasn't recognized by your captors? There was a churning knot of real fear in my stomach.

The third cadre, a taller, pale-complexioned, older man, who spoke less distinct English, informed us that we had already attended the political school in the other camp, referring to the mangroves, and here we would be brought up to date on the latest facts concerning the war in order for us to "know clearly the situation." Goldie gave a brief lecture on the policy of the National Liberation Front, referring to the small pamphlet we had been shown in the mangroves. His emphasis was on the paragraphs which began. "The Front protects the life of and grants lenient treatment to US and other Alien surrendered officers and men it gives proper care to the wounded," and "The Front takes care of the POWs' material and spiritual life, creates conditions to give back freedom to them when conditions permit it." The recital of these points seemed to be another effort to create the image in our minds of the idealized policy as reality rather than the "now you have it, now you don't" condition.

The meeting was concluded when Mr. Hai, the cadre seated in the middle, drew out of the papers on the desk several long sheets of lined paper and two sheets of questions. He held them up and spoke to us, gesturing with the papers. "You will take these questions and answer them for me. Write for me what you can know about the various questions as clearly and completely as possible. Do not write short as before. When you have completed your work I will review what you have done." With that he handed the sheets over the table to Smiley, who had gotten up and stepped in front of us. I was handed the sheet of questions, a ball-point pen and three folded sheets of lined paper for my answers. Mr. Hai's expression hadn't changed from the cold, imperturbable mask; only his eyes betrayed emotion and they weren't pleasant at all.

"Do you have anything to say?" he asked, not really expecting anything. Neither of us spoke. "Go back to your house." We were dismissed.

Leo escorted me back to the hut and made certain I had an

empty five-liter kerosene can to use for a desk while I wrote. Smiley came down to visit and see how I was progressing even before I had read the questions. That noon we received one of the infrequent noon meals, this one a treat of sweet soup which was delicious. The psychological preparation we were undergoing and had undergone for the past month to set us up for this confrontation with Mr. Hai was transparent as hell. I wondered how short they thought our memories were. Then again, the mind tended to blot out extremely unpleasant memories, retaining the less painful thoughts and anything good that might have happened.

My first action after lunch was to borrow a needle and thread from Smiley in order to patch my clothing, not knowing when the logistics channels would begin to function again. I spent that day repairing my black pajamas, much to Smiley's consternation when he discovered I was ignoring the questions. He encouraged me several times to turn my attention to important matters and I assured him nothing was more important than a prisoner maintaining his clothing. His smiling attitude began to fade.

The next day Mr. Hai came by to see me, inquiring if the report he had received about my lack of compliance with his directives was correct. I had already evaluated him as not being one to mess around with and told him quite frankly that this was the first opportunity I had gotten to use a needle and thread to perform much-needed mending on my clothing. This caught him off balance, which surprised me. I think he expected either a flat refusal or weak excuse which he could batter down. The clear need I had to patch my deteriorating clothing fell under "takes care of the material and spiritual life" portion of his own policy and caused him to stop and think. I filed that reaction away for further reference. I was told to devote my attention to the questions and "do the mending after." It was a mild encounter, but he made sure I was looking at the questions.

The new questionnaire was entitled "My Revelation." Beneath that heading, the questions were broken into groups, each numbered and requiring single answers for the biographical and military background data and essay-type answers for the new set of inquiries. The basic declaration Plato had attempted to get filled out was repeated and amplified. What Vietnamese officers, government officials and civilians did I have any dealings with while at Tan Phu? What were those dealings? What subjects did I study at the Engineer school at Fort Belvoir? How many days total did I spend at Tan Phu? How many operations did I go on, where did they go, and what were their results? Had I killed members of the Liberation Armed Forces in combat? (He was a dumb son of a bitch to think I'd ever consider answering that after he said, "I can kill you, I can torture you.") What are your qualifications and duties as "Second Officer" (my term for an executive officer) at Tan Phu post?

The essay questions dealt with religion, political beliefs and opinion on the economic and social system within the United States. Questions on the subjects I had studied in high school and college seemed out of place and unimportant, but must have had some value to him. The loaded questions dealt with my opinion on the war in Vietnam and the determination of a "just and unjust cause." I was to answer the latter "based on what I had learned from the cadre of the Front," which would have left little room for personal opinions and resulted in an endorsement of their viewpoint and program. Mr. Hai had stated that the format of these answers required that each page be signed at the bottom after it was completed, which could have been either for verification of "sincerity" or for use in attaching a signature to extracted material for propaganda use. The final question was "What are your desires and wishes?"

I read and reread the questions, fitting my cover story into the framework and contemplating the new questions, trying to determine which were probing for new information and which concerned verifiable facts that could be used to check my truthfulness. My first instinct was to stall, and I accomplished this by printing two full pages to describe the subjects I had studied in high school and adding a few I hadn't taken just to fill space. An unsmiling Smiley checked numerous times during the day, urging me to hurry and submit what I had finished. He and the other young English-speaker who was working with Dan acted as interpreters, translating what we had written into Vietnamese for Mr. Hai and the other cadre. It was not so much for their understanding, since they also spoke English, but for evaluation of content in the language which would be read and judged by the non-English-speaking Central Committee.

I accomplished several things by stalling that I wasn't then

162

aware of. Mr. Hai was on a time schedule and had a specified period of time to deal with the Americans in this area. Dan and I had been alloted nine days and Mr. Hai's young interpreters were pushing to meet the time limitation. The second effect was when I began at the end of the "Revelation" instead of the short-answer initial part. They had anticipated getting the short answers first and having the POW deal with the more important questions in decreasing numerical order, leaving the garbage queries for last in case they didn't have time for completion. I began with the garbage questions and was merrily scribbling inane comments about Home Economics, Woodworking, Mechanical Drawing, Drama and the other actual and fictitious courses I took in high school.

A frowning Smiley appeared shortly after taking my first effort for translation and grabbed the question sheet, pointing to the military questions and telling me to do them first. After he left, I plugged the answers I had give Plato in the first declaration into the proper slots, thankful I had made them simple and easy to remember. That left Mr. Hai with a duplicate of what I'd given Plato. The new questions were not so easy and I added to the cover story, stating I had spent little actual time at Tan Phu since I was required to travel over Vietnam, inspecting other civil affairs projects in order to improve our efforts to help the people around Tan Phu. (This one really frosted Mr. Hai when it came time to talk about the crimes against the people and building a dispensary, running medical patrols and improving sanitation became "crimes.") I couldn't remember Vietnamese names very well and could only give him the nicknames I had assigned the people with whom I'd had contact, much as I was doing with the guards now. He got a list that included "Sam Spade, Mr. Lucky, Digger O'Dell and Amos Hoople."

When it came time for the essay questions, I drew on everything I could remember from my classes on Economics, Comparative Governments, Comparative Religions, and History, to include the United States, Europe and Asia. I created a written picture of a heterogeneous society, stressing the broad spectrum of races and beliefs that made up the population of the United States. The concept of liberty, equality and justice as a basis for our form of government, even though imperfectly developed, was portrayed as the foundation necessary for a man to achieve a place in the society based on his own capabilities and limitations. I was angry with myself for not having been more familiar with my own country than I was. I found areas of political theory versus political reality that I wasn't able to resolve in my own mind and wished that as a member of the military I hadn't been encouraged to disregard the desire for political awareness. I was confronted by an enemy who stressed the interrelationship between military and political, both serving to achieve a political goal, and even though exposed to political theory at West Point, I was unable to cover myself against the oncoming attack. It was a case of knowing what I was against, but failing to define clearly what I was for. I stopped in the written dissertation before I got over my head, and attempted to convey only the idea that I was satisfied with the basic structure of my government and confident in the ability of my society to continually improve itself. This potential was based on the contributions from each of the diversified cultures represented within the society.

The question on the war was a short answer: "I am a member of the United States Army, captured during armed conflict and not required to answer this question, under provisions of the Geneva Convention concerning POW's." I left only the number of the question and a "No opinion" on several questions requiring me to divulge my thoughts on U.S. policy and the credibility of the government in Saigon. The latter was factual since I had been acquainted only with the Diem government and knew nothing about his successor other than the information given me by the cadre. I felt there would be an adverse reaction from Mr. Hai and found myself wishing he couldn't read what I'd written.

A hostile Smiley picked up my completed efforts on the Revelation and immediately handed me a new set of questions to complete. Mr. Hai apparently had several sets of questions to be answered in sequence and my slow answers to the first part prevented him from giving me more than this one additional list. The new questions involved the treatments for napalm burns, white phosphorus burns and poison gas attack. I noted that poison gas was outlawed, in the sense of war gases such as mustard, lewisite and phosgene, therefore there was no treatment for a gas that was not used. The only thing I knew to do for napalm and white phosphorus, I said, was to cover the burned area with a heavy grease to replace skin moisture and bind it tightly with gauze to keep air away and prevent infection. I added that I wasn't too knowledgeable on the subject, hoping they would try my treatment. The list also contained a question about my repentance for my "misdeeds" which received the same answer I'd given Plato, "I am sorry if any innocent Vietnamese civilians suffered from my actions while at Tan Phu," which was true.

On 9 April, a totally antagonistic Smiley picked up the final single sheet of one- and two-line answers, taking the ball-point pen but missing the sheets of extra paper I'd put in my mosquito net. He ordered me to fold up my belongings and prepare to move to a new camp. His attitude indicated my performance wasn't appreciated and I had fleeting thoughts of being more liberal in some of my answers, but wiped the thought out. It was finished and all I could do now was tuck up and take whatever came. I thought about my renewed sense of duty, thinking of the part of the Code of Conduct that stated, "I will avoid answering questions to the best of my ability," and wondering if I had done a good enough job. I decided that the one brief chance I had to see Rocky was the biggest factor in my resolve. I wasn't going to let him pull all of the shit down on his head. He needed someone to divert a little of it.

One of the questions on the last sheet had been to write the Code of Conduct. I thought about that a long time before writing, "I am an American fighting man. I serve in the forces which guard my country and our way of life. I will keep faith with my fellow prisoners. I am bound to give only my name, rank, serial number and date of birth. I will trust in my God and in the United States of America." I felt that was all Mr. Hai ought to know.

Late in the afternoon, Leo came to get me for the "critique" of my work. I walked to the school hut, entering and finding Dan already seated. As I sat on the floor beside Dan, I could sense the animosity from Mr. Hai.

The tall cadre, Major Bay, began by giving a short talk comparing the present revolution with the American Revolution of 1776. It was an eloquent, but hardly factual, account of what they felt to be the basic similarities between struggles for national independence and liberty from foreign domination. The Geneva Accords of 1954, as interpreted by the Front, were

165

used to substantiate their assertions of U.S. "aggression" in the same spiel Plato had recited during the indoctrinations in the mangroves. The major theme was the inevitable final victory of the revolution.

I found myself barely listening as Major Bay droned on in his carefully rehearsed presentation. My attention focused on Mr. Hai as he leafed through sheets of paper I recognized as my "Revelation." When Major Bay finished there was a long silence as Mr. Hai continued to study the papers. I was beginning to feel cold all over and the taste of bile came up in my throat. Finally he looked up, his malefic stare locking my eyes to his. "I have studied your revelations." He was speaking in the plural, but directing his remarks to me. "You have displayed what you can know about this cruel and dirty war and your part in it. The Front sought to know better your thoughts and your repentance so as to judge your cases and act according to your beliefs and your attitude. You realize clearly that you are in our power and we have full right to punish you as we determine, because you are an aggressor in our country, having committed grievous crimes against our compatriots. You have enjoyed the lenient policy of the Front which springs from the humanitarian spirit of the fourteen million South Vietnamese people and their only true representative, the National Liberation Front."

My palms had begun to sweat and I was experiencing a curious sense of lightheadedness as if my mind were divorcing itself from my body and stepping back to observe the proceedings. He continued, his voice flat, unchanging, "The Front cannot afford to show leniency to those who are unrepentant of their crimes." He picked up my Revelation, "I have spoken with Pitzer before and now speak to you." His voice had become softer, but even more intense. "You choose to persist in your attitude." Suddenly he slammed the papers down on the desk. His eyes flamed. "This is useless! You have not shown repentance or understanding! You continue to resist the Front!" His voice lashed out, carrying a physical impact with each word. I fought to keep from cringing back against the wall. I hadn't expected anything like this! "I can no longer allow you to live under the lenient policy of the Front!" Without realizing what that entailed, I felt a relief that he hadn't said I was to be executed. "You will go to a camp where your conditions

166

will reflect your attitude." He sat back, breathing deeply, watching my face intently. I felt my knees beginning to quiver and concentrated on keeping them still, holding my face in a fixed mask.

"May I say something, Mr. Hai?" I asked in the silence.

"No!" he snapped. "You have had your opportunity to speak." He looked to Leo standing in the back of the hut. "Take him to his hut." I arose, looking down at Dan, wondering how he'd been able to bullshit his way past this guy, then followed Leo back to my hut.

I sat staring at my few belongings, tied together with a length of vine, and wondered what twist of ill fortune had caused this. I thought back to my home and tried to picture the living room with Mom and Dad sitting on the couch in front of the fireplace. How I wished I were with them. It was so difficult to look at myself—bearded, dirty, covered with fungus infection, bones sticking out all over—and think that I once had sat in that living room. The two worlds were so far apart, and my chances for bridging the gap had just decreased radically.

My meditation was interrupted by Major Bay, who stooped under the low roof of the hut and squatted near me. He had a long face with a high forehead and heavy drooping lower lip. His eyes were rounder than is usual in a Vietnamese, but he had the characteristic broad nose. He had seemed to be a quietly intense individual the times I had seen him, but I couldn't really categorize him. His manner was milder than Mr. Hai's, which made his presence not unwelcome right now. He paused to roll a cigarette from the packet of tobacco he carried, placing it in his mouth and reaching into the shirt pocket of the black peasant garments he was wearing, searching for a lighter. Having found it, he lit the cigarette and drew a few puffs before speaking.

"You have displayed a bad attitude before the cadre of the Front and must surrender your right to live under the lenient policy granted captured officers and men," he began. "Do you understand why you can no longer enjoy the lenient policy?" The only reasons I had were that I wasn't subscribing to their concepts of how this war began; how it was being conducted and who was right and wrong. I knew of no requirements, other than those established by them to accept these people's ideas.

167

It had become apparent that "rules" like the Geneva Convention and international law didn't carry much weight if the Front didn't recognize them, and in this situation, the rules of the Front were more easily enforcible than any others.

"I suppose, Major Bay, that I haven't met the requirements set by the Front in order to live under the lenient policy," I answered, thinking that life under the lenient policy hadn't been that much of a good deal and people had been close to dying then. There was no telling how much worse it could get. I wanted to ask why the Front didn't print in their little policy pamphlet, which made a POW's life look like a moderately well-cared-for commodity, that not all POW's were granted similar treatment. I thought that they should state that, based on a POW's political views and response to the "requirements of the Front," he might or might not be entitled to some or all of the provisions of their policy.

He smoked for a moment, staring into the deepening shadows, so preoccupied it was almost as if I had ceased to exist. He looked back at me, "You must use this experience to correct your attitude and strive to progress so that you, too, may be released to return to your home." I nodded, the thought of release more pleasant than ever before. "Versace," my attention immediately sharpened when he mentioned Rocky, "displayed a very bad attitude." He was speaking in a musing tone, almost to himself. "He resisted against the cadre of the Front and now the Front cannot release him. He must rest here a long time." "Lord, help Rocky," I prayed. He had stayed in there against Mr. Hai and was in worse shape because of it. Major Bay stood and prepared to leave. "Consider your actions in the future," he cautioned. "The Front must judge you also." He was walking away as the guards came to take me on the walk to the new camp.

Dan and I retraced our steps together. My hopes began to rise as we neared the camp, thinking I might be placed in a separate cage, but in the same camp with the others. The thought of going to a separate camp as Rocky had done last April was frightening. It was one year since the bloody clothes had been arranged for us to see.

We took a short break just north of the second camp we had noticed to the east of No-K. Dan sat next to me and offered that he hoped we wouldn't be split up. I don't think he knew how much I was hoping the same thing. There was a sense of security in being near other Americans, knowing that if something happened to you, at least someone would know. Alone, you were at the mercy of the guards, who couldn't care less if you were alive.

"What in the hell did you write that pissed him off?" Dan asked.

"Nothing," I replied candidly, figuring that was my point of conflict with the cadre. The guards rejoined us and indicated for me to proceed to the south toward the second camp, while Dan was taken back to No-K.

It was a brief walk through the waist-high grass and reeds to the clump of trees. I was following Cheeta, who, along with Base, Porky, Chinh, Showboat and two other members of the "animal squad," "Slim" and "Pock," had been assigned to guard Rocky in the different isolated camps he had been in. I had an idea of what was waiting, wondering if I could take it. Mr. Hai had made a definite point in the meeting. He wasn't messing around when he made a threat and the days of Plato were over. The presence of this group of guards was enough to make me wish there were some magical way to transport myself to another place, any other place.

The final light from the sun was casting a reddish glow on the base of the clouds stacked up in the western sky when I entered the small camp, consisting of four huts, one of them a familiar cage which became my home. The bars on one side, facing a narrow porch, were newly nailed in place. It seemed that the bars had been taken down for some reason, then replaced. The other three huts were the typical guard huts, except these had no sleeping racks built along the walls. There was an absence of log walks which were used during the rainy season, but deeply worn paths, obviously walked on while the ground was underwater and muddy, indicated the routes used in the camp. The roofs of the guard huts had been repaired, but were mainly pieces of used thatching, which added to the run-down and temporary atmosphere of the whole camp.

As I arranged my sleeping mat and net in the cage, all of the guards gathered around the porch, watching me. I could feel their eyes, but continued to work. When I had finished, I turned and squatted outside the bars, willing to converse if they were and perhaps that way find out what the attitude here was.

I was determined not to repeat my previous mistakes of resorting to open physical signs of resistance since the odds of my accomplishing anything positive, other than getting myself in a worse bind, were slim. I was counting heavily on stoicism to create the necessary mental environment for survival.

Showboat, the most talkative of the group, squatted on the porch and asked if I knew why I had been sent to this camp. I replied that Mr. Hai hadn't been pleased with what I had written for him, but other than that I knew of no other reason. I hoped he'd give me an idea of what other mistakes I'd made along the line, but he merely nodded. Cheeta joined him in front of me and launched into a rapid speech on the leniency of the Front, his harsh breath, spiked with the odor of *nuoc mam* and nicotine from the weedlike tobacco he smoked, blasting me in the face. I told him halfway through the dissertation that he spoke much too fast for me to understand. Instead of slowing down, he raised his voice several decibels and continued as if speaking louder would get the idea across. The other guards crowded nearer, watching my reactions, except for Porky and Base, who hung back at the edge of the group.

A short time later, Showboat and Cheeta got up and walked away, the others following. Base stayed behind and when the group was out of hearing, he squatted beside me and in a serious voice, speaking slowly in order for me to understand, explained that I would have to realize clearly the just cause of the revolution and learn the truth of the situation in Vietnam so I might criticize my actions in the past and become a true friend of the Vietnamese people and the Front.

After that he gave me a short talk on the history of the revolution which I recognized as being almost a duplicate of the spiels Plato had given. Before he could continue, Slim came down with a set of leg irons, the anklets clanking on the long bar as he walked. Base arose with a sheepish expression as Slim asked him sharply what he was doing at my cage. Base mumbled a reply and, looking down at me, snapped, "*Cum lai!*"—put on your irons.

I was startled by the sudden change in manner, but put the irons on without comment. Slim fingered my net for a moment, asking, "*Muoi, khong?*"—do you have any mosquitoes inside? I assured him I didn't and he left. Base had stalked off immediately after his outburst.

The next morning I was unlocked before daylight and told to come to the kitchen to get my rice. I followed Pock, a constantly wisecracking camp jester, to the kitchen, a tumble-down remainder of what had been a rather large kitchen and mess hall combination. Poles, thatching and chunks of dried fireplace clay were strewn around the intact flooring and the small remaining portion of the fireplace on which blazed two low fires. He packed a heaping serving of steaming rice on my plate and placed a sauce of *nuoc mam* on top of the pile of rice. "*Khong co do an*," he said pleasantly.

After I'd eaten, as the sun was breaking over the trees, Showboat came down to the cage to explain the camp routine to me. I would be included in camp details and required to work with the guards since I was no longer granted lenient treatment. My spirits leaped. If this was all that was to happen, I was straight. I would also be given classes on the revolution so that I could understand the situation and realize my mistakes. I had heard that line so often that I almost began to think there were mistakes to realize. The relief of not winding up in a total pile of shit as a result of the encounter with Mr. Hai was almost as overwhelming as when I hadn't been killed after capture. The sun-helmeted cadre we had seen come through No-K Corral came by the hut while Showboat was there and inquired about my health, indicating that medical facilities in this camp were limited, but he would do his best to see that my diarrhea was taken care of. I hadn't mentioned the diarrhea, so it was obvious that he had been briefed on my condition. I couldn't understand why medical facilities here were limited when No-K Corral, 150 meters to the west of us, had been the site of numerous treatments for Dan and the rest of us.

That day I went on a firewood-gathering detail with Porky and Pock, picking up and carrying bundles of sticks and small limbs, dead wood dried by the intense sun that was used to build the virtually smokeless fires required to escape observation by aircraft. Porky said very little, other than telling me to pick up a certain bunch of wood or to take an armload to the kitchen.

After their lunch, the guards returned to their huts and slept until about 1400 hours when some of them went out on a fish-catching detail. Cheeta came down to the cage, greeting me with a stained-toothed smile and asking what I thought of the "*lao dong*"—the labor. I replied, truthfully, that it had been more enjoyable than sitting in a cage all day as I had done in the mangroves.

After a few minutes of idle comments, he drew a well-creased spelling tablet from his pocket and placed it in front of his feet as he rolled a ridiculously slim cigarette, using more paper than tobacco. He lit it and picked up the tablet, leafing through until he reached the desired page. Seeing me watching the pages, he turned the open tablet toward me, asking if I could read what was written. The page was decorated with freehand, sloppy semi-gothic lettering that included several sizes of letters in one word. The text of what was written, however, was in precise, clear script that indicated much practice. I told him that I couldn't read it, but it certainly was beautiful handwriting. He swelled noticeably and proudly told me that he had done all of it himself.

He began reading from the page, pausing after every sentence to explain for me, asking if I understood what he was saying. It was, verbatim, the same thing Base had given me last night: the beginning of a three-week course in the justification of a revolution and condemnation of those who oppose it.

In the atmosphere of the camp, free of the unknown retaliation and punishment I had dreaded, responding to the "eat together, work together, study together" attitude of the guards, I discovered myself more responsive to the lessons than ever before. Had I been ostracized and punished immediately, I would have closed down completely, but the unexpected turn of events caught me unprepared. It was a feeling of association, not mattering with whom.

Either Cheeta, Showboat, Pock, or Chinh conducted the classes. Porky kept to himself most of the time, joining in the work details but avoiding the gatherings of the guards unless it was a class or scheduled discussion. At night, he would lie in his net with a NLF newspaper, reading by the light of a kerosene lamp and singing the words in a frail, high-pitched voice.

Base tried to join in all group activities, but it seemed that he was more of an outcast than I was. The other guards joked about his lack of coordination and frequent blunders in performing the easiest of tasks. I began to feel sorry for him because he was trying so hard to gain acceptance within the group, but always managed to foul something up just in time to be noticed by one of the sharper members. He wasn't allowed to give me any of the classes, but every evening, when the other guards were relaxing after supper, he would walk over to my cage. Under one pretense or another, he would begin a conversation and inevitably lead into a lecture, repeating what I had heard that morning, but presenting it as if he were the instructor and I were hearing it for the first time. He was so intent on displaying his knowledge and asserting himself, if only to a POW, that it was pathetic.

At the end of April 1965, I was having a severe problem with the *lac* fungus infection. I found myself perspiring heavily during the morning hours, which aided in lowering the salt level in my body but irritated the splotched raised areas of fungus terrifically. The itching sensation was deep and continuous over the broad area covered by the abominable disease. Bathing was difficult because the canal was practically dry and I had to dig a hole in the middle of it in order to get enough murky water to rinse off. Even if I had had soap, it wouldn't have done any good, since the water did nothing more than replace dried perspiration with a light coating of silt. The diarrhea had slacked off a bit, but maintained a two-to-three-time-per-day regularity. Nevertheless, I was deeply tanned on the patches of skin not ravaged by the fungus and felt as if I could continue for several months at this pace before my system collapsed.

I had been sitting and listening to the lessons for about three weeks, paying attention as never before and becoming acutely aware of the structure of the revolutionary rhetoric. There were facts scattered throughout a tangle of distortions, bolstered with half-truths and a controlling Marxist dialectic. There was no allowance for questioning or contradiction within the instructional technique. I noticed with the guards in their classes, it appeared to be a case of not needing to understand, just memorize, repeat, and believe.

In one of Showboat's presentations on the utopian society created in North Vietnam after the Communist takeover, referred to as the "Socialist reconstruction" since the cadre stringently avoided any reference to "Communism" or "Communist" as a description, I asked why, if it were such a desirable en-

173

vironment, did nearly one million Vietnamese people flee to the "oppression in the South of Vietnam"? I went further to include world Communism, asking why there were refugees fleeing the "utopian societies" created when the Communists took over a country, many of them risking their lives to escape. Why, if the United States was suffering under such cruel oppression, didn't refugees flee from our shores to the more desirable Socialist countries? He was at a total loss, never having considered the question. He left that afternoon, a disturbed young man. "Sun Hat," the cadre, was unable to answer and the question must have gone up the line to whatever command political level could deal with this "reactionary" query.

Within a week, Sun Hat, Showboat and Cheeta came to the cage with the answer. "The exploiting classes within a country which had undergone Socialist reconstruction were threatened by the anger of the freed working class. Those who flee a Socialist country are the capitalists and exploiters, running to escape death at the hands of the people." I thought of the U.S., and how many of us "capitalists" would have to flee should there be a successful Communist revolution in America. I wondered where there would be to go if the U.S. should ever fall.

The guards went through a two-day session, taught by Sun Hat, to correct and align their thinking on this question, assuring that the answer from the political cadre was thoroughly accepted. I learned that there could be no questioning of the party line.

At the end of April Showboat appeared one afternoon with several sheets of lined paper and a new ball-point pen. I was told that I could now write what I had learned from my lessons in this camp in order to "display" my progress. I realized that this was another case of written acceptance or rejection of the same ideas that had been put forth by Plato, and then Mr. Hai. I was hesitant to refuse because of the trauma that accompanied a refusal, remembering the mental anguish which had come with each such decision. My mind was already slipping back to the previous incidents, re-creating vividly the fear I had felt. My hands were sweating and I suddenly felt very sick to my stomach.

He left the paper and pen, saying he'd be back to pick them up when I finished. That evening, I was given a cup of sweet soup which didn't taste so delicious as it had once, even though

174

it was the first time in months I'd had it. This time, I realized why I had been given the treat and it wasn't because the guards were in a benevolent mood. "Every action has its reason or purpose," as Mr. Ba had once told me.

I took a day to make my decision, fighting the urge to give in and quit resisting this system which controlled my physical environment and could inflict such mental pressure. It was a combination, I think, of pride, remaining sense of duty, and devotion to what I believed to be right that made me write only that I had been given the opportunity to live in close contact with my guards and had learned valuable lessons from them. I stressed the viewpoint I had gotten from working with the guards and being treated as an individual, allowing me to regain some of the respect for my own abilities and intellect which are denied to the average POW in a stagnant situation such as had existed in the mangroves.

I noted that the guards represented a small cross section of the Liberation Armed Forces and I had learned that the individuals within an organization reflected not only their basic traits, but also the instilled characteristics from the organization. I admitted that the guards had been fair in their treatment of me, much fairer than I had expected, and through this, had provided me with a new evaluation of the revolution. I refrained from stating that I attributed the more charitable and sincere traits to the individual and his upbringing, with credit to his family, rather than to the system which used him to fulfill a political mission. It was a weak effort to put at least something on the paper and, perhaps, keep them off my back for a couple of days. The thought of escape was again growing strong in my mind.

The paper was picked up and within a couple of days I knew the reaction from the cadre who had evaluated it. Those two days had been forty-eight hours long. I counted every hour as I sat in the cage, uncalled upon for the firewood details or for classes, assuming the worst was coming.

It began with the "Nightmare Alice" walks away from camp. There had been air activity to our south with AD–6 dive-bombers hitting targets quite a distance from us. They had drawn little or no concern from the guards, but the third day after the paper was submitted I was taken out of camp on an "air raid drill." The guards, in the event of an airstrike or threatened airstrike on the camp, would walk five hundred to a thousand meters from the camp into an area which offered no targets, and sit until the threat passed or the attack was over. They would then return to the camp. I was taken, on the first day, a distance from camp by Cheeta and Chinh. I accepted it as part of the precautions against airstrikes as they had said, but found the walking extremely difficult as we traversed large areas covered with the sharp stubs of reeds which had been cut close to the ground. It was like walking on a carpet of broken bottles since most of the reeds had been cut with a downward slash of the knife and had hardened enough not to break easily when stepped on. The guards, their feet toughened from years of going barefoot and experienced in walking this type of terrain, traveled rapidly. I found myself stumbling and half running to maintain their pace, unable to avoid the treacherous reed stumps. I asked several times for a slower pace, which was denied because of the need to get a sufficient distance from camp.

We rested some five hundred meters from camp, and I examined the cuts which had been opened on the bottoms of my feet. They weren't too bad, but bad enough to make me dread the walk back. That night, after our return, I had an extremely painful pair of feet and was happy the walk was over.

The next morning, after an early breakfast of rice and *nuoc mam*, Porky and Showboat came by the hut and told me that we were going out again. This continued for four days. I'm not certain if the real reason was to protect me against airstrikes, but the fourth trip, with all the guards going, took me to the west camp, beyond the No-K Corral where Dan, John and Dave were also taken by their guards. I was hobbling, the bottoms of my feet reduced to pieces of bloody hamburger. I had torn strips of bark from the trees near my cage and tried to make sandals, tying the strips to my feet with lengths of vine, but without too much success. The agonizing stinging pain caused by walking wasn't eased at all and all I could hope was to keep dirt and debris out of the cuts. I had broken a pole near my cage to use as a walking stick and I can imagine the picture I must have presented, with my ragged black pajamas, growth of beard and fungus-eaten skin, hobbling along, leaning heavily on my stick. Hardly the same athletic, 165-pound first lieutenant who had been captured in 1963, less than two years before.

My thoughts for escape were demolished by the air raid drills. It was a chore to walk from my cage to the new kitchen, which had been built by the guard hut, some twenty meters away. The healing was slow and it was weeks before I could walk at more than a shuffle without wincing.

The biggest change was the food. My "ration" became the familiar two plates of rice per day, but *nuoc mam* became scarce and fish even scarcer. The diet was reduced to one angel-fish-sized "*ca sac*" per meal, the little fellow looking more like they should have left him in a fish bowl. When there was no *ca sac*, I received a handful of rock salt to go with the rice. Eating became more and more difficult as the work details were stopped and I had to sit in the cage during the day. My appetite dropped immediately. I couldn't allow myself to become weakened to a helpless state as Dan had been. Here there were no other Americans to help me, and if I had to depend on the guards, my chances of survival would be nil.

On 13 May, the whole camp went into action. One of the guards from the Corral came down just before breakfast and held a hurried conference with Sun Hat, who left at a dead run for the other camp. The other guards in the camp here, chattering among themselves, went quickly to their hut and got weapons and ammunition. Sun Hat returned and the guards gathered for a briefing. I strained to catch what was being said, failing to hear. Within half an hour, my guards, with the exception of Base, had left in groups of two, heading to the east.

There was a river or large canal to our east, we had discovered after moving to the Corral in January. Motorboat traffic was clearly discernible during the night and early morning, indicating a major waterway.

For the next two days there was a constant flow of guards through the camp, those coming back, tired and wet from walking through reeds and the forest, and rested groups going out. It seemed as if several camps of guards had been mobilized as I saw faces that I had put out of mind. The question asked of the returnees was always "*Gap chua*?" and the answer "*Chua*."—Have you found yet? Not yet. I wondered, "Found what?"

On the fifteenth, my answer came when one group of exhausted guards returning replied "*Gap roi!*" Whatever they had been looking for was found. There was little rejoicing because the guards were so tired and I discovered the next morning what the object of the search had been.

A bedraggled, weary, but still defiant Dave was brought into camp, arms bound, escorted by Leo, Sun Hat and Cheeta. The other guards had already gone to work constructing a tiny cage between mine and the kitchen. It was going to be barely long enough, or wide enough, to contain a mosquito net. Another set of leg irons appeared, these with a heavier iron bar and two heavy anklets. I got an opportunity to catch his attention shortly after he arrived and gave him a "What happened?" gesture. He shook his head slowly, closing his eyes for a moment. He had tried to escape from the Corral and after evading for two full days, had been recaptured. I wondered if Dan and John had gone with him and what had happened to them.

The cage was completed rapidly and Dave went in, spending the entire day in irons, and the next two days as well. He refused to eat, his already weakened system revolting after the strength-draining attempt for freedom. Cheeta made it quite clear to me in a short lecture that Dave had committed a serious "crime" against the Front and I was not to try to communicate with him at all. I nodded, wondering how to get a message drop started with him.

On the nineteenth, Dave and I were taken back to the school area where a hastily recalled Mr. Hai, along with the rest of his traveling circus, conducted an inquisition concerning the escape attempt. I was placed in the same decaying hut I'd stayed in during the recent "Revelation" scrape and was ignored except by Major Bay, who came by to restate his admonition to improve my attitude and "progress." Dave had overshadowed my lack of cooperation, pulling their attention to him.

Dave spent long hours in the school hut while Mr. Hai and Major Bay threw question after question at him. "Why did you try to escape? What was your plan of escape? How long had you considered escaping? Who helped you?" There was a strong effort to discover why Dave had attempted to escape when he had been promised release by the Front. It was inconceivable to the cadre that anyone would endanger his life in an escape attempt when he could be released without danger of harm. To not believe the Front's promise of release was almost as severe a "crime" as the physical attempt to gain freedom for oneself.

The second area of great interest was the part played by Dan and John in the attempt. Dave sat there and pulled full responsibility onto himself, denying any assistance from the other two. Mr. Hai refused to believe this, since Dave and John had been assigned one large mosquito net for the two of them. The sleeping John had remained in the net after Dave departed, not giving notice that he was gone until morning, when they got up for breakfast.

This questioning went on for two days and Dave was taken out of the camp, leaving me in my hut. He had been gone not more than fifteen minutes when Dan and John were brought into the camp and placed in the same larger hut Dave had been in.

Mr. Hai confronted them with an accusation of helping Dave to escape and demanded full details of the planning that had gone into it. He was upset that Dave could have gotten out in the first place, and also, that he could have eluded the searchers as long as he did. Dan and John gave nothing during the first interrogation while Mr. Hai dropped false statements, allegedly made by Dave, implicating them. I wrote out a short note, outlining the sessions with Dave and letting them know he had kept them clean as far as being accessories to the escape. The paper I'd scrounged during classes and the first interrogation was coming in handy. On the way by their hut to bathe at the canal, I let Dan see the note as I palmed it. He watched me place it under a log by the canal and later, when he went down for a bath, picked it up. Mr. Hai could rant on because the word was out.

In the next days, he got nowhere with the two of them and they were taken out. I returned to the camp which had now been named the "Salt Mines," joining Dave. The statement made by Mr. Hai (whom we now referred to as "Mafia") about "conditions reflecting your attitude" wasn't an idle threat. The diet, which had consisted primarily of rice and salt after my failure to meet the requirements of "progress," continued, with the scattered meals of singular *ca sac* becoming less frequent. The light work details were reinstated for me, but Dave was kept in the cage. It was not so much the physical labor involved, but the exposure to the broiling midday sun that began to sap my remaining strength. The daily perspiration was a blessing in disguise, however, as I was able to tolerate the high salt content of the meals, needing it to replace what I lost. Dave, on the other hand, was in his net during the day, getting out only to take his rice at mealtime and to go to the latrine. Within a short time, he experienced a total revulsion to salt, but the rice, a monotonous necessity, was too difficult to push down by itself. He began throwing up when he attempted to eat and was soon undergoing extreme physical as well as mental strain.

I had a brief bout with heat exhaustion early in the new schedule, returning to my cage in the middle of the day, perspiring more heavily than usual with accompanying headache, dizziness and blurring vision. The great difference between the deep shadow within the trees and the sun-drenched open patches of reeds was evident as I staggered to my cage, feeling as if I had stepped inside a refrigerator. I lay on the straw mat in my cage, trembling with chills and sudden weakness, knowing what was happening and that it would pass, but still sickened by the fact that I was helpless and alone. It was the first time in this camp that I had been unable to take care of myself and the thought that something worse could happen with equal swiftness made me realize how close death could be—in the case of serious illness, by the time the guards reacted, if they did at all.

Two and a half months of utter desolation and hopelessness followed, knowing that we were slowly starving. The guards no longer mentioned release, a dream both Dave and I still retained. Illness was given minimal attention if at all. When the fungus threatened to cover my face and possibly threaten my eyes, Sun Hat waited almost a week and brought in one of the tiny bottles of "*Ong Gia*" which I used sparingly to push back the infection. This was timed with the onset of the rainy season with its hours-long downpours. The high humidity seemed to increase the activity of the fungus and I knew there would be at least six months of rain. Dave had recurring attacks of salt revulsion which would throw him into violent paroxysms of vomiting or dry heaves.

After the initial deluge of rain, we had a period with bright sunshine and cloudless skies. We had gone through a series of days when the guards had declared that there was no water available for drinking, leaving Dave and me to lick dry and cracking lips with equally parched tongues. I imagined that the reservoir had gone dry and water was quite scarce, leaving the alternative of sharing with the prisoners or stretching it a little further by rationing it only among the guards. Dave and I found ourselves depending on the moisture in the boiled rice for our only input of fluids. One day without water at first, then three the next time. Finally, a four-day stretch with only a couple of jiggers' worth on the second day made dehydration a very real, new threat. I had refused to do any work which would have caused me to perspire, as if I had anything left to perspire with. I could feel the lining of my mouth tightening and drying as the days passed. There wasn't enough saliva to make an attempt to wet my lips worthwhile and I found myself shoving mouthfuls of hot rice down at mealtime to prevent the escaping steam from depriving me of its precious moisture.

The rains came again and I stood out in the wonderful cold wetness, head back, letting the water revitalize my depleted system. As soon as my cup filled with water, I would gulp it down, repeating the process until my stomach was distended and I couldn't force another drop down. Had the rainstorm not come at that particular time, it is entirely possible that both Dave and I would have become dehydrated to a point that our systems would not have been able to recover. After two days of drenching downpours, driven by a ferocity characteristic of midseason storms, the premature rain ceased, the clouds cleared, and the burning dry season sun returned. It was a week or so later that the actual rainy season began. Our need had been answered, but not by the guards.

Airstrikes near the camp forced the guards to move us away during the day several times. Dave and I traveled in the same boat, though forbidden to talk to each other. Once located in a safe area distant from the camp, we were placed on two sections of the flooring from the boat, seated in a patch of reeds facing one another and ordered not to talk. The guards stayed in the boat about five meters from us and slept until time to return.

Dave and I waited until we heard them gently snoring and leaned forward to talk. The first words from each of us were almost identical: "Let's get the fuck out of this shit!"

We both knew that we were becoming too weak to survive much longer and an attempt to escape, no matter what the result, would be better than rotting in the camp. I'd been planning for months, working out all possible contingencies including our physical condition. Dave was a storehouse of information on the terrain since he had covered much of it on his first attempt. I learned that he had eluded the guards for two long days and nights, having them pass within feet of him on several occasions as he lay hidden in the reeds. He had crossed the river, thinking it was a large canal, and continued to the east, trying to reach Soc Trang or nearby outposts since this was the only area he was familiar with in the delta. If only he had known to turn north or south on the river and follow it until he hit one of the cloeer outposts, he might have made good the escape. Instead, he crossed the river and was recaptured by guerrillas in a village on the other side, a bitter disappointment after getting as far as he did.

We spent three hours the first day and a couple of more hours during the second trip out to lay the groundwork for our escape. The guards were in deep slumber most of the time. I sketched the pattern of canals on the piece of flooring with a reed dipped in water. We would leave the camp, proceeding along the small north-south canal behind the camp until we reached the larger east-west canal number twenty. Turning east on it, we would travel in the canal until we reached the river. After that it would be straight south in the river until we came to an outpost or reached the artillery position we had heard to the south. Because we would pick an extremely dark night with rain to cover our departure from camp, we would need the canals for direction. The one-kilometer squares, delineated by the crosshatched canals, were a tangle of reeds, vines, large ferns and groves of trees. It was easy to become disoriented in the forest even during daylight travel.

Back at the camp, I managed to get a couple of messages to Dave, using blood from full mosquitoes for ink, pieces of bark for paper, and a sharpened reed for my pen. The need for some strength motivated both of us to consume all of the *ca mam* given us and request extra rice at each meal. Initially the guards were surprised, but since there was no extra *ca mam* for us and the amount of rice they had left over was sufficient to give us more, there was no undue concern. The biggest problem was slipping the leg irons and avoiding detection once having done so. I tore strips from my rice-sack blanket to make a short rope for linking us once we went into the river, preventing possible separation. I had saved a few dried fish from the noon meals Slim had given me, hiding them in the thatching above my head. When I retrieved the pieces I discovered that the small ants living in the roof had all but devoured them, leaving me with no rations. I decided we could live off the land should we be out for a couple of days. The cattail roots, nipa palms and numerous edible greens that grew away from camp would provide some nourishment and water would be no problem as soon as we got away from the contaminated water standing in the camp area.

By 24 August 1965, we were ready. I had one pair of black pajamas patched so they could be tied at the ankles and used as a flotation support once we entered the river. This would be accomplished by first soaking them in the water, then whipping them over my head, thus inflating the tied legs with air which would act as two floats as I lay between them. Anything of mine that I felt would be of value, I wrapped in my extra shirt, making a head pack which would allow me to keep it above the water as we traveled. I included the small diary I had been keeping on pieces of paper since the days with Plato. I had memorized important dates and events in case the diary should be lost, but wanted to bring it and the information out intact. We waited for a suitable night.

The night of the twenty-seventh was perfect. The rainstorm rolled in from the west at half-hour intervals, each passing downpour lasting about ten minutes. The sound of the wind and beating rain would cover any noise we might make as we made our way out of camp. The guards were all in their hut by the kitchen, the storage hut having collapsed earlier in the month for some unknown reason. That left the path to the canal open. With my last bit of hoarded ink in an old piece of ball-point pen filler, I drew out an escape route leading from this camp past No-K Corral and to the north, as if we were planning to head in that direction, taking an overland route which would parallel the canal. It was detailed enough to look as if it had been made and then revised to make travel easier because of our condition. This I was going to drop in the water near my cage as we left, hoping they would find it and assume it was our route. If they did, it would keep them off of our backs for a couple of more hours.

As we had planned, singing would be our means of communication in the camp. The guards were accustomed to hearing us sing to ourselves during the days and at night as we lay alone in our nets. My signal to Dave would be a bit of "Tonight," from *West Side Story*, indicating I was set to go and was checking to see if he was ready. An affirmative from him, which would come fifteen to twenty minutes after I finished in order to dispel guard suspicion would be "Old Man River." A negative reply for any reason would be "Just One of Those Things." We generally hummed or whistled, and this aided in keeping the guards unaware since no words were used.

That afternoon, after watching the building rainstorms to our west, I whistled "Tonight" as both the opening and closing for fifteen minutes of time-wasting semi-musical endeavor. Dave answered later with "Old Man River" and there was a wild feeling of exultation as I realized we were nearly ready. I could almost taste the first cup of coffee at the outpost as we waited for an American helicopter to pick us up. The thought of freedom was enough to double my strength. I bore no illusions about it being easy; in fact, it was going to be a regular bitch even making it to the river. Nevertheless, the thought of escaping this situation and getting back to Americans made any hardships en route worthwhile.

The storms began just before dark, lashing the trees with a pounding rain and making the guards rush to get us locked up so they could return to the relative comfort of their hut. The mosquitoes were undaunted by the rain and Chinh was slapping furiously as he locked the iron. I prepared my things after he had gone, stuffing brush under my mat, forming a hump which would look like a reclining body to a hurried guard in his midnight check. I sat, waiting for Dave, my heart hammering against my ribs, finding it difficult to breathe except in rapid gulps. The tingling edge of fear was there, like just before a fire fight.

Perhaps an hour later I heard Dave singing, the melody indistinct, but my spirits crashed. It couldn't be anything but a negative. Something had gone wrong. "Just one of those things . . . one of those crazy things," the words drifted to my cage and I sank back on the mat. I realized how keyed-up I'd been when the shivering started in my legs and worked its way up my body until I lay shaking as if I were having a chill.

The next morning as I sloshed past his hut in the calf-deep

water, he held up his leg iron as if examining it. He hadn't been able to slip his irons. I took my rice and sliver of *ca mam*, wishing I weren't here to have to eat it. Back at the cage, I sat pondering the reasons for our not being able to try last night. Perhaps there was a reason for our not going last night, perhaps some guiding power had decided we shouldn't make it, perhaps we were destined to fail. Pessimism flooded my thoughts, driving determination to succeed before it. Then, in a moment of reevaluation, I thought of who and what I was. The importance of never losing my identity in this one-dimensional world of spirit-warping degradation. I was an Officer, a West Pointer. I was a member of the Special Forces, I was an American. I was not geared to die in a forest prison, my body covered with infection, under the control of a group of individuals whose only interst in me was that inspired by their political cadre. If they wanted me dead, they were going to have to put out more effort than merely watching me starve.

I went back over our plan, searching for faults. We had decided not to kill any of the guards in the escape unless it was necessary to save our lives. I remembered reading that POW's in attempting to escape should avoid killing unless absolutely required. I had picked up and hidden one of the long, straight stakes the guards had sharpened a short time before to be used as *punji* stakes. It would serve as a walking stick while we traveled as well as being a spear if I needed it.

The day seemed longer than usual and it was almost time for supper when I heard Dave whistling tunes from *West Side Story*. The third tune was "Tonight!" It was on for tonight! After supper I asked for additional rice, taking it back and wrapping it in a small piece of plastic I'd taken from the kitchen. I hummed "Old Man River," thinking how I wouldn't mind "gettin' a little drunk and landin' in jail" providing it was Jack Daniels and an American jail.

The rain continued from the night before, sporadically through the day, increasing as the night cooled the air. It would be good cover for us again. Base was on guard and almost caught my slipped iron, but the mosquitoes saved me as he took a quick look at the seemingly secure anklet I raised near the net for him to see. Bravado paid off as he grunted and hurried back to his net where he would spend the night, supposedly awake, watching the prisoners.

I was ready and waiting just after dark, the feeling of excitement building. The rain washed over the camp time and time again. It was getting later and Dave hadn't appeared yet. He was to come to my cage and we would leave from it. I found myself dozing, with my mind creating fantasies in which I was carried above the trees and swamp, above the stinging mosquitoes. I was seated in a bucket seat like I'd had in my TR–3 and could watch the treetops gliding below me, all in perfect silence. I awoke with a start, finding myself still in the cage, hating dreams like that because they made this place seem even worse.

It must have been almost midnight when Dave's voice came softly from outside of my net: "Ready, Nicko?" I jumped at the sound, then pulled up the net so he could come in. We checked our gear and then slid into the night.

The rain beat down on us, soaking us before we'd gone ten steps. The paper with the false route was lying on the porch as if I'd dropped it accidentally. I glanced at the guard hut and saw Base in his net, silhouetted by the flickering kerosene flame of his lamp. He was curled up on his side, asleep.

We felt our way along the well-worn rut that marked the path to the canal, depending more on our feet underwater to guide us than trying to see. It took us about ten minutes to cover twenty meters to the reed-lined canal, as any noise now would be the end of the escape. Once in the canal, we moved more rapidly, but found the canal less clearly defined the further we got from camp. Reeds had grown down from the banks, making the canal irregular in shape and blocking our path numerous times. We crossed an intermediate canal which was used as a link between our camp and the Corral, proceeding to canal twenty, which we'd estimated was another two hundred meters or so to the south.

The longer we traveled the more clogged with reeds and floating plants the canal became. The depth, which we'd estimated to be hip-deep at a minimum, became so shallow we thought we were walking in the field. Trees closed in around us and soon we were wondering if we hadn't strayed from the canal at some point, entering the forested fields on the east of it. There was no way to retrace our steps. The night was totally black with overhanging clouds blotting out the stars.

We had decided to keep conversation at a minimum, but

the situation required a decision. Dave suggested heading overland, going what we thought would be due east until we hit a larger north-south canal which we could follow to canal twenty. I considered the extreme difficulty of navigation, but thought if we could maintain a reasonably straight path we would have to hit another canal which couldn't be worse than the one we hoped we were on. We decided to try it and turned left, finding ourselves immediately in a tangle of ferns and reeds. It would have been a task to get through them in daylight and trying it in absolute blackness was a nightmare. We sounded like a herd of elephants as the reeds snapped and broke. I would have sworn that if we'd been able to see we could have taken a five-meter detour and avoided the whole mess.

Once through the tangle, we found ourselves wading through a chest-high patch of tubular grass, so thick that it forced us to fight every step of the way. The water was calf- to knee-deep and posed the least of our problems. The mosquitoes were like a second skin, driving their stingers into every square inch of our bodies. The rain had plastered our thin garments to our bodies and gave us no protection. I was constantly slapping to keep them out of my mouth, nose and eyes; the rest of my frame would have to accept the punishment.

We tried to move faster. Our plan had called for an early start, about 2100 hours, to give us maximum time before daylight when the search would begin; instead, we hadn't gotten away until midnight or shortly before. We had five and half hours before the guards would get up and find us missing. Those three hours we had lost could be crucial.

I began to tire rapidly, feeling the effects of malnutrition robbing me of power in my legs. Dave was slowing considerably, his breath coming in rasping jerks. I asked him if he would be able to make it. "I don't have the strength, but I've got enough determination to get me to that river!" he gasped. "Don't let me stop." He pushed on through the high grass, reeds and clumps of trees, driven by the thought of freedom.

After an hour or so, the rain stopped abruptly and the cloud cover broke slightly, showing brief patches of sky above. It was lighter now because of the stars which speckled the heavens and I could see the swarms of mosquitoes swirling around me. Their humming had been audible even above the sound of the rain and since the rain had stopped their volume had increased tenfold. I paused to slap and flail away with my towel, killing some, but succeeding only in making room for new ones. I was getting numb because of their bites, with the deep chill from the rain and cold wind adding to the feeling of misery.

We had been guiding on trees after the clouds broke, attempting to keep a reasonable straight path. When we came upon a canal at a 30-degree angle instead of hitting it perpendicularly, we didn't know if we had hit a north-south canal or an east-west one. The canal was relatively wide and well used, so we decided it must be east-west since they were main communication routes. The next question was, were we traveling east or west when we came upon it? The canal was on our left and was the first one we'd come to. This meant it must be canal twenty-one and we were heading west. With those assumptions, we turned what we had designated as being east and slipped into the canal, following it until we reached an intersection and heard voices on both sides of us. Guards from another camp were putting out stakeouts to catch fish and would be by here soon. We climbed back into the reeds and paralleled the canal, still moving toward our east.

It began to get lighter, but the cloud cover prevented us from determining which direction was lightest. We moved into the trees and grassland away from the canal to avoid any possibility of contact with the guards who would be searching along the waterways. Our path had taken us across three other canals, but it was difficult to determine what in the hell we'd done because of the clouds which had again blocked out the light from the stars during the night.

I was nearly exhausted; in fact, my strength had gone long ago, but my mind was so tired it couldn't register the fact. I could feel the raised spots all over my body from the mosquito bites. The fungus, irritated by the mosquitoes, added its itching to the already tormented skin. Walking was trying to lift one lead weight after another as my legs felt completely dead and heavy. The water clung like quicksand. I hurt, but I wasn't going to stop.

The sky continued to lighten, bringing the surroundings from the realm of black shapes to gray outlines, then to dim, full-dimensioned trees and brush, and finally the addition of color as morning came. We were traversing another large patch of the grass, with a grove of trees to our left and a closer one to

188

our front. I decided to get a bearing on the sun so we could head due east, putting us much distance as possible between us and the camp before we holed up for the day.

We should have been traveling eastward. Our path for the last forty-five minutes, at least, was in what we thought was east. I climbed a dead tree to see above the other trees, checking for the sunrise that should be ahead of us. The sky was darker in front of me than behind. There was almost a desire to cry as I turned and looked behind me, the way from which we had come, and saw the first spreading rays of sunlight breaking through the clouds on the horizon. We had been traveling to the west.

Worse than that, I saw the distinct path we'd left in the tall grass. It marked our trail just as if we'd left road signs telling the searchers to come this way. We were in a world of hurt right now and it was going to get worse before there was even a chance for it getting better. I slid down the tree, trying to come up with a quick, relatively easy way to foul up the trail we had left. Dave had sensed our problem, but didn't want to admit to himself that we had been traveling to the west.

"Could that be a false sunrise?" he asked in a tired, quiet voice. He was beginning to sag, his initially low strength completely exhausted and the determination which had kept him going now suffering a mortal blow. It had taken one hell of a lot of guts to try a second escape after an unsuccessful first attempt, particularly with a lack of physical conditioning against him. The urge to try to comfort him was strong, to assure him we would still make it, but I wasn't too certain of our chances right now. "We're in a hurt right now, Dave, but we'll screw them up a little, then head due south. There's no telling how far west we are. We could be west of the camp, or parallel with it. Rather than trying to go east, we'll go south, try to get out of the search pattern and look for the river tonight." He nodded listlessly, his face so swollen with the marks of hundreds of mosquito bites that it almost obscured the flickering light of hope in his eyes.

I tramped out several false trails from our main path, terminating each in an area where the grass stopped and we could conceivably have continued without making a distinct trail. It would take them a little while to check these out and, I hoped, throw a touch of confusion into the problem. We then backtracked along our path and about a hundred meters from the false trails we turned to the right, heading due south, making certain to carefully cover the spot at which we turned off and close the grass back over our path as we moved away. That would leave them with a dead-end trail and no indication of where we had gone from the false trails. With luck, they would choose the more likely of the false trails and be searching to the west or northward, while we went south.

I cursed at our slow pace. We couldn't travel faster than a stumbling walk and I could picture the guards, like a bunch of bloodhounds, rapidly sweeping the area, closing on our trail. I hoped they would follow the map. That would occupy them for a few hours. We came to a narrow canal and after observing in either direction, we crossed, wading up to our waists before climbing out on the other side and entering the reeds. I could hear distant sounds of voices.

We had traveled another hour when we heard voices in a boat along the canal we had crossed. They were making no attempt to be quiet and were apparently calling to others who were following our path in the tall grass. They had gotten near us too damn fast. It was going to be hard to shake them if they came this way. I had lost my walking stick-spear sometime during the night and was looking for something to use for a weapon in case we had to clobber one of them. Their high-pitched shouts and chattering sounded like the yelping of hounds on the trail of an animal. I knew what a fox must have felt like in a chase and wished I were as fast as he.

The sound of an oar knocking against the side of a boat came from in front of us. Sound carried in the quiet morning air and whether or not the sound was intentional, it let us know there was someone ahead of us. We decided to push on, getting as far into this block of trees and vegetation as possible, screwing up the trail and then picking a place to hide until the searchers passed. It was certain that if we continued to move, they would spot us. Dave and I were making a false trail to the west, into a clump of trees, when an excited burst of chatter from the canal behind us indicated the discovery of our exit point from the other block and entry into this one. The reeds had been bent as we broke through in leaving the other side and broken again on this side, indicating where we had passed. The guards in the boat were calling to the group following our trail that we had crossed to this side. Soon the voices were coming noticeably closer. They were on our fresh trail.

I couldn't think of anything that would aid us in slipping them now, aside from a tremendous amount of luck. The guards in the boats had traveled along the canals looking for a broken area in the reeds that would indicate someone entering one of the blocks of forest, then they would circle the block to see if they could find more broken reeds indicating the exit point. They would then search for another entrance point and another exit until they came to a block that had been entered, but showed no signs of an exit point. Their quarry would be in that block and the pursuit element, following any fresh trail that had been found, would be called to pick up the new trail at the point of entrance. They were close on our track now and it wouldn't be long before they were in sight.

Dave and I covered the narrow trail we had made into a dense clump of ferns, lying out flat in the water, covered to our necks with our heads pressed in close to the stalks of the ferns. I smeared mud on my face and stuck grass to the mud, breaking up the outline and flesh color. All we could do was wait.

I could hear my heart thumping as the voices came closer. I thought of the movies I'd seen as a young boy about the war in the Pacific and how the hero had always miraculously escaped, no matter what the situation, or how bad the odds. From our viewpoint, we were always the heroes, but what happened in real life? I was hoping we had the hero's luck. I thought of the long grass that had given our trail away and how neither Dave nor I had considered it in our plan. His escape had been during dry season when the grass was withered and brown and he'd followed trails which left the guards with nothing to follow. Rainy season had brought the grass to full growth and the water had concealed the paths. The guards traveled primarily by boat along the canals, so a path through the grass was obviously ours. The decision to leave the canal had been our big screw-up.

Cheeta broke into the patch of grass from the treeline, his Russian burp gun carried in a ready position. Behind him came Yes Yes and Frank Lloyd, moving at a rapid slog through the water and clinging grass. My throat tightened and I didn't dare breathe. More voices from the south! Another group of guards was sweeping in to link up. Their voices were rapid, excited. They were close and they knew it. I wriggled lower in the water, my nose just above the surface, as I saw the first bunch pass within ten meters of us, following the trail. "Please let them follow the path. Please let them keep going." The silent thoughts kept running through my mind.

They reached the trees and stopped. Yes Yes proceeded while Cheeta and Frank Lloyd circled the area this side of the trees, looking for another trail. Yes Yes called that there was no trail and they began to backtrack, searching carefully on both sides of the original trail. My stomach knotted. I wished I could draw myself into a tiny ball and hide in the fern itself. The utter futility of the situation crashed down on me. I was suddenly very tired, very sick.

Leo's voice called to them from my left, not more than twenty meters away. Cheeta answered that they were almost on top of us. He didn't know how right he was. Leo's group moved forward, sweeping through the ferns and grass that branched into our hiding place. I pulled my head back from the ferns and took the diary in its plastic wrapping, pushing it underwater at the base of the fern. The length of knotted cloth went underwater also. There was no reason to let them have any idea of what we had brought with us.

Cheeta shouted in alarm and jumped back, his weapon trained downward. He had almost stepped on Dave. The others rushed over, covering Dave with their weapons. Cheeta was yelling for Dave to stand up slowly. The muzzles of all the weapons were trained on him as he unwillingly got to his feet, his torn clothing looking even more pitiful as it clung to his bony frame, dripping muddy water and slime. Cheeta determined that Dave was unarmed and fired three quick shots in the air, followed by four more. The other searchers would converge on this area if they were nearby.

"Where's Ro?" Cheeta demanded.

Dave shook his head slowly. *"Toi khong hieu,"* he replied in a lifeless voice—I don't understand.

Cheeta began gesturing around the area and yelling, *"Ro dau ai?"* Dave glanced back at me, his hand making a "go away" gesture. He would keep them occupied, giving me a chance to possibly back away and avoid them. The immediate question was, "Can I leave him alone to take the punishment for this?" This was his second unsuccessful attempt and he wouldn't have a chance.

When Dave refused to disclose my location, not more than six feet from him, the guards became angrier and Leo gave a quiet order. The guards with Mossin-Nagant carbines unlocked the folding bayonets on the muzzles and swung them into place. They began to tramp through the ferns, slashing and jabbing the water with the spike bayonets. I was sliding backward through the ferns, moving as quietly as possible, when Sun Hat, whom I hadn't seen or heard, tripped over me as he backed through the dense clump of ferns. Instantly there were muzzles and bayonets all around my face.

I was ordered to my feet and stood beside Dave, my mind numb to what was happening as if it had shut itself down. Leo stood several feet away from us, his face contorted with anger. Cheeta and Frank Lloyd searched us, taking the bundles of items we had wrapped in our extra shirts. Leo kept snapping questions at us in Vietnamese which we ignored, not fully understanding him and not really caring. This seemed to make him angrier and he leveled his burp gun at our stomachs, threatening to shoot. Neither of us knew if he was serious, but Sun Hat and Cheeta instantaneously moved to stop him. He pushed Cheeta back with his free hand, then pulled the bolt back on the weapon. Up to this point I hadn't felt any overwhelming concern, but the burp gun fires from the open-bolt position and will empty its 35-round magazine of ammunition in a matter of seconds. Leo was serious about shooting us. I could feel my stomach tensing, expecting the impact of the slugs.

"Shoot, you little monkey! Go ahead, shoot!" Dave spat out, his voice suddenly vibrant. I could see Leo's muscles tensing in his forearm; everything became slow motion. Sun Hat reached over, very slowly it seemed, and placed his hand over the muzzle of the weapon, pulling it to the side. The other guards stood by watching the action unfold.

Leo barely contained his rage, but allowed the older cadre to pull his weapon away from pointing at us while talking softly and urgently to Sun Hat. The resolute head shake, no, from Sun Hat indicated that whatever Leo wanted was being rejected.

Dave sank to his knees, crippled by the complete letdown caused by our recapture. Leo was immediately shouting for Dave to stand up, once again pointing the weapon at the defenseless prisoner. I squatted beside Dave, putting myself between him and Leo, figuring there would be less chance of him shooting me. Dave was slipping into unconsciousness, his overtaxed system near collapse after the magnificent effort. I lifted his eyelid and saw nothing but the white; he was passing out.

Not knowing what the guards intended, I asked if I could help Dave since he was in serious condition. Leo told me to get away and leave him alone. Cheeta and Frank Lloyd concurred. Sun Hat stepped closer, probably suspecting a trick of some kind, but when he saw Dave's face, ashen under the swelling mosquito bites, he ordered me to get Dave on his feet so we could be marched to a boat. I pushed my towel underwater and squeezed it over Dave's head, mopping his face gently. His eyelids fluttered, but didn't open.

"Can you make it, Dave?" I asked. I was worried that Leo would shoot him if he couldn't walk and I wasn't about to let that happen. I got a mumbled indistinct reply. He was really out. I told Sun Hat and Cheeta that Dave could walk, but I would have to help him. Sun Hat nodded and snapped an instruction to Yes Yes, who pulled my towel from my hand and, after Frank Lloyd had pulled me to my feet, tied my arms at the elbows. The towel ripped. Leo took his towel and tied my elbows tightly. Dave had started to slump over and I bent to catch him. Leo insisted that Dave stand without assistance.

"Dave, get up," I almost begged. He remained leaning against my leg, breathing in shallow gasps. Leo was watching with a triumphant smirk. "Get up, man, they'll do you in if you don't get up." It looked hopeless. I was lost. What in the hell could I do? He wasn't responding at all.

"Sergeant Davila!" I snapped. The guards' expressions were ones of total shock at hearing the sharp command coming from the filthy, tattered figure standing with his arms tied behind his back. "Get on your feet!" Dave drew a shuddering breath. "O Lord, please let him stand up," I prayed.

"Grab my leg and pull yourself up!" His hand moved, grasping my calf weakly and feeling upward for my knee. I bent my knee, giving him a place to hold. "Come on, Dave," I cursed to myself. "Grab on and pull yourself up! I can't help you." My voice sounded harsh even to my ears.

"Don't quit in front of these fuckers. You're better than all of them. Don't give up now!" Dave was on his knees. Deep strain pulled the muscles in his face, and his mouth twisted with the struggle to rise. I bent to the side, lowering my arm for him to grasp. His hand searched until it reached the bend in my arm and locked on.

"Pull up with me!" He responded as I straightened, getting to a crouch before his legs gave way beneath him. The guards stood silent watching this awesome display of human will-power.

We tried again and Dave clung, pulled, and with his face contorted almost beyond recognition, stood upright, leaning heavily. "Damn good, Dave!" I felt like cheering. They never thought he'd make it, but he showed them! Son of a bitch, he showed 'em!

Leo pointed for us to proceed. The walk was a torturous retracing of our steps back to the canal we'd crossed into this block. Dave somehow managed to keep his feet moving, leaning heavily across my shoulders, until we reached the reeds bordering the canal. There whatever source of strength he had called on gave out and he collapsed completely. The guards helped me drag him to the boat and we were taken back into the small canal we had left from. Boatloads of guards were pulled up next to the banks along our route. There were more than I had seen at any one time before. Curious eyes studied Dave and me as our boat glided past.

When we reached the vicinity of the camp, there were more guards along the banks. Dave tried to sit up, suddenly alert again, but lack of strength kept him from rising. We were taken out of the boat and began the short walk back to our cages. The crushing disappointment of having tried and failed was more depressing than anticipation of what lay ahead. I was numb to physical shock now, the mosquitoes, malnutrition and total exhaustion having done their work. The dysentery which had continued throughout my time in the Mines had caused me to stop three times during the night. The few tablets of sulfa-guanidine I received after a week of prolonged runs hadn't even slowed the flow and I had this as added reason for trying to get back to Americans and a hospital. Now we had failed.

Dave managed to stagger to his cage, leaning on my shoulder and grasping handfuls of reeds to pull himself along. Once he reached the miserable structure, he sprawled out on the flooring, lying quite still. Cheeta and Slim pulled me over to my cage where an older man in his late forties stood watching from the small porch as I approached. I crumpled on the poles, my legs completely transformed to rubber and unable to support my weight. *"Sao anh di tron?"* he asked indifferently—Why did you try to escape? I didn't answer immediately. He continued, "Did you think you could successfully escape?" I sat up and faced him.

"Chung toi o day sap chet doi," I began, slowly, seriously—We were about to starve here—then went on, "Escape was our only chance of living because to stay here meant to die. You cannot expect a man to surrender his life without a struggle and the conditions in this camp forced us to attempt to gain our freedom."

He was listening more intently as I spoke, catching the words for starvation and the idea that the conditions forced us to try to escape. "Do you know that the people would have killed you if they had caught you?" he asked.

I thought for a moment and the reply was evident: "Would it not be better to die while attempting to regain one's freedom than to lie quietly and rot of disease and starvation? Would a soldier of the Liberation Army give up his life without fighting to keep it?" He sat quietly, looking at me, and then stood and walked away, splashing through the calf-deep water to the guard hut.

I looked around and immediately saw Base standing in the trees, away from the others, glaring at me, his eyes filled with the hatred of one who feels he has been betrayed. I realized then that Base, in talking with me over the weeks, had come to rely on me as a neutral element in his own hostile environment. The guards in the other camp would chase him with sticks when he made infrequent trips to pick up rice from their main supply. He had found that an American prisoner was his one means of establishing his status as a guard or as an individual, and last night he had been on guard, responsible for security of the camp, and had fallen asleep. The Americans had escaped and the security of the entire area was threatened. I had betrayed him by taking advantage of his laxity. As far as his shattered ego was concerned, it had been a direct effort to disgrace him. The punishment for sleeping on guard duty is as severe in the Liberation Army as in ours, and Base was subject to whatever disciplinary action the cadre determined suitable, including death.

Chinh and Slim arrived shortly after the cadre left, carrying a plate of rice and a large serving of mushy *ca mam*, and another set of leg irons. Chinh set the plate down on the poles and told me to eat quickly. His normally placid face was stern. The cadre had told them to give Dave and me some rice immediately. Slim stood by, holding the long iron rod and two U-shaped anklets, impatiently waiting as I shoveled down the putrid-tasting mess, my stomach almost revolting as the first mouthful slammed in unannounced. I was so hungry that I didn't care what it tasted like.

When I finished, the guards ordered me to get in my cage and prepare my mosquito net. My mat and net, which I'd left behind, had been exchanged for an older, patched net and partially unraveled straw mat. I was conscious of the exchange, but didn't really care at the moment. Once my net was up and I was inside, my legs were thrust into the regular iron I'd been using. Then Slim grabbed my arms and, fitting the U-shaped pieces over my biceps, ran the long bar under my back, through the loops in the anklets, fastening my arms to my sides. I watched with a detached interest as he proceeded to pull the bar up under my shoulder blades, canting the anklets back at a 45-degree angle and fastening the two ends of the rod, making it impossible for me to do any more than bend my arms at the elbows. The leg iron was pulled downward until I winced with pain.

"Dau, khong?" he asked without emotion—Is there pain? I nodded, yes. He grunted and gave it an extra tug, sending spikes of pain into my already cramping muscles.

It was already late afternoon, and after locking me up, the guards returned to their hut for a conference. I heard them talking in low tones for hours, continuing into the night. Dave was silent and I couldn't move to see his cage. I hoped he was all right. Complete physical exhaustion overcame the discomfort of my position and I fell into a deep sleep. Sometime that night I dreamed that Dave and I were on the way to freedom. We had hidden in the cramped space between decks of a Vietnamese boat and were waiting only until the boat docked at Camau, when we would abandon the painful traveling position and go directly to the MAAG detachment. The thrill of being

197

so near freedom was fresh in my mind when I awoke.

The horror of waking up in irons was magnified by the taste of freedom from my dream. My muscles were cramped and aching fiercely, particularly my neck muscles which were bunched from the unnatural position forced by the arm irons. There was no way to relieve the cramps, and twisting within the restriction of the irons only made them worse. I had to crap and waited for the guard to release me as they normally did before breakfast. I wished he'd hurry; I didn't want to call out, asking permission. It seemed best to stay as much out of their attention as possible. The pressure of the gas built up rapidly, causing my already tender and inflamed intestines to feel as if they'd burst. I locked the cheeks of my ass together, trying to block the liquid excrement. I wasn't going to be able to hold it.

"Thua Anh Giai Phong," I called, *"cho toi xin phep di cao?"* The required format for asking permission from a guard, "Please Mr. Liberation, may I request permission to go crap?" There was no answer from the guard hut. I repeated the request a little louder. I wouldn't be able to make it to the latrine even if he did come now, but I might get clear of the cage.

I heard Cheeta's voice: *"Di cao di!"*—Go ahead and crap!

I called out, saying I couldn't move because of the irons. There was silence once again from the guard hut. I turned my head wildly from side to side, wondering what in the hell I could do. Then came the creeping warm flush of shame and revulsion as the hot, stinking mass burst out, spreading in my trousers and on the mat. The times in the past that the diarrhea had caught me before I reached a latrine prepared me for the physical shock of crapping all over myself, but then I'd always been able to attempt to clean myself up. I was immediately wondering how I'd get this mess cleaned up, never thinking that Cheeta might have been stating the policy for the days to come.

By the time Chinh arrived with my pan of rice, the particularly revolting stench of bacteria-filled feces had permeated the net and he almost gagged as he unfastened the arm irons so I could eat. I asked if I could clean up the cage before eating. Chinh shook his head, no; I wasn't to be allowed out of irons except to eat two meals a day which the Front would give me. He left the plate of rice and retreated to the guard hut, where an excited discussion erupted. Chinh seemed to be urging that I be allowed to go crap when necessary. Cheeta argued that the instructions didn't provide for that. Slim and Sun Hat argued that feeding me was enough.

I leaned as far out of the net as I could, eating the still-hot rice, happy that there was no *ca mam*. I couldn't have taken it along with the rotten odor that surrounded me. I took the minutes of release to revolve my neck, easing the taut muscles, and to work out the cramps in my legs that had knotted up like ropes. Chinh came to get the plate, giving me a sip of water that barely covered the bottom of the cup. Then I allowed him to put the irons back on, something that was to be endured since there was no way for me to effectively resist at this time. I had failed and would have to take whatever came, keeping my eyes and mind fastened on the next time, whenever it might be. The most important thing was to continue to eat, no matter what the conditions. Rice was the key to survival.

After he had gone, I remembered that I hadn't checked Dave's cage out. I had heard him talking to Chinh, but couldn't make out the words. He was more weakened by the escape attempt than I was and could be in bad shape if they kept this up for very long.

That day I lay with my thoughts. No one came near the cage during the afternoon and my anxiety began to mount. Would they refrain from shooting us when we were recaptured only to starve us in this type of punishment? Was it a temporary punishment while the higher cadre made a decision whether or not we were to live? I knew that the guards weren't doing anything more than they had been told to do. They might add a little harassment, but there would be no leniency from them unless some cadre ordered it. The bit about not being allowed to go crap was obviously not considered when the cadre had told them I was to be in irons except for eating. Chinh had proposed a solution which was, to me, logical, but strict interpretation of instructions had blocked the idea.

Supper that night was another pan of rice, a smaller amount than I normally ate, topped with a few chunks of rock salt. I was so thirsty that I avoided the salt. Two more crap runs during the day thoroughly saturated the sleeping mat, making the whole area totally repulsive. After forcing myself to ignore the foulness and eat the pan of rice, I scooted my ass near the bars and splashed water, which was at a level just below the floor, up with my hand, trying to clean off. I managed to thoroughly inundate the mat, net and myself before Chinh came back to lock me up again. I was wet, but a little cleaner. I had dozed during the afternoon, allowing my system to relax and regroup, so I wasn't immediately sleepy that night. There had been no water with the meal and my thirst grew all out of proportion as I concentrated on it. The mental picture of a tall glass of iced tea, frosted, with droplets of water trailing down the sides became fiendish torture as I allowed myself to want it, realizing there was no earthly way for me to get it. In a matter of minutes, I had intensified my thirst to the point that I was ready to cry out. It was past midnight when I finally dropped off into a disturbed sleep, the pounding of rain on the thatched roof my only calming factor.

The next morning I got a glance at Dave's cage, seeing only his mosquito net, white against the darker background of the bars and surrounding trees. I wondered how he was doing, wishing there was something I could do to help. The VC dealt with prisoners on an individual basis, trying to break down any unity that might develop. The concept of each prisoner fighting for his individual survival and completely dependent upon his captors for basic necessities was their ideal situation.

Back in the Corral I had composed a letter to the International Red Cross, giving our names, ranks and dates of capture as well as synopses of our health. I requested food and medication recommended by Dan, and signed the letter "Senior American POW."

In one of the encounters with Mafia at the school area, he had lashed out at me because of the letter, claiming I had criticized and condemned the Front. I learned then how far letters got. "Who elected you the 'Senior American POW'?" I answered that we were still members of the U.S. Army and I was the highest-ranking POW; therefore I bore the responsibility to the men under me to see to their well-being. Within the limitations placed on us, I would strive to obtain that which we needed to survive.

Mafia's reply was a classic: "You are a prisoner. You are no longer a soldier. Each prisoner should be responsible for himself to the Front. You must no longer feel responsible to your government which has sent you to die in Vietnam. You

200

are not a 'Senior American POW,' you are another prisoner just like the others because there is no rank among prisoners." He stressed the "democratic structure" of the prison camp and its "equality," which if accepted by the POW's would create a breakdown in the establishment of a chain of command and reduce the men to individual, and sometime isolated, struggle against their captors.

The strength gained from a unified struggle was never more apparent than in a prison camp. American POW's during the Second World War were noted for their unending resistance and harassment of their captors. The Americans' unique sense of humor, when supported by a feeling of unity, brought them through great hardship. Korea brought the first cases of POW breakdown and, accompanying that, the highest death rate of American POW's since the Civil War. In this situation, the VC were exploiting the weaknesses of individuals who are unsure of many things except their desire to remain alive. In depriving them of any interrelationship or interdependence, the cadre could work on individual anxieties and attack the loyalties which the man had formed under different circumstances. Over a period of time, loyalties, if not deeply rooted and well formed, can be eroded. Without unity, there is no method of maintaining the validity of one's beliefs while the cadre works to destroy them.

In the afternoon, Cheeta came down and squatted on the porch, well away from the smell. I was asked if I knew why the Front was forced to punish me. I replied that I had tried to escape and had been recaptured. Cheeta shook his head violently. *"Khong!"* I was being punished because I had foolishly endangered my life as well as the lives of the guards who had gone to search for me. I was confused. He said that the Vietnamese people would surely have killed me had I come in contact with them. I thought back to Plato and the wrong-way *punji* pits. Cheeta went on to say that the guards had taken great risks in searching for me and only their desire for my safety had caused them to take such risks. I was shocked. How dumb did he think I was? Leo certainly hadn't been too concerned with our safety when he had leveled his burp gun at us and Cheeta had been standing right there. Obviously, whoever wrote out this script for him hadn't been aware of the incident.

I was told that the Front felt it necessary to strongly impress

201

upon me the crime I had committed against myself and the Front so I could criticize my actions and correct my thinking. Cheeta then went into a series of questions which assumed that Dave had planned the entire escape. Cheeta offered me the chance to absolve myself of guilt, since the Front knew "Vila" had planned the escape. Dave's second escape attempt had, without a doubt, put him high on the VC shit list and they were going to cement the allegation if they could. I told Cheeta that they were incorrect. The escape had been my idea since I was sick and starving in the camp, knowing I would die if I stayed. Because I was an officer, I had ordered Dave to go, telling him I couldn't make it alone. Cheeta was furious, snapping at me that the Front already knew that it was Dave's plan and I had just gone with him. I began to think that perhaps Dave had told them it was his idea in order to pull the heat off of me as he had done with John and Dan. It would have been like him. If so, Charlie was going to wind up with two guilty parties.

I stayed with my story, telling Cheeta that only because the conditions here were causing us to die slowly did we risk death at the hands of the civilians. He didn't like the line of reasoning, but continued with the next part of his speech. If I repented of my crime and promised that I would never try to escape again, the Front could be lenient with me. I thought of the time in the fourth grade when I had been caught taking marbles out of a fishbowl in the classroom so I could play marbles at recess. My hand had been slapped, I was told to put them back, apologize, and say that I wouldn't do it again. This was a ludicrous analogy, but the idea seemed the same. I told him I was sorry I had tried it the way I did, thinking more that I was sorry that we were recaptured, but I couldn't promise him I wouldn't try it again because I'd rather die trying to regain my freedom than starve in a prison camp.

Cheeta seemed astonished that I felt I had been starving and assured me the Front would see to my material needs even though I had been a bad prisoner. He repeated the terms of his bargain: repent, say you'll never do it again, and we'll ease up. I felt an urge to crap and punctuated my negative reply with an odious passage of gas and excrement. Cheeta straightened immediately and splashed back to the guard hut.

I lay there the rest of the afternoon, wishing someone would come by to talk with me, even if it were Cheeta. I had passed the point of being able to ignore the filth in which I was lying and found the constant restriction of my entire body a psychological problem as cramping, unrelieved muscles forced my mind to seek a means of avoiding the increasing pain. I had recited the names of the fifty states over and over, had tried to remember the names of the state capitals, and spent several hours singing songs from old movies and Broadway productions. I recalled the first eighteen lines of the prologue to Chaucer's *Canterbury Tales*, in Middle English just as I had memorized them in an English IV literature class in high school: "When that Aprille with his shoures sote. . . ."

Even so, I thought about the knotted muscles, and they hurt worse therefore. I had developed a headache from the unnatural position of my neck caused by the arm irons and the initial annoyance had grown into the full-scale torment that only a bad headache brings. I was filthy and stinking and I hurt. More than that, there was nothing I could do to change it. I thought of an aspirin; how I wanted one aspirin! I thought of water and how much I wanted a taste of cool, clean water. I thought of how different all of this would be if Dave and I had escaped and felt myself biting my lip to keep from crying out. It was only the second day and I felt like calling for Cheeta to come back so I could promise him I wouldn't try to escape again and please take these damn irons off and let me get clean, let me have some water.

The afternoon dragged on. I was almost at the end of my endurance. I could feel every separate pain in my body intensified by my awareness of its existence. I could feel my mind reaching out to the momentary blessed relief that would come when the guard unlocked my arms for supper, but it was so long before he'd come, so long.

Splashing from beside the hut caused me to turn my head in time to see Base step up on the porch, wearing a pair of black shorts and torn black shirt with one sleeve missing. His face was expressionless as he squatted at the edge of the porch, staring at me as I lay restrained in my own filth. His eyes were cold, without emotion, but a tiny smile began to play at the corners of his mouth as he surveyed my punishment. I wondered if he would say something so I could determine what he was thinking, but he remained silent. I stared back at him for a moment, trying not to show the extent to which this was affecting me, then looked up at the top of the mosquito net, trying to ignore him. I found it impossible and spent several minutes of confusion until I realized that he was probably getting some sort of perverse pleasure out of seeing me in this situation. I felt a stirring of ego or pride which refused to allow me to submit to this inspection without some show of defiance, some evidence that I was as strong in my resistance as they were in their pressure. I couldn't think of anything I could say which would be effective. I'd look like an ass if he refused to answer. I could feel his gaze and his revulsion at the sight in front of him. Then, almost as a reflex action, without thinking, I turned my head toward him and smiled. It was unexpected even for me. The expression on Base's face was one of un-guarded surprise. I felt the smile spreading, my cheeks begin-ning to crinkle, the anguish wiped out in the joy of a real smile.

Base regained his deadpan expression and stood up, looking back at me with a quizzical glance as he stepped off the porch and sloshed away through the water. I felt like chuckling. Suddenly the headache and the pains weren't so bad, and the sense of a victory, no matter how small, was sweet to taste. By the time supper came, I was ready to do what I could to clean up, make the situation a little more bearable, and hang with it a little longer.

The "corrective action" went on for six days. On the fourth day, Cheeta having gotten no promise from me about not trying to escape again, there was no change. The cadre had apparently felt that total restriction, straight rice diet and little or no water would achieve the desired results. The daily lecture from Cheeta reiterated his initial points.

While relocking the arm irons on that morning, Slim had checked the tautness of my restrictive clamps, pulling down on the leg irons until the rough-surfaced ankle bar cut into flesh and I winced. The iron bar under my shoulder blades was fastened securely and I felt myself being stretched even more cruelly between the two rods. My arms were being pulled back and downward while my feet and legs were stretched in the opposite direction. It was like being on a rack. *"Dau, khong?"* Slim asked. I couldn't answer as I tried to arch and pull a little slack without success. All I did was tear two raw spots above my arches as the iron rubbed sharply.

"Thau Anh Giai Phong," I said as levelly as possible, *"toi co dau nhieu."*—I have a lot of pain.

He looked at me a moment, then grunted, *"Ua,"* and splashed back to the guard hut. The new tension on my already strained and cramping muscles was unbearable. The guards needed something to report to the cadre, and were probably using this as a means of persuasion without going into "physical torture" which their policy forbade. It was true, no one had come down and physically tortured me in the sense of beatings or ripping my nails from my fingers, but who the hell needed to? They could sit in their hut, relaxing, and let the restraints do their work.

I was hurting now as I never thought possible. My neck muscles were jammed by the hunched shoulder position the irons forced me into by pulling upward at the biceps, close to my sides. At the other end, my legs felt hyperextended, as if my kneecaps would pull apart. If it hadn't been for Base, I would have promised Cheeta that I wouldn't try to escape again. I was already a liar with the declaration, so one more wouldn't hurt; in fact, I'd feel much better afterward, particularly after they took these irons off. The incident with Base, however, had awakened a wild desire to hold out.

The night after the leg irons had been extended, I had tried to sleep, but found it virtually impossible with the splitting headache and cramps from shoulders to calves. It was already dark when I felt more than saw someone step up on the porch. The guards were in their hut, reading aloud and singing. I couldn't tell who it was and watched as the figure stepped up close to the bars, peering down at me, silhouetted by the small kerosene lamp burning by the foot of the cage. The face was indistinct, but I got a crawling sensation up my spine when I recognized the slouching posture as Base's. He stood watching me for several minutes, not speaking. I was never so conscious of my helplessness as at that time. The sharp tingling sensation of fear burst in the middle of my back, spreading its waves throughout my body.

He remained motionless for some time, then stepped quickly to the small opening that served as a door and slid inside the cage between the net and the bars. I had no time to think as he lifted the net from under the mat and kicked viciously. The first contact was at the base of my ribs. Pain shot through my

205

stomach, my head slammed back into the mat. The second kick was higher on the rib cage, bringing another lancing pain. My eyes were closed in agony as I tensed for the third kick, but it never came. I felt the porch shake gently as he stepped off, disappearing into the night.

I lay panting, with the sharp pain rocketing through my stomach and chest, wondering what that had been all about. I thought about calling the guards and telling them what had happened. That was out because they would side with Base and most important, this was between Base and me now. One day, someday, things would be evened up and Base could take me on then. I'd look forward to it.

The next day I decided enough was enough and told Cheeta that if it meant both Dave and I would be given lenient treatment, I'd promise not to try to escape again. He received this pronouncement calmly and told me to wait for a minute. I thought, "Well, since I don't have anything special to do right now, I guess I could spare a minute of my otherwise busy time."

I heard a rapid exchange in the guard hut between Cheeta, Chinh and Sun Hat. Moments later all three appeared with a piece of paper and ball-point pen. I was told to write, date, and sign my repentance and promise, which I did. They took the paper and Chinh left the camp, shouting at Sun Hat that he'd be back soon. I hoped he would hurry.

That evening I received a half-full cup of water with my rice and spent more time savoring the clear, sweet-tasting rainwater than scooping the rice down my throat. The irons were moved closer together that night, giving me a greater degree of movement and, particularly, relaxing my neck. The relief from the total agony made partial agony seem like a blessing. I fell asleep.

At noon the next day, Chinh and Cheeta came to the hut and removed the irons, telling me to go and bathe. Chinh handed me a piece of soap and a new towel. I got a sudden catch in my throat and turned away, ashamed at the urge to cry. The relief was so beautiful and now soap and a new towel! I found it difficult to walk because of my stiffened legs and had to cling to branches as I hobbled to a clear spot of water near the cage.

I looked toward Dave's cage and saw him sitting by the

door. He was a skeleton. His shoulder bones protruded from taut flesh and the rib cage was clearly defined, each rib looking as if it were bare bone. I glanced at my own body, seeing where the reduced diet had cut muscle away, but the presence of beri-beri, which I'd picked up again earlier in the month, masked much of the loss with fluid buildup. I was weak, but I was in much better shape than Dave. The escape had really pushed him to the limit, but if anyone could come through it would be him. His system must have been made of cast iron; he kept going where an average man would have been finished.

The guards were grouped around him and Intern was checking his chest with a stethoscope. It was the first time I'd seen the young medic for about two months.

I washed myself until the soap was gone, never quite getting rid of the odor of excrement, but feeling much better. The mat and net were next for washing and were hung in the weak sunlight to dry. I cleaned out the cage and was beginning to feel human again. My pajamas were dry by suppertime and I brought everything in, arranging the still-damp mat and putting up the net. I sat, waiting for the rice and fighting a renewed hunger.

Porky brought my plate to me, heaped with steaming rice and topped with a large chunk of *ca loc*. I was devouring the meal before he had time to step back off the porch. He stopped a few steps from the hut and turning, asked with a shy smile, *"Ngon, khong, Ro ay?"*—Is it good, Rowe? I looked up, surprised, and nodded vigorous assent. His face broke into a pleased grin and he walked away. It was so much easier when you cooperated a little bit.

The next three days, Dave and I received large helpings of rice and portions of *ca loc* and *ca ro*. I ate each meal as if it were to be my last, stuffing my shrunken stomach to the bursting point, sensing the energy and strength returning. The guards were all quite affable, going out of their way to ask if the food was good and if I had had enough to eat. I decided to try them and asked for more fish. To my amazement, I received a larger second helping than my first. Cheeta and Showboat came by the cage and asked if I would help them with learning English. It was an opportunity to kill time, and to get my hands on a pen and some paper, so I said I would be happy to help. The feeling of pseudo-camaraderie was quickly erasing immediate memories of the preceding days. My mind was quite willing to grasp more pleasant sensations.

On the evening of 7 September, only ten days after we had attempted to escape, Sun Hat told me to prepare to move to the camp with John and Dan. I looked at him, disbelieving what I had heard. Just before dark, Dave and I were taken back to the No-K Corral. I couldn't understand what these people were doing.

Sun Hat led Dave and me over to the hut where Dan and John were already in their mosquito nets. The guards all stood around on the log walk, watching us enter the hut and probably expecting some joyous reunion scene. They must have been disappointed as Dan greeted us with a noncommittal "Welcome back." John was more enthusiastic, but nevertheless somewhat restrained. Dave and I returned the greetings and looked for a place to put our nets. John was in leg irons as a result of Mafia's certainty that John was an accessory to Dave's escape attempt in May. Dan had avoided being placed in irons, perhaps because of his continuing illness.

We learned that the conditions here had dropped off after the school with Mafia and had continued at a low level until Dave had tried to escape. After that they had dropped to abysmal depths.

John, who had been in the net with Dave when he had escaped, had been immediately placed in irons because he hadn't told the guards when Dave left. It was immediately established by the cadre that every prisoner was responsible for the activities of every other prisoner. If one or more escaped, the ones remaining would bear full responsibility whether or not the escapees were recaptured. As I was told soon after my arrival, "It is the duty of each prisoner to inform the guard as soon as he becomes aware of any other prisoner breaking or contemplating breaking any camp regulations." If this had been followed, even in our small group, it would have destroyed any hope for mutual support among the Americans. You wouldn't know who you could trust; therefore, you wouldn't trust anyone. It was fortunate for us that none of us had ever been too good at following instructions.

I noticed a curious anxiety among the guards after 20 September. Something was brewing and none of us could figure it out. We had been involved with two serious illnesses in our group. John went very low with pneumonia, becoming almost totally incapacitated and responding only after Intern was able to obtain penicillin which Dan took responsibility for administering, along with solucamphor, a stimulant. Dave went down with another bout of salt repulsion, and he hadn't yet recovered from the escape attempt. We fought it through with Dave as he began to force rice again, but there was no real relief in the form of direly needed food.

On 25 September the guards brought the radio over to our hut and told us we were to listen to Radio Hanoi. This was unusual and we took it as a sort of treat, since there was some reasonably good music if one listened long enough. The news broadcast was what we were to hear, and other than reports of more victories by the Liberation Armed Forces there was nothing of great importance. We thought we heard a scrap of news as the station was dialed, mentioning a Sergeant somebody who had done something, but the guards missed that part. Afterward, Sun Hat, now renamed "Carpenter," asked me what we'd heard on the news. It had been the English broadcast, making it impossible for the guards to understand; they knew it was coming from Hanoi only because of the place on the dial and the song "*Vietnam muon nam*" which ended the broadcast. I related the little I could remember and he seemed disappointed. He said we would listen again the next day.

On the twenty-sixth, we heard the beginning of the broadcast, catching the phrase "The execution was carried out at ten o'clock," then static and again, "in retaliation for the murder of three patriots in Danang," static, "Captain Humbert Roque Versace," static, "Coraback." I sat stunned, the rest of the broadcast a blur of meaningless sound. Dan stared at the radio, disbelief on his face. John looked at us, his eyes questioning.

Carpenter demanded to know what had been said. The other guards sensed as well as saw our reaction and crowded close to hear my answer. I mumbled that it hadn't been too clear, but there had been an execution. It was difficult to say, because I hadn't really accepted what I'd heard. Carpenter knew that what we were to hear was being broadcast and told us we'd listen again tomorrow. They left, talking excitedly among themselves. The harsh sound of Leo's laughter carried over the top of the other voices.

There was silence in our hut as the realization grew: Rocky

209

was dead. They had executed him, murdered him. It couldn't be! Rocky and death didn't fit. He was too alive, too vibrantly alive to be dead just like that.

John broke the silence. "Was that the Versace that was with you?"

I wanted to say no. Rocky wasn't just with us, he was one of us! Dave looked questioningly at me, his dark eyes serious and concerned. I nodded slowly. "Yeah, that was Rocky." The questions flashed through my mind, seeking a shred of logic in what had happened to him. What did he have to do with Danang? How could he be held responsible for the deaths of three terrorists? Rocky was a prisoner of war, a noncombatant, unable to protect himself, and they had killed him.

Tumbling flashes of thought fragments whirled through my consciouness; Rocky at Tan Phu, the day he got off the chopper, the baseball cap canted to the side of his head, the relaxed, happy grin; then his anguished face right after he'd been hit on the operation, his endurance and spirit under physical and mental stress, his desire only to go back to his family, his faith that remained strong; and the most tragic of all, Rocky, back in the first camp as he looked up with that open, warm smile and said, "Aren't these wonderful people!"

> He stood as others dream to stand;
> He spoke as others dared not even think;
> From soul deep faith, he drew his courage,
> his granite spirit, his ironclad will.

> The Alien force, applied with hate,
> could not break him, failed to bend him;
> Though solitary imprisonment gave him no
>   friends,
> he drew upon his inner self to create a force so
>   strong
> that those who sought to destroy his will, met an
>   army
> his to command.

> Phrases of his I shall not forget,
> spoken sincerely, filled with truth:
>   All I wish is to return to family, home and
>   those I love;

For I am young and life is dear,
but to bargain for this life of mine when the price
     you ask
requires of me to verify a lie
and sell my honor short,
makes clear the choice between the two;
a life with honor, a life without;
With me, you see, life without honor is no life at
    all,
so I will not comply with what you require and
    choose to suffer
whatever may come.
    This is my answer at this time,
this is my answer in times to come;
I only pray that I shall not weaken, for I am right
and with God's help, I will have strength to
    resist whatever means you use
while attempting to fulfill your evil scheme.

    Thus his fate was surely sealed,
for such a man, standing firm
defeated them on their own ground
and for him to live and tell of this
was a thing that could not be.

    I saw him not the day he died,
for, I imagine, as he lived alone,
so they arranged for him to die alone;
But in my mind there is no doubt,
as he stood while he was alive,
Duty bound, Honor bound, Unswerving in
    allegiance,
so he stood the day he died . . . a Rock.

The next day, Carpenter and the guards came early to be
certain we heard the broadcast. Even with the accompanying
static the broadcast was clear enough for us to hear the report
of the executions of Captain Humbert Roque Versace and Sergeant Kenneth M. Coraback, carried out at ten o'clock in the
morning, in retaliation for the execution of three "patriots" in
Danang, by order of the High Command of the Liberation
Armed Forces of South Vietnam. "Coraback" was a mispron-

unciation of Ken Roarback, a member of our Special Forces brother team, who had been captured at Hiep Hoa post less than a month after our capture in 1963. We had lost two friends and two good soldiers. I wondered why they would take a prisoner on the battlefield, grant him his life and demand gratitude for the act, and then take his life from him as a prisoner.

Carpenter hung on every word as I told him we had learned of Rocky's execution. He immediately asked what we thought, the question bursting forth, as if he had been waiting for days to ask. Dan nailed him on the spot by saying we expected the same fate since the Front's policy obviously allowed the murder of prisoners. Carpenter was shaken and retorted that Versace had been a criminal and had been punished for his crimes. I countered that we were equally guilty of the crimes of which Rocky had been accused and therefore could expect the same fate. John winced as he understood what I had said. Carpenter found his question had gotten him in a hole and began to tell us that the Front regarded us not as criminals, but as misguided individuals. He assured us that the Front had no intention of killing us and we should continue to "progress" so we could be released to return to our families. He was smiling, an ingratiating expression that fitted the hollow assurances.

I glanced at Dave, seeing in his eyes the reflection of the last months in the punishment camp, the slow death there, the near quick death in front of Leo's submachine gun, and now this. It was a tightening vise that left a man no place to turn, no hope for maintaining the shreds of individuality, self-esteem, beliefs without paying with your life for that privilege.

The second year ended on 29 October 1965.

5

YES YES, ONE OF THEIR OWN, WAS DISPOSED OF. IN AN encounter with Carpenter and the other guards he had been told to go to market to buy goods for the camp. He protested because it would entail traveling in an area where Government troops were present. The protest became a refusal as he challenged the squad cadre's right to send him into danger. The instructions to purchase items, some of which were to be given to the POW's, became the central point of his argument. If it were only for the guards, he said, he would gladly go, but he wouldn't assume risk for a POW's benefit. Carpenter and Leo were backed by the other guards and it was evident that Yes Yes was being ostracized by the group. He declared suddenly that he was through with the squad and was leaving.

There were immediate warnings for Yes Yes to reconsider, which he ignored. He emerged from the guard hut with his belongings and sleeping mat under his arm, walked past our hut, pausing to glare at us, then proceeded to the canal where the boats were tied up. I heard the oar knocking against the side of the boat as he poled it up the canal to the north.

The loud, frantic discussion in the guard hut after his departure tapered into mutterings as Pock emerged, hurried to the canal and left in another boat, traveling south. The guards continued to discuss the incident until Muoi arrived. He sat in their hut talking with them for almost an hour and departed.

Later that night, Pock returned. The first question was: *"Gap chua? Gap chua?"*—Has he been found yet?"

Pock's answer was tersely worded: *"Nghi lang. Can bo gap roi. No sap chet."*—He was in the village. The cadre have him. He's about to die. There was no escape from the system, particularly for one of them. We never saw Yes Yes again, nor was he ever again mentioned by the guards.

On 9 November 1965, we were moved back to the school area. Our camp was completely dismantled, and John and I carried the precious heavy flooring planks, upon which the guards slept, to the boats. We spent the day dragging and pushing the cumbersome lengths through the water and mud, while the guards watched and played cards, joking as we struggled. Our only laugh, insignificant as it was, came when Cheeta asked me how one said plank in English. Thinking of the unbelievable weight of each plank, I told him, "Lead, Cheeta, pure, solid lead." He spent the rest of the time repeating his new English word to the other guards, telling them, "Son, Ro to car-ri led."

John and I were forced to walk to the camp, while Dan and Dave were allowed to ride in the boats because of their reduced strength. On the walk, I became acutely aware of a muscular strain in my abdomen from trying to carry the heavy planks. The pain, which had been sharp after I attempted to lift two of the planks at one time, became almost unbearable. I cursed my stupidity and began to think seriously of a possible rupture, which would have been disastrous under these conditions. Adding it to the diarrhea, the fungus, the malnutrition and the accompanying mental strain gave me a bleak accounting of my status. John was still recovering from the bout with pneumonia and the fact that we were considered the "healthiest Americans" was evidence of how far we had sunk from the condition in which we'd been when they captured us.

The school area had been completely reworked since we last saw it during Dave's inquisition. The old huts had been torn down and a series of new ones built. We were placed in two separate huts built about five meters apart, close above the water. There were no bars on the walls. Father along the walkway which ran in front of our huts was a third hut, a cage large enough for a mosquito net and a half. There was room for someone else as Dan and I were placed in the middle hut, with Dave and John in the outside hut.

The tall, slender figure of Major Bay approached from the

larger of the two guard huts near the canal. He was almost cordial in his welcome, stating that we were here for an extended series of classes designed to give us a clear picture of the situation in Vietnam so that we might be able to realize our mistakes and thus be released to return home. His quiet, imperturbable manner was effective as he said that he had been delegated by the Central Committee to see to our welfare and to report our progress directly to them.

New towels were given us, as well as soap chunks and bottles of tooth powder. It looked like another buildup period, so we chanced it and asked for new toothbrushes. The ones we had been given were almost ten months old and quite useless. The request was granted, as Major Bay seemed to display a sincere interest in caring for our needs. The gestures weren't registering with me as purely humanitarian. Too much had happened to allow an idealistic appraisal and Plato's words kept coming back, "Every action has its reason or purpose."

One of the first surprises in the camp was haircuts for the Americans. There had been infrequent tonsorial butcherings in the past, administered by the inept novice guard barbers, using a pair of hand clippers and dull scissors. I was treated to a good haircut by Major Bay himself this time and felt much better with the neat cut. He attached a short lecture to the haircut, directing my attention to the fact that a political cadre, of some stature in the Front, was cutting the hair of a POW. This was to indicate the equality that existed among the cadre and guards as well as the treatment afforded a POW in this new camp.

Razor blades, which had been issued before at two-to-four-week intervals, were given to us and we managed to shave after the major portion of the beards had been whacked away by the clippers. Spirits began to rise in proportion to cleanliness, and by that evening, we were feeling semicivilized.

The first few days were devoid of any indoctrination. Major Bay acted like a paternal host, checking at least once a day to see that we had gotten sufficient rice and a portion of fish. The guards went about their camp chores in a constant jovial mood, catching fish, gathering and chopping firewood. Carpenter was squad leader, followed by Cheeta, Showboat, Intern, Clem, Chinh, Pock, "Bunny Boy" and "Bud." Cheeta and Showboat continued their efforts to learn English, having me write English words for them with a phonetic spelling in Vietnamese and a definition. This was written in a copybook and sometimes illustrated by Dan, who had established himself as an artist with the guards. His freehand sketches delighted the guards while providing the Americans with several ball-point pens and paper lifted from the copybooks.

Major Bay began our indoctrinations with a series of bulletins on the war, proclaiming great victories for the Liberation Armed Forces on all fronts. The "Enemy out of combat" column bore staggering figures to substantiate their claims of entire Government battalions being wiped out. We were assured that the war would not change from its present course because the invincibility of "people's war" was a historical fact. He reiterated the theme that we had heard first from Plato. "The Front can differentiate between the cruel ruling government in America and the unfortunate, misguided soldiers who were sent to die in a far-off country, only to enrich the capitalist-imperialist warmongers." The idea was for us to accept our assigned role as "misguided sons of honest members of the working class" and repent our past misdeeds, realizing the truth of the situation as the Front presented it. The mention of "our release" was a repeat of the now-ragged promise they had dangled before us since we were captured.

By 20 November, 1965, I had become so swollen that I looked like a series of water-filled balloons linked at hips and shoulders. My eyes were almost closed, particularly after a night of lying on my back had given the water a chance to distribute itself over the entire body. During the day it would build in my legs and waist. I called Intern and told him I was having a valid problem. He examined me and decided it wasn't serious enough. Not more than fifteen minutes later he observed me as I stood on the walkway, trying to piss, my fluid-bloated, stallion-sized genitals hanging grotesquely. I looked up in time to see his shock-widened eyes staring. He obviously had never in his life seen anything to compare with what I had hanging this day.

He sped back to where I was standing, almost missing a corner in his haste, and demanded that I try to take a piss again. I did so and he spun about immediately, went directly to the boat dock, and poled rapidly down the canal. I waddled back to the hut and sat down. It was tiring to stand with all the extra weight bearing down. I felt as if I had a couple of unseen elephants sitting on my shoulders.

That evening he came by and said he had gotten some herbs and would brew up a pot of *thuoc nam*—which could mean any kind of herb medicine—for me to take in the morning. It was guaranteed to make me begin to urinate and drop the fluids. At this point, anything would have helped and I looked forward to the remedy, whatever it was.

Clem unlocked my irons and told me there would be no rice for me this morning; the *thuoc nam* had to hit an empty stomach. Intern called for me to come to the kitchen hut and I proceeded to get a cup of evil-smelling, greenish-brown liquid. The taste was slightly bitter and citric, about what I assumed boiled rotten lemon peels would taste like. I drank it and returned to the hut, waiting for results.

It took only a half-hour before I was forced to drag my bulk down the long single-pole walk to the high platform latrine, barely making it atop the precarious perch before the rush of acid, yellowish-brown fluid sprayed out as my intestines voided the putrid liquid. No urination, but the intestines were turning inside out.

I finally finished and managed to stagger to the hut without slipping off the walkway. I was so weak my hands trembled as I grasped the trees to steady myself. I felt so nauseated that if there had been any fluid in my stomach, I would have vomited for certain. I reached the hut and dropped to the mat, a cold sweat covering my face. Intern's cure had been worse than the swelling and I still had a lot of swelling left. I knew I wasn't taking any more of the herb cure; I couldn't stand another five hours like I'd just spent. The next thing out of me would be kidneys and stomach; I must have dropped everything else this morning.

Intern came by later in the afternoon, asking if I had been cured. I told him what I thought of his prescription and told him in no uncertain terms where he could stick the rest of the potful. He thought for a few moments as he studied my pained expression and then his face brightened. He blurted that he had forgotten to add the coconut husk to the concoction thus leaving it unbuffered and harsh to the system. I assured him it was quite harsh and said he could add all the coconut husk he wanted, but I wasn't drinking any more. I asked to see Major

217

Bay to request medication and Intern left.

On 25 November, I received the first in a series of injections of the strychnine sulfate and vitamin B_1. Strychnine was their standard for breaking the fluid loose, with B_1 to meet the deficiency. The swelling continued as I fought an increased thirst. There was water available for drinking and my body demanded it. Beginning on 2 December, I measured myself, using a piece of string and comparing the lengths with a portion of a centimeter scale that Dan had picked up somewhere. The conversion to inches reflected the following dimensions: chest (normal: 39 inches; 6 months after capture: 36 inches), 2 December: 39 inches; 5 December: 40.4 inches; waist (normal: 30 inches: 6 months after capture: 27 inches), 2 December: 36.5 inches; 5 December: 37.6 inches. I gained a maximum of nearly 4½ inches around my chest and over 10½ inches around my waist during the fluid buildup.

On 9 December, one month after the attack began, I began to drop liquid again through urination. The period of time it lasted was a continuous nightmare of extreme leg pains, insomnia and constant fatigability. Relief, when it came, followed increased cramping as the fluid drained from my body, leaving me shriveled and bony.

The indoctrinations continued on a low but incessant level. The guards conveyed to me the idea that they had all the time in the world and we could stay until we either learned or died. Execution wasn't the only way to go. Disease and malnutrition were our constant companions.

On Christmas Day 1965, we were allowed to eat a special meal together in the guard mess hall, sitting at the long table. I had requested, on behalf of all of us, an opportunity for us to eat together and perhaps have a special meal. Major Bay had indicated because the Front "respected the religious beliefs of POW's," it would allow us to worship as we chose, and would help us celebrate Christmas. I found that my thankfulness at Christmastime was a very personal thing and Major Bay's promise of a celebration meant only a chance to get a meal instead of fish and rice.

We gathered at the table and John gave thanks for our lives and what health we had. I quietly asked a blessing for Rocky and Roraback in my own mind. We received an entire *ca loc* apiece that night with fried rice, which was still fish and rice, but a delicious change. It was the first meal I'd had in over a year after which I felt filled with something beside boiled rice. We were given some small cakes, and they created almost a festive air as we devoured them, savoring the sweetness.

On New Year's Eve a messenger came into the camp late at night after I'd been locked up and caused a great stir among the guards. The next day we were told to prepare to move out of the camp and within a couple of hours we were on our way to spending over a month in a series of temporary bivouacs in the forest. We slept in the open with only a piece of plastic over our mosquito nets at night, with reduced sanitary conditions, with the same source of water for cooking as for bathing and washing our plates, with little or no soap or tooth powder, and with a decreased ration of fish.

Seven days after we moved out of the camp we met our first new American POW since Dave had joined us, twelve and a half months earlier. Late at night on 7 January, I was awakened by the sound of a deep voice coming from the guard area across the fifteen-foot reservoir beside which we were camped. It was speaking English that sounded too much American to be VC. Whoever it was spoke very slowly, asking when he would arrive at the place he was going. The answer was indistinct and silence soon settled over the area. I went to sleep wondering who the new man was.

The next morning, we all heard the voice and were aware of the extreme slowness of speech, almost as if the man were drugged. Dan was called over by the guards and the rest of us waited impatiently for him to come back with word of what was happening. There was a great deal of talking and then words of instruction from the guards, apparently to Dan, about helping someone to walk. As Dan rounded the end of the reservoir, plodding through the standing water and mud, he called me to give him a hand. I hurried along the mud bank on which we were camped, ducking the low-hanging tree limbs and brush, reaching him just at the beginning of our area. I caught my breath in shock.

There, clinging to Dan's shoulder, was a hulk of human wreckage. The hunched form was a huge bone structure covered with tightly stretched, fungus-infected skin. What must have been a grin of absolute joy at seeing other Americans looked like a leering death head. The deep voice echoed from the cavernous chest, "God! Americans! I can't believe it!" I was ashamed at the repulsion I felt.

Near our mat he squatted down Vietnamese fashion, his broad, bony shoulders touching his knees, buttocks resting on the ground. This was our introduction to Tim Barker, Captain, U.S. Army, captured a year before near Khai Hoang in an ambush. The bones, so prominent in his arms, were as big as my entire wrist and had there been flesh on those bones, this man would have been a giant. I learned later that he had weighed nearly 225 pounds when he was captured and stood six feet two inches or so tall. In a year of captivity he had been reduced to little more than 130 to 140 pounds at the most and his posture was so wrecked by constant enforced squatting that he was unable to straighten up. I am five feet eight inches tall and I could look levelly into his deep sunken eyes.

I was overwhelmed by his reaction to being with Americans and a strong feeling of kinship and responsibility toward him swept through me. His black pajamas were filthy and worn almost through. The infected skin and strong stench of dried pus from the open ulcerations made the first step clear. He had to get a bath and get into clean clothing. Dave and John began straightening out his few belongings after he said he had soap that he could use, while Dan and I took charge of getting him bathed.

He had a new chunk of the lye soap which he said he hadn't used because of the extreme stinging it caused when in contact with the infected skin. I encouraged him to bear with it since the fungus would never heal if it wasn't kept clean. I then discovered that he was too weak to stand while he bathed, so John carried water from the ditch-type reservoir to a spot on the other side of the bank where I helped him scrub two weeks of crusted filth and dried pus off of his body.

I fought the urge to vomit as the water and soap loosened dark yellowish cores from the eruptions covering his back, chest and legs, allowing fresh purulent discharge. He was covered with the same type of fungus we had developed, but his had been complicated by obvious excessive scratching and lack of washing. The infection had gone deep and the ulcerations were large enough that I could have inserted the tip of my little finger into any of them without touching the edges. It was going to take a lot to get him cleared up again, without even considering what we would do about the critical malnutrition. Walter Reed Army Hospital, with its virtually unlimited facilities, would have had difficulty bringing this man back.

In the days that followed it became evident that Tim was going to die. His short-lived joy at being with Americans gave way to depression when he saw our conditions. I had never encountered total mental defeat, but the VC had managed, in one year of imprisonment, to destroy this man's will to live. In conversations with him we learned that shortly after his capture he had attempted to escape while being moved in a boat. He was recaptured and placed in a camp with only Vietnamese prisoners. He had been deprived of food and kept in irons, had developed the fungus infection and went untreated, was shunned by the other prisoners because he was "unclean," and had rapidly lost hope for ever getting out. The deterioration in physical condition had reached a point that he felt he could never recover. He came to us a dead man in his own mind. It took the body exactly twenty-eight days to succumb.

In the meanwhile, the five of us were taken back to the school area for one night in order that Mafia might meet with us. The strong cage that had been built adjacent to our hootches had obviously been for Tim. The VC always allowed great lead time in advance of any operation and he had been expected. In this instance he stayed in the hut with Dave, and John drew the cage for the night, much to his displeasure. Mafia met with us in an atmosphere of pseudo-formality, befitting his status. He produced a newspaper-wrapped package of *banh bo*, a steamed sweet bread, and another type of cookie. After lecturing us on the requirement for us to bear up under the hardships of our present conditions as a sign of our "progress," he launched into an account of U.S. troops being committed to the war in 1965, and the "obdurate and perfidious schemes of the U.S. imperialists" as they sought to prolong the struggle.

I felt a surge of elation when he said U.S. troops were in action, even though I had reservations about the truth of the statement. I knew that if American troops were getting into the fight, Charlie was going to get torn up. My concern was why American troops were sent in. I had hoped that the Vietnamese would have been able to handle the war by themselves by this time, but obviously some imbalance had occurred.

When he finished talking, he asked if we had any requests.

221

My first one was medication for Tim and enough food for him so he might begin to regain his strength. Mafia conferred briefly with Major Bay, who was sitting beside him, after which he asked Tim what medication he needed. Tim had no idea and Dan interjected a list of vitamins, antibiotics and the fungicidal liquid we'd been given. He also stressed Tim's need for nourishing food to supplement the rice diet. Mafia and Major Bay both nodded as he spoke, replying that they would ask permission from the Front to provide the necessary items. Mafia then rose and indicated for us to go ahead and eat.

Bud brought over a small pot of tea and the cadre sat for a few moments watching John's barely contained eagerness as the sweets were unwrapped and the rapidity with which they disappeared. I spoke briefly with Major Bay in Vietnamese, trying to tell him that there was no time to waste if they held any real desire to save Captain Barker. I didn't want Tim to understand what I was saying; he had enough problems. Tim asked for a Bible, which Mafia refused to provide.

The next morning we were moved back into the forest, and on 13 January, medication began arriving for Tim. Vitamins B_1, B_{12} and C; hepatana, the horse liver extract; solucamphor; and a number of bottles of "*thuoc lac, Ong Gia*," the fungicide. The vitamins were in small vials to be injected, as were the solucamphor and hepatana. Dan was given a syringe and a couple of ancient needles that had been sharpened many times either on a stone or the bottom of a rice bowl, leaving their points rough and dull. We were also given a dozen bottles of the red medicine to be used on the infection. The medication, in itself, wasn't even a beginning toward what was required to bolster Tim's depleted system; moreover, the vitally needed food wasn't given.

This time, as before when one of us had gone very low with some illness, the first step by the VC medic had been to provide a half-kilo of white sugar and a couple of lemons. In special instances, the Front would purchase a small can of sweetened condensed milk, but one had to be almost immobilized for this. The purpose was to encourage the prisoner to continue to eat rice, supposing that the sugar and milk would aid him in getting it down. Tim received his sugar and lemons, but he was still mobile, so no milk.

Our days were now a struggle not only to keep ourselves

alive, but to aid Tim in every possible way. The most frustrating aspect of this was Tim's lack of desire to live. We were putting out more effort to keep him alive than he was. A week or so after he arrived, Dan and I discovered we had begun to develop deep ulcerating sores on our arms. Washing his clothes and helping him bathe had exposed us. His fungus, on the other hand, was clearing up in the wake of repeated washings and applications of the flesh-searing *lac* medicine. The deeper infections were still serious, but improving. I had hopes periodically that he'd pull through; however, his refusal to eat enough rice, except during Tet when the guards shared some of their delicious holiday pastries and pork with us, forced his already weakened system into a state of collapse.

One of the cadre who had been in the camps since we moved into the forest came by one of the final bivouacs to check on us. We were called individually to get haircuts, and when I had to practically carry Tim to the cadre, the VC finally realized he wasn't going to survive. The cadre was stunned and immediately blamed us for not properly caring for our friend. He stressed that the Front had provided medication and sugar for the POW in the tradition of humanitarianism. We were to note that Tim had been treated well by the Front while he had been with us, in order that we could verify that "his death was not a result of mistreatment." After that, they sat back and waited.

On the morning of 4 February 1966, Tim awoke early and called out to me, asking what we were having for breakfast. I jokingly answered, "Buckwheat cakes and sausage," happy to hear him express an interest in the meal we were cooking. Minutes later I went to his net to help him get out and eat. He was crouching at the rear of the net, his eyes enormous, the pupils dilated. "I don't want any rice! I won't eat it!" He was almost antagonistic in his refusal to eat. I had spoon-fed him on a couple of occasions before when it had looked like he would expire on us and I considered doing it again. I returned to the fire to get a pan of soft-cooked rice with some of the rice water on it to make it slide down easier.

When I reached his net, he was curled in a tight ball, lying on his side. I thought he was sleeping again and pulled his net up to wake him. Then it hit me! He was spasming from the waist down, his legs twitching and jerking. I dropped down beside him, calling for Dan to "get the fuck over here!" Tim's

face was ashen, his breath coming in shallow rasps. I grabbed
for his wrist, feeling for the pulse. It was faint and fluttery,
barely strong enough to be detected. Dan slipped in beside me
making a quick assessment. He called for John to get Intern
fast, telling John to pick the little son of a bitch up and carry
him if he wouldn't hurry.

Tim's eyes had rolled back in his head and raising the lids
showed only the blood-traced whites. A strange gurgling came
from deep in his throat. I cleared his mouth. He had nearly
swallowed his tongue. I thought of the drowning victim I had
tried to revive one summer without success.

Dan was busy counting as he timed the pulse. I looked at
him and he shook his head slowly, his eyes calm as he worked
with the same coolness he'd shown in the stress of combat.
Tim's body was cold, like a corpse, but his face was burning
up. Dave brought a towel soaked in cool water and gently
swabbed Tim's face, wiping the parched lips and moistening
them.

John came back with Intern trotting behind him, carrying
his ammunition box of medical supplies. He took one look and
hurried back to the guard area, returning with a syringe of
solucamphor and injecting the respiratory stimulant before we
discovered what it was. He watched for a moment as Dan placed
a folded towel under Tim's head and made certain no clothing
was binding him. Intern turned and left without a word, taking
his medical box with him.

Tim's chest began to heave rapidly for a moment, then
slowed and stopped. Dan immediately checked respiration and
pulse. Tim wasn't breathing and his pulse was almost gone.
We rolled him onto his stomach and with Dan by his face,
checking throat clearance I began artificial respiration. His
body was so wasted I felt as if I could crush his ribs and had
to fight the urge to push hard, trying to pump life back into
him. "Don't . . . die! Don't . . . die!" The rhythm went through
my mind as I applied pressure, then released.

Dan nodded when Tim began shallow breathing again and
I stopped the aid to his respiration. The gurgling sound was
more pronounced and I thought of the death rattle when un-
cleared fluids gather in the throat. There wasn't a damn thing
we could do except wait.

Intern came back and told us to bring Tim to the canal,

224

where he would be put in a boat and taken to a hospital of the Front. It was a certainty that he'd die here, and even though I doubted a hospital existed, it was worth a try. Anything to try and save him. Dave helped me as we made a hasty litter out of two poles and two of the rice-sack sheets. Intern led Dave and me, carrying Tim on the litter, to the canal where Bud stood waiting in the back of one of their boats. As we placed him in the bottom of the boat and shaded his head with his sleeping mat I knew it was the last time any of us would see "the Bear," his nickname before capture.

Bud and Intern shoved away from the bank, poling quickly down the canal and out of sight. I watched, thinking how this man had so terrified them with his size and had been systematically broken down until he chose to die rather than try to exist. He had maintained a strange dignity through it all, like a huge wounded stag, sinking to his knees just before he dies. Dying, but leaving no doubt of his strength even though destroyed by a force he couldn't really comprehend. Dave watched silently, his eyes reflecting deep understanding.

On 9 February 1966, only five days after they took Tim out, another new POW arrived. We only got a brief glimpse of him at first, since Major Bay, who arrived with him, kept him separate from us while the "requirements of the Front" were completed.

From a distance the stocky, cherubic-faced Negro looked almost fat. His cheeks were full and his black pajamas were well filled. I immediately thought of beri-beri and hoped he wasn't in bad shape. We couldn't handle too many more sick POW's. Major Bay spent a good deal of time talking with the prisoner and I could hear the new man's soft mirthful chuckle as he conversed with the cadre. I wondered what was next.

Dave thwarted Major Bay by slipping up to the new man's net one afternoon when the guards were asleep and speaking with him briefly. Dave related that the new man was Staff Sergeant Ben Wilkes, he had been a POW for about a year, and this was his first contact with Americans since his capture. Dave went on that Ben had been in an all-Vietnamese camp, but unlike Tim, had been well fed, getting the same rations as the Vietnamese. His diet had consisted of the ubiquitous rice, supplemented with potatoes, corn and fish, and he was, in fact, carrying a good deal of fat. I shuddered to think of what our diet would do to him after meals like that. He would probably want to go back with the Vietnamese again after he ran into our cooking.

One week after his arrival, Ben was allowed to eat with us, giving us the first chance to get to know him. He was an immediately likable person, soft-spoken and with a quiet, bubbling sense of humor that seemed right below the surface, ready to break out at the slightest opportunity. He had been captured on his first operation, fresh in the country and unaware of the ambush tactics so effectively employed by the VC, and he had barely escaped with his life. His first year of captivity had been more of a "storage" effort by the VC than exploitation. He had eaten well and had encountered only minor illnesses which his body was able to handle without need of excessive medication. We were happy to learn that he was in good health, much better than ours.

Dave was having another problem with rice. He would eat and vomit, try again and vomit again, until he finally got the rice to stay down. He had developed hemorrhoids, but because of his dislike for the mosquitoes, he would hold off a crap run for several days, avoiding going out of his net. The resultant impacted stool would break him loose and bleeding would occur. It was painful and increased the pressure on him. He had stopped eating for a couple of meals in February and once again began to weaken.

On 21 February, we moved into a new location within a couple of kilometers of the river, with Major Bay again the camp commander. The new area was well covered with trees and the canal had fresh, relatively clear water flowing past. The guards began construction of a camp on the twenty-second, and by the twenty-fifth, there were five huts completed and one near completion. Pole walkways went in during the next few days and by the twenty-ninth, the camp was complete. Dan and I were again placed together in the one hut, John and Dave in another, and Ben in a separate one. There weren't more than three meters between any of the three American huts and we could talk freely. The guards were separated from us by a good forty meters and only the periodical checks at night reminded us they were still around after dark.

226

Because the dry season had caused the water level to sink, we were cooking in the bottom of a shallow ditch which ran in from the canal. During rainy season, it would be completely underwater, but at present it was usable. The guards began seining the canals, using old mosquito nets or regular seining nets and catching large numbers of fish. We normally got the ones the guards didn't want, particularly the "*ca lac,*" a flat, silver fish with a tail that tapered to a point rather than spreading into a tail fin. Its flesh was filled with hundreds of hairlike bones which made it unpopular on the VC menu; hence the Americans could expect to get all the *ca lac* caught. We had no means of preserving them unless we cooked them up at night and left them overnight for breakfast. They were tasteless and difficult to eat. The other discarded fish we were given were the *ca sac* that Dave and I had received in the Mines. He wouldn't eat *ca sac* and his problem with rice became worse.

Dave Davila began to slip into physical immobility. He had developed a serious case of diarrhea and had been given sulfaguanidine, which relieved it slightly. The hemorrhoids were bleeding more profusely after the outbreak of diarrhea and Dave was noticeably concerned. He began to stay in his net except when he had to go to the latrine and even avoided frequent trips by using the *nuoc mam* crock during the day as well as at night when he was locked up and unable to go to the latrine. The crockful of diarrhetic excrement was nauseating as well as unsanitary. To prevent John from getting any sicker than he already was and to keep Dave moving I required him to make runs to the latrine during the day, just like the rest of us.

Dave's refusal to eat had a frightening similarity to Tim Barker's. After he'd gone three days without eating, I talked with him, seeking the key that would unlock the man's desire to live and break this momentum toward inevitable death. I had watched one man die and could see the same fate opening up in front of Dave. I went to see Major Bay, telling him another American was going to die of malnutrition and disease if we weren't given adequate food soon. I suggested pumpkins, remembering the lifesaving effect they'd had back in the mangroves. His answer was an apologetic refusal. Pumpkins were out of season and conditions of war made life in the forest very difficult. I was reminded that my American aircraft were bombing the countryside, destroying the crops and bringing hardships

227

to the POW. In seconds, he was pouring out a volume of propaganda that I could have well done without. I reminded him of Tim's death, using the word "death" in opposition to Major Bay's report of Tim's being in a hospital. He accepted my statement and replied that Dave was young and could return home to his family if he would progress and learn to live with the conditions imposed by this dirty war conducted by our government. I tried again with an appeal for food and got another lecture on the war. It was so damn frustrating, such a feeling of helplessness to have one of your men dying, for you to know he was dying, and not be able to influence the situation.

I went back and talked with Dave again, giving him the straight word on what he could expect in the way of help from the VC and what we could do to help him. From a physical standpoint he could have whipped the problem, but it was psychological as well and the brief contact with Tim Barker had provided Dave with his answer to escaping the oppressive environment.

Major Bay spoke with Dave on 12 March, telling him there was nothing for the POW's but rice and what fish the guards could give us. I think Dave had held a slight hope that something would be provided if the situation became serious enough. Major Bay torpedoed that idea with his speech. I watched Dave's face become a mask and his eyes retreat into the past, blotting out the awful reality. I could almost hear the surf crashing on Waikiki Beach as Dave walked back to his hut, ignoring the three of us around him.

I made one more effort for food, making it almost a plea for a man's life as I told Major Bay that without some type of change in diet, any type of food, he would have another dead POW from his camp. He thought for a moment on the last point, deciding finally that his previous answer would hold. No food, eat rice.

In my diary I made the following notations on Dave's condition:

15 Mar—1 meal, facial swelling, on posterior again
16 Mar—1 meal, stool worse, frequency increasing—more mucus, blood both clotted and fresh
17 Mar—no eat, swelling increasing, stool BAD—*drank canal H$_2$O on 15th or 14th instead of boiled H$_2$O—weakening*

Dave was weakening to the point that the disease began to take over. He complicated matters by drinking water straight from the canal. I began feeding him after this, hoping to stall the process of deterioration until something happened to change our situation. I had no idea how long that would take.

18 Mar—1 meal, no longer mobile, chest congestion, weak— message to Bay for medication

I wrote a message to Major Bay informing him that Dave was going into the terminal stages and unless food and medication reached him immediately, he would die. I sent it out with a guard early in the day, making certain Intern was aware of the degree of seriousness that existed. Late that same night Dan and I were awakened by Chinh, who handed Dan a packet of vials and me a note from Major Bay, stating he sent the medicine I requested, three glucose, ten vitamin B_1 and ten vitamin C, and telling me to advise Dave to "eat much the rice." It was a gesture, but not enought. Dave was going to need blood-expander soon and enough antibiotics to knock the exploding diarrhea. More than these, he desperately needed food.

*19 Mar—Fed Dave 2 meals, stool—much mucus—dark clotted blood; very weak, facial swelling to point eyes difficult to open, sporadic incoherency. 3 streptomycin w/ glucose, 3 B_1 3C—needs IV fluids—*FOOD.

Dan gave Dave the streptomycin and it didn't even faze the runs. The vitamins were lost in the rapid passage of fluids from his body. We were cleaning the mat in Dave's hut almost every hour as he was unable to control the flushing action of his body and dropped globs of mucus and blood along with watery feces.

I wasn't going to let Dave die! He'd been the guy with enough guts to try a second escape right after an unsuccessful first attempt. He and I had gone through the Mines together, lived through a botched-up escape attempt, made it through the "correction period." He had gone through too much to just give up now. I prayed for guidance, some idea of what I could do to help this Kamaina get back to the islands he loved.

That night was Dave's last night. It was hard to lie in the

leg irons and listen to a man die, calling the names of friends he had known before, muttering, his mind a thousand miles away from this hell and getting farther away each second. The spirit was struggling to break from its mortal bonds, fighting to rise from the filth and degradation, climbing away from all that bound those of us who remained behind.

*20 Mar—Unable to take H$_2$O orally—90% incoherent, (began last night)—many runs during nite—mucus (golden yellow) blood, white/cloudy globules. Needs IV fluids—blood/ expander—food—*SOON.

I tried to feed Dave in the morning, but it was impossible. He couldn't get a cup of water down without gagging. Ben Casey, the medic from the mangroves, came in and made a rapid evaluation of the case. There was a rapid discussion between Intern and Ben, the older medic speaking sharply to the younger Intern, pointing to Dave, obviously upset by what he saw. Dan was called over and Ben told him Dave should be moved to a hospital as soon as possible. My immediate reaction was that if I were going to die, I'd want to die with Americans. The thought that possibly, just possibly, there was a hospital and Dave might be given treatment made me reconsider.

John and our Ben were watching from their hut as the drama unfolded. I realized I had no right to deny a man whatever chance existed for him to live, and the chance that there was a hospital was sufficient to give him that opportunity for survival. The second consideration was the other men here. To expose them to the chance of infection was unwarranted, particularly since there was no indication that any treatment would be available here.

Dan helped me wash Dave and clean him up. I gathered his belongings and made a small bundle for him. His rice-straw sleeping mat was of no value now because of the constant washings and still-present traces of the diarrhetic stools. Our Ben helped me carry Dave to the canal where the boat was waiting. I had an unpleasant sensation in my stomach as I looked at Bud standing in the back of the boat as he had done with Tim. Ben Casey stood in a narrower boat in front of Bud's, his belongings stored neatly under a poncho. As we lifted Dave down into the boat, he clung to my forearm, the strength of his grip far beyond anything I imagined possible. I found myself gripping his forearm and realized it was the ancient warriors' arm clasp, as if Dave was bidding a farewell.

The boat disappeared down the canal. I found myself praying. Praying more sincerely than I ever had in my life for blessing on those who had gone from us and guidance to bring those of us left through whatever lay ahead.

Dave's absence was felt. Whereas Tim's arrival, period of decline and subsequent death made him seem transient, Dave was part of our group, and the impact of this second death, within two months of the first, drove already sagging morale to abysmal depths. On the twenty-first, Major Bay came by to talk with us and met a quietly hostile group of Americans. No matter how they applauded their own leniency and humanitarianism, no matter how they tried to utilize the threat of our punishment as "criminals" to enhance the flavor of life, its bitterness inconsequential relative to death, none of the rhetoric, that in the first months of captivity had seemed feasible, reached me now. I had been involved with the deaths of three Americans in the past six months and had experienced a period of enforced slow starvation in the Mines. There had been a violent rending of the screen of hypocrisy that had been held before us and the insidious manipulation of human beings under the cloak of "humanitarianism" stood naked and ugly.

I spent long nights after that analyzing my thoughts and reactions. I had felt bitterness and hatred building, feeding off the constant frustrations and anxiety. I could destroy myself if I allowed negative emotions to dominate my thinking, and partially from a strong sense of self-preservation, partially from a sense of responsibility to the other men, because I could offer them no solutions if I could find none for myself, I turned to the one positive force our captors could never challenge, God.

My religious background included Sunday schools, vacation Bible schools and church attendance as a youngster. I had never questioned religion nor had I ever really accepted it. It was something I lived with because that's the way things were done. There had never been a time of trial serious enough to make me consciously depend on a Supreme Being except when I felt some interest of mine was beyond my direct influence. Once I achieved what I had set out to do, God was given a pragmatic

231

"thank you" and forgotten until my next need arose. My closest association with the development of faith came at West Point. Four years of compulsory chapel each Sunday, the idea of "having to go," failed to diminish a growing sense of peace and communication I discovered within the quiet majesty that was the interior of the Cadet Chapel. In the stillness of the Chapel I began to look at faith, not in terms of ritual and sectarian dogma, but as a very personal communication between one man and his God. After graduation, I had no time to develop that which I had begun, but evidently the foundation was still there.

I found myself returning to and drawing from that foundation in this situation where I was stripped of all material assets, leaving only the intangibles which form the core of our existence: faith, ethics, morals, beliefs. It had become a test of whatever inner strengths I possessed against the total physical control exercised by my captors. Were I to survive with my spirit intact, I could only turn to faith in the Power I believed to be so far greater than that which imprisoned me. For the first time in my life the words of the Twenty-third Psalm were a source of strength and consolation. From the loss of Dave on, I began to believe: "The Lord is my Shepherd; I shall not want."

John was having problems with the diarrhea he'd picked up in February and the sulfaguanidine he had been given wasn't helping. On 6 June, we were visited by a pleasant, very friendly individual who told us he was Bac-Si Hai—Dr. Hai. It was my first contact with anyone from the Front who even alleged he was a doctor and my hopes soared. He carried the same U.S. .30-caliber ammunition box for a doctor's bag as the local medics. Once he opened it, however, his status was evident. Besides carrying a Belgian Browning Automatic pistol, like a high ranking cadre, instead of the American .45-caliber pistol that local cadre wore, Dr. Hai had a new stethoscope, two pairs of blunt surgical scissors, several encased syringes and various types of vitamins and antibiotics in distinct contrast to the meager equipment carried by Intern or Ben Casey. He spent over an hour examining us, paying particular attention to John and Ben. I was extremely relieved to see John with some hope of getting his diarrhea cured. Dr. Hai spoke to Dan and me about the course of the war and said it was just about over.

His cheerful attitude aided him in getting through to me when he mentioned release and return home. Dr. Hai encouraged us to keep eating and maintain our health so we would be ready to go home when the time came. He urged us to keep taking P.T. because it "cleansed our bodies."

Showboat and Cheeta continued a low-key indoctrination, developing the theme of unflinching sacrifice and boundless courage on the part of the Liberation Armed Forces as the key to total victory. "The spirit of man can triumph over any weapon." News reports of U.S. defeats throughout the country were used to emphasize the point, although the distorted casualty figures and equipment losses detracted from what might have been a plausible demonstration of spirit over weaponry. Showboat quoted from a news bulletin, dated 30 April 1966, giving the following U.S. losses in SVN:

> 1961 — 30
> 1962 — 443
> 1963 — 962
> 1964 — 2,506
> 1965 — 17,964
> 1966 — 27,834 (1st 3 months)

I realized the firepower available to an American unit and even if it were a war of attrition, the LAF "unflinching sacrifice" team was going to get bloodied up something awful, particularly if the U.S. was taking those casualties.

I asked Showboat for figures of Liberation Armed Forces casualties in order to have a basis for comparison. If we had lost ten men in a battle and the enemy lost twenty in the same battle, we would have been better off than he was; however, if all I knew was that we lost ten men, there would be no way of evaluating who had suffered the most. Showboat failed to appreciate my logic, stating that any losses suffered by the Liberation Armed Forces were kept secret to prevent the enemy from correctly estimating the LAF's strength. I agreed with him that it was a good idea not to release casualty figures and asked where they got a tally of our American losses. He ignored my question and continued with the quotes, stating that U.S. troop strength had reached 270,000 men and we had over 2,300 aircraft in South Vietnam. I listened, making mental note of

233

the figures he was giving so I could refer back to them during the next rehash of the war and see if their figures tallied from one time to the next.

This camp had been named "the Neverglades" because of its general undesirability as a permanent habitat, but I hadn't known when I was well off. On 30 June, we moved to a new camp, traveling to the west, then south, away from the river into a more inaccessible area. The boat we were in barely passed through the overgrown canals, forcing Carpenter to get out and push. The trees alongside the banks seemed to crowd the evening sky out of sight, increasing the sensation of being closed in.

We traveled south about two hundred meters along a slightly clearer canal after crossing a well-used east-west canal and saw, under the thick canopy of leaves, the first huts of a large complex. The boats pulled up beside a bank which had a broad path, camouflaged by bending trees over the top and nailing the rows of trees to horizontal poles so their branches apread over the bare path below. Log walks wound their way back into the trees on both sides of the canal. Several large, raised structures were visible from the canal, all of them extremely weather-battered and in need of repair. The camp had apparently been deserted for a period of time.

Our guards were met by Muoi (now called "Mom M."), Frank Buck and Ben Casey, who had been here for a while, judging from the sacks of rice and equipment in the kitchen hut where they were standing. We four Americans were led along a series of well-constructed log walks, four or five poles wide, tied down with cross poles and wire; much better than any we had seen previously, indicating this camp at one time must have been considered relatively permanent. We were led to a long, substantial-appearing building, its sides and ends heavily barred, one of the few totally intact buildings in this part of the camp. The others lay destroyed in the water.

Dan turned and looked at Cheeta as if there had been some mistake. We had lived in open huts in the Neverglades and now, in a remote location, more distant from the river, which to me meant less chance for escape, we went back into a cage. Cheeta motioned for us to enter. Since it was almost dark and we had eaten before leaving the last camp, we were told to put up our nets and go to sleep. I was happy to get inside my net because of the almost deafening hum and accompanying stings of the unbelievable swarms of mosquitoes. The school area had been renamed "Mosquito Junction" because of its mosquito population, but this place was worse. We quickly strung up the nets inside, noting the woven reed mats covering the floor and indications of attempts by the previous tenants to make it more comfortable and watertight.

Cheeta waited, locked John's and my irons, then locked the cage door. The sudden change to stricter security seemed to portend some unpleasant occurrence of which we were not yet aware. Dan had confronted Major Bay in the last camp with a serious question which dealt with equality of prisoners and the Major's answer cleared up doubts which were in all of our minds regarding the treatment we were receiving.

The treatment of all POW's within a given camp was equal, based on the Front's assigned equality of status among the POW's. Major Bay had referred to my time in the Salt Mines as a period during which I was not allowed to enjoy the lenient policy and developed this into an example of humanitarianism by pointing out that Dave and I, even after trying to escape, had been allowed to rejoin Dan and John. Life in the camp was difficult, he admitted, but death in an escape attempt was a more serious threat to us. It was a matter of sticking with the conditions that existed, making the best of them, and depending on the Front for release, which Major Bay assured Dan was coming. It wasn't that much of an answer, but he didn't have to give much more to make his point: Things are not too good, but they can get worse if you try to beat the system, so live with it and hope for release.

I was called down the next day for a conference, and because with me he could lapse into Vietnamese when his English failed, Major Bay went into an explanation of the same subject in order that I might "tell Phit and the others the policy of the Front and calm their fears." He showed me Dan's note and, in a short speech, twisted the entire meaning and purpose into an appeal for better treatment, trying to portray Dan as one who misunderstood the "great equality and democracy" of the policy toward POW's. I was a poor target for his speech, particularly since Dan had explained his intentions to me before Major Bay got the note. It appeared that the cadre was using the note as a ploy to create more dissension among our group, driving Dan and me apart. That evening we got a chuckle out of the conversation as I related it to the others, even though the "hope for release" didn't include how to stay alive until it occurred.

Shortly after the conversations, the guards had built a volleyball court in a semi-cleared area near the camp, leaving stumps scattered around where they had chopped down some trees. We were to engage in sport with the guards, as specified by the policy. Major Bay had stated that, because of "conditions of war," certain parts of the policy could not be fulfilled. This volleyball game was his effort to give more credibility to what remained of the functional policy. Unfortunately, the early rains flooded the area and it looked as if the "sport" would be canceled.

We underrated the cadre's persistence, for we found ourselves playing a muddy game of water-polo volleyball against an enthusiastic group of guards. Our popularity didn't rise when the team of Slim, Major Bay, Clem, "Phit," "Son" and "Ro" soundly trounced a nine-guard team, five games to one in three days of play. John's hitherto undisplayed athletic ability stood out as his height and sharp spiking drove the shorter guards into a frenzy. Because of our physical weakness we played a less frantic game, depending on setups and the height-advantage spiking to create confusion on the other side of the net. We stopped each day after two games because of the telling effect on our strength, but with bolstered morale because of our triumphs.

We learned in the next days that this camp was a blessing, the sleeping accommodations and security excluded. It had been a work camp for ARVN and civilian political prisoners and their innovations to make it more livable provided us with sources of nutrition we had lacked before. Long mounds planted with sweet potato vines lined the canal, running twenty-five meters in one direction and about ten or fifteen meters in the other. The potatoes had been taken long ago and digging around the base of the vines showed no new growth, but the abundance of leaves provided us with sorely needed greens. We were able to supplement our diet with soup made from the nutritious leaves and to break the monotony of rice and fish or rice and *nuoc mam* each meal.

The routine here was much like the one we had followed in the Neverglades. Get up, cook rice, eat, and sit or try to catch small fish with a borrowed pole and live until time to cook and eat our supper rice. Then, back to the cage.

The days went slowly, with only our activities to keep us busy. We spent long hours talking about things in our past, places we had been, places we wanted to go; things we had done and things we wanted to do. Food was a main topic as we recalled our favorite dishes, creating mental images of what now were like the zenith of epicurean delights. I never realized how utterly delicious a crunchy peanut-butter-and-strawberry-preserve sandwich had been until now. Oddly enough, sex was far down on the list of topics, coming up only in conjunction with past amorous exploits, real or imagined, related as a part of a longer story. At this point even the thought of sex was exhausting and not really involved in our survival, although it was another reason to survive.

The guards would bring the camp radio over for us to hear the English broadcast by Radio Hanoi, which was a news coverage of the war and the political and military aspects of its developing intensity. It was supposed to keep us abreast of the conflict so that we might evaluate the validity of the lessons taught us by the Front. We listened in amused silence to the sweeping claims of military victories, noting the lack of any setbacks for the Liberation Armed Forces. We learned that the 1st Infantry Division was engaging the VC, and the frequency of their mention indicated a lot of problems for Charlie. Hanoi's broadcasters used the phrases "totally annihilated, soundly smashed, completely routed" to describe the effect of their actions against the American units while labeling their own attacks as "heroic, glorious, tempestuous, undaunted." For our ears, accustomed to straight reporting of facts, the flurry of editorial adjectives and adverbs was superfluous, whereas their usage in the Vietnamese news broadcast for the guards brought gasps of appreciation and more complete understanding of what was being said. For them, it was not so much a matter of getting all the facts, but having the ones given them sufficiently draped in appealing modifiers to make the news worth remembering.

News of an antiwar movement in the United States was of interest to us. We had seen several leaflets indicating dissent

237

and protest against the war, but put them in the context that there hadn't ever been a war we had fought that somebody didn't like. Hanoi reported protests on campuses across the nation, which we took as a normal exaggeration, but it stayed with us where the battle reports didn't. I recall the female announcer saying that the "students' association in struggle for a democratic society" had been a leader in the growing movement and wondered who in the heck they were. I was to hear and read more about them in the days to come.

Major Bay appeared after about a week and gave us a summary of the war news out of which we learned that the 1st Air Cavalry Division was in country and, according to Major Bay, was in the process of being "totally annihilated." He conducted several classes on "the just cause of the revolution and the injustice of the U.S. dirty war of aggression," using the same basic lesson plans that Plato had used, with an attempt at updating by discussing "limited war" as begun with the introduction of U.S. combat units.

Major Bay emphasized the importance of our recognition of the "just cause of the revolution" in its march toward peace, democratic freedoms, independence and reunification of the Fatherland. The overall effect was of an old, scratchy record which you didn't particularly like (even though you've memorized most of the words), being played for you at a party which you didn't really want to attend. Afterward, we were given pen and paper and told to write what we had learned from the lessons. My first reaction was that I had an opportunity to snatch a little more paper since my supply was running low.

Then came the question of what I had learned. Major Bay made certain that we were separated during the answering phase so there would be no exchange of ideas to foul him up. I began by challenging his contention that the NLF was the "sole genuine representative" of the 14,000,000 South Vietnamese people, since that was supposed to be the entire population of the South. With simple arithmetic, I added the 1,000,000 refugees who escaped from the North after Ho Chi Minh took over, the 500,000 or so ARVN soldiers, their 1,500,000 or so family members and the 100,000 government officials with their 300,000 or so family members for a rough estimate of at least 3,400,000 people who I felt quite certain didn't accept the NLF as their "sole genuine representative."

238

I agreed that the Vietnam situation should be decided according to the will of the people, but not influenced by the North. I also agreed that the terrible destruction and death caused by war was a crime against the innocent civilians, but it took two sides to make a war. My outlook on the development of the war was that I was only hearing one side of the story and, as Mr. Ba ("Plato") had told me after I was captured, "Every bell has two sounds." I was careful to write most politely, making my points more probes of his lessons than outright contradictions. I wasn't ready to give up the lenient policy of the Front just yet.

On 21 July, Dr. Hai visited us again, bringing his beaming optimism, this time talking about an exchange of prisoners. We were immediately excited because this sounded more like what should be happening. One of the greatest fears was that no one on the outside knew we were still alive. There had been no mention to our government by the VC of our status as far as we knew and the thought of being forgotten was a basic terror. We knew that the Army would do all it could to get us out, but not if they didn't know we were alive.

The cheerful doctor gave antibiotic injections for various infections and went so far as to check my eyesight, which had grown worse after the years of vitamin deficiency. He assured me he'd get some vitamin A for me shortly and get my eyes in good condition. Ben had picked up a case of diarrhea and got sulfa for it, which was the fastest any case of the runs had been treated.

After Dr. Hai departed, our conversations bubbled with the thought of an exchange. I was confident that this, unlike a release, would include me since the lists of prisoners would be agreed upon before the exchange took place and if the Americans asked for me by name, there was a damn good chance I'd go home. We tried to recall how the exchanges in Korea were handled, wondering how long we'd have to wait. The next days passed rapidly as our spirits, at a high point for 1966, made everything more bearable. After all, we weren't going to be here that much longer!

Major Bay came in on 23 July with a new set of lesson plans which he wanted me to go over with him to check for proper English. I questioned myself about giving any sort of help to a cadre, but decided to see what it entailed before refusing. The new lesson plans were revisions of the ones he had used on us with explanations of the points I had made, or the questionable portion of the original omitted. Other additions included the American people's support for the just cause of the revolution and opposition to "Johnson, McNamara and Co.'s illegal, immoral and unjust war."

I asked him about these "American people" who supported the just cause of the revolution, asking if he believed that dissent in the United States against a government policy necessarily involved support for the other side in the case of the war. To him, condemnation of the American government's policy was a sign of support for the revolution just as the solidarity movement in Cuba, Communist China, and Russia supported the struggle against "U.S. Imperialism." There was little hope of explaining freedom of speech and assembly and the right to criticize the government to a man who had never experienced them in his life.

We had heard, in late 1965, that the U.S. had begun bombing North Vietnam, but after a bitter round of denunciations by the guards and cadre the topic slipped into the background. Major Bay now brought it up again and Radio Hanoi kept us up to date on the air war. Major Bay brought in figures of U.S. aircraft losses, remarking about the accuracy of the North Vietnamese weapons and the heroism of their pilots as our losses climbed steadily toward 1,000. The condemnation of the U.S. for bombing nonmilitary targets in the North had grown since we had come in this camp and we decided the Air Force and Navy were really pounding the area to get such violent protest. President Johnson took a scathing denunciation for something new each day from the Hanoi editorial staff. I figured any man that could cause them that much trouble must be doing a good job. He was "Public Enemy Number One through Ten" with this group of guards and cadre, which was a compliment indeed.

None of our guards had caught John's last name as being the same as President Johnson's until Dr. Hai brought it up on his last visit. Even he stopped smiling when he said "Johnson." John's name was unofficially changed by Dr. Hai to "Dong," which never stuck. We liked Johnson.

Major Bay had also denied the presence of any North Vietnamese troops in South Vietnam, stating it was an insult to the Liberation Armed Forces to insinuate they were not as capable fighters as their Northern brethren. With regard to Communism, the liberation movement was a broadly based nationalistic movement in which the Communist party played only an equal role with the other political, religious and miscellaneous groups.

There was specific instruction to the cadre to deny any link with the Communist Party of Vietnam, headed by Ho Chi Minh. This was the first thing an American prisoner looked for to justify his own beliefs and if they could successfully deny the presence of a Communist-inspired insurgency, the rest of the POW's beliefs could be attacked. Once doubt in the validity of outside Communist presence was established, the "gratitude reaction" and survival instinct began to work within the bounds of the Front's policy. The most devastating thing for a POW is to feel he has been betrayed by those for whom he is fighting. Invalidation of an "enemy presence" substantiates the Front's premise that the American soldiers are "misled," therefore, betrayed.

Had I not understood some Vietnamese, I might have missed hearing the daily political classes attended by the guards in which the doctrine, *"Mác-xit, Le-nin-it,"* was taught to even the youngest of them. It was incongruous to hear the cadre teaching the Marxist doctrine to the guards one hour and to deny any connection with Communism in the next, when talking with the Americans. The fact that Communist indoctrination was drawing the guards into the inescapable fold, and that the cadre felt the need to lie to us about it, strengthened my conviction that I was right in my beliefs.

On 8 August 1966, Mafia returned to the camp. I hadn't seen him since the meeting shortly after Tim Barker had arrived and had been much happier because of his absence. He brought a small package of brown sugar, half a kilo of peas and some rice starch candy for us to make sweet soup. It was a pleasant surprise and we thoroughly enjoyed it with our rice that evening. It cost us a thank-you note to the Central Committee about the treatment we were receiving: the standard "I have not been beaten or physically tortured," which was automatic by now; and "I have received sufficient food and medication to maintain my health," another reasonable assessment if one considered what little we had as "health." I wrote that I had been given a sleeping mat, mosquito net, sheet and clothing which was adequate for the climate. My black pajamas were still in fairly good condition and there were no gaping holes in my mosquito net at present, so I was in good shape.

He spoke with us in almost a bored fashion, telling us of the new successes of the Liberation Armed Forces on the battlefields, the hopeless political situation in Saigon, and the growing support for the NLF around the world, particularly in the U.S. He brought out the problems of discrimination, unemployment and poverty in the United States as internal problems going unsolved while the large corporations "reaped huge profits" from the war; thus making it a capitalistic enterprise while the working class suffered at home. He stressed that not only were the American people struggling against the government, but opposition was coming from within the Congress itself. He was almost sneering when he said, "Very soon the Johnson government will be forced to withdraw from Vietnam. As you know, they cannot win."

He leaned forward, more intent, staring at each of us in turn. "What now of you? Surely you can see clearly the aggressive war carried on by Johnson and McNamara will fail and our revolution will decisively succeed." He sat back again, studying us. I wasn't going to say much. I'd learned to keep quiet with this guy.

"And now." He paused. "You must consider carefully your thoughts on the situation and write for me what you can know. Think before you write, as the Front must judge your progress." His tone became conciliatory as he finished: "Do not waste your lives in an unjust war that brings no happiness to your dear families. The Front wishes to release you and allow you to return home so that you may tell the truth of the situation to the American people."

We were dismissed after receiving several sheets of paper and two pens for the four of us. Mafia said he had to go now, but would return later. Morale was lower after this session than at any time since we had arrived in this camp.

Jim Jackson, Special Forces medic captured near Binh Hung, southwest of Camau, only a couple of months previously, came to our camp on 13 August, wearing a pair of knee-length black trousers, a defiant grin and clinging traces of the bewilderment

242

that follows loss of freedom. Dan immediately recognized Jim because of a medical course they had taken together at Fort Sam Houston, Texas. The separate cage was indication that Jim, like Ben at first, would be isolated until the cadre could get to him, leaving it up to us to get communication set up.

Jim almost strangled on his first plate of rice when he took a bite, failing to see the small folded piece of paper, wrapped in a piece of cellophane, tucked in the middle of the pile of rice. The mail had gone through with Clem as the delivery boy! Jim had a wide grin for all of us as we trooped by his cage en route to ours for lockup, giving us the feeling that we might have helped him a little.

The cadre started interrogating him immediately and si-multaneous indoctrinations left him drained at the end of the day. He must have upset Mom M several times during the sessions, judging from the familiar siren-pitched, whining voice that carried over to our kitchen where we sat.

Not long after, Mafia sent Showboat to pick up the papers we had written. I realized a serious mistake I had made during this period. When the papers were written for Mafia and Major Bay, each man did his own writing without consulting or really discussing with the others what he had written. We had become four separate minds, each striving to cope with the situation in our own way. The goal was to return to our families. The necessary conditions for achieving this were to "understand the truth of the situation in Vietnam and repentance." This writing was the test of our understanding of the "truth," our ability to say we recognized the just cause of the revolution and the unjust "U.S. war of aggression." Mafia had demonstrated his ability and willingness to influence our conditions in whatever manner he felt necessary to make us more receptive to "the truth." Whether we actually believed it or not, he wanted it down on paper. All of the cadre and guards worked to instill a sort of "cooperate and graduate" attitude, making their requests sound so simple and beneficial: we would "discard our false impres-sions, become awakened and lose the title of 'U.S. Aggressor' to take the new title 'peace soldier' and defend world peace." In addition to the "self-improvement," we would be allowed to go home if we progressed sufficiently. With all those good deals, they probably wondered why we hesitated in the least.

I had been able to take a devious course, because of my

substantial knowledge of certain parts of revolutionary theory and literature, and a touch of psychology. Each man was limited or aided by his educational and military background and was not necessarily equipped to deal with the problem except in terms of "Yes, I agree," or "No, I disagree." My failure to stop for a moment in the preparation of my own paper to give some positive guidance to others allowed Mafia to better exploit our fragmented group.

In our own discussions about the lessons there was no doubt that the swaying of our loyalty to our country was impossible. The "truth" we were being taught was thoroughly picked to pieces, leaving no doubt that each man had evaluated what we had been told in the light of his past experiences and exposure to an American education. Each found that the lack of objectivity and the contradictions and faulty logic in the Front's presentations far outweighed the strands of truth that were woven through the lessons.

I had lost two men for whom I was responsible to malnutrition and disease, under conditions which were better than I myself had experienced in the punishment camp. I could not, because of my own conscience, influence a man to write something that might cause him to be sent to a camp like the Mines. I could and would attempt to set a proper example, but the individual would decide for himself whether or not he followed. I was senior in rank, but junior in age except for Jim Jackson. My advantage in age gave me a greater ability to handle the years of physical hardship, of diarrhea, beri-beri, fungus and a tour in the Mines, none of which had knocked me to my knees. John was in his forties, Ben was thirty-nine and Dan was in his mid-thirties, and only Ben wasn't seriously threatened by sudden extreme malnutrition and the disease which immediately followed.

After the cadre finished with Jim's sessions, he was allowed to come into the kitchen and we were free to talk. Cheeta and Showboat accompanied him over for the first meeting with us and squatted on the floor, beaming with satisfaction, as the five of us engaged in a spirited conversation. The guards constantly urged us, *"Dung buon. Dung buon"*—Don't be sad—encouraging a happy attitude no matter what the situation, except when a cadre determined that mental depression was required to achieve certain results. In this instance, there was no need to urge us to be happy. Jim was a breath of fresh air, bringing news of America and filling us in on what was actually happening in the world outside.

The first topics were results of combat actions we'd heard about: the Special Forces camp at Hiep Hoa which the VC overran in 1963, claiming four Americans captured and nine killed, according to Mom M. Dan and I had good friends on the American detachment there and were overjoyed to learn that there were no American deaths, although John Colby had been badly shot up. I had hoped that he and Doug Horne, the detachment commander, as well as the rest of the team hadn't been killed. Of the four captured, Ken Roraback had been executed with Rocky, and Isaac Camacho had escaped from the POW camp. The VC had reported that he had been released, which was another of the many false reports; the '65–'66 Dry Season Counteroffensive had put Charlie and the North Vietnamese units (nonexistent, according to Major Bay) up against American firepower, and although our people had taken some nasty casualties in ambushes around An Khe and in Tay Ninh Province, the VC and NVA displayed their "heroic spirit of sacrifice" under pounding from our artillery and airstrikes, losing men at such a rate that I could understand why Radio Hanoi never mentioned it. The LAF was depending on its mortars and rockets to hit our air bases and supply depots, trying to neutralize the force that was dealing them the worst losses they had suffered since the conflict began.

We learned that the 25th Infantry Division had joined the 1st Air Cav., the "Big Red One," and the Marines, giving the war a whole new look. The first American units had come in country in March 1965, just at the time Dan and I were meeting Mafia for the first time. He had been confident of the LAF's ability to defeat ARVN, giving the NLF political domination of the country. "Final victory" had been within their grasp when the contest suddenly took on new dimensions.

There had been attacks on our base areas around Cu Chi, Lai Khe and Long Khanh as well as terrorist attacks in Saigon, which had been well publicized over Radio Hanoi. I began to realize that what we heard over Radio Hanoi wasn't total lies. In this propaganda effort, the mixture of truth and distortion was in such proportions that the desired image was conveyed without completely destroying the veracity of the source. The

245

report of a battle occurring would be substantially correct, but through amplification of enemy losses and omission of their own losses, with proper adjectival emphasis, the propagandist created a highly inaccurate and favorable recounting of what might have been, in actuality, a stunning defeat. I wondered in how many battles the results were so decisively against the LAF that they couldn't be reported at all. Theirs was the advantage of only having to portray one side of the picture, selecting and altering the available facts to substantiate whatever theme they were declaiming.

So we learned that the situation on the outside wasn't a fraction as bad as we would have believed had we accepted Hanoi's reports. There was a lot of winning to be done, but the first step had been taken. The "final victory" which Mafia had felt was so close had been jerked away. The VC and NVA were good soldiers and their leaders were experts in guerrilla warfare, and we were fighting on their terrain. With the sanctuary afforded them in Cambodia and Laos, it would be a hell of a conflict. I hoped no one was looking for a quick win back home, because that wasn't the way these people fought. Their leaders were, no doubt, already evaluating our strengths and weaknesses and determining how best to undermine our strength and attack our weakness. I had renewed faith in my country's ability to meet this challenge and not to fold up in the face of Mafia's "War of National Liberation." The attempts by the cadre to create a picture of hoplessness for the Government of South Vietnam and U.S. efforts had been fruitless to begin with, but this exposure of the basic element of deceit had wiped out any chance they might have had to create doubt in our minds about the military situation.

To vary our menu, I encouraged everyone to experiment with cooking, trying to devise new ways of preparing the fish and leaves. Monotony of rice and fish, rice and leaf soup, rice, fish and leaf soup, rice and *nuoc mam* was a certain killer of appetites, and none of ours was too strong. We discovered that the *ca sac* intestines were lined with fat and that by rendering down the fat from thirty or more sets of tiny intestines, we could get enough grease to half-fry a few fish. By fastening the flat-sided *ca sac* between a split bamboo reed, we roasted them over the hot coals until they were as crisp as potato chips, then dipped them in the salty *nuoc mam* to add flavor before

246

eating. The advantage of roasting them was that the sharp, tiny bones, which would otherwise have to be picked either out of the fish before eating or out of your gums afterward, were charred to the point of edibility. Fish bones, when eaten, provided a source of calcium, otherwise difficult to get. Occasional supplements in the form of different wild greens from the guards provided a change from the sweet potato leaves.

We learned to take wild grapes which grew in thick bunches along the canals and, squeezing the sharp, acid juice from the green grapes, use it to flavor our water and leaf soup, sometimes adding *ca sac* for body. The guards contributed a pasty, yeast-like rice mush which was used to flavor soup, and which they called *com me*. It consisted of cooked rice, placed in a covered crock with a special type of bacteria working on it for a period of days to produce the tangy paste when the rice grains had broken down. This became one of our mainstays on the menu since it could be used in water, by itself, to make a sauce to pour over the rice. An infrequent snake, given us by the guards, was reason for a feast because of the solid meat and the fat from the intestines that could be used for making grease.

In September, I began to have brief, vicious bouts with dysentery again as the normal diarrhetic stool broke into blood, mucus and pus, accompanied by the same rolling abdominal cramps I'd had before. During this same time, John, still troubled by the runs he picked up in February, began to feel weaker and experienced headaches, which had been a problem because of his eyes, but became more serious now. Jim and Dan checked John and me, discovering the initial traces of yellow pigmentation creeping into our eyes and tinging my skin. It was a liver malfunction and both of us had it. Within two days, our eyes were a deep yellow and I had a pronounced yellowish cast to my skin. Our appetites hit bottom and coupled with the continued diarrhea, we were rapidly approaching a critical stage. I again went to the guards and requested medication for the jaundice. Intern had enough training to recognize the symptoms and over several protests from the other guards because I had interrupted their card game, he went to check John and talk with Jim. He departed in the afternoon, leaving us to spend an especially miserable night with the leg irons adding enough restriction to prevent me from finding one comfortable position in which to relax between crock bouts.

In the morning, Intern was back with vials of "hepatone," another variety of the horse liver extract used for all liver ailments. John and I took a total of 26 cc in three doses, spread over nine days. By the fourth day, my appetite was back and as soon as I began eating the normal amount of rice, I felt my strength and energy returning. We had taken as much precaution about cleanliness during this time as possible because of the possibility of food or utensil contamination, spreading the disease to the others. Luckily it was restricted to the two of us and we recovered quickly once we resumed eating sufficient rice.

The importance of eating rice, as we had just established, was lost with Ben. He had been dropping weight steadily since he joined us, finding our diet and conditions extremely difficult to adjust to. The signs were clear long before his problem in eating rice reached the danger point of near shut off. I made a first entry in my diary on 18 October 1966:

"down on rice—Joined us on 9/2/66 after 1 year in ARVN POW camp w/ much & varied types of food—difficulty adjusting to local US POW diet of rice w/ some occasional fish."

The thought of Tim and Dave was motivation enough to make me search for a means of heading off the problem before it developed any further. I requested stakeout lines from the guards so we could put the twin-hook lines around the camp area, trying to catch something bigger than the *ca sac*. It worked well for a while as each man took a turn at putting out the stakeouts and providing fish for the meals. The first days provided us with catfish and a few *ca loc*, a most welcome change to the menu with the larger, more edible pieces of fish aiding Ben in pushing down a pan of rice. We cleaned the area of hungry fish; others that remained refused to bite our hooks and we had to wait for more cat and *loc* to find their way in.

In mid-November, I requested permission to convey a message to Major Bay through Carpenter, who had assumed the command of the camp. Carpenter listened carefully as I told him of Ben's problem with rice and how he needed some type of food before he became too weak and disease hit him. Carpenter asked if Ben was sick now. I replied that he had diarrhea now, but that wouldn't be anything compared with what he'd have if he dropped much more weight. Intern had given Ben some sulfa for the runs and he had them under control, at least at the present. I stressed that we'd had two Americans die already and we didn't want to lose another one of our friends.

Carpenter flared briefly at the last statement, regaining his calm expression after muttering something about "American aggressors." It gained nothing when I assured him it was urgent that Major Bay be made aware of the situation. If the Major thought he'd get his ass in another sling like he did in the Neverglades, there might be hope of getting food for Ben. In the meantime, I requested extra fish from the guards that we would give to Ben, making certain he had something to replace the rice he wasn't eating. Carpenter decided Ben was still healthy enough and didn't need extra fish. He assured me Major Bay would be certain that Ben was cared for and told me not to worry. I returned to the American area quite worried.

In the next weeks we kept Ben active, urging him to stay out of his net and avoid the temptation to withdraw. He and Jim engaged in conversations and the two of them would chuckle and laugh softly over something they'd said, lighting Ben's face up and opening up his broad grin. There was a strong rapport between the two of them and Ben seemed to rally, drawing from Jim's adaptability and calm acceptance of the conditions here.

Ben suddenly declared on 27 November, that he couldn't pull his cooking duties anymore. He had developed a swelling in his abdomen which was diagnosed as beri-beri by Intern. A slight case of the runs also bothered him and he received sulfaguanidine and vitamin B_1 for the illnesses. I didn't understand his change in attitude, not liking to see him concentrate all of his attention on his illnesses. The more you thought about them, the worse they seemed to get, and with our situation, it was much better to keep your mind on something else, while at the same time doing all possible to get the ailment cleared up.

From that day on, Ben's decline was more noticeable. He spent more time in his net as he grew weaker.

Mafia and Major Bay came in about a week before Christmas and I thought it was in answer to the appeal for food for Ben. We were all called over to the guard kitchen where Mafia would speak with us. I, personally, didn't want to see him because each visit meant either a lecture, an interrogation or a require-

249

ment to write something for him. The less contact I had with him, the better, but this was a chance to get the food so necessary for Ben's life.

Walking over, Ben stumbled and almost fell. Jim and I helped him into the hut where Mafia and Major Bay were seated behind a low folding table. Mafia surveyed us with casual disinterest, motioning for us to sit on the floor in front of the table. Major Bay's eyes fastened on Ben as we helped him to sit down, then swept across the rest of our faces, studying each of our expressions.

They had come, we learned, to plan for a Christmas celebration which the Front would give us in order that we might "practice our religious beliefs." We would be given a special meal and whatever decorating material we desired to prepare our kitchen for the festivities. The immediate impact was the hope of getting real food. I don't believe any of us interpreted it as an opportunity to "practice our religious beliefs," because you can't ever stop a man from praying. The basic concept of thanksgiving and joy for the birth of Christ was something that required only a man's thoughts and spiritual rejoicing.

Major Bay told us we should be aware of the great leniency of the Front in allowing us to celebrate not only Christmas, but also New Year's. Both were holidays foreign to the Oriental people, who were other than Christian and who celebrated the lunar New Year instead of the solar New Year as we did. Had they only sought to allow us to celebrate and enjoy a meal, representative of what we might have had at home, it would have created a thoroughly favorable reaction among the recipients. The overtone of political expediency dampened our enthusiasm for all but the food.

After Major Bay had finished, I asked if he had any word on the possibility of an extra ration of food for Ben to counter the oncoming malnutrition. Mafia glanced at Ben, asking dryly, "Are you ill?" Major Bay's face fell noticeably as Ben related his inability to eat rice and insufficient fish to make up for the loss and told of the diarrhea he'd had and the one or two runs he was still making each day; not serious, but potentially dangerous if he got any weaker. Mafia nodded, his face unchanging.

I asked Major Bay if he had received my requests for food for Ben. He and Mafia both replied, almost in unison, "I did not know Wilkes was ill." It was my fault for not putting the request in writing and trusting Carpenter with his "There is no need to worry." He had probably been covering his own ass, by not letting the higher cadre know that the POW's were asking for food. I doubted that Major Bay could stand a report of another POW death going to his superiors, but I decided to hold the fact that Carpenter had failed to tell Major Bay about Ben.

On Christmas Day we received one chicken, two heads of Korean cabbage, three small papayas, manioc root, some grease, a handful of peppercorns and a type of French roll. A packet of coffee and white sugar topped off the Front's contribution to our Christmas. I had declined decoration material, thinking back to the propaganda photos that had been posed in the past and realizing how happy and content, well treated and adequately provided for we'd seem on this day. I saw no reason to dress it up any more for a photographer should he appear. One day out of 365 was hardly representative, but a photograph would last a long time. I did request a candle for each of us as a part of our observance. They were normally impossible to obtain and were surreptitiously used to kill errant mosquitoes in our nets at night after we'd been locked up. The total outlay of funds for a five-man celebration might have reached five hundred piastres—say five dollars—but to the five of us, it was a priceless opportunity to partake, savor, and rejoice.

Dan and I killed the chicken, instructed by the crowd of watching guards not to chop off its head, but to cut its throat, catch and save the blood for cooking. In Vietnamese cooking, particularly in the countryside, everything goes in the pot except the lower intestines and stomach. This includes feet and head. Back in the kitchen, John was cook of the day, with Dan and Jim assisting in preparation of the chicken.

Ben offered grace before the meal, which was observed and commented on by the guards. Showboat explained to them that this was the custom of our American religion and instead of making offerings or burning incense, we talked. I told him we also made offerings, indicating the plucked and boiled chicken head with its glazed eyes as I pulled it out of the soup pot and offered it to the god of the fireplace, tossing it among the burning sticks. I couldn't find the feet, somewhere among the limp cabbage leaves. We ate as if this were the last meal we would ever have.

The next morning we all had diarrhea as the greasy food

hit our unprepar   systems, and Ben took a nosedive, thinking his earlier diarrhea was causing his new runs. He had some sulfaguanidine left and took eight tablets, attributing the end of the runs the next day to the medication, even though the rest of us also ceased passing the loose stools at the same time without medication. He was back to a third of a pan of rice per meal, leaving him one and a third pans short of the minimum requirement at the end of a day. He was noticeably weaker although still able to walk. I prepared a crock for him, knowing he would soon be unable to make it to the latrine. He got the remaining papaya and sugar in an attempt to bolster his appetite, but without success.

We were back on what fish we could catch and the regular "ration" from the guards. I decided to chance our health after talking with the other three and getting their consent. We would give Ben from a third to half of all the fish we had each meal in an attempt to get some nourishment down him. The remaining fish would be split four ways, with the shares equal among us until one of us weakened physically, at which time the other three would give him the large portion, continuing the apportionment until we were unable to continue to perform our chores.

I reported the situation to Carpenter, not asking for help this time, but demanding it. I made certain there were no other guards around when I talked with him to avoid a confrontation where he'd have to maintain "face," most likely at the expense of the POW's. I received a lecture on the leniency shown by the Front in giving us the Christmas meal even under the conditions of war. I agreed and expressed our thanks, but reiterated how all the good would be invalidated if Ben died. I was told to return to my cage and Carpenter would take care of the matter.

Intern appeared to examine Ben and departed the camp after finding Ben unable to walk, barely able to sit up by himself. The next morning he returned with a package of medications and instructions for Jim and Dan to administer them. There were vials of vitamin B$_{12}$, Urotropin, a bottle of "levomycetin," which the label indicated contained chloramphenicol, excellent in treating the increasing diarrhea Ben was experiencing once again, since his system was unable to resist the bacteria and dysentery was almost certain to develop, and finally, a tube of

252

twenty concentrated chocolate tablets for "appetite." Cheeta bought a *ca loc* over at mealtime for Ben and he got it down with almost a full pan of *"chao,"* rice cooked to the consistency of gruel.

The *chao* was a standard diet for guards and POW's alike when they were too ill to eat regular rice. The Cream-of-Wheat consistency made it easier to consume, but the total nutritional value much less. With regular cooked rice, we used one cup of grains per man per meal. A pan of *chao* required only one-quarter cup of grain rice: thus, Ben in eating a pan of *chao*, got only a quarter of the required rice and a lot of water, which was of no practical value. Nevertheless, his spirits rose with the appearance of the medication. It seemed that the Front was going to provide the necessities for his survival.

That evening as I was helping him eat, encouraging him to get as much of the *chao* down as possible, in addition to the second medium-sized *ca loc* from the guards, Ben sent a shiver of apprehension up my back when he pushed away the remaining third of his *chao*: "I can't eat a pan of rice!" I looked at him, seeing Dave's face as he had said the very same words only days before he had left us. I lay awake that night, my net within an arm's reach of Ben's, listening to his shallow irregular breathing and trying to push out of my mind the awful finality of what was happening.

On 30 December, Intern brought vials of vitamins B_1 and C, camphorsulfonate and a can of milk. Ben's runs were increasing and the teaspoonful of levomycetin per meal wasn't helping. Dan reread the label and we realized that it wasn't going to help at all. The bottle Ben had been given was "levomycetin palmitate," a special preparation for pediatric usage. A dosage of 1 to 2 grams per day could be used and Ben was getting only 250 milligrams.

Jim was checking vital signs as Ben turned worse on the night of the thirtieth. He had a slight fever and was running a pulse of 100 to 120. He began to drift mentally and would black out if his head was elevated. He began to pass a lot of fluid in his stools, now virtually uncontrollable, and didn't have the strength to get to his crock. The pattern was so clear and so damned, damned irreversible.

On the morning of the thirty-first, I fed him a full pan of *chao* with a pan of milk. The only fish we had to give him

253

were two small *ca lac*, our "ration" for the meal, difficult to eat because of the bones and hardly worth the effort for their food value. He received the entire spectrum of injections: vitamins B_1, B_{12} and C, camphorsulfonate and Urotropin. The levomycetin was increased to two spoonfuls per meal. The chocolate tablets didn't taste good to Ben and he almost refused to take them, but Jim convinced him they at least provided some energy. He rallied slightly during the day as the combination of stimulant injection and sugar from the sweetened milk gave him temporary vigor.

That afternoon, one of the area's cadre brought in the ingredients for our New Year's meal: sugar, beans, rice starch candy for the sweet soup, coffee and sugar, and a small package of cookies. I had asked Carpenter if the money to be spent on the New Year's celebration could be diverted to buy food for Ben, hoping to get some type of meat, or perhaps eggs. He had replied that the Front was providing medicine and food already for Ben and the celebration would also be provided. We were given new sets of black pajamas and new sleeping mats, which we'd requested through Mafia because ours were almost unserviceable. Had it not been for Ben's condition, the Front would have provided us with a memorable and enjoyable holiday season.

Just before supper, Mafia and Major Bay arrived and sent Showboat over to tell us we would meet with them after supper. I took Ben's pan of *chao* and milk down to him before eating, figuring I'd get him straight before shoving my own rice down. He was in a neutral mood, somewhat incognizant of his surroundings, mentioning some movie he had to see, but aware of my attempts to feed him and the fact he didn't want to eat anything that tasted like rice. I had gotten a few spoonfuls of *chao* and milk into his mouth when John came to the door of the cage, saying Mafia was ready to see us and wanted me there. I told John that I had to finish helping Ben first and to tell Mafia it was more urgent that Ben eat. He understood immediately and left to relay the message.

I had gotten seven spoonfuls of *chao* and a quarter of the milk into Ben when John returned, stating Mafia had said that he would decide what was important and I could feed Ben afterward. I was to come immediately for the meeting. I left the pans beside Ben, urging him to try to eat some of it himself, knowing he wouldn't, and followed John to the guards' kitchen where Jim and Dan were seated in front of the two cadre.

After I sat down, Mafia inquired about Ben's condition, asking if the medication had helped. I replied that Ben was in serious condition and we were worried about his chances of living. Major Bay nodded seriously as I spoke, his brow creasing as he understood what I was saying. I had never tried to exaggerate the seriousness of our conditions when speaking with the Major and I believe he realized I wasn't in the present case. Mafia waited until I finished and began a spiel on the two celebrations the Front had arranged for us in accordance with its policy toward POW's. The provision for respect of our religious beliefs and the issue of new clothing and mats were proof of the validity of the Front's concern for the welfare of its captives. We were to clearly realize the facts before us and write them in a letter, stating the treatment afforded us.

He had assumed the propitiating air that John had noticed nearly always accompanied a soft-sell requirement for us to write something for him. We took the sheets of paper and pens, wondering how he could ignore what was happening to Ben and ask us to write about the Christmas meal and clothing. It was like looking at the fire-blackened bottom of one of our cooking pots, rubbing two small clean spots in the center and asking someone to write about them as a description of the condition of the pot bottom.

We returned to the cage, where Ben was stretched out in a restless sleep. I put his pans outside his net, untouched except for the little he'd eaten before, thinking that I'd have to get a lot down him in the morning to make up for missing tonight. Dan peered through the net, reaching under to feel Ben's temple and check his pulse without letting mosquitoes under the net. He withdrew his hand, tucking the net back under the straw mat. "Fever," he said quietly, "pulse is fluttery, too damn fast." Bud appeared in the doorway and told us to get in our nets. It was totally dark in a few minutes and each of us was alone in the rectangular world of his mosquito net; there wasn't anything for us to talk about. I woke up once during the night, groggy, hearing a frightening rising and falling low sound coming from Ben's net. It was eerie, almost as if he were trying to sing. I dropped back into slumber with the sound in my ears.

Just before dawn broke through the trees, Frank Lloyd opened

255

the cage door and unlocked my irons. I was on cooking duty and hurried to empty my nearly full crock and take my early morning crap before washing up and preparing breakfast. I glanced at Ben's net as I left the hut and saw him on his back with his hands folded on his chest. His right leg was slightly bent at the knee, leaning across the extended left leg. I wondered what the sounds he had made were.

The rice was cooking and I was putting Ben's *chao* on the second three *nuoc mam* crocks, keeping it above the flames, when Dan came into the kitchen. I looked around as he squatted beside me. "Ben's dead."

Something was squeezing my guts, twisting and pulling. I sat back on the pole floor, unmindful suddenly of the swarming mosquitoes about my unprotected feet. Dan reached over and swatted them absently with his folded towel. "I checked him when I got up. No pulse, no respiration. Rigor mortis is setting in. Jim's with him now."

I felt tears welling up in my eyes; sorrow, frustration, anger; but I couldn't cry, no matter what I felt. I wiped the dirty sleeve of my torn work clothes across my eyes and stood up. "You son of a bitch, Mafia. You miserable, rotten son of a bitch. I could have at least gotten a meal into him before he died, at least done that for him, but I had to come and listen to your fucking shit about the fucking leniency of the fucking Front." All the venom welled up in me as the thoughts of Mafia and last night raced through my mind. I walked out of the kitchen and down the log walk toward the cage. Dan shifted the kindling under the rice pot, stoking the fire.

John met me as I passed Jim's cage, his face set in lines of anguish. In the cage, Jim squatted beside Ben's mat, the mosquito net pulled up from the edges. There was a cold strangeness in the body lying on the mat. It wasn't the Ben I'd known. He was gone. "He went peacefully," Jim said softly as I squatted beside him. The face was calm, almost relieved, the hands folded loosely across the chest. Ben had detested the filth of diarrhea. A puddle of yellowish fluid lay beneath his shrunken buttocks, globs of clear mucus and blood floating in it. His right leg was bent at the knee, raised away and across the left leg as if to avoid contact with the liquid.

"We'll get him cleaned up and his new blacks on him. I don't want the guards to see him like this." Jim nodded as I spoke. We might have to live with filth, but they weren't going to see Ben dead in it. Dan came into the cage to help us. John was taking care of the rice.

When we had washed him and straightened his meager possessions, I left to tell the guards. I was torn between anger and frustration as I approached the canal and log bridge leading to the guards' kitchen. The helplessness of our situation, of watching my people die and not being able to do anything, was choking me. It must have been equally bad for Jim and Dan who, as medics, knew what should be done, what was needed, but couldn't help either.

I walked into the hut where the guards were gathered, squatting around a large pot of rice with their bowls and chopsticks, picking at a smaller pot filled with chunks of *ca loc*. Conversation stopped abruptly as I entered without the required permission. Heads swiveled toward me, the eyes hostile and questioning. I searched the faces until I located Carpenter at the far end of the group, locking eyes with him. *"Anh Giai Phong, Wilkes da chet roi"*—Wilkes is dead.

Carpenter's bowl, poised at his lips as he shoveled rice into his mouth, sagged, spilling the white grains onto the mat. There was silence, eyes fell away from my face as guards' glances dropped to the floor. Carpenter couldn't disengage his eyes as my statement registered in his mind. His lips began to work, but no sound came out. His eating bowl hung from his fingers, the rice continuing to spill onto the mat. I turned and walked out, returning to our kitchen where the others were gathered around the cooking fires.

We squatted beside each other, watching the flames dancing under the pot of water John was boiling. "I wonder if they'll let us bury him?" Jim broke the silence. The sound of approaching bare feet on the shaky logs outside interrupted us. Intern, Cheeta and Carpenter appeared in the door. *"Wilk dau ay?"* Cheeta demanded.

Jim stood up slowly and led them to the cage where Intern took one look and turned to Carpenter, speaking in low, rapid Vietnamese. Jim came back with them and Cheeta told me to prepare Ben to be taken out for burial. I told him we would rather bury him ourselves since he was our friend. Carpenter vetoed this immediately. The Front was responsible for the interment of the dead and our only responsibility was to get him ready. Argument hadn't saved his life and it wouldn't get us permission to bury him.

The final twist of their knife came when we were told to take his good blacks off and clothe him in an old pair. The Front wanted the new pair back. Jim helped me carry the sleeping-mat-wrapped remains to a boat by the log bridge.

Ours was a quiet farewell to soft-spoken, gentle Ben Wilkes, a beautiful human being who could find no existence in this harsh, hypocritical world of imprisonment. The uncomplicated essence of his easygoing nature found release in the final dignity of death, the untouchable realm, free from the oppressiveness and aggravation that existence here carried with it. Ben was clean and free, his bubbling, mirthful laughter rolling forth once again. "Please be happy with him, Lord," I prayed. "He's a good man."

6

On March 4, 1967 we were taken from the camp we called "Hanoi II," leaving behind the physical reminders of that period of imprisonment, but each of us bore the mental scars that, though invisible, would ache in the long nights ahead. The short boat ride brought us back to the No-K Corral, where we found relatively sophisticated new construction had altered the old layout.

We four Americans were placed in a single, low-ceilinged cage, barred on all sides, top and bottom. There was barely enough room for our individual mosquito nets to fit side by side and our sleeping mats overlapped partially, creating the feeling of total restriction. The pole flooring was unusually uneven and we piled strips of bark under our mats in an effort to gain some sort of minimal comfort. The barred ceiling was perhaps three and a half feet above the floor, forcing us to crouch when entering the cage and limiting our movement. It was a terrific relief to be able to leave this cage in the mornings and stretch, after the leg irons were unlocked.

The guards were still at work completing the camp and we found ourselves forced to carry logs and peel the bark from them as the guards used hundreds of the poles in construction of their kitchen, a guard mess hall, two guard huts, a small POW kitchen and a long hut to be used by the Americans as a mess hall and school hut. It was exhausting work and we found our strength quickly draining, although the guards gave

259

no indication that they noticed. The baking hot sun seemed to sap our energy as soon as we stepped out of the shadowy tree line and there never was enough water to satisfy our punishing thirst. Only at night, when we accepted the restriction of the cage, was there relief from the heat.

I noticed the reappearance of older guards. Thanh was back, as were Porky and Base, each of them evidencing changes in their attitudes and manner. Thanh was now a talkative, solicitously smiling squad cadre, his appealing, boyish sincerity and simplicity replaced by the brash, clamorous arrogance of newly assumed authority. Base and Porky had both been assigned as boat handlers and bodyguards for higher-ranking political cadre. Exposure to the dedicated political leaders of the revolution had provided Porky and Base not only with individuals to be emulated, but also with the rhetoric to support their new identities. Both were virtually unrecognizable as the inhibited, frustrated young boys we had known before. It was unfortunate that in losing their prior weaknesses, they had developed the veneer of fanaticism that often shields the developing revolutionary from the full spectrum of human reaction and interreaction, leaving him merely an automated shell with only revolutionary responses functioning.

Major Bay visited the camp and introduced a new cadre who was to be in command of the camp. Mr. Sau was hardcore; there was no doubt of this from our first meeting on. He was a Southerner who had gone to North Vietnam for training at the political schools in Hanoi and had infiltrated South Vietnam in 1962 or 1963 to carry out his duties as a political cadre. His eyes were like narrow pools of ice water, totally devoid of any emotion. His voice was low-pitched and soft, but each word snapped like a slap in the face. His manner was one of a man who could give the order for his child to be beheaded and smile as it was carried out. In talking with us, he displayed an arrogance we hadn't detected in the other cadre. The impression was that we were the Caucasians who had dominated his country, in the form of the French, and had felt superior to him as a Vietnamese. Now he, as a Vietnamese, was in complete control of us. My misgivings about existence in this camp were increased as a result of the meeting with this cadre.

We established the same cooking and chore routine we had followed before with Jim Jackson filling the fourth slot. Dan,

John and I were familiar with the layout of the camp and soon had made our conditions as livable as restrictions would allow. Fish were provided by the guards and we discovered edible greens around the camp that partially replaced the potato leaves in our diet. After Ben's death in the last camp, we had been given a larger ration of fish for almost a month, but as in times past, the extra food had ceased and we were back on a bare subsistence level. Major Bay had assured us that conditions in this camp would be better than before and we earnestly hoped he was telling the truth.

In April 1967, there was a concentrated effort by the guards to provide fish for our meals and we found ourselves eating an average of one and a half *ca ro* per man per day, about two mouthfuls of fish per man. It was a great assistance in eating the rice and raised our hopes for survival. We were also given glutinous rice, *com nep*, which had a flavor somewhat like oatmeal, if one stretched his imagination. It was much easier to eat than the regular rice and I found myself able to eat a greater quantity even without fish to push it down.

Thanh undertook the task of digging a trench around the camp and with almost no help from the other guards, completed a seventy-five- or eighty-meter length of ditch, one meter wide and an average of two meters deep. The dry-season water level was substantially below surface in this area and he appeared to dig with little trouble. Even so, I was amazed at the strength and endurance. The other guards, when they infrequently helped him, became tired rapidly while the lithe, hard-muscled young cadre worked on, oblivious to heat and exhaustion. I listened one evening after completion of the trench as Sau praised the example set by the squad cadre and urged the other guards to do equally well in their tasks. I recalled that Thanh had, on several occasions, encouraged the other guards to do their part in the digging without any real response other than halfhearted appearances to toss a dozen or so shovelfuls before they disappeared to get a drink of tea. It was a case where the guards could either help or go about their own work and studies, leaving Thanh to complete the task he undertook.

We speculated about the purpose of the trench and decided it was to be a moat for *punji* stakes surrounding the camp as a barrier. Dan commented sarcastically that, as in the mangroves, it would probably be "to keep the people out." As it

261

developed, *punji* stakes were sharpened, but they were taken out of camp to be used elsewhere. The mound of earth piled beside the ditch was used by the guards as an area for planting manioc and a type of aquatic edible green. The mound would be above water during the rainy season, thus making it an ideal garden as well as a path around the camp. Unfortunately, our erstwhile gardeners hadn't considered the fact that the good humus, the decayed leaf material that Thanh had dug through in breaking ground, was at the bottom of the mound and they were planting in the claylike mud he had dug from the bottom of the ditch.

In mid-May, we were seriously concerned when Dan and John were told to prepare to move out of the camp. They left on the evening of 15 May with Sau, Base and Bud. Jim and I were left in the camp with no real idea of what was happening although we had been told that our two friends would be going to a village with Mafia. I could think of nothing I would enjoy less than being near Mafia, but the thought of being in a village with food was tempting. There was a period of difficult readjustment to the sudden void in our small world.

The immediate question was what the reason for the split was. Jim had not given the VC what they wanted after his capture and had been subjected to the "helicopter ride," suspended from a roof beam by a rope around his arms which were tied behind his back. Mafia tried to "influence" the tough young NCO to fill out the declaration with this type of pressure, but succeeded only in pissing Jim off. After he passed out several times, falling face-down in mud and water and nearly suffocating once, Jim caused Mafia to try the long-term approach. That was why he had come to our last camp. Nor had my attitude been exemplary by VC standards. We concluded that the decision to have us remain together in No-K Corral hadn't been for our benefit and we set about planning an escape.

Our evaluation was verified as the supply of fish was cut drastically and we found ourselves eating whatever greens we could scrounge and an increasing diet of the rotten *ca mam*. The dry season had dried up the canals and the guards were eating the fresh fish themselves, leaving Jim and me with the *ca mam* that had been made in the camp. I had found that the fermented fish were difficult to stomach even when properly made, and our guards had also managed to thoroughly foul up

262

the batch of *nuoc mam* they had tried to make. The blue-black rotten flesh clinging to the bones we were given was totally inedible.

We had watched the process as large piles of fish, seined from the reservoirs, were scaled, partially or wholly gutted, and packed in cement urns. Salt water was poured over them and the top of the urn sealed with dried banana tree bark. Within days, the stench was enough to create a strong desire to vomit and the flies swarmed in clouds above the urns. The problem at that time was that the guards were using what was supposed to be our mess hall as a storage shed for the vile-smelling urns and we were unable to eat near them. Rice was difficult enough to eat without the added handicap of the rotten smell and flies. The guards couldn't understand why we refused to eat in the mess hall and crowded into the tiny kitchen hut.

Several weeks later, the tops were removed from the urns and Carpenter, the local connoisseur of *ca mam*, inspected the maggot-covered mass of decaying fish. More salt was needed in the brine, he declared, and grain rice was roasted, then crushed into a rough powder to be used as a coating for the fish when repacked. Once the fish were coated with the rice powder and repacked in the urns, the brine was poured back over them and the urns were resealed. Somewhere the process had failed and now Jim and I were given the resulting mess as a ration.

In mid-June, Mom M arrived with the report of an impending execution. Jim and I were worried as the aging cadre spoke of an ultimatum issued by the NLF to the South Vietnamese Government that the execution of three Vietcong in Saigon would cause a retaliatory execution of American POW's. I had no doubt that the Front would carry out their threat and began linking our separation from John and Dan with it. The possibility of the two of us being selected was strong and I only wondered why Muoi would tell us. We were reminded that our attitudes had been bad, and in an offhand manner, Muoi mentioned that the Front would select POW's who had failed to recognize their crimes and progress. He dropped the subject after he was certain we had realized the full implications. I found myself hoping the three VC would get jail sentences rather than the death sentence.

We began working seriously on the plan for escape as the

pressure built, but fortune slapped us down. Jim had been forcing the *ca mam* down as we sorted through our ration to get what fish was not rotten and cooked it with leaves to make a sort of gravy that could be poured over the rice. After seventeen straight days of *ca mam* without a break, Jim's system revolted and he vomited his guts up. For nearly two hours, his stomach turned inside out, racking him with dry heaves when there was nothing left to barf. My stomach convulsed as I tried to help him and I fought to keep my rice down.

When the spasms passed, Jim was completely wrung out and his mental resolve was shaken. He had encountered for the first time the body's resistance to the only food we had available to us and knew what would happen if he couldn't force himself to accept the rations. It was terrifying for me to watch the horrible pattern emerge once again. I went to the guards and found Carpenter, telling him that Jim needed fresh fish. His immediate reply was that there were no fresh fish available yet, but some responsive chord must have been touched because he asked if Jim was sick. The story of the *ca mam*, related in front of Sauser, brought a promise of gill nets which I could use to catch fish in the canal. It was more than I hoped for, and the early rains which brought water back into our camp canal provided us with a beginning of hope for Jim's survival.

With Jim and me struggling to keep our heads above water, pushing rice and making all possible efforts to provide sufficient fish to keep ourselves going, 17 July marked Dan and John's return to the camp. There was immediate happiness at seeing them again and the sudden relief of tension as Jim and I knew Muoi's talk of POW executions in this camp would be less likely to be fulfilled now that the other two were back. Both of them looked well, although John had run into serious problems with diarrhea while away from the camp.

I learned that they had, in fact, been taken to a village in a Communist-controlled zone where they had spent two months. Mafia had conducted a series of indoctrination sesssions for them in conjunction with a school in which he taught English to members of various groups within the NLF ranks. It had been Mafia's effort to force concentrated indoctrination on them and exploit their status as POW's by exhibiting them to his students and on an occasion, to the villagers in the area.

Dan related the carefully staged trip through the "liberated

264

zone" on which he and John were shown an area sprayed with defoliant, the site of a B-52 strike, a maternity hospital, a cemetery for dead war heroes, a school and a meeting place. The people in the areas had obviously been coached for their roles as they displayed a threatening attitude and, on cue from the cadre, denounced John and Dan for their "crimes." Dan mentioned one instance where a young man jumped from the canal bank into the canal waving a knife and showing all intentions of slicing him and John to ribbons. A local cadre intervened from the canal bank and the action ceased, leaving Mafia to explain the complete respect and obedience the people showed to the Front and its cadre. Both John and Dan recognized the underlying fraudulent note in the people's responses as the cadre guided and aroused the crowd at each site, thus structuring the scenes to fit their needs. They also noted that the responses and outbursts were turned on and off like the flicking of a light switch, indicating more of a rehearsed than a spontaneous reaction. I filed the comments away in my mind, fitting them into the growing picture I was getting of the methods employed by our captors.

Jim Jackson began the death process on 20 July 1967. Only three days after Dan and John had returned, causing our meager supply of fish to be divided further and bringing *ca mam* back on the menu, Jim's fragile grasp on discipline slipped. It took the mention of *ca mam*, only the words, to slam him back into the full gut-spewing paroxysms. On 22 July, he was vomiting after almost every mouthful of the gruel-consistency, soft rice *chao* we were preparing for him, but he fought to keep eating. Diarrhea set in rapidly and his body fluids were draining.

A new VC medic appeared in the camp and prescribed a type of local medication that looked like double O buckshot. Jim took several of the pellets and in two hours was pouring a greenish bile from both ends. The "medicine" must have been a highly toxic substance. The medic insisted that the medication would cause the bacteria to be rapidly flushed from Jim's intestines, but failed to consider the effect of further dehydration through massive fluid loss.

On the twenty-third, Jim was in low spirits. He made one attempt to eat the morning *chao*, but pushed his pan away after vomiting. He knew what would follow, the certain death, but he had reached the abysmal depths of hopelessness and his

265

words were like an awful echo from before, "Why prolong it? I can't eat rice!" God how I hated those words! How I hated the tiny oppressive sphere in which we struggled to exist. The simple, terrifying equation of eat rice and live, refuse and die.

There was a measure of concern from Sau and Major Bay which resulted in an appearance of medication. Jim received vitamins B_1, C, and B_{12} along with the stimulant solucamphor and Nivaquine tablets, a malaria treatment. As usual, the medication was a shotgun effect with no attempt to isolate the cause of the illness and eliminate it. The guards and cadre refused to accept the fact that adequate food was all that was necessary to reduce if not eliminate the malnutrition and disease among the POW's. How many times I had heard, "the Front provides adequately for your livelihood." If only they would recognize that we were not able to adapt as easily to the diet of rice for our staple as they were, and that the appetite-crippling monotony beat us all into collapse. The superficial attempts to provide medication might as well not have been given if food didn't accompany it.

Jim fought to eat as his spirit surged up, unwilling to be crushed by the conditions forced upon us. He asked the VC medic for specific medicine which he knew would be effective in treating the amebic dysentery, and after some discussion and conflict between cadre and the medic, Jim was given two vials of Emetine and a native version of paregoric. The medication took effect and the runs slowed. We convinced the medic that something was needed to boost Jim's appetite and he received the can of milk and sugar we had hoped for. The calories would give his body something to burn while the rice was made easier to eat. I began to see a chance for the crisis to pass. Jim wasn't going to quit, he was fighting to stay alive!

I was preparing the *chao* for him and refused to accept his inability to eat a full pan. Each meal I brought a heaping pan and set it in his net as if I expected him to consume the contents without trouble. It became a challenge to him and within three days he was able to force down two full pans of *chao* each day. By rationing the milk and sugar, he was able to stretch it out for four days before we were faced with an empty cupboard and the prospect of giving him *nuoc mam* again.

Jim's spirits were high as he felt himself countering the initial onslaught of dysentery and the inability to eat. I had watched and prayed as he battled himself, conquering the despair and hopelessness that had fatally weakened the inner resolve of our friends. Once he determined that he wasn't going to let himself die, it became for me a matter of doing everything in my power to help him breach the barrier of readjustment to the diet. Jim, in deciding to rely on his own resolve, his own inner strength to survive, had found the answer. A man who depended on his own will to live, using whatever our captors provided as an assistance, not a necessity, could surmount the obstacles to survival posed by the environment. The night Jimmy was at his lowest point, the night he was at the crucial point of living or dying, I woke up to hear him in the grip of the cramps and agony of one of his many violent passages of bacteria-laden excrement. As he lay back on his rice straw sleeping mat, panting in pain, his voice was a poignant plea, "Dear Lord, don't take pain 'cause it makes me know I'm still alive. Please, Lord, please give me the strength to bear it and the strength to keep going. Don't let me quit." I added my silent prayer for him to be heard. I knew the pain, the weakness, the anguish, and it was a battle each man had to fight within himself. Prayer was the only means we had to reinforce ourselves and it was the best.

The day Jim was to eat his first meal with nothing but *nuoc mam*, I heated up pots of water so he could take a warm bath, a luxury which lifted his spirits even higher. His obvious joy while sponging with the warm water and washing with a bar of carefully hoarded good soap we had swiped from the guards brought an air of celebration into the POW compound. He was going to make it! He had been knocked to his knees, but had gotten up and was going to live! I had no doubt that he would eat and begin to rebuild his strength. It was so damn good to have him alive and determined to survive.

By 30 July, Jim was eating regular cooked rice again and had set up a program of easy exercises to regain muscle tone. His first urge was to get out of his mosquito net, to escape the "cotton coffin" that had entrapped Dave and Ben. The crisis had been weathered and now we had to work to prevent a recurrence.

Our efforts to catch fish provided us with some food as the rainy season progressed and more fish appeared in the area. The guards gave us their discarded gill nets, and after spending

267

hours mending the tears, we put them to use. We picked up hooks and line from the stakeouts that had been abandoned by the guards and put them out around the camp, further supplementing our diet and bringing us up to the two small fish per man per day level. An occasional snake in our nets provided a special feast, although it destroyed the weak threads. The restrictions imposed by the guards hampered our ability to adequately provide for ourselves, but we were getting a little elbow room and knew that if we could be allowed a little more freedom, there would be a good chance for survival. Some of the greens planted by the guards were beginning to grow, but were taken by the guards for their meals almost as soon as they sprouted. We used forest greens and edible plants, and occasionally we would find some of the planted greens untouched by the guards and use them for our soup.

The long period of *ca mam* before Dan and John's return, coupled with the rice and *nuoc mam* diet during Jim's illness did their work on my already weakened system and on 3 August 1967, dysentery slammed into me with fever, nausea and violent cramping. I had managed to hold on until Jim was out of danger so there wouldn't be two of us down at once, but with the sudden onslaught of dysentery, provoked by malnutrition, I found myself facing another crucial test in my own battle with disease. The cramping spasms that accompanied the ten or fifteen crap runs I made each day were old enemies of mine, as was the fever. The greatest threat was the nausea that could prevent me from getting enough rice down. My intestines felt as though broken glass was being forced through them and the continuing pain throughout my abdomen made eating extremely difficult. In a moment of reflection one afternoon as I sat in utter misery on the latrine, I thought how fortunate I was to have gotten this disease early in captivity, when my body was still strong, and to have learned to accept it. Had I gotten the disease as a new ailment after more than three years as a prisoner, it was doubtful if I could have forced my mind to accept and deal with the pain and the filth. How low I've sunk in conditions of living, I thought; or more exactly, conditions of existence, of survival. A sudden drop to this level would be enough to destroy any man's will to live.

The fluid loss and inability to contain any food very long further weakened my system and I noticed the edema which indicated beri-beri again. The VC medic, now identified as an "Y-Si," or physician, came in to examine me after Jim and Dan had reported the seriousness of my condition to Sauser. With both of the Special Forces medics standing close by, aiding him in diagnosing the problem, he concluded that I had dysentery and "*thung*." Dan gave him the words "beri-beri" and he picked them up as "American medical terminology," adding to the few French medical terms he knew. After that, his every visit included mention of "Beri" and earned him that as a nickname.

Sauser was asked to pass on the political aspect of medical treatment. It seemed that the VC medics could suggest medication to be given for a particular POW's disease, but the political cadre would have to decide on the political qualification of that POW. Based on the POW's attitude toward his captors and their indoctrinations, whether or not he was "living under the lenient policy of the Front," and other related factors, the cadre could either approve or reject the suggestion. Whether or not the medication was immediately available also counted heavily in what the POW could expect to receive. It could be the prescribed medication, a lesser type or a lesser amount, depending on the cadre's decision and the supply.

I received a tube of twenty sulfaguanidine tablets, which had failed to knock my intestinal problem during the past three years, and a sack of "*gao luc*," grain rice with some of the husk and the bran unremoved, providing thiamine to counter the vitamin B_1 deficiency. Fortunately, the sulfa slowed the dysentery, but the rice grains even after being cooked acted like roughage with the remaining husk coating tearing through my very tender intestines faster than a load of commercial laxative in the packages. Everything passed through too rapidly for my body to absorb the vitamins and I decided to hold off on the rice and ride with the beri-beri for a while, letting the sulfa take care of the runs first. Once the bacteria count in my intestines was down to a workable level, I would go back and try the rice again. Jimmy was having his day now as he made certain I forced down a pan of regular rice each meal, no matter how long it took to eat. Again, that was the key to survival.

Mafia and Major Bay appeared on 9 August, checking on the reports that the Americans were having a bad time with disease. All four of us stressed the importance of at least the bare minimum of nutritional requirements to enable us to keep going. There was a flicker of understanding as they heard basically the same request from all of us. Major Bay seemed amazed that we were not able to find enough food for ourselves and I pushed the opportunity to ask for more gill nets, stakeouts and a chance to fish in a larger area. Mafia said he would check with "the commander of the camp," who happened to be Sauser, sitting across the hut from him, but it was made to sound very official. We left the hut with at least a hint of a chance to provide for ourselves.

Shortly after that the guards began a larger effort at planting greens, manioc and even several pepper bushes. Two chickens were brought into the camp and the guards began to supplement our fish with some they had caught. There had obviously been an order from the cadre to keep the Americans alive and the guards responded with the usual initial vigor which rapidly slipped through grudging compliance to disregard. We ate well for almost a week as the guards contributed one or two large *ca loc* or several large *ca ro* for our meals each day. After that it was the castoffs from their daily haul, most of which were overripe, having died and gone rotten in the gill nets before the guards picked them up. On one day in particular, Cheeta came down with a can of about twenty fish for the four of us and out of the total number we salvaged three that were edible. I took the fish to show to the guards, telling them there was no sense in bringing the rotten fish to us because we couldn't eat them. Base told me to cook them in a lot of salt water and the taste wouldn't be too bad. Cheeta snapped out that *"Anh Giai Phong* eats fish like that." Realizing I couldn't argue with them, I set the bloated, smelly fish on the floor of their mess hut and told Cheeta I was returning them and perhaps *Anh Giai Phong* could have them for supper since the Americans didn't want to waste food.

The rooster and hen that had been brought in were establishing themselves as favorite characters with the Americans. We dubbed the rooster "Calhoun" and the hen "Miss Pris" and spent many of the long hours watching the hen drive Calhoun to the verge of frustration as she ignored his attempts toward male dominance. Aside from his developing status of a true henpecked male, our feathered alarm clock had a malfunction in his timer and ignored the rising sun, choosing to crow roughly between eight and ten o'clock at night, depending on moonrise. On nights of a full moon, we could lie in the cage and listen to Calhoun out on a walk around the area, probably convinced that it was daylight. Miss Pris, clucking and grumbling to herself, followed reluctantly behind the knight of our small barnyard.

By early September, I had the runs under control and was again able to eat a normal amount of rice without too much difficulty. The cadre sent in extra fill nets for us and informed us we could sell extra fish we caught by giving them to the guards when they went to market. Our first concern was to catch enough to eat, but the thought of having a little buying power was tempting. We planned all the items we would buy, letting our imaginations far exceed any possibility we had of making the actual purchases. It was wonderful to dream.

In the hours we spent sitting and talking in the kitchen or the "*nha mam*,"—the "house of *nuoc mam*—I remembered an idea I had begun to fashion back in the mangroves as a time-killer and tossed it out for group discussion. It was a plan for a resort, to be built after I got out of the prison camp, and it provided a wonderful topic for all of us to consider. Jimmy was keenly interested, and once his attention turned to the development of the idea, his recovery from the illness became more rapid. He had something he could contemplate and focus his attention on and the mental activity was like a release from our surroundings. John and Dan added their ideas, based on past experience, and the concept grew. It became a composite of all the activities we would want in a resort, all the conveniences and a setting, a perfect location to accentuate what we had created. It was this basic plan that I drew from and expanded to create the "Hacienda del Sol" complete with menus, advertising campaign and staff during the long months that lay ahead of me. It became my vehicle for reaching the outside world, one of the many dreams.

Radio Hanoi was our source of news and added nothing to raise our spirits. There was an increasing use of U.S. news reports and editorial comment on them by the North Vietnamese to validate their stand on the war. The dissent within the United States gave them a means to encourage their followers, influence the uncommitted, and challenge their opponents. Just the fact that the reports were in good English and came from Americans whose protests to the war took the form of support for the enemy was enough to create a feeling of hopelessness. Radio Liberation, the "Voice of the NLF," used the propaganda program "Radio Stateside," which was taped in the United States and sent to them for broadcast to U.S. troops. We listened to the American commentators condemning our government, urging support for the militant groups in America, and praising the actions of the NLF. It was as if our country was being turned upside down and we sat listening, wondering what we would find in America if we ever did return. Chinh and Cheeta joined Sauser in giving political lectures to us at odd times, using no set schedule, but emphasizing the reports that had come over the radio.

Our fishing ventures enabled us to sell fish on two occasions, although our requests to buy food were denied. It was another case of the inflexible contention by the cadre that "the Front provides adequately for your livelihood." We were encouraged to buy tea, sugar and cookies as treats without considering any of the possible purchases which would have contributed nutritional value to our meals. It was difficult to comprehend their reasoning until Cheeta inadvertently gave us the answer. "The Front is charged with providing for your material welfare under its lenient policy toward POW's. If you were forced to buy your own food, you could claim ill treatment under the policy." His logic stunned me. As long as they maintained the facade of providing for us, even with men dying under their "lenient policy," they could claim compliance, leniency and humanitarianism. It was frightening how they depended on the worthless words of their policy to form the mask shown to the world when reality here in the prison camp, unseen by outside eyes, formed the ugly face under the mask.

We bought raw brown sugar, black pepper, and two cloves of garlic with our first fish money after rejecting a packet of white sugar, several ounces of tea and twelve cookies the guards had elected to buy for us with our money. Sauser allowed us to exchange the items after I protested to him that we didn't need the items the guards bought and wanted condiments and the cheaper brown sugar, thinking of quantity. It was a grudging concession on his part and I found myself marked as a troublemaker by Sauser for my actions. The incident with the rotten fish, my contention of points of illogic with the guards in indoctrinations, and now the refusal of the guards' purchases were not in keeping with Sauser's concept of the subservient American POW. I was claiming basic rights that a POW didn't have.

On 14 September, the first indications of some big event began to unfold. A group of party cadre, a journalist, the dried-up little VC major who was said to command this particular series of camps, and Sauser gathered in Sauser's redecorated guard mess hall for a conference with the American prisoners. Dan and John went together, then Jimmy and I were called separately after they had finished. I passed Jim as he left the forum, catching his negative shake of the head and finger over his lips. He wasn't smiling, so whatever was in store couldn't be good.

I was told to sit on one of the benches which ran the length of the table in the hut. Across from me were the cadre and the journalist. Sauser sat at the end of the bench to my left and the little major perched on a stool at the end of the hut. Chinh and Bud squatted near the door at the other end of the hut. The journalist spoke enough English to be understood and began by telling me that the representatives of the Central Committee had come to visit the camp to determine the conditions of the American prisoners and to review their progress. He offered me a cup of sweetened cocoa, which I accepted and drank with great delight. I noticed a tape recorder on the bench beside the journalist and was immediately on guard, understanding what Jimmy had been telling me as we passed on the log walk. When the first question came on my health and the conditions in the camp, perfunctorily asked by one of the cadre, I took the opportunity to review the history of our small group of Americans, outlining the problems we had encountered with disease and malnutrition. As the journalist translated, the cadre nodded, and one of them asked Sauser about measures taken to offset the problems. Sauser pointed to the remaining plants along the mound of earth, mentioned the chickens, and told the cadre that we had recently sold fish to purchase sugar, condiments and tea. Eyes focused on me and I realized what had been structured to catch such a complaint as mine. I had dropped into Sauser's trap and his position must have looked quite secure to the cadre if they really even gave a damn.

The questions shifted to the war and what I knew of the

273

situation. I noticed the tape recorder was switched on, and I began by asking in Vietnamese if I might use their language so the cadre could perhaps understand more easily. There was surprise on their faces and no one spoke until an older man on the end who had been totally disinterested told me to go ahead and use Vietnamese. The tape recorder was turned off and it became clear that they were just killing time and following a script with my appearance here. They were probably willing to record anything that might be worked in as propaganda, but the attitude was one of boredom. I gave them a five-minute recap of the latest action reports from Radio Hanoi before the journalist told me it was sufficient. He asked a question which seemed to emanate from his personal interest about my knowledge of the language and what I understood of Vietnamese culture.

I was able to recall portions of Vietnamese history, mentioning Tran Hung Dao and Le Loi, two early heroes of the Vietnamese people who developed guerrilla warfare to defeat the Chinese, and Nguyen Du, who wrote the great literary masterpiece *Kim Van Kieu*, a poem which was translated into many Oriental and Occidental languages. There was complete attention from all of the men as they heard the three names and my brief comment about each man's fame. Several other questions came from the cadre, directed at what I knew of the antiwar sentiment in America and whether I believed the Front would gain final victory. My only comment was that if they could force the Americans to withdraw from Vietnam and then carry out their pledge to fight until final victory, it seemed logical that their sons or grandsons might see final victory. The journalist translated my last statement, made in English, omitting the "sons and grandsons" portion. The cadre seemed more bored than before and I was told that my attitude had been judged by the "commander of the camp" (Sauser) to be unsatisfactory because of conflicts with the guards and failure to follow camp regulations. Sauser sat looking out the side of the hut and the little major absently swatted mosquitoes. I nodded and waited as the journalist looked to the others for something else to say. No one was listening and he spoke to Sauser, telling him I was finished. Sauser told me to go back to the hut and not discuss what had been said with the others. Before I left, the journalist stopped me and told me if I wanted to write a letter to my family, he would see that it was sent through the

Liberation Red Cross. I acknowledged him and walked back to the kitchen wondering why they had even bothered to call me over.

The next day, John and Dan had their photographs taken and the cadre who had stayed overnight departed. For the next several days we discussed the possibility of release and could pinpoint no reasons for the selection other than the obvious reasons for my being rejected and Jim's short period of captivity. It was certain that outside influences which we couldn't evaluate were responsible.

We had been given glutinous rice for our meals and found it was actually beginning to level our weight off. On several occasions we received bunches of a type of cabbage and manioc, which greatly improved the menu. Chinh brought down bananas and a coconut for us and helped us to make curry one evening. It was a period of better food and rising hopes for building our health.

On 22 September, John suddenly declared he couldn't eat and began vomiting when he tried to push rice down. It was a shock to all of us because he had been the strongest eater during our nearly four years even when he had run-ins with diarrhea. He missed both meals on the twenty-second and immediately began making an increasing number of crap runs.

Ben Casey came in with Beri to check John, and with Dan's and Jim's help determined that John needed specific medication to knock the runs and build his body's resistance. Ben had his own ideas about what medication would be given, but the two Special Forces medics put him on the right track. I took it from there and spent several hours with the two VC medics trying to convince them of the need for food in conjunction with the medication. Ben soon agreed, but Beri contended that the food wasn't available, relating his stand to the times in the past when we had literally begged for food for our dying friends and had received none. Ben will remain in my thoughts as the one who placed the issue of a man's life ahead of whatever political restrictions existed. He told Sauser that John was going to die if food wasn't provided. His word as an *Y-Si* apparently carried weight as he further told Sauser that he was recommending to the higher cadre that John receive a special ration. I saw, for the first time in four years, the political cadre bend in compliance with a humanitarian request.

Medication came into the camp in amounts and types that

exceeded anything we had seen in all the other years combined. Vitamins B₁, C, B₁₂, B complex, solucamphor, atropine, penicillin G, Emetine were the first of the medications, but John continued to grow weaker. On 30 September, he was going through sporadic choking, coughing spasms and his stools were showing blood strains as well as the mucus. He managed to eat a bowl of pork soup in the evening which marked the beginning of my feeding him. I had seen Jimmy Jackson come through with little help from Charlie and I knew it could be done.

The first of October was the crisis. John's pulse was around 125, his breathing shallow, rapid and strained. He was fully coherent and aware of all that was going on around him, but the racking spasms of coughing were wearing him down. His stools showed dark blood and golden-yellow mucus, a turn for the worse which we prayed would be countered by the antibiotics. It was going to be close.

On the third, John got the first meal of sweet potato and banana soup, which he ate with unusual vigor and delight. These meals were to continue with a steady supply of sweet potatoes and bananas doled out by the guards and several meals of chicken soup added. By 6 October he was eating enough of the soup that a pronounced gain in his strength was evident. His runs had dropped off to one or two per day and the blood and mucus had disappeared. Ben had added chloramphenicol and Diamycin, both to counter John's diarrhea, which combined with sulfaguanidine and Emetine covered a broad spectrum of intestinal diseases. There was virtually no escape for a bug in that environment. Cod liver oil capsules were added to the vitamins and Isotonique solution for fluid balance. I had been adding salt to his soup in small enough amounts that he couldn't detect the taste, but would have some intake to replace the loss.

The combined food and medication appeared to bring John out of the illness, although he seemed convinced that he had little chance of improving. Sauser required daily reports from Ben and made his own inspections. While I was feeding John, Dan and Jim were administering medications and helping John with his beginning mild exercises to gain control of his muscles again. All three of us helped to bathe John and wash out his mosquito net and mat, and still had to take time for fishing and basic chores to keep ourselves going. But John wasn't improving fast enough for the cadre, and Dan, Jim and I found ourselves being severely reprimanded. Sauser was working under pressure from his superiors, and we were the only whipping boys he had.

By 17 October, it became evident that John, if left in the camp, would not survive. The guards were already grumbling about the amounts of potatoes and bananas given to the POW and were encouraging us to get him to eat rice again. I knew that John wouldn't be able to go back to rice and fish; he had turned them off completely. I told Ben that it was essential to keep John on the food mixed with a little rice in soup to add more bulk. Ben reported to Sauser that the picture was getting darker. John had been able to walk across the mess hall and had been sitting for longer periods of time with Jim's help, but a relapse would erase all of the progress.

Dan, Jim and I had been so busy managing all the duties in our area that we had little time for anything else, but the idea of a release had prompted us to discuss possible contingency plans which could be used to help those left behind. One of them was the possiblity of an operation back into the area to rescue the remaining POW's. Dan felt certain he could identify the area from the air and once spotted, he could lead an operation in to spring Jim and me loose. The signal for us in the camp would be an L-19, flying to the south of us and gunning its engine two or three times, circling and repeating the process. That would mean that an operation would be coming into the camp the next morning and those POW's in the camp would have to get out of their cages that night and make it to a point fifty to a hundred meters away from the camp so they couldn't be hit when the camp was zapped. Once the operation began, they could signal helicopters or link up with friendly forces. Jim and I began rehashing our plan for an escape, knowing that the two of us would have better than a fifty-fifty chance with any luck at all and those odds would be better than if we stayed. If there was a foul-up on the rescue operation, we would try to escape ourselves.

Mafia arrived on the morning of 18 October with Major Bay and a high-ranking cadre. They paid an immediate visit to John to determine if he was able to travel. That was the tip-off to what followed. Preparations were made by the guards for a trip and Mafia spent a great deal of time talking with Ben and Sauser about John's condition and chances for recovery. The activity brought John's spirits up and the next day he was able to walk around a little. A session was held in the forum in the early afternoon with Dan, Jim and John attending. I sat back at the kitchen feeling more alone that I ever had before. There was laughter from one of the cadre and Mafia's voice even carried a note of mirth. After about thirty minutes, Bud came to get me and I followed him to the forum. The others stood waiting on the earth mound beside the walkway with Cheeta and Chinh. There was a long silence as I passed and continued to the forum. Mafia told me to sit on a stool at the near end of the table when I entered. The older cadre who had arrived with Mafia was sitting at the other end of the table and on either side of the table sat Sauser, Major Bay, the little major and the guards. They were sipping cups of tea and candy wrappers lay on the floor.

The older cadre began to speak and Mafia translated: "You are POW Rowe and you are here to learn of the decision of the Central Committee of the National Front for Liberation of South Vietnam. Your comrades are no longer prisoners. They are to be released under the lenient policy of the Front and allowed to return to their homes and loved ones." I knew this was coming, but it was still a shock. They were actually going to release them and I was going to stay. Jim was with Dan and John! Then it hit me! I was alone!

The cadre continued in a more severe tone, "You have shown a bad attitude toward the cadre of the Front and toward the soldiers. You have violated camp regulations and you have foolishly tried to escape. You cannot recognize the just cause of the revolution and you do not realize your misdeeds against the Vietnamese people. For these reasons you cannot be released and must rest here a long time until you are able to know the truth of the situation in Vietnam and know clearly the crimes of your government as well as your personal crimes."

I felt like shrinking through the floor poles. It was almost as if I had done something wrong and my mind was trying to discover just what. The thought of staying here until I died was terrifying. The cadre paused a moment and then added, "Do you think that merely because the war ends that you will go home. You can rest here after the war." The door slammed

278

shut on the only light I had seen in the darkness that was around me. I had forgotten about escape or rescue and was totally involved in the control these people had over me. I had wildly thought that the war couldn't go on much longer and all I would have to do is hang on until it ended. Now that too was closed to me.

Mafia pushed a cup of tea over to me and the cadre's voice became almost gentle. "The Front wishes to correct your mistaken thoughts about our revolution and gives you the opportunity to learn in the coming days so you too might be released and return to your dear family. Do you think of your family often?" I nodded, not trusting my voice. Mafia pointed to the tea. "Drink. It is for you." I took the cup and sipped the weak brew, thinking it must be the second or third run-through for the leaves in the pot. "Major Bay and Mr. Hai will be in the camp with you after I leave to insure that you have the proper chance to study, and I encourage you to correct your attitude and struggle to learn the truth. Do you have anything to ask of me while I am here?"

I couldn't think of anything and just wanted to get out of the hut and back to the others. Mafia spoke up. "You must not try to talk with the others. They are no longer prisoners and cannot share the house with you." I was isolated even with the others still in the camp. "You can go now. I will speak with you later," Mafia concluded.

I walked back to the kitchen in utter despair. Jim and Dan were gathering their old belongings from the cage and checking out the new mosquito nets and clothing that had been given them. John was sitting in the *nha mam* as Ben checked his chest with a stethoscope. Cheeta, Chinh and Base stood on the walkways watching. I walked into the kitchen and squatted in front of the fireplace, staring at the cold ashes from the morning's fire, feeling as though I had ceased to exist. Everything was happening around me and I was excluded.

Major Bay came in behind me and coughed. I stood and turned to face him, not really seeing him at all. "You will cook the supper meal for your friends tonight before they leave. They are no longer prisoners, so you must take responsibility for the duty." I acknowledged the order and turned to scoop rice into the cooking pot. Jim started over as if to help, but was stopped by the guards and reminded that we were not to

279

talk. He and Dan went over to help John prepare for the journey as I began cooking.

Before the meal, I asked Major Bay if I couldn't eat this last meal with the others since it might be the last time we saw one another. I was determined to get a chance to send a message back to my mom and dad if nothing else and this was my chance. He agreed and sat in to monitor our conversation, allowing us to talk for a brief time. Dan let me know that there was a message he had written stuck in the kitchen area and then went on to a brief spurt of slang reassuring me that he'd do everything he could to get an operation in to pull me out. Jim seconded it and Major Bay sat smiling, not understanding a word. I gave Dan a message for my parents and then wished them both a heartfelt Godspeed on their journey to freedom. I got permission to say goodbye to John and was thankful he had his chance to live.

After it became dark, we were all put in boats and taken to a camp several kilometers away where propaganda films were being shown for the guards in the area. John stayed in the boat during the films while Dan and Jim sat away from me. I was with Major Bay, who, with Chinh, had brought me to the films in a separate boat. It was almost as if there were already miles separating the Americans, and we were no more than fifteen feet apart.

When the films ended, I managed to get one last handshake with Dan and Jim before I was put back in my boat. The last request I had for them was: "Get John home alive. Don't let him die on you." I knew that if it were at all possible, they'd do it. They climbed into the larger boat and were gone.

Thoughts after four years

Time is infinite and creeps on knees,
made stiff with age, so slowly does it crawl;
But looking back, the years have flown,
each so useless, each a void.

Perhaps it is this that makes it so,
the painfully slow, yet rapid flight,
of many days, none with a face, none with its mark;
one like another in long endless procession.

What fate is it that holds us so,
suspended in this abhorrent void;
surrounded close by an alien force,
while all around us life flows on.

I seek the light that issues forth,
from that which I knew and those whom I love;
that which now seems like a dream from the past,
and forms my greatest hope for the future.

With faith and hope, I will survive,
determined not to falter, not to die;
a promise to myself to stay alive
swearing that to oneself, one cannot lie.

So, oh infinite time, creep on, creep on;
or speed like Mercury, as the wind;

for though suspended, imprisoned, bound,
my mind reaches out to touch the light.

And somewhere in the surrounding dark,
the light I seek already glows;
perhaps from here 'tis only a glimmer,
but at the source, it is sunbright and strong.

So span I will the time between,
and at time's end I'll touch the light;
for I have felt the Lord's strong hand,
and with his help, I cannot fail.

7

THE CAGE WAS SO EMPTY. THE DARKNESS AND SILENCE in the camp created a feeling of utter loneliness. Only the mosquitoes greeted me as I stooped through the low doorway, finding my net drooping from one corner, a huge tear in one side. It was too much. I sat down on my mat, partially covered by the ripped netting, and put my head down on my knees, not feeling the insects that covered my exposed skin, as I was overwhelmed by a rush of thoughts:

Jim and Dan and John. All the days we'd spent together, fighting to stay alive, hoping to go home. And now they were on their way; I was left behind. There would be no American voices, no friendly presence other than my own. They were going home, going to stay alive, going to see their loved ones, going to eat real food. They had broken through the barrier and were breathing free air while I continued to gasp for each breath in this closed, oppressive atmosphere, my nothing world.

Finally I shook the almost overwhelming depression, knowing it would return but forcing myself to turn to immediate matters of need. My net was ripped from top to bottom along one entire side; far more than I could repair. Miss Fit, the camp watchdog, must have gotten inside and tried to get out, or else she was trying to get inside, away from the mosquitoes. Either way, she'd wrecked my net. I draped part of Dan's old net over the side of mine, covering the tear, and tucked it in after I'd crawled under.

Bud came by to lock me up soon after I'd gotten the mosquitoes inside the net killed off. He attached the lock to the leg irons and squatted for a moment, swatting mosquitoes with his hand, *"Ro co buon khong?"* he asked seriously—Are you sad? *"Toi chua buon,"* I replied, *"ma khong vui"*—I'm not sad yet, but I'm not happy.

That night was a series of vivid dream sequences in which I found myself facing a tidal wave roaring toward me, and I had no place to go. Jim and Dan were standing on a high bank to my left, far out of reach, shouting and waving to me, but their voices were drowned out by the roar of the oncoming water. John lay on his straw mat on a bank on the other side, also above the raging water, just watching. My footsteps seemed to be bogged down and I knew there was no hope for outrunning the water; there had to be some solution, some way out, and the others couldn't help. An idea was developing in the haze of the dream, bringing a surge of relief that I would have an answer, when I awoke. Chinh was unlocking my leg irons; it was the dawn of my first day alone.

The silence in the hut was like a vacuum, with only the sound of my voice when I muttered to myself breaking the void. It was going to be a problem to readjust to solitary existence. The fear of becoming seriously ill with no one to help was a very real threat and the near knockdown in early August was still vivid in my mind. Loneliness was the least of my worries; I had the forest animals. And, more important, I was responsible just for myself; being alone had some good points. After feeling the depression of being left behind, I began to experience the exultation of knowing Dan, John and Jim would be free, would be back in America—and the word would be out that I was alive and still kicking. Our idea of an operation into this area to break out the remaining POW's, now reduced to myself, was my greatest hope. I knew that Dan could locate this area and aerial recon would pinpoint it. As soon as I heard that L-19 fly to the south of here and gun his engine a couple of times, I'd be on my way that night, leg irons or not, to link up with the operation that was coming in the next morning. I knew I had a damn good chance now.

Major Bay was my daily companion in the weeks that followed, talking of his days as a young revolutionary, the hardships and rewards of his years of service and his hopes for the future. I renamed him "Uncle Ha," a takeoff on Ho Chi Minh's nickname, and began to develop a growing comprehension of the background and beliefs of this political cadre as he opened his memories and thoughts during our discussions. It was the first actual rapport I had established and I sought to develop it, seeking to find a replacement for the communication I had lost when the others had been released.

On 3 November, Ha said Dan, Jim and John were in Cambodia, meeting with representatives of the Central Committee, American peace emissaries and reporters of the international press. He added that I would soon go to visit the liberated zones and would be given clothing and medication to "improve my conditions of living."

I had passed my fourth year of captivity on 29 October 1967, thanking God that I was still alive and that three of our group had been released in time for their lives to be saved.

I knew that none of them had bought any of the line that the cadre was throwing at us, and the period of time that Dan and John had spent with Mafia in the Liberated Zone hadn't seemed to have changed their minds about our being right. The basic question of right and wrong was not in doubt, even after the VC began bringing in their reports of a "second front" in the United States that was growing in its support for the NLF. Our association with the Vietcong had proven beyond a doubt where the source of hypocrisy and evil lay. The insidious nature of our captors' doctrine, and their method of dealing with other human beings, was ample evidence of our country's reason for opposing its spread.

The escape Jim and I had been planning before he was released was still in my mind. We had planned to execute it after Dan and John were released, having anticipated their freedom because of the attention focused on them by Mafia and the need to get them away from Jim and me for a period of time. Our influence was regarded as "reactionary," thus forcing Mafia to attempt to exploit the other two and satisfy his prerequisites in an environment where he might strongly influence them without fear of counterinfluence. It had definitely been a shock to Jim when it was announced that he was to be released also. I maintained the desire to escape, but put it off because of the rescue operation that I was certain was coming.

Thanh, "Andy Gump," from a nearby camp, Porky, Chinh, and Base were in the camp with Ha, Sauser and "New Three," a hardened combatant turned cadre, forming the cadre roster. The traffic in and out of the camp was so heavy that I noted in my diary, *"4/11/67, local scene like Chink fire drill—need traffic cop on canal."* The attitude of all guards and cadre was extremely happy, primarily because of the successful movement of three Americans into Cambodia for release. I was generally ignored except by Ha and Sauser who spent hours each day talking with me about the revolutionary theory and goals in the context of its application to South Vietnam. I didn't have to feign interest because I took this as an opportunity to study Communist cadre on their own ground and probe their thoughts and method of thinking in an environment where they spoke freely, trying to portray their beliefs either as a time-killing device or actually to enlighten me.

On 6 November, Ha called me to the "forum" to receive the first of five lessons. It was an all-day session, sitting on the pole floor, listening to the same lesson on the history of the revolution I had received in Hanoi II.

An oversimplification of the economics of capitalism, described as the governing motive behind "foreign aggression," was the need of capitalist countries "to sell the surplus goods that they do not completely sell at home." The well-worn example was given of the maker of ball-point pens who, in a capitalist country, overproduces to make a larger personal profit, exceeds the "one pen per person" demand, and is forced to invade a foreign market to peddle his goods in order to pay the taxes forced upon him by the evil ruling regime. The skeleton of French colonialism was dredged up and thrown into our closet with the label "neo-colonialism." The flat denial of North Vietnamese presence in the South was a counter to the basis for U.S. commitment. They questioned the policy of foreign obligations having a higher priority than problems within the U.S. and incorporated the challenge of America's right to stand as a representative democracy in the world with its racism, poverty and inequalities. The rising opposition to the U.S. involvement at home and in the world coupled with the growing strength of the NLF and the revolution were offered as one part of the reason the Front was assured of final victory. The split between the American people and the American government was considered as essential for Vietnamese as well as worldwide victory, and Major Bay projected the "defeat of

U.S. imperialism by all wars of national liberation, even in America."

Some of his points were valid, drawn from the actual shortcomings of our society, but they were placed in an unresolvable context, wherein our system created the inequalities and perpetuated them without hope of ever reaching a solution. I realized the faults; however, I believed that our system of government provided the means for each of its citizens to achieve his rights alongside any other citizen, effecting whatever corrective measures were required through due process of law. If fault were to be found, I felt it would be with some of the self-centered, self-perpetuating members of the bureaucracy that hampered the proper functioning of our system. I would not accept our system as being at fault; instead, I attached blame to individuals within the system.

The denial of North Vietnamese presence was an admission of guilt in the cadre's attempt to attach the stigma of guilt to Americans in South Vietnam. If the North Vietnamese were not illegally entering the South, why would both the NLF and Hanoi deny their presence? Their strongest argument against "U.S. aggression" was the indigenous nature of the LAF, the "people's army" opposing us, the "fourteen million South Vietnamese people, rising up as one to throw the invader from their shores." By this time there were North Vietnamese units fighting on all fronts except in the delta region, yet their presence was blandly denied.

The second written lesson was "Ten Year's Crimes of U.S. Imperialism and Lackeys in Saigon." It had been annotated with a list of "crimes" which included: "On January 21, 1965, just the first of lunar new year, the US and Thieu-Ky clique brought 47 men to the Vinh Trinh dam, cutting their tongues and ears, plucking out their eyes, desemboweling, liver plucking, burning with gasoline tying together, hanging rucks and throwing down to the Vinh Trinh dam." (Spelling as from the lesson plan.) A second item informed me, "In Phung hiep district, one US adviser beated barbarously Mirs. Lan."

I listened to Major Bay discuss the incident at the dam in gory detail, thinking that all it took was a VC death warrant, naming a person an "enemy of the people," and slaughter became legal and praiseworthy. Their chosen example of the alleged Vinh Trinh dam incident included most of the mutilations that the VC normally performed in their "lessons to the people," and I imagined that if all the acts had been committed on each individual, there wouldn't have been much left to throw "down to the Vinh Trinh dam." As usual, the English used and the vague attempts to substantiate their allegations made the lessons ineffective. Ha didn't have to convince me that war was brutal and ugly. I had seen what his people had done to our wounded, to innocent villagers singled out to be "examples," to the entire family of a district chief, including his two young daughters and wife. I had seen the bestiality and inhumanity that had been displayed by these people who now, suddenly, became the judges of what they alleged were "U.S. crimes" against the Vietnamese people.

I was told to answer four questions pertaining to these two classes:

"1) With that motive would one assert that the aggressive war of the US Imperialists in SVN is unjust and certainly will be defeated?

"2) Why is the war of the SVN people just and will succeed?

"3) What are the crimes of the US Imperialists with regard to the SVN and American people in 11 years ago?

"4) Yourself had any crimes toward the SVN people?"

The first was like "Have you stopped beating your wife yet?" The third involved the issue of exploitation of the American soldier by "U.S. Imperialists." According to the lessons, not only the SVN people were victims, but also the American fighting men and their families. I considered the moral issue involved, questioning the validity of war at all in the perspective of man's inhumanity to man. There is no moral basis for war. Wars are fought to establish one man's superiority over another or one people's dominance over another; more specifically, one government's superiority over another. War is a function of expediency and policy, not morality. The responsibility of morality must be shared by both sides, and if it is equally shared, then the basis for conducting the war is eliminated and peace will prevail until the next policy impasse is reached.

Here, the question of morality was raised by those whose goal was world domination. All morality was ignored, except when their code of morality contributed to furthering the cause of revolution. The only answer offered, according to this doctrine was submission to its control, since its followers were pledged to war until their goal had been attained. If I questioned the moral issue in war, which is inherently immoral, then acceptance of their solution was the only means of establishing morality—morality through surrender.

I found the long hours of repetition in the lectures made me quite tense. By failing to answer the questions in a satisfactory manner, I was faced with breaking the fragile rapport I had established and compromising any freedom of action I might have. I had already questioned Major Bay on his weak points in the last camp and he had either removed them or strengthened his presentation with additional "facts." I was determined not to give him anything usable as propaganda, but had to show some comprehension.

Three other lessons followed in the next four days. The final lesson was "The Duty of US P.O.W. at Home after Being Released by the Front." The "duty" of the "Struggle for repatriation of the US expeditionary corps and satellite troops. Propagandize and with activities to convince friends to demand for withdrawal all US troops from VN." The POW was encouraged to "tell clearly the truth" about the U.S. "aggressive war," the National Liberation Front and its support from the 14 million Vietnamese people who were "not afraid to sacrifice and suffer for determined to fight and win," and the "lenient and humane" policy toward POW's. The "Struggle Form" listed included:

—"Use the radio, television, books and papers to tell the truth.

—"Demonstrations—slogans—meetings—leaflets for struggle.

—"Refusing to eat—holding strikes.

—"Truthly participating in all struggle organization of the American people.

"Revolting and reaction. . . ."

One paragraph near the end of the lesson said, "Our just war is being supported by our friends throughout the five continents including the US peace loving people supporting actively our efforts."

I was certain that the POW's who had been faced with this ideology could discern the difference between fact and falsehood. We had watched the cancerous eating away of individuality and free thought, the creation of one mind to serve all of its followers, the sharp contrast between utopian promise and totalitarian reality. I hoped the "peace loving people" back home weren't supporting a cause they didn't understand.

Opposition to our government was understandable in a country where dissent is allowed under law and the right to question our government's policies is something Americans take for granted. The American people do love peace, but that love is not restricted to any one element in the society. We had enjoyed peace on our shores longer than the other countries in the world and it, like the freedom we enjoyed, might have become somewhat commonplace. I wondered what Major Bay would have to say if he could experience one month in my home. I wondered what the demonstrators I had heard about on some of our campuses would have to say if they'd been Hungarian or Czechoslovakian students protesting a government policy in those countries. My greatest hope was that if dissent existed, it would be in an attempt to improve our policy or our country, but not to support our enemy and destroy our country.

I waited through the passing days, listening for the L-19 which would indicate my chance for freedom. The water level had begun to drop as dry season approached and my ability to catch fish was severely hampered, making the consumption of enough rice extremely difficult. The number of *nuoc mam* and rice suppers increased. I broke one molar on a piece of shell fragment in my rice one evening and spent the next four days in the misery that only a toothache can cause. The root finally became numb and not so sensitive to heat and cold. There was no dental care except that which I performed, using bamboo sticks to bleed my gums and vine fiber as dental floss and brushing with crushed charcoal.

On 21 November, Thanh arrived with two puppies, two ducks, some baby chickens and a boatload of bananas, entire stalks of green bananas. The puppies and eight or ten stalks of bananas stayed. Porky brought a stalk of the small, unripe fruit to my kitchen for which I was thankful. I had been catching water snakes in my nets the last five days and combining their livers with the smaller livers taken from the few fish I was catching. This nutritional supplement was small, but better than nothing. The bananas gave me the chance to bring a little flavor and change into a meal.

The next day an L-19 was all over the area, obviously checking out Hanoi II to our west, this camp, and the float-in movie area to the southwest where I had watched the last film with the others before their departure. That evening he came back and flew over the area to our west once again, probably having spotted the buildings in that camp under the foliage which was still sparse and recovering from the recent caterpillar damage. Sauser and the guards were prepared to move out of the camp if he put smoke in, but there was no need to leave as he departed after the second look at Hanoi II. I knew it had to be either Dan or Jim and I'd get the signal in the next few days to move out. My spirits were soaring! I was going to get out of here and Americans were going to do it!

The two pups came down the long log walk for their first visit to the American area, and I fed them leftover rice and fish bones. Every animal in Vietcong camps eats rice, from rats through cats, and these two little slick-coated black pups were no exception. I found I couldn't get them to leave my side and when I went into the cage that night, they followed. The guards didn't object and I was very happy to have them around for companionship.

The mosquitoes bothered the thin-skinned little pups at night and they would cry pitifully when the guards would leave them in an open box overnight. I decided to give them a night of relaxation and brought them into my net with me after I had been locked up. They tumbled all over themselves in the pure ecstasy of not being covered with mosquitoes and almost destroyed the inside of my net before I got them quieted down and curled up at the bottom of the net, by my feet. I had named them "Turn" and "Bounce" because of the gymnastics they went through in their playing. Turn wasn't satisfied with the bottom of the net and I awoke with him curled snugly in the bend between my shoulder and face as I lay on my back, with his little head propped across my neck. He was snoring a little puppy snore of contentment.

I didn't want to move him, but I detected an extremely repulsive odor coming from him, like the stench of rotten fish. I had just moved his head when his little stomach began to rumble and I was shoving him out of the net just as he began to vomit the obviously decayed fish he had eaten in the guards' kitchen. I could see why the pups preferred American cooking. I had gotten two loyal moochers that day and they were a source of many hours of real enjoyment for me.

A new guard appeared on 12 December with several recruits, none of whom would have passed his fifteenth birthday. One of them, an arrogant, mouthy youngster with the coldest eyes

I'd seen on any of the guards, was reputed to be a "*dung si*" with American kills to his credit. He was about thirteen or fourteen years old. That afternoon the L–19 checked to the west again.

The next morning before I'd cooked rice, the L–19 was back, this time with smoke rounds slamming into the vicinity of Hanoi II, some two kilometers to our west. Within minutes, the jets were overhead and making their first passes on the target. New Three, Chinh, Cheeta, Base and "Music Kid," a pleasant-faced student who had recently been inducted, were in our camp, and they had their gear and me in tow and were into the area across the canal before the jets had made their first bombing run. We followed an indistinct trail which led along the same line of bunkers that Jim and I had followed in June '67. The bunkers were more tumbledown and deteriorated with the overhead mud cover looking as if it wouldn't stop a .30 cal. round. I was taken almost to the edge of canal twenty-one and told to get under cover and wait until one of the guards came to get me. I looked at the water-filled trench with the six-to-eight-inch clearance between the water and the bottom of the overhead poles, deciding to stay outside.

The L-19 was circling to the south, out of the pattern of the jets as they swept in to drop their ordnance, watching the area and checking for possible new targets. I sat on top of the bunker roof with some leaves pulled over my head watching the show. I was a one-man rooting section for those American jets as they poured bombs, rockets and then machinegun fire on the unfortunate camp. I was seeing all Ha's victory claims reduced in importance by one very close, very personal defeat for each of these guards; even more so for the guards in the camp under attack. I hoped there were no American prisoners over there.

That afternoon, taking enough time to refuel and rearm with a possible break for lunch, the jets were back. The L-19 arrived shortly before them and the whole show began again. Thanh and Andy Gump had appeared, to report that their camp was in bad shape and to take Cheeta to help them sort through the wreckage. Cheeta had a personal interest in the search because he had recently lent Thanh his prized transistor radio, which he'd purchased on the trip to Cambodia with John and the others. Somewhere amid the wreckage was his radio or what remained of it and he took it upon himself to find it.

I was sitting on my bunker seat, watching the jets as they

banked almost directly over us. I could see the pilots' visored faces as the planes lined up for their bombing runs; they were close. The guards were firing away with every weapon they had, including the burp gun Base was firing, which was accurate up to about one hundred yards maximum with a marksman using it. With Base, I feared more for the guards around him than the aircraft.

The strike had been going on for the bomb stage and the rocketing was just beginning when I lost sight of one of the jets. The other continued to make its passes. I immediately considered the missing plane might have been hit by a stray burst of firing, but the L–19 didn't seem concerned as he circled lazily to the east. There was no sign of the second aircraft until I heard the sudden sharp series of explosions coming my way. Fast! They were detonating in a path that was unmistakably along canal twenty-one and I was within twenty-five meters of that canal. I dove for the water-filled trench with one horrifying thought in my mind, "CBU"—the cluster bomb units which spread hundreds of steel-pellet-laden canisters that explode individually, covering the area with a deadly rain of large buckshot.

I hit the water head first, plunging all the way under, but not before the sharp stinging in my leg and buttock, followed by numbness, indicated I'd been hit. I managed to get my feet under me and my head above the filthy water, damn thankful that I'd been able to get to it. The guards were yelling excitedly, almost frantically, that someone had been hit and that the others should stay down. The jet had probably reacted to word from the L–19 that people were bugging out along canal twenty-one and he had laid the CBU's down to take care of them. He came close to taking care of one American POW also and even though he didn't know I was down here, I began to feel a strange animosity toward that pilot.

I checked my wound and found two flesh wounds, one of them a glancing blow which had cut, but not left a fragment or pellet embedded. I wiped them clean with my towel, stopping the blood after it had flushed the wounds. I began to consider the fact that if Dan and Jim had gotten the word back, there was no reason for those pilots not to know I was down here. What in the hell were they doing throwing air-strikes in on top of me? Confusion and disbelief overwhelmed me as I let myself think that perhaps the information about these camps had gotten

293

out and had been accurate, but that the decision had been not to come in after me, but instead, to bomb the camps out of existence, myself with them.

The next two days we got up long before dawn, cooked, and moved away from the camp to the east, arriving in a concealed position before first light. The first of those two days, the L-19 was back early and we had just gotten settled when the roar of the jets echoed in from the east, behind us. The strike went in on the approximate location of the float-in movie and the L-19 made circles directly in line with the No-K Corral while the fighter-bombers unloaded on the primary target. I was certain that he had spotted the Corral and it was only a matter of time before it was hit. If anyone was trying to rescue me, this was a dumb way to do it. I began to feel an affinity toward the guards as we all shared the same danger, the threat of "my" American airstrikes. My morale sagged to a horribly low level as I saw the rescue I had counted on becoming another threat to my life. I was thinking, "If you guys aren't going to help me get out, then please just leave me alone; don't you try to kill me too."

In the following days, the observation plane directed strikes to our north and east, checking his two targets in this area but ignoring the Corral. My morale was still sagging as the big plan for a rescue operation faded in front of me. I was going to have to get myself out and it wasn't going to be easy. I fought the depression that was dragging my thoughts strictly into the negative. The feeling of hopelessness was returning and was worked on every day by the guards or by one of the cadre as they talked about the release and how I could work to secure my own. The Front had "demonstrated its sincerity toward U.S. POW's and the fact of its release of three American POW's is proof of the lenient nature of the Front."

I planned to celebrate Christmas no matter what the circumstances. My theme song during this entire episode had been, "God rest you merry, gentlemen, let nothing you dismay . . ." During the air raid drills, I hadn't been allowed to check my gill nets in the canal, and I now discovered that they had been all but wiped out when the guards had camouflaged the canal by breaking trees over it. Somehow the trees snagged my nets when they dipped into the water. I had to resort to catching baby *ca ro* with hook and line, but it was food. On Christmas eve I spent the morning catching enough of the tiny *ca ro* for a substantial surplus, without having to catch more; I was declaring the next day a holiday. I washed out my kitchen and made a wreath out of tree branches and pieces of colored thread. Purple wild grapes took the place of holly berries and I thought it looked damn good when I finished. Better than anything else in the area.

After making certain all was in readiness in my kitchen, I went back to the cage and slept until time to cook supper. I was softly singing Christmas carols to myself, picturing the brightly lit tree covered with ornaments and glittering tinsel, the table spread with food, the fruitcakes, the eggnog, and most important, the people. The fireplace in my living room at home was the window through which I saw my family, seated on the couch, as the small, dancing flames of my cooking fire became the roaring blaze on our hearth at home. I was strengthened because I knew this Christmas, unlike any of the others since 1963, they knew I was alive and that knowledge would make this a special Christmas for me, as well as for them.

I had already gone to bed with irons fastened and door locked when Cheeta woke me. Mafia and Ha were in "to organize a celebration for me and allow me to conduct mass," and I was to come to the forum immediately to meet them. I made my way to the forum and was told to be seated on one of the benches across from the two cadre. It was the first time I'd seen Mafia since his departure on the release trip and he was almost bubbling over with the news he was to give me about his handling of the trip.

The first order of business was to celebrate midnight mass, Mafia informed me. He produced a candle and told me to burn it at midnight; I had permission to conduct my religious service. I looked at him somewhat stupidly and replied that I was a Protestant and didn't exactly require a "midnight mass" for Christmas; in fact, I'd already held my own personal thanksgiving, in accord with my beliefs, and was ready for tomorrow. Mafia was determined, "You will take this candle and you will burn it during observance of your midnight mass." He paused a moment before adding the reasoning behind all of this, "The Front respects the religious beliefs of U.S. POW's and you must celebrate your religious holiday."

I was on the verge of grinning, but managed to control the twitching corners of my mouth and accepted the candle. He told me that the Front had also given me tea and cookies so I might have a party after celebrating mass, "just like we did in America." Cheeta would be assigned to stay up and "assist" in my service, performing the minor task of locking me back up when I was finished.

I took the candle and small packets of tea and cookies and returned to my kitchen, followed by Cheeta, grudgingly carrying out his instructions while Base and Chinh were sleeping soundly in their nets. He turned in Radio Hanoi for a time check and the question of making it Saigon midnight or Hanoi midnight arose. The hour's difference between the two gave Saigon its first edge over Hanoi since I had been captured, with a guard voting for earlier Saigon time so he could get to bed. While waiting for midnight, I squatted by my fire, fanning smoke back over my feet to keep the mosquito population down, boiling water for tea. I watched Cheeta's discomfort as he sat on the log walk above the dry mound where I chopped wood, writing in his notebook by the flickering light of his kerosene lamp. He was puffing furiously on his cigarette, blowing the acrid fumes to ward off his mass of insects.

I asked him if he would like to come into the kitchen where there were fewer mosquitoes. "No. The mosquitoes do not bother *Anh Giai Phong!*" "Merry Christmas, Cheeta," I thought, "hope all the rest of yours are the same."

At Cheeta's announced midnight, I lit the candle while squatting in the kitchen, thinking for a moment of all the beautiful significance that could be attached to the lighted candle, the symbolism that here was without meaning. In this environment, which required that I communicate with my God unaided by the accouterments of ritual, I found they soon lost their significance and were not a necessity. I extinguished the candle, saving it to use later, killing mosquitoes in my net.

I poured the tea and divided the cookies into two piles, small but equal, and took tea and cookies out to Cheeta. It was Christmas and sharing was a part of the spirit, particularly when it was a portion of something very valuable to you. The only things I could share with Cheeta that he would understand were the cookies and tea, and I was happy to even be able to share them. He was surprised when I asked if he'd like them. Normally, the guards would refuse to accept any portion of a special treat we had been given by the cadre, but Cheeta took the cup of tea and sat munching the cookies in obvious enjoyment as I walked back to the kitchen.

296

When he finished eating, he folded his notebook, put his pen away, and told me to return to my net. After the irons had been locked and Cheeta had gone, I lay listening to the sound of the mosquitoes and thinking that this wouldn't be such a bad Christmas meal tomorrow after all; I had saved three cookies and had half of the tea left.

The next morning, after an intentionally sparse breakfast, saving the *ca ro* for my evening feast, I was called to the forum for a conference with Mafia. He related the events of the release trip, the stay in Phnom Penh and the meetings with Tom Hayden, the peace group representative who had come to receive the Americans. Mafia seemed more impressed with his own actions than any other aspect, telling me of the attention he received as a cadre of the mysterious revolutionary forces in the U Minh Forest region, the legendary U Minh battalions, the Forest of Darkness. His ego had definitely been inflated, and his prestige among the cadre of MR III had no doubt gone up, because of the successful operation. He wasn't too impressed with Tom Hayden as an individual, but was enthusiastic about the movement Hayden represented. He said he had asked Hayden to write me a note of encouragement, but the time had been so limited that Hayden hadn't been able to.

I asked about John's health and learned that as soon as they reached Phnom Penh, a Cambodian doctor had run tests on John and provided medication which brought him out of a slump and enabled him to travel home. The trip had been difficult for John, but Dan and Jim had helped tremendously to keep him going. Mafia spoke in glowing terms of riding in "new Mercedes automobiles" from the Cambodian border to the capitol, a gesture, he said, of solidarity toward the NLF.

My three former cagemates had been given a small amount of spending money and were allowed to do a little shopping after being registered in a hotel. Dan bought a pair of shoes, as did John, while Jim picked up a tea set. I could almost feel the clean sheets and luxury of a hot bath. It must have been like a tiny piece of heaven to them.

After the formalities and exchange of speeches of mutual support, the flight to the United States began; the Americans were returning home, and Mafia, along with his guards, began the long journey back into the forest.

The lesson to be learned was that release was possible for those who believed in the Front. I was told that now I "must

297

do my share," do what I could "to end quickly the war." Mafia grew serious for a moment as he said, "Before, you have done nothing, and now you must contribute your share in order to enjoy the lenient policy of the Front." The concentrated effort to get something on their side of the scoreboard was underway. I thought of the imprisonment up to now and wondered what could be added in the way of harassment or pressure that hadn't already been tried, aside from outright, systematically inflicted torture designed to break me physically. With the threat of disease and hardships of the environment, they wouldn't have to exert much effort to make it really miserable.

Mafia and Ha gave me a rundown on the war, claiming a total of five B-52's shot down over North Vietnam and over 2,300 aircraft shot down since the bombing had begun. They talked about growing racial violence in the U.S., mentioning Newark and Detroit as major scenes. Radio Liberation had broadcast a tape recorded program called "Radio Stateside," prepared in the U.S. by an obviously dissident group and sent to the Front for use in its propaganda efforts against American troops, particularly the Negro soldiers. Stokely Carmichael was quoted as saying, "Violence is the only solution for American Negroes." As Mafia mentioned twenty-six Negroes who had died in violence in major cities, I wondered why anyone would advocate violence as the "only solution." I wondered if he'd ever put his life on the line for whatever cause he supported or if it would be the "other guy" who was the victim of that violence.

Chinh and Cheeta took charge of the daily indoctrinations, spending at least an hour each day with me, discussing some aspect of the revolutionary struggle. I gathered from their off-the-record comments that a new POW might be moving in. I began to look for further indications, hoping they would bring someone else into the camp, making it easier to resist them, and ultimately, to escape.

Mafia came in on 30 December with an announcement that there would be a "ceremony" the next day for my New Year's Day celebration. I was given a small young hen, a number 12 can of green peas, four rolls, some grease, black pepper and a package of coffee and sugar. Along with the items for my meal came the word that the answers I had given Ha on the five lessons had not been acceptable and the Front was not pleased with my attitude. That was all it took to start a reaction in which I found myself searching for a way to appease the cadre and still maintain my perishable status quo.

The next day there was a crowd in the forum as the guards and cadre from two camps assembled for the program. Mafia, Sauser, Ha and New Three were present, and stacked into the long hut were Chinh, Cheeta, Base, Music Kid, Thanh, Beri, Buck's Boy, and two other guards, "Clark Gable" and "Ri." Mafia had a tape recorder, which I had seen the day before as the guards examined it, and Beri had a 35mm camera. The stage was set for my appeasement, but I had anticipated the requirement Mafia threw at me for a message to the American people, proclaiming my desire for peace. Extemporaneous speech would have contained some of the freshest thoughts in my mind on the subject of peace—which would probably have been the revolutionary rhetoric Chinh and Cheeta had been feeding me during the past week.

Fortunately I had taken a few minutes the day before and scribbled a broad appeal for world peace from the unbiased view of a POW who just wanted to go home. When I pulled my piece of paper from my pocket, thanking Mafia for the opportunity to express the exact thoughts I'd had in mind for several days, he knew he had been jocked out. The guards were open in their approval of my willingness to cooperate and only the cadre were frowning. Beri took several photographs during the short program, which ended more abruptly than planned because of my message. Mafia was ready to leave immediately once he knew there would be no propaganda this trip. I went back to my kitchen, breathing a sigh of relief; I had bought a little more time, but it wouldn't work again.

The fungus infection had been developing into a serious problem. It had covered most of my body except for my face and head and the crawling, itching sensation was so aggravating I had begun virtually attacking it with the scraping stick or any convenient piece of wood that would serve to tear and gouge until pain replaced that infernal itching. My fingernails had been eaten away by the infection and I had only three toenails remaining, leaving me with the feeling that I was being devoured. What sleep I might have gotten, between the mental gymnastics of fighting anxiety and frustration, was ruined by the itching, tormenting fungus. I would dread the coming of night with its leg irons, physical inactivity and ample time for torment.

In early January, I noted in my diary: *"6/1/68, ... Loss of sleep affecting strength, disposition, morale. Now working on mental buck-up before trouble sets in. Can't fight on multiple fronts—political is enough; add fatigue, strong homesickness, extreme tiredness of POW life plus the chance of health breakdown and the picture is not bright. Tonite the buck-up begins, tomorrow a new day, a new, brighter outlook."* The political lessons had become almost more than I could take as I had to sit and listen to the guards degrade my country and voice their conditioned confidence in our defeat. From the diary: *"Poop sessions getting nasty. Remember to keep mouth shut, hands holding top of head down. Think of pleasant things."* It was a bitch to have to sit and listen to garbage like the guards were passing out without a chance to rebut the inaccuracies.

One method I'd discovered to fight the frustration and anxiety was to physically exert myself to the point of near exhaustion by chopping wood, making constructive improvements in and around the kitchen hut, and engaging in any other positive, constructive activity that needed to be done. I made a personal pledge to perform only positive actions and improvements in order to negate the adverse reactions to frustrations. The resulting exhaustion allowed me to drop into periods of deep slumber at night, interrupted only by the itching, irritating *lac*.

In solving one problem, I aggravated another. I wasn't getting enough calories to support extra activity, and the diarrhea went wild whenever the lower abdominal muscles were strained at all.

I was becoming tense and irritable, my temper rising to almost uncontrollable pitch on several occasions. I feared the possibility of total loss of control in the presence of the guards; first, because of the futility of striking out at one of them, and second, because it would give the cadre firm proof that the pressure was, in fact, affecting me and could be exploited to gain what they desired. As long as they were forced to guess about my mental state, they would have to fish for means of influencing me, possibly scrapping an effective method in order to try something new. I had no doubt that over an extended period, they could hit the right combination through trial and error, with their greatest weapon being my inability to remove myself from the tightening vise. Isolation was their key.

Constant reference by the guards to a new POW gave me

hope that I'd have someone soon with whom I could communicate. My diary reflects the optimism and hope I felt and the recurring letdowns as time passed and no one came. I tried to keep my morale at a median level, uninfluenced by the up-down effect caused by the guards' references to alleged coming events, but with only partial success. I found that my American upbringing and desire to trust made me unable to comprehend the effectiveness of hypocrisy as a tool. The compromise of ethics and lowering of standards in order to compete against this system were, in themselves, a source of mental anguish.

I turned to prayer when my resources had been exhausted. My relation with my God was such that I'd try until I felt I could go no further or I was in need of special guidance. I didn't want to call on Him at every turn, and even though I asked for His guidance in all my actions, there were days of special need. Perhaps it was my acceptance of His presence and the predetermined path on which I walked that gave me the greatest comfort. I received comfort when none was indicated by my conditions, none was provided by the material surroundings. The quiet, inner calm which would settle over me was not a function of this earthly environment.

I found the carefree little pups a source of keen pleasure as they explored the strange world which surrounded them. Turn's first encounter with a sharp-finned *ca ro* that refused to play as Turn thought it should, and their rollicking chase around the mud bank after flittering butterflies gave me the ability to look ahead, at times to come.

On the night of 13 January, I was taken to a camp some two kilometers from the Corral, traveling a devious route to confuse me as to its exact location. When I entered the camp, I noticed two cages, smaller than mine, capable of holding two men each. They were empty, but two well-used crocks lying beside them indicated they were occupied. I saw most of the older guards there along with all the "Mice," the new young recruits. A movie screen was set up at the far end of the small clearing and all were in attendance for another series of propaganda movies.

I was made to sit in the rear of the crowd and not allowed to look around the gathering. This instruction aroused my curiosity and during the interval between two of the films, I stood up to stretch and took a good look around before Base saw me and shouted at me to sit down. There were three men sitting in front of the crowd, just back from the screen, and they were Americans! The broad shoulders, the bearded jawline I saw on one as he turned his head to talk to one of the others, the sandy brown hair of the one in the middle all indicated Americans. I sat down with the desire burning inside me to rush up and join in their small group. These must have been the other POW's the guards had been talking about. I wondered if I'd ever get to see them again.

Four movies were shown that evening. The first was a color and sound documentary on industry in Communist China, stressing the production of agricultural and industrial machinery and consumer goods. The guards were enthusiastic when they saw the Chinese production of radios, watches, cameras, clothing and automobiles. These things were stressed by the cadre in a summary, stating that only through a successful Socialist revolution could Vietnam ever hope to achieve the status of their Chinese brothers. The second film was entitled *"Guerillas of Cu Chi"* and showed the actions of the Vietcong guerrillas around Cu Chi as they fought against American units. The bunker complexes, the booby traps, the raids on militia posts, the ambushes of American units and the support given the guerrillas by the people were applauded by the assembled group. The third film, another color and sound production also produced in Red China, was a ballet dedicated to the Vietnamese resistance against the Americans in both North and South. The scenes included a strategic hamlet being resisted by its inhabitants and finally destroyed; guerrillas destroying a road and killing a drunken, lecherous American sailor who was supposed to be on guard and was lured away by a beautiful young girl guerilla; Liberation Army Forces ambushing an American-advised ARVN unit, with cowardice among the Allied forces, particularly the American, contrasted with the ultimate in bravery by the VC; Nguyen Van Troi, the NLF martyr who had been executed for his attempt on the life of Robert McNamara, showing their version of his death as he shouted "Down with the Imperialists and traitors, long live Ho Chi Minh"; and finally, a scene involving the antiaircraft gunners in North Vietnam destroying a screenful of American jets.

The film was quite good from a viewer's standpoint, filled with beautiful female dancers, heroic soldiers and a dedicated filmland populace. The guards were wild in their applause and cheering as the film glorified war and their part in it. I liked the music and the choreography, particularly that involving attractive females. It was refreshing to see what a woman looked like again. The final film was a long black-and-white sound production on the Communist takeover in China about 1947. Once again, the glory of revolutionary struggle was emphasized, the honor of enduring hardship, the heroic sacrifices, and the inevitable victory bringing peace and happiness to a grateful nation. The guards were truly inspired as we went back to the camp, each of them promising the heroic acts he would perform when his chance came. My only thought was that war was always more glorious when you watched it on film.

The sight of other Americans so near to this camp made my feeling of loneliness even stronger. The idea that the cadre would isolate Americans in order to better influence them was repulsive to me. If the idea they were trying to get across was so valid, so "just," so essential to securing world peace, why did they have to create conditions which would influence a person through mental and physical pressure to accept it?

The indoctrinations continued, combining broadcasts from Radio Hanoi, Radio Liberation and the tape-recorded programs from "Radio Stateside" with the daily lectures from the guards. I was troubled by the increased use of American sources to substantiate the revolution and the violence that seemed to be erupting across the United States. I began hearing more statements alleged to have been made by U.S. senators and congressmen, not only opposing our presence in Vietnam, but supporting the stand of NLF. They were quoted as allegedly condemning United States violations of the 1954 Geneva Agreements and of the U.S. Constitution and the U.N. Charter as well; the statements went on to label our own troops as aggressors and deride the Vietnamese government in Saigon. Alleged commentary by AP and UPI made mockery of American troops' actions and gave strong credit to the VC. The news reports of racial violence, clashes between police and demonstrators, and the growing antiwar movement were blows to my jealously guarded faith in the American people and our government's ability to represent them. I couldn't believe that these statements were actually being made, but their consistency and repeated new reports of dissent and violence indicated that a problem of some magnitude did exist.

The guards and cadre made maximum use of these commentaries, realizing the valuable weapon they had been given

303

in their efforts to break down the will of an American prisoner to resist. "Radio Stateside" was one of their favorites for me to hear since it "came from my country and would allow me to learn the truth from my countrymen." I began to hear of the Black Panther Party, of planned violence to gain civil rights; names of individuals began coming up time and time again: Rap Brown, Stokely Carmichael, Eldridge Cleaver; of the desertions and draft-card burning and support for those who opposed service in the Army. I tried to create a valid picture in my own mind of what actually was happening, allowing for the distortions I had learned to expect from the Communist sources, and still came up with a disturbing set of conclusions.

Chinh made a statement, in one of the lectures, which I wrote in my diary, stunned at its implications and concerned because of the correlation with which I could see growing in the United States, *"16/1/68 . . . Poop for today—'Commie* WORLD REVOLUTION *is solution to world peace—and* IS *coming. Overthrow of capitalism & imperialism, a prerequisite to world peace. After VN—Laos, Thailand, Philippines, Indonesia, Korea, etc.—after Asia & Pacific—Latin America—then U.S.A., England, Australia, France.' The word is out."* The "Second Front" the cadre had mentioned in the United States, the outbreaks of violence, the senseless killing in our cities, the dissension, the breaking of loyalties to the country under whatever guise, and now the open declaration of revolution beyond Vietnam, beyond the Pacific, through the United States until it encompassed the world, the picture was frighteningly clear. I thought back to the Salt Mines and my question about the refugees fleeing a Communist takeover within a country and the answer, "They are the capitalists and imperialists fleeing the wrath of the freed working class." I was familiar with the VC "death warrants" for "enemies of the people," and after hearing the guards' explanation of the refugees it was no longer humorous to think: "There will be a lot of us capitalists leaving the United States if this ever happens there." Where would there be for us to go?

I made a decision to try an escape, unaware of the reaction it would bring. The first thoughts of actually attempting, once again, to gain my freedom, had barely circulated in my conscious mind when I was seized by violent nausea. I vomited, the stench of diarrhetic stools in my nostrils even though I was nowhere near the latrine. I began trembling and could feel my calf muscles knotting into cramped ropes; the urge to crap was suddenly very strong. I barely staggered to the latrine before bursting loose. My stomach was beginning to cramp and I continued to convulse in wrenching dry heaves.

I made it back to the cage and collapsed on my mat, pulling my folded net over myself, not bothering to try to string it up. When my back touched the mat I cringed as my legs began to straighten out and my shoulders tried to hunch up, drawing my elbows in close to my sides. It was the Mines! Oh God, I'm back in the Mines! The rotten putrescence of my own filth, the irons, the cramping muscles, the pain in my neck, in my head, the flies walking on me, their tiny feet racing patterns on my skin. I turned my head as I vomited again.

It took hours, I don't really know how long, before I could get up and walk to the kitchen. The nightmare had passed, leaving me weak and drained, feeling as if I'd been hooked up to a strong electrical current and suddenly cut loose. I sat on the floor in the kitchen, trying to calm my still-rolling stomach, wondering what in the hell had happened. The re-creation of the trauma of the "correction period" was a thoroughly frightening experience, particularly since I had done it to myself. I tried to analyze it, finding no reason other than the link between escape and the effects of the correction. It was an unpleasantness I dealt with during the next two days as I hurriedly devised a plan.

The ground was dry enough for travel overland and I was going to use a direct line, following the general path we'd taken to the east in December, avoiding the airstrikes, and making it as fast as possible to the river. When it got dark, I'd make the final approach to the water and turn south, swimming for the posts I knew had to be there. There would be no need for food and I didn't need any of my gear except the diary and extra trousers for flotation.

The entire plan depended on my being able to leave the camp before or during the noon sleeping period of the guards and be far enough away when they discovered my absence so that I could reach the river when it got dark. Overland travel would be rapid in daylight with the risk of being accidentally spotted as my greatest concern. I noted my attempt on 26 January, *"R out after breakfast."*

Leaving the camp was no problem as I asked permission to

look for firewood. Porky and Base grunted a simultaneous *"Ua,"* giving me the green light. I walked through the guard hut and out of the camp to the east, passing just north of the Mines as I put distance between myself and the camp. The guards might call for me sometime soon and panic when I didn't answer. I had to be at least a couple of clicks away before that happened, or else I'd be in bad shape.

As I walked along the narrow path I noticed how short of breath I was, even though I'd traveled less than a kilometer; it was going to be a rough trip because my condition was apparently worse than I'd anticipated. The few tests, push-ups, deep knee bends and sit-ups, that I'd given myself to check strength, had not been an accurate evaluation. My legs were tiring rapidly and I slowed my pace, deciding to make a long, steady haul rather than a short, fast one. I was kicking myself mentally for not taking physical weakness into consideration.

The feeling of freedom, if only to be out of the trees, was exhilarating and I felt my spirits climbing. It was spur-of-the-moment chances like this one that worked, I thought to myself, beginning to feel more confident. It was going to be so simple to just follow the path to the river, jump in and swim to the south. It might take a while for the swim, but I'd make it.

The sun was directly overhead and I'd crossed two canals, traveling more slowly now as I became more tired. I stopped to rest periodically, conserving my strength as much as possible for the swim. I suspected that the guards were already alerted to the fact that I wasn't in the area assigned to me and a search was underway.

I was past the spot at which we had stopped during the airstrikes and had to pick my way through reeds as the path ended abruptly. I noticed a smaller path running to the south, but I was going due east and decided to break my own trail here. As I broke through the patch of reeds and high grass, I found myself in a thick clump of trees which I'd seen from a distance, not realizing how dense the overhead canopy of leaves was. I had taken only a few more steps when my breath caught in my throat! A hootch! I looked around! Another hootch, a third! Oh shit, I'm in a camp. My stomach was turning over as I began to backtrack toward the reeds.

"Dung lai!"—Stop! I froze. A curious face peered at me from the door of the nearest hut, probably seeing the black pajamas, darkly tanned face and dark hair in the initial glance.

The face became incredulous, then began calling for other guards. I'd been recognized as an American. Stocky, well-fed soldiers appeared from the huts, some of them carrying weapons: "Russian AKs," the thought registered as I stared at the Soviet-made assault carbines carried by these soldiers. They clustered around me, showing more curiosity than anything else. All of them tried to talk to me at once, asking if I was an American, what I was doing here, did I speak Vietnamese.

I felt my knees trembling as I glanced around, looking at the physical condition of the men, their weapons, the equipment some of them wore. This was a part of a main force unit! These soldiers were part of the hard core and I was right in the middle of them without a pot to piss in; I couldn't have fouled this up any worse if I'd tried. My mind worked around the problems I was creating for it and I found myself answering their questions in Vietnamese and grinning at the ones who seemed the friendliest.

Within the space of four answers: "Yes, I am an American, but a prisoner of war; I was out gathering wood so I might cook my food in the prison camp and got lost; I came into this camp, thinking it might be members of the Liberation Armed Forces, to get someone to help me return to my camp; I saw the huts and I was afraid I'd run into a group of civilians who would kill me because of the hatred they have for Americans. That was why I was backing toward the reeds."

Smiles broke out in the group and I released my breath, watching them check me out, examining this strange creature who had broken up the monotony of their routine and was obviously in need of guidance. I told them my camp was to the west of here about two or three kilometers, but I wasn't certain exactly how far I'd wandered and I had no way of telling direction. They thought it humorous that I couldn't use the sun to tell direction. I was going to be the dumb, funny American if that's what scored points with these people and it obviously was because they sent two of their people out to find my camp while I waited.

Porky and Chinh arrived with the two soldiers who had gone out and immediately were collared by an older-looking member of this group who had said nothing since my arrival. He spoke with them in low, sharp tones and I got the idea that they were getting the word about their prisoner wandering all over the countryside. I dreaded their reaction, but was in for a surprise when we departed and the group of soldiers said goodbye to me and told Chinh I was a good prisoner who knew his lessons well, referring to my relating the lessons I'd gotten from Ha as I'd been caulking the seam on the boat. Chinh was surprised and evidently was influenced by the comment or other factors unknown to me because upon return to the camp he told me that I was not to go out of the camp for anything from now on, I would be locked up early for several days and I was not to mention where I had been to anyone. I think there was a little negligence on the part of a guard being covered up.

That night, I found that I was so happy to have gotten out of the situation with my skin that being back in the camp didn't bother me that much. The disappointment of failing was there and it was deep, but the thought of how much crap I could have gotten myself into was enough to dull the ache.

I pondered the attitude of the soldiers, thinking how they had responded to an American who spoke their language and could spout their political ideas. What if I hadn't been able to, I wondered.

Tet, the Lunar New Year celebration, was approaching and provided a perfect diversion. I was anticipating the food and sweets that would accompany the guards' celebration. There was an air of expectation among the guards as 29 January neared. They seemed to have forgotten about the twenty-sixth completely. The indoctrinations stopped for a number of days and there was an exchange of pleasantries between the guards and their American. I enjoyed the period of political inactivity and turned my thoughts to the cakes and possible pieces of pork to come in the next days. If they would forget and celebrate, so would I.

I noted in my observations that the seven-day cease-fire, proposed by the NLF, would be a time to be extremely cautious. The broadcasts from Hanoi and Liberation Radio urged the ARVN and militiamen to take advantage of this "humanitarian" gesture by the Front and return to their villages to celebrate Tet with their families. No weapons could be carried by the men to their homes if they lay in a liberated zone and, I thought, it would be an ideal time to catch ARVN with troops dispersed and without weapons, a terrific advantage with which to begin an offensive. The Communist stations condemned the Government in Saigon for not matching the Front's cease-fire order and encouraged the Vietnamese soldiers to go home anyway. I noted that spring began right after Tet and if there was to be a winter-spring "total victory" campaign, then Tet would be the time to launch it.

On 31 January, I heard that the NLF had hit major cities over the length of Vietnam. Hanoi's broadcasts were filled with glowing reports of victory after smashing victory for the NLF. Kontum, Pleiku, Ban Me Thuot, Danang, city after city was being overrun; ARVN was disintegrating, the American command was in turmoil, the "People's Forces" in complete control of all battlefields. What a "humanitarian" gesture, I thought, wondering if many ARVN had actually taken advantage of the cease-fire.

The next days were ones of high excitement among the guards as the victory reports continued to pour in. On 3 February, my guards felt that total victory was assured. From the diary: *"3/2/68...Kiddies partied hard/late—already celebrating "total victory"—premature, I believe. Mat [Mat Trang—the Front] can't maintain tempo of attacks much longer—and he has it* ALL *hanging out—if only Sam has a big stick left."* If Uncle Sam had the stick, Radio Hanoi certainly wasn't mentioning it; the staggering reports of Allied casualties continued to come in. Hue, Saigon, Can Tho all were in bad shape. Reports that General Westmoreland was to be relieved and that the U.S. was now spending 66 million dollars per day in SVN added to the picture of turmoil.

The NLF must have been taking a few losses themselves because A5, my squad of guards, got the word to get ready for war. The older soldiers, Carpenter, Leo, Old Moon, Clark Gable, New Moon and their contemporaries, were the first to go, having gathered at the Corral before departure for the last pot of tea with the younger guards. I hadn't seen some of them for months, but they had apparently been somewhere in the area and were now on the way to a unit. The next increment was already preparing and included Cheeta, Clem, Pock, Showboat, Thanh and Base. Porky, Chinh and Bud stayed with Sauser and Major Bay to hold this camp.

"10/2/68 R. Hanoi...Western, US news sources quoted—very critical of US situation." The pessimistic reports continued to flow in; no one seemed to think we could hold out, particularly the journalists I was hearing from. I couldn't believe that the situation was as bad as Hanoi made it sound; the American Army didn't just fold up and if the issue hadn't been decided by now, the VC would have blown their cork and we

could begin to mop them up. Then came the commentary from the United States. "We have obviously lost." "The Government in Saigon cannot guarantee security. The question is no longer in doubt; we have lost." "Pull American troops out immediately." The senators and congressmen again in alleged statements calling on President Johnson to stop bombing the North, to get American troops out of Vietnam and let the VC take over. I began to listen to the names of the senators and congressmen, wondering if they could be serious, if they really knew who the VC were and what a victory for them would mean. The use of "neutrality" as a ploy to secure a "coalition government" was no more than a slight detour to the same goal. The Communists wouldn't sit for very long in a coalition with members of the present Vietnamese Government; it was total victory or continue to fight as far as the Communists were concerned.

Major Bay presented a lecture on the situation in the United States and Vietnam, drawing exclusively from sources I recognized, not one of them in Hanoi or in the NLF. I hoped the statements were inaccurately quoted, because the picture they conveyed was one I tried not to accept. I wrote the points down so I might check them with later stories, seeking loopholes. He began with the elections held in September of 1967: "The forthcoming elections in South Vietnam might be an exercise in futility because they seem likely to perpetuate the present unpopular military regime in power"—alleged statement by Senator T. Morton—Reuters, 13 August. "The military junta has set up a military commission to seize power in spite of the majority of votes won by candidates in the forthcoming elections"—alleged statement by Senator S. Young—AP, 8 August. "After publication of results, Candidate Truong Dinh Dzu said Thieu-Ky list won by fraud. Demanded National Assembly invalidate the 3 September election. He would submit a report with proof offered. He was supported by Phan Khac Suu, President of National Assembly, who, with 5 civilian candidates, is preparing to bring it before the National Assembly"—alleged BBC broadcast—5 September. "Tran Van Huong planning to set up a neutralist government faction in opposition to Thieu-Ky"—alleged AP—4 September.

Statements which were also condemnatory came allegedly from Senator J. William Fulbright and Senator Mike Mansfield, whom I recognized as leaders within the Democratic Party, but even though they had been quoted before by Radio Hanoi and the cadre, I totally refused to accept the validity of the indictments of our policy and the elections. My regard for these members of our government was too high to allow me to accept their employment as propaganda tools.

The antiwar movement in the United States was of major importance to the political cadre's development of his lesson and he drew from the following to illustrate his points:

"More and more the U.S. people seriously lose confidence in the Government and are discontent with the war in Vietnam. They are calling for a change in the present policy"—alleged Chicago *Sun-Times*—22 June 67.

"Points of conflict within the United States are: High war budget, tax increase, deficit, additional troop and expenditure requirement, anti-war movement, Afro-American problem"—alleged AP—no date.

"Public opinion in the U.S. is openly urging LBJ to revise the whole of the U.S. Foreign Policy, first and foremost in the Southeast Asia area"—Alleged *U.S. News and World Report*. From alleged AP and UPI sources: "7 week torch race, (27 August-21 October), 4,800 kilometers from San Francisco through 190 towns to Washington, D.C. protesting the war."

"NYC Committee for Immediate Withdrawal of U.S. Troops from Vietnam, collecting thousands of signatures. (Late September results, 93,000 signatures.)"

"20 September—Women for Peace—demonstration, Lafayette Square—end the war."

"27 September—New York—'Businessmen for Peace in Vietnam Assn.'—300 factory owners, businessmen in 44 states—statement demanding LBJ stop the war."

"17 September—133 writers and publishers signed statement refusing to pay income tax in protest against the war."

"15 April [the date of the broadcast]—New York—'Student Mobilization Committee'—response to 'Vietnam Week'—workers, intellectuals, religious followers, peace militants. March to UN building. Rev. M. L. King denounced war in Vietnam as illegal, unjustifiable."

"San Francisco—100,000 of same type—same poop."

Major Bay then went to the implications of the U.S. policy: "There is no way other than stalemate"—alleged *U.S. News and World Report*—7 June 67. "U.S. prewar Allies have either left the U.S. or are abandoning it."—alleged *U.S. News and World Report*.

A small booklet entitled "U.S. People Against U.S. War in South Vietnam," published as propaganda for American troops, had as its front cover a photograph that I found difficult to believe. Its caption was, "In the Nov.-27-1965 march to Washington, the SVNNFL's flag was hoisted beside the U.S. flag, symbolizing the South Vietnamese and American peoples' friendship." I was fighting back the bile that rose in my throat as I looked at the pictures of Americans giving support to this conglomeration of Marxists, revolutionaries, soul-crushing atheists; this system, this ideology that pledged itself to destroy the very liberties those people were exercising. Dear God, I was thankful Tim and Dave and Ben weren't here to see this. At least they died believing the American people supported the cause for which we were going through this hell; believing that someday their deaths would have gone toward accomplishing something worthwhile, even though they wouldn't be here to see the realization of our dreams. Perhaps while we were living, the mundane aspects of our daily existence blanked out any higher aspirations, but the approach of death makes a man want to have died for something, not to have squandered his life.

I leafed through the pamphlet while Major Bay sipped a cup of tea, preparing for the next part of his dissertation. Draft-card burnings, self-immolations, soldiers refusing to go to South Vietnam, deserters in Sweden, "May 2 Movement," "Women Strike for Peace," Senator Ernest Gruening, Dr. Benjamin Spock, "Committee for Non-Violent Action," "The War Resisters' League," "The Catholic Worker," "The Workshop of Non-Violence." The pictures of the signs carried in the demonstrations, "Withdraw U.S.Troops," "War on the KKK, not Vietnam," and the one that showed me the greatest naïveté of the bearer, in a march under the large banner, "We come from Selma for freedom in Oakland—peace in Vietnam," a young lady with the sign, "We must not fight our brothers." I hoped she was referring to our Negro citizens as "brothers" rather than my captors.

Major Bay began with the news of the Tet offensive, commenting that the opposition to the war and the hopelessness of the U.S. position that I'd just learned about was all prior to the general uprising of the fourteen million Vietnamese people under the glorious banner of the NFL. "What can the position of the U.S. imperialist be now that it and its lackeys in Saigon have suffered total defeat?" he asked. I was at a loss for words. The events as I had heard them left me with no place to turn. I couldn't base any statement on my personal faith in my country and our government; I had no facts from which to draw. He was almost smug as he realized my silence indicated my confusion.

The advantage was his and he drove the points home with reports of the NLF entering every major city in South Vietnam. Saigon was the scene of bloody fighting. Hue had been captured and the citizens of the ancient capital had risen up to punish "the cruel agents and henchmen of the imperialists and their lackeys." He paused for a moment to leaf through a sheaf of papers, selecting one from the stack. "In Hue, we have proven the invincibility of our revolution. The people have risen up, thousands as one, to overthrow the evil ruling clique and even now, the traitors are being severely punished by the people. It is a just action against those who have committed barbarous crimes against the people." He pointed to the sheet of paper, "I receive the documents from my commanders, telling me of the successes of our people in their struggle for national liberation and I tell of them to you so you might better understand the just cause."

Faced with the worsening situation in Vietnam, Secretary of Defense McNamara had been "rejected" by President Johnson as he sought to bring some change in the situation. General Westmoreland was blamed entirely for the U.S. defeat and he would "walk the same path as Navarre, Lattre de Tassigny and De Castrie." The war was "unjust and immoral" and was recognized as such by "the world public opinion and the progressive, peace- and justice-loving American people," thus dooming the U.S. imperialists to defeat.

Even my optimism and belief in our ability to win suffered a hell of a blow in the days that followed. The guards were all in high spirits, talking to me about their coming visits to Saigon while the NLF took over and how I'd soon be able to go home. I found myself leaning toward the thought of going home, thinking of the relief I would have when this question was finally decided.

I had never really considered the political aspects of a war in the past, since I, as a member of our military, was bound by the traditional separation of military and political in our system. I had learned and trained in the methods of conducting warfare as the right arm of foreign policy without questioning the political issues involved. Yet here I was forced by my enemy to question the ethics and policies of my own government. I, like the rest of the American POW's, was ill prepared for the political warfare involved in an ideological struggle. It was difficult enough defending my country, my government and its policies against the specially trained Communist political cadre without having to contend with the opposition from my own senators. I tried to ignore the almost daily references by Radio Hanoi, Radio Liberation or the guards and cadre to new condemnation coming from the United States, but found my morale and resistance dropping lower.

I developed another bad case of dysentery in the days of new indoctrinations, beginning after I had spent several sleepless nights trying to resolve the questions in my own mind, and becoming progressively worse.

To complicate my situation, Sauser came in and gave me a requirement to write an "appeal" to U.S. servicemen to go home. I refused and asked him for medication for the dysentery, receiving instead a lecture on "my duty to the Front" and my requirement to "do what I can to end the war." He carefully stressed the need for me to "contribute my share" in order to be able to "enjoy the lenient policy of the Front." His meaning was clear: write and I could get medication. I decided to try and ride the dysentery out by getting more sleep and pushing down more rice.

The next two days were total misery. *"Wake up run loose, loose. Colon pain during nite very noticeable. Lac now in* BAD *shape, am gouging chunks of skin at night while scratching. Comb useless—tried scrape stick—30% effective. Only relief comes after raking an area and inflicting pain—lasts till Lac knocks nerve ends and itching begins again. Chance of infection high—many scabs. Mid morn run mucus/blood 1cc. Afternoon run mucus/blood 1-2cc. pre chow run mucus/blood."* There was no sleep and no relief. Sauser called me down and repeated the requirement. I decided to make the trade for the medication and write a screwed-up appeal that would take days to be translated. Since Sauser didn't speak English, I calculated that by the time it came back down the line, I would be reasonably well and could argue it out with him then. I noted my writing in my diary, *"Message from Tu Binh My* [American POW] *to no one in particular. Quoted Radio Hanoi, NLF cadre—footnoted and in quotation marks."* That evening I got to listen to Radio Hanoi; no medication. Included in the news: General Westmoreland was being relieved, President Johnson was upping U.S. troops to one million and my diary comment, *"Western, US newspapers quoted—very critical of US situation."*

I discovered the next morning that Sauser was having Chinh, who had studied a little English, translate my appeal for him. My diary reflects the situation: *"M translating my 'appeal'— damn dictionary has 'duress,' 'conjure,' etc. M might be onto my line of thought, Bluffed this* A.M. *on several key words to throw him off—Admin & Report officer. etc. Afternoon—nasty day—Sau turned down my appeal (thought he might) he plays no games—whipped an 'appeal' on me that he had written. After translating it into English, I had to tell him it was a 'no go' for me. Appeal to US Officers and Men & ARVN. 'I am a representative of a number of POW's—who? Urge US troops to disobey orders. Sau highly displeased. Off to Shangri-la. Chinh says I have the mind of an aggressor and don't understand—told him O.K.—if he says so, then so be it. After 4 years I would cease trying to understand since it was so obvious I did not. Things could get nasty with Sau at the helm."*

That night, the pressure was almost beyond my control. I could see the trap closing in and there wasn't an exit in sight. My system reacted severely to the strain: *"6 runs between period 2000-0500, all 3L with mucus/blood. Wake up run 3L mucus/blood. After chow run mucus/blood 2cc, midmorning run 3L mucus."* That afternoon Mom M, who had come in the day before, gave me a one-kilo *ca loc* for my supper. The unexpected gesture by this seemingly callous old cadre caught me by surprise and I expressed my sincere thanks for his generosity, wondering what had prompted it.

Sauser was back the next morning with a slightly toned-down appeal, but still containing the "disobey" clause. I had questioned the "representative of a number of POW's" part since I was the only POW in the camp. Sau showed me a set of three initials under a statement, obviously printed by Chinh, agreeing to my being a "representative." I told him it was still worded too strongly and I couldn't write it. I noted that evening in my diary, *"Sau getting nasty—'I owe it to the Front for all the lenient treatment I've gotten.' Will at least stall him for a while—I hate to get this far in the ballgame and fumble."* I knew I was weakening and would soon make my first big mistake, but couldn't build the determination to flatly refuse. The nights got worse as I condemned my weakness and inability to push him on the point. The greatest agony came from my grasping at his statement that "if this turns out well, the Front might consider you for release." I wanted to go home. Lord, how I wanted to get out from under this pressure.

The dysentery reached the point it was unbearable. *"Mucus/ blood 2cc, mucus/blood 1cc, colon pain* VERY *sharp—diaphragm tight, burning—like a solar plexus punch. Gut pain, gut pain—spiraling. Mucus/blood 2cc."* My last entry that day was *"This is ridiculous! At this rate I'm not going to last very long—hope they have comfortable latrines at Leavenworth prison."*

I wrote the appeal as Sauser had put it down, leaving every inaccuracy I could in the message. The appeal portion was worded as follows:

"Dear to the realization of peace and total victory for the NLF is the US GI. For if the US Forces cease to fight, there can only be a total defeat for us and an end to the war. The NLF wants you to partake of its lenient policy, to put an end to the war by the following actions:

"Do not go on operations killing innocent Vietnamese people.

"If you surrender on the battlefield or cross over to the people's side, you can be repatriated to any country of your choice whether it be Russia, Siberia or even Sweden."

I felt lost after I handed the paper to him. It had begun, "I am Rowe, James, 1st Lieutenant, captured 29 October 1963." I had now taken the first step toward the most confused months of my life.

I received ten sulfaguanidine, which served to reduce the runs to a controllable level. The Front had let me continue to "enjoy the lenient policy."

I heard a BBC broadcast when the guards were tuning the radio searching for Radio Hanoi, *"Peace talks—Moscow, London, Paris agree that war is over—LBJ could prolong suffering with additional US troops, but the issue has been decided."* My mind accepted the concept of peace talks; the suffering had gone far enough. I felt committed and hoped that the war would end before that appeal could be used. Even though it was screwed up, they still might use it on ARVN; an American would be able to detect the foul-ups, but translated into Vietnamese, it could be re-arranged.

The guards were all extremely friendly now and I was included on a fish-catching expedition to one of the reservoirs where the water had sunk low, trapping the fish. We brought back about a hundred pounds of fish and I received two large *ca loc* for my supper. This continued for several days as we returned to catch more fish. I could feel my strength returning with the vastly improved menu. I was using all the wild greens I could get my hands on to make soup for my meals. The exertion of carrying the heavy bags of fish for the guards broke the diarrhea loose again, but I received sulfaguanidine immediately and that quieted it down.

Bounce, who had stayed in camp after Turn was taken out, had adopted my cage as hers after the first nights I'd let her and Turn sleep in my net. Miss Fit had been out to a village and brought back a load of fleas which Bounce inherited. Within a couple of days, I was being attacked myself, and I was killing from a minimum of two to a maximum one-night kill of 85. This kept up over a period of a month, adding a new dimension to discomfort and forcing me, at one point, to shave my head to keep them from nesting. The guards and Sauser were horrified at my bald head, but failed to accept the fleas as a discomfort. In a sixteen-day count I had killed 513 fleas, wounded twice that number and put another undetermined number into a missing in action category.

Radio Hanoi added its note of discouragement quoting General Westmoreland as stating the VC suffered a twelve-to-one loss ratio in the Tet offensive, making them three times weaker than when it began. This brought my spirits up off of the floor, but they were smashed when Hanoi went on to quote AP and UPI knocking General Westmoreland, claiming he was "daydreaming." If we don't believe in ourselves, I wondered, who in the hell will?

In the midst of the flea episode, a more dangerous threat developed. A large fire was burning to our east and heading this way, pushed by the dry-season winds. The ground had been dried out by the hot sun and the vast areas of withered brown grass would burn like tinder. The trees were green-leafed, but a fierce enough blaze could ignite them and turn this entire section into a burned-out wasteland. It was early

March and the rainy season was too far away to be able to help; this was going to be a bad show no matter how you looked at it. Water was scarce already and the reservoir near camp where we got the cooking water was low and dirty. Bathing was a luxury and I was hoarding my precious supply of rain-water in the drum, using a minimum each day for drinking, trying to stretch it out. I had no idea where we'd go if the camp should be destroyed, but things could only get worse.

Some of the guards became edgy with the spread of the fire along a line running from north to south without a visible break. Smoke, which had been a haze on the eastern horizon, rolled in clouds toward us.

I sat on top of one of the camp bunkers one evening with Bud, watching the orange-red glow in the sky to our north where the fire was already sweeping beyond us to the west. In the course of idle conversation, I asked him about the guards who had gone out to fight during the offensive and hadn't returned. The answers from Chinh and Porky had been that all were safe and still carrying on the fight; however, Bud in his unconscious manner told me Leo had been killed in an airstrike near Can Tho, Carpenter had been seriously wounded and was back in his hamlet, out of the army, Clark Gable had been killed in an attack on a militia post, and Old Moon had died in an artillery barrage. Thanh had been hit in the lung during another artillery barrage and was in a hospital being treated. Bud mentioned he had been to see Thanh and he would soon be back with us here.

Clem had been killed and was the sixth of seven sons in his family killed in the revolution. Bud commented that Clem's father, who had fought with Ho Chi Minh against the Japanese and the French, had said that as soon as his youngest son was old enough to fight, he too would go to the revolution like his brothers. If he were to die, the old man swore he would return to the revolution himself. I began to add the losses out of this camp and extrapolate to the other camps, thinking that General Westmoreland might not be far from correct in his kill ratio.

The next morning the fires were closer and the guards began taking walks into the surrounding forest to check on its prog-ress. I had convinced Sauser that the fleas actually existed in the cage and received permission to sleep in the *nha mam*, the curing shed where *nuoc mam* was put to sit in the huge crocks as it rotted. I spent the day making the irregular pole floor more comfortable, finishing in time to prepare to cook supper.

I was squatting in front of the packed-mud fireplace in the cooking hootch when I heard Porky and Bud laughing as they returned through the brush surrounding the camp. They walked up on the clay bank that encircled the camp, and as Bud proceeded on to the guards' kitchen, Porky came toward me. I could see he had something clutched in either hand. I felt the log floor shift slightly as he stepped into the back of the hootch. I turned, and Porky held out two bundles of fluffy down, each with a beak and pair of bright, round, unblinking eyes attached.

"Ro, here, *Anh Giai Phong* gives you two birds to feed. Soon they will be big and you can eat them." I looked at the two creatures rather dubiously. Porky must have sensed my doubt and he continued, "They are *con au*, and are very fine birds. *Anh Giai Phong* shares them with you."

I was thinking, Thanks a hell of a lot, Porky. I can barely find enough food for myself and you dump these things on me. I learned that Porky and Bud, while out in the forest searching for crane eggs, had come upon the nest of a forest eagle and had taken these two babies since there was a chance that the fire burning to our east would sweep through this area and the mother eagle would not be able to save her young.

"What do they eat?" I asked.

"You can feed them small pieces of *ca sat*. Soon they will eat many animals," Porky replied as he walked out of the hootch, leaving me holding the two orphans.

Well, I thought, you two little fellows are in worse shape than I am, so let's see what we can do about food and a place for you to sleep. The little creature in my left hand expressed his feelings about the whole affair as he made a soft chirping sound, looked up at me with those enormous eyes, and crapped all over my hand. That was my introduction to "Herc" and "Ajax," my two eagles. When they were young, they proved to be oversized stomachs with beaks, covered with down, then pinfeathers, and finally full plumage as they became young adult stomachs with beaks attached. Never have I encountered such voracious appetites, inquisitive natures, or complete self-confidence. The world belonged exclusively to them.

The day after Porky presented my two clowns to me, I learned through overhearing the guards' conversation that the fire burning to the east would, in fact, sweep through the area, and it was possible that our camp would be burned out. After hearing this, I returned to the *nha mam*, fed Herc and Ajax for the umpteenth time that day, and sat down to decide what items among my worldly belongings could be abandoned should I be forced to move out rapidly. Smoke was now a gray blanket over the entire area and it was obvious that the fire was progressing steadily.

That night I went to sleep with the smell of smoke all around me and the sky in three directions an eerie, flickering orange.

It was still dark, the smoke was choking. Bud was unlocking my leg irons and telling me to get up and prepare my rice. Bud's normally languid manner was disturbed by an air of urgency which, with his poor coordination, caused an impossible situation. He was shaking so hard he couldn't fit the key into the padlock. Finally he gave up, handed me the key and had me open the lock.

"Rung chay gan day; nau com di"—The fire is very near; you must eat now.

With that, Bud grabbed the key and moved off in the darkness toward the guard kitchen, his lamp the only light in the area, but all around me the sky was red. I pulled the leg iron free, took down my mosquito net, and put all my belongings into the rice sack I used as a pack. Looking around the floor, I said a mental goodbye, then picked up the lamp, and made my way to the guards' kitchen to get the light Bud had forgotten to give me. All of the guards were in the kitchen, their gear stacked on the low board seat nearest the thatch wall. Sauser was speaking rapidly with frequent gestures toward the approaching fire, as the guards listened intently.

"Thua, Anh Giai Phong, cho toi xin phep doc den." The familiar request came out without my thinking: "Pardon me, Mr. Liberation, may I request permission to light the lamp?"

All heads snapped toward me and the looks were as if I had been the one responsible for the fire threatening to destroy the camp. Porky stood up and walked over to where I stood. "Why haven't you cooked rice yet?" he demanded.

"Because I had no light in my kitchen," I replied.

"Uh," Porky grunted as he lit the small lamp and I turned to go. "Cook rapidly," came Sauser's voice from the hootch.

That morning and for the next four days, I got a close look at a minor Hades. The fires raged in the grass and reeds on all sides of the camp, burning the saplings, but failing to ignite the larger trees. The Mines were completely destroyed as the rampaging flames roared through the dense thickets of tangled vines and reeds, leaving only the blackened trunks of the taller trees with their withered leaves. Before the main blaze reached us, the guards had burned a firebreak around the east side of the camp which slowed the fire sufficiently to prevent it from destroying our camp. The ditch and mud wall which surrounded the camp were an added protection, as the sub-humus burn was prevented from working its way into the camp proper.

I worked alongside Porky or Bud on most of the days when the camp was under immediate threat, using a wet rice sack to beat out any fires that might threaten the thatch roofs or the grass inside the wall. After the fire had been beaten back for the moment, the guards would retire to the forum where Sauser sat directing their efforts while he drank tea. I remained along the wall or went back to my kitchen to rest, taking frequent sips of boiled water to wet my parched lips. I was covered with perspiration, dirt and a layer of soot and ashes, feeling dirtier than ever before. The *lac* reacted to the salty perspiration and dirt, making the feeling of filth and irritation more intense. There was no water for bathing, and for the first night I climbed into my net after nineteen hours of battling the flames, dirty, grimy and exhausted. I objected to having my leg irons locked because of the threat of fire inside the camp while we were sleeping and my inability to flee. There was no reaction from Chinh, who was equally tired and had no time to argue the question; he locked the irons and left.

The smoke had become so heavy that I couldn't see twenty meters in front of myself. Breathing was difficult and my eyes felt as if salt had been rubbed in them. During a three-hour battle against the fire coming in from the Mines to our east, Porky was overcome by the smoke and I found him gasping and choking, clinging to a tree trunk near the ditch. I lowered him into the ditch where the air was a little clearer and wet his towel with water from the U.S. canteen he carried, placing it over his nose and mouth. I began to think of the possibility of suffocation if the smoke got any denser. The burning reeds literally flared like gasoline, creating huge clouds of the lung-searing gray smoke, and there were hectares of reeds left to burn.

Fortunately the fire burned all available fuel in the area and subsided, leaving our camp an island of green in a sea of charred wreckage. I began to assess the damage and my own require-

321

ments for the coming days. Water was crucial. The hole Sauser had dug was almost dry and the water was unfit for use, even to wash pots. Our camp reservoir was an ash-covered mud puddle, totally unusable, leaving only the canal twenty-one reservoir as a source of water. It was about a three hundred-meter walk to that reservoir and I would have to carry the water, one five-liter can at a time. The task that lay ahead of me was going to be a bitch! Six-hundred-meter round trip, eleven trips to fill my water drum, twelve counting spillage, for a total of seventy-two hundred meters, over seven kilometers of carrying water so I could drink and cook rice. It had to be done, and I spent two days lugging the heavy can, finding myself completely exhausted afterward, but with water to use.

I discovered all the homeless birds, reptiles and other animals had gathered in our oasis of green trees. Herc and Ajax had, by this time, realized that this was their domain and as young as they were, gave every indication that they would soon be protecting their oasis against all trespassers. Herc was the bad ass of my two "Rogles." (A baby eagle, raised by "papa Rowe," became a "Rogle.") He kicked hell out of Ajax two or three times a day with additional sparring on the side. Ajax was intimidated, but not so much as I was when I wrote in the diary, *"Never stand behind an eagle when it craps—blast like a 75RR—2-3 meter range. I know now."* Ajax finally asserted himself several days later. *"Ajax has found eagle type vocal chords—let brother crow get in area scrounging scraps, then stood up on his 2 still scrawny legs and* 'SCREAMED!' *(scared me at 1st) Brother crow left feathers, anus and eyeballs as he rocketed out of range—like an Honest John launch. Evasive maneuvering was obvious till he went out of sight. Ajax then turned, dropped Herc on the head (1st time I'd seen this happen) & settled down for a nap."* My two young idiots were developing unique, individual personalities and, with Bounce, gave me the only real companionship I had.

My refusal to sleep in the cage any longer because of the fleas, startled Sau until I called him on "mistreatment" under the policy. He told the guards to build a new cage for me, and once again I was used to carry the logs. The work made the fleas seem like the lesser of two evils as diarrhea once again nearly incapacitated me. My temper was surging up and down

322

as lack of sleep and the disease tightened my nerves to the breaking point.

The work details continued after the log-carrying. I was detailed to go with Bud and Base to carry firewood, ending up carrying the majority of the heavy, fire-charred logs to storage sites in preparation for use in the rainy season. I was almost in rags, with only the set of blacks given me at Christmas to wear. My others were the remnants of Jim and Dan's cast-offs and my own year-old set. The work details were particularly difficult because of the blistering sun and the effect of roughened logs on my bony shoulders. I asked on several occasions for clothing, but got no response from the guards. The supply system left much to be desired around here.

I found myself beginning to treat the depressing news reports as normal, having heard the same basic theme so many times. The Vietcong continued to maintain pressure on all the cities, destroying my premise that they couldn't keep it up; Khe Sanh was being touted as another Dien Bien Phu and our troops were reported to be taking a pounding from the enemy artillery; the idea of "peace talks" seemed to be a key issue, with Uncle Ho calling for "complete and unconditional halt to the bombing," the NLF calling for "withdrawal of all U.S. troops," and the antiwar groups in the U.S. echoing the two demands.

President Johnson's answer was reported to be 35,000 more troops, $5.1 billion added, and limited bombing. From within the government came opposition: *"24/4/68 R Hanoi . . . many voices (including Sens. Kennedy, McCarthy, Mansfield, et al.) raised vs. LBJ's 'lack of good will' in stalling initial contacts between US & NVN. After stating 'anytime, anywhere' LBJ is tossing in conditions—rejected Phnom Penh, Warsaw."* The only light point in the news was the report that *"General Westmoreland is personally commanding large operations in the fire Provinces surrounding Saigon."* For a man who had been "relieved" three times already, he certainly clung to his position.

The major claims by the guards in the lectures now were that the U.S. would be forced to cease bombing North Vietnam because of the terrific losses we were suffering. Radio Hanoi had already celebrated the two thousandth American jet shot down and they were trying for three thousand. Second, the turn of events in South Vietnam had sealed the fate of "the Johnson

323

war," leaving the U.S. only one alternative. As Major Bay put it, "In 1954, we triumphed over the French, but offered them a method of saving their honor. We now offer the same method to the government of Johnson by allowing him to meet with us and discuss peace." The final point was the immense base of support enjoyed by the NLF right within the United States. "Johnson is isolated from the people and his government no longer represents the will of the American citizens." Once again the great volume of material that was available to the guards and cadre from AP, UPI, the *New York Times*, the *Washington Post* described the antiwar movement's growing strength and the government's problem in dealing not only with Vietnam, but with the internal strife also. Racial violence, the assassination of Martin Luther King, the tragedy of the aftermath: "*8/4/68 . . . 46 cities, NYC, DC, Chicago, Boston, etc. hit hard by Negro rioters—houses, cars burned—sniping—police and national guard and reserves used. Stokely Carmichael calls for 'guns and more guns, violence and more violence.'*"

I began to form a picture of my country that was unlike anything I had ever imagined could happen. Could I have been so wrong about the cause I supported? Could the government have actually changed so much between the two Presidents? The overwhelming opinion in the United States, particularly in the news I had heard, was so antiwar, antigovernment. Even though it was still coming from Radio Hanoi and the guards, the big change had occurred in the sources. The Communists no longer wrote their own English broadcasts, they merely selected from Western news agencies or from prominent individuals who were saying what Radio Hanoi wished to put out.

I tried to maintain my objectivity, telling myself that it was not our system in America that was being challenged, only our policy in Vietnam. I considered that I might have been mistaken about our involvement, particularly from a political or legal standpoint, since my main concern had been the military aspect. I had come when Ngo Dinh Diem was president of South Vietnam and President John F. Kennedy had sent me to act as an adviser to the Vietnamese Army. Since that time, President Kennedy had been assassinated, President Diem had been overthrown and killed, the war had exploded from 17,000 advisers to 500,000 U.S. combat troops, the Strategic Hamlet program had been wrecked, and "special warfare" had given way to "limited war." Now the American people were deciding we shouldn't be here, they were flying VC flags back home, and another Kennedy was saying, "Get out of Vietnam." Perhaps it was time to go home; before it was too late. My country was coming apart at the seams and I had a greater interest in preserving it from direct threat than beating a dead horse in Vietnam.

Herc and Ajax were my source of relief. They were feathered already and learning to fly. I wasn't exactly certain how a mother eagle would go about giving flying lessons, so I improvised, using a clearing and a mound of bark peelings upon which I'd stand to toss the birds, one at a time, up into the air, watching as they hurtled upward, wings tucked, enjoying the ride. At the peak of their ascent, they'd suddenly realize that the ride was over and roll belly-down, unfurling their powerful, reddish-brown wings and gliding back down beside me. Herc took the lessons as a matter of fact, doing well in his glide phase and displaying a rare grace, even at his young age. Ajax, on the other hand, seemed to take it as a game and I was constantly dodging as he careened past, trying to land on my shoulder, but not judging his distances correctly. He was a little clumsier, less eagle-like than the dominant Herc. Ajax, after crashing and burning on several beak, belly and butt landings, began to pick the pile of bark to slam into. He may have been a clown, but he wasn't dumb. The bark was a lot softer than the ground.

After the fire in mid-March, there was a very short supply of fish until the rains began and the water level started up in late May. I received a cucumber from Chinh and planted the seeds, hoping to supplement the diet of greens upon which I was depending. I had transplanted some of the guards' manioc in hopes of getting the leaves and had planted a cutting from one of the guards' pepper bushes, in an attempt to grow my own condiments. The cucumbers did poorly until the rains came and then everything sprouted! The fire-blackened earth around the camp broke open as fresh green shoots pushed through, the cucumbers climbed head-high up the trees within a week, and the pepper bush cutting produced its first tiny leaves. The manioc leaves and various wild greens were my chief source of nourishment during this period of time as I made "weed soup" almost every meal to avoid eating plain salt with my remaining rice. But the fire had done quite a bit of damage to

325

the edible greenery, and the rice supplies had burned along with camps in the area.

On 18 May, Mafia appeared with a summary of the situation in South Vietnam and the United States, repeating the same points I'd been hearing for the past weeks. I found that the constant repetition of the themes had fixed them in my mind, and as Mafia spoke, I found myself keeping up with him, silently matching his points one for one; I knew the spiel as well as he did. Repetition was the key to indoctrination of the guards: "No need to understand; just memorize, repeat, believe." I had passed through the memorize and repeat phases.

Mafia asked me questions regarding my opinions on the war since I had been studying the course of events. I told him quite frankly, I was surprised that the NLF had been successful in the first offensive and had launched a second. It indicated more preparation and strength than I thought possible. He smiled slightly. "As you know, we can end this war in two or three months. The Liberation Forces have entered every town." He chuckled mirthlessly. "Why, the puppet troops dare not even resist when we come to storm their posts. They know that to surrender is better than to die." Only the "end the war in two or three months" stayed with me. I could hold out that long; I had to hold and stay alive. I set my timer for August, thinking I'd be home for Thanksgiving this year and how wonderful it'd be.

He went on with his questioning and I responded almost verbatim from Ha's lessons, causing Mafia to blink in surprise at the knowledge I hadn't shown before. After I was sent back to my cage, Ri came down with a tube of the *lac* medicine that had been effective when I'd tried it in 1967. The infection was so bad now that I wondered if the tablets would work. I was willing to try anything for relief and began taking them immediately. Ri mentioned the purchase of condiments such as black pepper and garlic to improve my meals. I couldn't believe that Mafia had set this up just because I spouted Ha's lesson plans; there had to be something else involved. I tried to get that three-month limit out of my thoughts without success. I was programmed for three more months and then home when the war ended.

Herc and Ajax were flying and creating all sorts of havoc with the wildlife in the area. I had taught them, from their earliest days of hopping from the *nha mam* to the kitchen, that the pole above the kitchen entrance was the place to eat. When they were fed, that was where the food would be. If they were hungry, I would find them sitting and waiting for me to feed them. As soon as they started learning to fly, I began catching rats, birds and snakes to feed them so they'd know that fish weren't the only edible game around here. Once they were flying, they were able to pounce their own food and the training became an unexpected benefit as they would bring anything they caught back to the kitchen pole to eat it. I sat in the kitchen and when they returned with an edible-sized bird or squirrel, I'd exchange a fish for the delicacy and list it under "training fees." Herc had good taste in squirrels and provided me with several tasty meals.

Several things occurred after Mafia's visit. The guards became extremely friendly, except for "Killer Mouse," the thirteen-year-old recruit who had allegedly killed Americans already, and the other young "Mice," recruited after the second offensive to replace men lost in combat. I was placed back on a diet of plain rice instead of the *com nip*, making each meal a struggle. The guards began emphasizing the end of the war coming and my chance to go home. All served to increase my anxiety over Mafia's three months till the war would end.

Airstrikes were going in on all sides of us during April and May, particularly to the southeast and east, indicating that the war wasn't quite over yet. The guards, who had been so certain that they'd be celebrating in Saigon, by now were hearing that the Americans were "obdurate and perfidious; clinging to their evil schemes of aggression" and the NLF and valiant Vietnamese people would have to fight on, making even greater sacrifices for the Fatherland.

I had a problem with the guards tormenting Herc and Ajax. It seemed that I was the only human the birds recognized as friendly and my kitchen and area were "the nest." Any intruders could expect to be greeted by two sets of dagger-like talons, mounted on a feathered bundle of defensive anger, and the guards initially gave the birds wide berth. After a while, Killer Mouse began taunting Porky and Bud about the birds scaring them. After that it was only a matter of days before Porky caught Ajax unawares and pinned him with a branch until he could grasp the struggling eagle's wings. Killer Mouse and Porky pulled the bird's wings apart and stood laughing and poking at him with a stick as he fought to strike with his talons, helpless in their grasp. Herc perched on the kitchen roof, his head switching from side to side as he glared at the scene below. I came running in from the spot where I'd been chopping wood as soon as I saw what was happening, but was blocked off by Bud, who stood watching. I was fighting back the rage that was building as I listened to Ajax's now frustrated cries of pain and anger and asked Porky, in as calm a voice as I could manage, to please let the bird go. Killer Mouse snapped for me to be quiet, *Anh Giai Phong* was playing with the *con au*. Porky laughed again as he jabbed Ajax in the chest, but his laugh was strained; it seemed as if Killer Mouse was the only one of the three who was actually enjoying the bird's humiliation. His small eyes were gleaming in almost perverse pleasure as he watched, not daring to hit the bird himself, but urging and taunting Porky to strike harder.

I watched for a moment longer, then my anger flared beyond control and I shouldered past Bud on the walkway, grabbed the stick from Porky and threw it into the mud. Killer Mouse screamed in outrage, but didn't dare release Ajax's wing. Porky went white when he saw my face and realized I was actually taking control of the situation. I grasped Ajax's wingtip from Porky's weak grasp and released the bird, shoving him toward Killer Mouse. "Play, you little shit, play!" I shouted at the wide-eyed, panic-stricken young guard as Ajax turned his released fury on his tormentor. Herc launched himself from the roof in a power dive, aiming for Killer Mouse and missing by inches as the guard tumbled backward off of the walk.

I stepped down beside Killer Mouse before Ajax pounced, and blocked the bird from the prone body of the guard. Herc made another pass, but pulled out as he came over me. I managed to get Ajax's feet and settled him on my arm. Herc was now circling above the trees, screaming the shrill cry of the breed. I told Porky to get the young guard out of the area before I let Ajax loose to attack him. They all departed, with Killer Mouse swearing to get his weapon and kill all the "animals" in the American area.

My birds began staying away after that and I was happier, hoping they'd fly and make their own home away from the camp. Porky gave me a sharp reprimand, but stopped with that when I threatened to tell the cadre about the bird's mistreatment, knowing that the birds were a point of interest for all visiting cadre in the vicinity. The eagles were supposed to be difficult to raise and I had not only raised them, but had succeeded partially in training them to respond to my whistle and to bring game to the kitchen after they'd caught it. Major Bay and Mom M took great delight in showing off the accomplishment of their American prisoner and I had counted on their displeasure at possibly losing the birds merely to satisfy the guards' streak of cruelty.

The rainy season came in with its high winds, explosive thunderstorms, breathtaking lightning displays and lashing rains. My hootch leaked badly, and the first really hard rain, which happened to come at night, I found myself bathing right in my net as the water poured through the sieve I had for a roof.

The news of the war and the United States continued to pour in. Khe Sanh held the military spotlight as the Communist news broadcasts claimed the U.S. government had declared that Khe Sanh would be defended to the last man and now we were being forced to evacuate in the face of enemy pressure. The assassination of Senator Robert Kennedy was carried on all broadcasts for several days with editorial comment strongly condemning the "evil ruling clique" for a "political assassination." I sat, stupefied, wondering what in the world was happening to my country. First, President Kennedy in 1963, then Martin Luther King, and now Robert Kennedy. The violence was unprecedented, the country facing an era of dissension and disorder which could cripple us if even half of what I'd heard had been true. The peace talks had begun and I looked to them as a solution to this problem in Vietnam, fearing that the Tet offensive had accomplished its goal and the Allied position in Vietnam was untenable. The loss of more lives could be avoided through a negotiated settlement and we all could go home. I was strongly influenced by the U.S. news services that were constantly quoted by the Communists, finding my morale sinking with each new condemnation of our efforts or pessimistic opinion of our chances for survival on the battlefield. I began to look at the Vietcong and North Vietnamese as stronger fighters than I had credited them with being.

In one of the lectures, Porky and Bud discussed the peace talks with me, presenting a view I hadn't considered before, but obviously one the cadre had conveyed to them. *"Progress at the peace talks is not important. The issue of South Vietnam will be decided by the NLF in South Vietnam and there will*

be total victory. The purpose of the North Vietnamese repre-
sentatives in Paris is to utilize that setting to expose to world
opinion the 'crimes and aggression' of the US in SVN—so that
the world's people will realize the 'truth.' The North Vietnam-
ese representative must repeat the truth many times so ALL
PEOPLE WILL BELIEVE."

In July, I began hearing frequent reports of the peace talks.
The North Vietnamese were unyielding in their demands: Stop
bombing of North Vietnam, totally and unconditionally; recognize the NLF; remove U.S. troops; and discuss problems of
South Vietnam with the Front. The U.S. wanted assurance that
the attacks would stop on the cities in the South, but the North
Vietnamese said talk to the Front. Pressure from within the
U.S. seemed to be in favor of the North Vietnamese stand as
the cry went up from what seemed to be the liberal element of
our government for the President to concede to the North Vietnamese demands. Major Bay quoted from what he claimed
was an extract from the *Congressional Record* on or about 7
March, in which the late Senator Robert Kennedy and Senator
Fulbright were highly critical of our presence in Vietnam, and
then went to a book called *The Betrayal*, by a Marine officer
who had retired shortly before publishing the work. The picture
drawn from the book was enough to make me question whether
the price we were paying was worth what was or was not being
accomplished by the United States and allies. Radio Hanoi
followed with quotations from the same book.

The news got worse. Violence in the cities continued: Cleve-
land, Washington. UPI and AP reported Khe Sanh as a "major
military defeat"; General Westmoreland was "blamed" for the
Tet defeat. Senator Fulbright, Senator McCarthy and Senator
McGovern were highly critical of U.S. policy in Vietnam; the
Republican party platform committee strongly condemned the
LBJ administration for war in SVN. U.S. gold reserves were
in danger. LBJ declared NVN must withdraw troops, stop attacks on cities in SVN before bombing halt; North Vietnam
repeated: "Total and unconditional halt to bombing before serious talks begin." Draft cards were burned; deserters appeared
in Sweden. Violence erupted at the Republican Convention in
Miami, and three Negroes were killed.

My United States was being turned upside down and there
was no solution in sight. I had only the eighteenth of August
to look forward to because it meant going home; the war would

be over, if the peace talks could begin. I was wishing they would start; the issues were too confused for me and I had no way to fight back.

My only substantial victory was over rats as they finally gave up after losing twenty-one of their number to my traps. They had laid waste to all the vines planted by the canal and I had transplanted my vines to my kitchen, but then they had directed their attacks against those vines and my rice supply in the kitchen and even my mosquito net as well. I awoke one night feeling something crawling over me and discovered a large rat had chewed a hole in my net and was inside with me. I knocked him off my chest, praying he wouldn't bite me, and flailed away until I finally killed him. I patched the net the next morning, only to have another rat inside with me that night. I managed to kill him without being bitten and rigged a deadfall in my cage which eliminated two more of them before the action ceased. After all of this, I managed to get two small cucumbers from my remaining vine, thoroughly enjoying the soup I made from the hard-earned vegetables.

Major Bay came in on 13 August and, along with two of the local cadre, encouraged me with talk of going home soon. I felt my spirits climbing as a ray of light grew brighter, even if it was a release. I had reached a point where going home was the important thing and release was the way to accomplish it. Escape was a remote dream since the Tet offensive had broken Government control of the countryside. Even if I did escape, there would be no place to go.

I was required by Major Bay to write a letter to U.S. troops in South Vietnam, condemning our efforts. I told him I couldn't write it. He repeated my "duty" to the Front and said I would reconsider after I had seen the "truth" in actuality. Mafia would be coming in shortly and I would learn more then. He was too assured that I would capitulate, and it bothered me. I wanted to go home, but still clung to the basic principles I knew to be right. The Code of Conduct was one thing I remembered as an unchanging guide. Even when the issues were totally confused, it provided the standard of conduct that should be maintained, and if I could comply with it, I would be right. The only problem now was to stay alive while following it.

The meals of *nuoc mam* and rice still outnumbered the meals with fish, but there was always the promise of better food and more fish, even though it never quite materialized. Herc and

Ajax had been able to fly and catch their own food until Mom M came in one day and decided they were flying too far. He took a knife and, with Porky holding Herc, butchered the eagle's left wing feathers. Ajax was luckily out of reach, but my best bird became earthbound. After that I had to feed both birds as Ajax refused to leave without Herc and the clipped wing totally wrecked Herc's spirit. He couldn't understand why he suddenly couldn't fly. I could feel his anguish as he would perch on the log walk, beating his one useless wing against the air, straining to lift away and managing only to flop clumsily around in a circle until he fell into the water below and I'd have to pull him out. The light began to die in his eyes in the days that followed.

I waited for the eighteenth, hoping that Mafia would come in with some news of the peace talks and my going home. I ignored the voice in my head that kept telling me to be ready for a ration of shit, not to expect anything good; my timer had been set, the whole situation was so screwed up that this war couldn't go on, nobody wanted us in Vietnam anyway and the big problems were in the U.S., not here. I wanted to go home and Mafia had said "two or three months."

It was the morning of the eighteenth when Mafia arrived, three months to the day. I heard him as he spoke with the guards in the kitchem before Base came down to get me for my meeting with the cadre. I put on my clean set of blacks and walked to the forum where he waited.

As I entered, Mafia glanced up and smiled briefly, indicating the bench on the other side of the table. "Sit down," he said brusquely. "There is much I must discuss with you." The tingling of apprehension spread along my spine, this wasn't going to be what I'd hoped for; it wasn't even going to be good. "How is your health?" he inquired.

Now began the initial inconsequential chatter about health, catching fish, the whole required line of bullshit, as if he really cared. "I'm OK, Mr. Hai," I answered. "How have you been since the last time I saw you?" I hated myself for the hypocrisy, wishing I had guts enough to say what was boiling in my mind; the days I'd crapped my intestines out with dysentery, the meals of rice and salt, the nights I'd almost gone up the side of my mosquito net with the mental anguish and torment, the daily hardships that had become practically second nature, the mosquitoes, the cold, the hunger, the weakness, the nausea, the constant threat of death. None of these would come out; they weren't part of this unwritten script of pseudocordiality.

"Oh, I am very well. Do the guards provide you with sufficient food for your health?" He sounded bored.

"I get enough rice, Mr. Hai, and I'm catching fish for myself. It's difficult trying to feed all the birds and myself too."

"Do you have vegetables?" he asked.

"I get the greens from around the camp, the leaves and ferns mainly," I replied.

"Then you have sufficient vitamins for your health."

The initial questioning was of little or no value as far as changing anything; he was asking almost without listening to my answers. I felt like telling him I was eating steak and potatoes each night just to see if there would be any reaction.

"Today I bring you a ration of coffee and sugar," he said, handing me the packages. I thanked him, ashamed of myself for grabbing the newspaper-wrapped packets. It took so damn little here to make a day into a real holiday. Then he began the spiel, just like before, no mention of the war ending, no chance to go home; the trap slammed shut.

I had allowed him to hook me with the promise of the war ending, building the idea in my own mind, placing my hopes on the peace talks, on the chance to go without any more requirements to write anything for the Front. Mafia had caught me straining to cross the finish line and closed the door on me. I felt as if all the blood had been drained from my body.

I listened as he went through his main points: "The revolution is the just cause; the United States is the unjust cause; the Front's policy is lenient and good. You must realize how we triumph on the battlefield and in the political struggle. As you know clearly, the longer we fight, the stronger we become. The longer the puppet army and the U.S. aggressors fight, the weaker they become. The great victories of our nationwide general uprising have caused the puppet army to collapse and the U.S. aggressors to withdraw into their small bases while the people's forces control both countryside and major portions of the cities. The puppet government is near collapse and is attacked from all sides. World public opinion strongly condemns the traitors and they will surely fall before us."

Tay Ninh, Khe Sanh, Dak To; names I'd heard on Radio Hanoi. The losses, the deaths, the hopeless struggle. The antiwar movement, the President's decision not to run for re-election, the American people's opposition to their government's policy, dissension within the government. I could feel the confusion building, the feeling of being trapped and having to defend something that wasn't defendable.

"And now," he continued, "you must reflect upon the situation in South Vietnam and write for me your thoughts on the war and how it can be resolved. You realize the futility of the struggle, the needless loss of American lives. As I have discussed with you before, the just cause of the revolution lies with the Vietnamese people and the National Liberation Front. You must recognize the unjust cause of the U.S. imperialists and their henchmen in Saigon who sent you to die a useless death so they might become enriched by this war. It is they who cause your suffering in this camp and keep you away from your dear family. I can report to you that the Front wishes to release you before the end of the war and I can help you to gain your release. You must believe that my recommendations are well received by the Central Committee, and if you show sufficient progress, you can be released as were the others." He paused for a moment, watching me, then pulled several sheets of lined paper from the .30 cal. U.S. ammunition box and placed them in front of me. "You can write for me now your thoughts."

There was an empty feeling deep in my stomach. The thought of release was strong and it was the only way I could see to come out of this alive. The reasons I'd had for being willing to hang on, no matter what came, had been torn away from me. Why should I die in this rotten camp for a cause that nobody supports anyway? I sat looking at the paper for long seconds before Mafia went on, "You must write your thoughts so the Front can study them and control your thinking. We must correct anything you do not understand."

"Mr. Hai, I can't write those things now." The words were out before I realized I'd said them. I panicked as I saw the coldness come into Mafia's eyes. "There are a lot of things that are still unclear in my mind." I was grasping for some way to soften what I'd said, some way to stall him until I could devise a way around this. I couldn't condemn my country and yet I didn't want to die for nothing, die for supporting a lost cause.

"You must contribute your share to ending this cruel war," Mafia declared.

"Mr. Hai," I said earnestly, "I'm just a POW, and who am I to say what is right and what is wrong?"

"You have learned the truth of the situation in Vietnam and you must have the courage to speak what you think." His voice softened to a less cutting tone. "Do not fear your government to punish you. You will be protected by the great mass of the American people; the government cannot resist the strength of the people."

"What if my thoughts are not according to what you believe?" I asked, pushing a little, trying to find an out.

"We have spent much time teaching you the difference between right and wrong. You are an aggressor, guilty of bloody crimes against our people, yet the Front has seen fit to spare your life and give you the opportunity to return someday to your family. You must do your share to end this cruel war. We cannot be lenient to those who are not sincerely repentant of their crimes. Consider your duty to the Front and the Vietnamese people."

"I can see where the Vietnamese people have suffered in some cases, Mr. Hai, particularly when they've been caught in an airstrike or artillery. I also know that the Americans don't put airstrikes or artillery in on civilians just to hurt civilians. There have to be troops in the area," I answered.

"You do not wish to write for me," he snapped.

"I can't write anything based on what you've said today," I replied; then, trying to soften the effect, added, "Perhaps if you could give me more information, I might be able to draw a conclusion."

He retrieved his paper without speaking. After taking an extra moment to return it to the ammunition box, he looked at me with a slight smile, confident in his control of the situation. "Go back to your house and do your work. We will talk again."

This was a break, I thought. I needed to check my nets and stakeouts to see if I'd have fish for supper. I got up from the floor and said good-bye, which he ignored, then made my way back along the log walkway to my kitchen hootch. The mosquitoes were clustered and waiting under the packed-mud fireplace. They swarmed over my bare feet as I squatted in front of the water pot to get a drink. My throat was extremely dry.

It seemed as if conversation with Mafia always made me thirsty.

I pondered the preceding events and wondered what would come next. Mafia wouldn't take a lot of stalling and my status was precarious to begin with. I finished the water and slipped out of my long black pajamas, preparatory to wading out to check the nets and lines. Now I was swatting with my towel as the mosquitoes attacked the newly exposed skin. I was happy that it wasn't raining today. That usually meant more mosquitoes and more exposed skin as I was unable to wear a shirt. I had only two and couldn't afford to get one wet unnecessarily.

I walked along the mud embankment to the path I had made to my stakeouts north of the camp. At the break in the trees where the path began, I stepped down into the cold, knee-deep water, reaching out to grasp a bunch of reeds and steady myself. It was always a shock to step into the water, because no matter how accustomed you were to it, it always seemed cold. I lurched along the uneven path, splashing water in front of me, hoping some of the mosquitoes would be knocked off and drowned. If mosquitoes could drown.

The first two stakeouts were bare. The *ca sac* had been taken, but it was evidently the work of some *ca ro* rather than the larger fish. The next one had a small *loc.* I could see the horizontal line dipping and the twin bamboo reeds at either end bending inward as the fish struggled to free itself.

I whistled to myself as I splashed my way back to the hootch, Mafia almost forgotten. The score from *West Side Story* was featured for the animals in the area. Part of my "Nick Rowe Cultural Appreciation Program" for the underprivileged animals of Vietnam.

As I was preparing to cook rice, Porky and Base came down to the hootch.

"*Anh Giai Phong* wants your mosquito net and clothing," Porky stated.

"What for?" I asked.

"*Anh Giai Phong* will wash your clothing and net with his. You will have the extra time to study and learn from Mr. Hai," Porky returned.

That's not a bad deal, I thought to myself, having the guards do my laundry for me. "OK, Porky, I'll go get it for you. Thank you."

Neither of them made a remark as I gathered up my mosquito

336

net and clothing, bringing it back to the kitchen hootch. "Here it is," I said as I handed it to Porky.

"*Ua*," he grunted as he handed it to Base and led the way back to the forum. I had just put the rice on to cook when Base came back into the kitchen. "*Anh Giai Phong* wants to wash the clothes you are wearing."

"You want to wash the clothes I'm wearing?" I repeated.

Base only nodded a strong affirmative. At this point my suspicions were not aroused, but my thoughts of standing or squatting around that kitchen without the protection of long pajamas and a shirt were frightening.

"What am I to wear?" I asked foolishly as if Base could give me any sort of answer.

"*Anh Giai Phong* wants to wash the clothes you are wearing," he repeated, even more determined.

There was no use fighting him over a pair of trousers and shirt. If he wanted to wash them who was I to stop him?

I stripped down to the ragged black shorts I was wearing as a stopgap effort against penetration of mosquito stingers through the seat of my threadbare pants, and handed him the shirt and pants. The mosquitoes were overjoyed. What do I do now? I wondered. The mosquitoes were like a dark cloud around me and not even the swishing towel knocked off enough to make an appreciable difference.

The meal was singularly unenjoyable due to my uninvited guests and my inability to deal with them. It would have been classified as less than a total success even without them. Rice and fish boiled in *nuoc mam* never did appear on any reputable menus.

After cleaning up, I went back to the cage to prepare for another night. There wasn't much to do since everything was probably drying by this time and the guards would have it back shortly. I relaxed for a moment, thinking about the events with Mafia and possible dodges the next day when he'd have a whole new pitch to throw at me.

As the sun sank below the trees, Base came down the walkway, keys dangling from his hand. "*Cum lai, Ro!*" he commanded—Put on your irons!

Purely in a reflex action, I started to reach for the long leg iron, then realized how I was dressed. "Wait a minute, *Anh Giai Phong*, where is my mosquito net? Where are my clothes?"

"Cum, Ro, lai!" Base commanded again, more strongly.

"I want to talk to *Anh Giai Phong* Quan if you won't answer me!" I retorted, realizing for the first time that I'd been tricked.

"Anh Giai Phong Quan is not here," Base snapped. *"Cum lai di!"*

Oh, oh. I thought. This is going to be nasty. "Where are my clothes and net, *Anh Giai Phong*?" I asked in a more civil tone. "The mosquitoes will be out soon and I need the net."

Base apparently decided I was obsequious enough and declared, "Your net and clothing are not dry yet. You can sleep like a soldier of the Liberation Army tonight without a net."

With that I was virtually tossed into the leg irons as Base made certain there was no further debate. After the lock went on, he disappeared down the walk leaving me to deal with the increasing number of mosquitoes.

Mafia, that son of a bitch, had set this up. A lesson for the uncooperative American, and I fell for it. There wasn't much I could have done even if I had caught on to what was happening earlier. The situation suddenly lacked humor. "Ouch! Die, you little bastards," I cursed under my breath as I slapped the first group of mosquitoes that drove their stingers into my exposed skin. The torn and frequently mended shorts were no good at all and my body was soon completely covered with swarming, probing insects. The first sensation of hundreds of simultaneous penetrations and injections of the insects' anticoagulant is almost an exquisite pain like the sharp bite of lemon juice on a fresh tooth extraction. It rapidly becomes an intolerable annoyance.

I could feel the pulpy mass in my hand each time I slapped at a concentration of stings and crushed another fifty or so of my tormentors. There was no spot on my body that wasn't covered now. They drove in at my face, neck, arms, legs with a fanatical urgency. Once in contact or near the source of human warmth they seemed to go beserk in their plunge to reach blood. I could sense the welts rising from the constant assault.

I couldn't kill them fast enough. Blood and crushed mosquito bodies smeared my skin and this drove the new arrivals into a wilder frenzy. The frequency of stings was so high that there was a constant reaction; numbness was beginning and I had a faint hope that it would give me a little rest. I had folded the towel and crammed it into my crotch trying to protect my genitals from the onslaught, but to no avail. There seemed to

338

be no position in which I could expose a minimum of skin space and still swat. I was almost ready to cry out and I hadn't been fighting them for more than half an hour. Oh Lord, this is going to be a long, long night.

The night wore on without a moment of relief. "Where are they all coming from?" my mind screamed. The constant, unrelenting torment was indescribable. Numbness had given way to a raw, open, sharp pain as the nerve endings writhed under the onslaught. The body's defenses were overwhelmed, the nervous system was flashing red lights all across the board.

Oh, how I wanted to get away from the stings. Exhaustion was creeping in to the already dismal scene as the need to sleep pulled at the frayed edges of my consciousness. I found myself slumping in momentary bursts of tormented slumber only to be awakened by a fresh wave of agony washing over my body. The leg iron seemed to be a living creature, binding my ankles, denying me the slight extra freedom to protect myself. Raw red strips marked the path of the rough metal resisting my efforts to loosen my legs from the tight clamps.

Twice I had tried to make it to the *nuoc mam* crock as my already inflamed intestines reacted to the violent battle against the mosquitoes, but the twisting and turning broke the diarrhea loose and twice I had been unable to reach the crock. The odor, the filth, the stings, the hopelessness of fighting. Yet I wasn't going to cry out. I wasn't going to give them the satisfaction of knowing what I felt.

"Screw you, Mafia, and all your ancestors!" That was my final coherent thought before I was aroused by Base opening my leg irons. The night had been scraps of consciousness, hallucinations, and nothingness.

Darkness still lay over the forest. Base showed his obvious disgust at the mess that met his eyes. Holding his piece of camouflaged parachute to his nose, he blurted out an order for me to clean up the cage, then turned and disappeared back along the walk, muttering to himself.

The mosquitoes had thinned tremendously with the coming of dawn, though by then I was too miserable to really notice. I continued to lie huddled on the now filthy rice straw mat, drawn into a fetal position in utter exhaustion. "O Lord," I prayed, "please give me strength to make it through today. I hurt, Lord, and I don't know what to do about it. Please give me strength."

Base's voice cut through the stillness: *"Nau com di! Ro, nau com!"*—Fix rice. Rowe, fix your rice!

I was so tired, so damn tired. I felt cruddy and stinking. The fungus infection on my back and arms itched unmercifully, yet to scratch would mean inviting worse infection and I couldn't chance that. My mind began to slowly take account of what was happening. It was like trying to walk chest-deep in thick maple syrup. I touched my arms and felt the welted surface. My face was the same. I made a halfhearted attempt to brush off some of the remaining mosquitoes, but they just flew up, then relanded.

The cage shook as Base stormed into the small section by the door. *"Thuc day nau com di!"* He seemed to be incensed that I hadn't moved yet, but at this point I really couldn't care less.

"OK," I answered. *"Mot chut"*—Just a moment.

"Di ngay!" he snapped, his brow furrowed in anger—Go immediately!

At this point I wasn't about to move. "I'm not hungry. I don't want to eat."

Base paused a moment, scowling; then, probably overcome by a combination of repulsion and indecision, whirled and stomped away.

I drifted into a state of semiconsciousness in which I was aware of all the sounds about me, yet dissociated from them. My system was already weakened by malnutrition and illness and last night was an energy drain I couldn't afford.

Porky was my next visitor. "Clean up your house!" he said after surveying the situation. "Why do you not prepare your food?"

"I'm not hungry and I'm very tired," I answered. I slowly sat up and asked, *"Anh Giai Phong*, why was I forced to stay out in the mosquitoes last night without a mosquito net and clothing? Am I being punished?"

Porky recoiled slightly, although his face remained impassive. "Your clothing was not dry. *Anh Giai Phong* can give it back today if it is dry." He was looking at the damage caused by the mosquitoes and, inwardly, was no doubt wincing as he imagined what it must have been like. His tone softened slightly as he said, "Go and cook your rice. You must eat to stay alive so you can return to your family."

As soon as he started the second sentence I could have

quoted it for him. How many times had I heard those words? "Eat much the rice." It was discouraging to realize that most of what came out of these mouths was a memorized speech or phrases to be used in conversation with American POW's.

"OK, *Anh Giai Phong*, I'll go in a moment." I replied. It was important not to miss a meal and particularly this morning.

"Go now," Porky continued, "soon it will be light and the *Dam Gia*"—the L–19—"will see the smoke. Be careful of your fire."

I nodded and got to my feet. First would be a trip to the latrine. I could wash off in the water out beyond it and take a bath in the canal after that.

I walked very slowly down the logs toward the kitchen, stumbling once as my foot slipped off the side of the precarious bridge and plunging up to my knee in the water. The burning shock of the water on my raw ankles cleared my mind. "All right, candyass," I chastised myself, "let's get organized and get your clumsy self clean and fed."

I found a spot near some of the burned-out trees where the water was clear and took off the shorts, dropping them to the side. The combination of raised splotches of fungus and welts from mosquito bites made my skin an ugly, lumpy reddish tan, and I ginerly splashed the chilly liquid over my shoulders. There was an immediate dual shock: the cold and the sting. The next time was even more severe as I took my sliver of soap from its cellophane wrapper and lathered as much as the high ash and lye content would allow. As the first bubbles touched my irritated skin I felt as if I had been seared with acid. The lye ate into the reddened skin with such fierce pain that I thought surely I'd blister. I waited a minute or so, convincing myself that it had to be done, and finally made a broad swipe down my chest and across one arm. I had to bite my lip to keep from cursing out loud.

After the first, it became almost a relief to counter the incessant itching of the fungus and irritation of the bites with a brand-new sensation. I imagined that every place the fungus was stinging, it was dying. This made bathing easier. With the completion of a thorough wash, or as thorough as cold water and VC soap would allow, I found myself feeling much better and made my way back through the camp to the canal for a second wash in cleaner water. As I walked past the forum en route to the canal I noticed Mafia sitting by the long table observing me. I could feel his eyes following me until I went behind the trees bordering the narrow canal.

The bathing completed and back in my kitchen, I set about preparing rice. My breakfast *loc* was still alive and things were looking up. As I was completing my rice and fish, Porky came into the kitchen.

"*Ong* Hai wishes to see you."

I had expected this and set my bowl down, preparing to follow Porky.

He shook his head. "*An com di. An roi, len nha*"—Go ahead and eat. When you're finished, come to the house.

He started out, then turned. "*Ro a, mac do. Hieu?*"—Rowe, wear clothes. Understand?

I wasn't surprised by the last bit. The guards often disregarded the most obvious things and my not having any clothes couldn't have been more obvious.

"*Thua, Anh Giai Phong.*" I spouted the familiar preface. "I don't have any clothes. You took them yesterday to wash them."

"*Ua,*" he grunted. "*Anh Giai Phong* will bring your clothes. Eat!" With that he moved away leaving me to finish my rice. There was a growing emptiness in my stomach as I contemplated what Mafia would have lined up today. The relief of not having to constantly battle the swarms of nighttime mosquitoes made me feel many times better than I had felt at dawn. The utter relativity of everything. I felt better than I had at dawn; therefore, I felt good. Not overall, but relatively. The thought of last night cut through my mind like a razor and I could remember almost every moment. My mind had such a vivid impression branded upon it that it could re-create the sensations on its own. These reactions collided behind my eyes and I felt as if I were turning inward to examine the repeated sensations without being affected by them. There was somehow a moment of complete detachment and introspection. It was too brief to draw a conclusion from what I saw, but self-analysis was there.

Porky broke into my thoughts when he returned with a bundle of still-wet clothing, a pair of trousers and the shirt. I thanked him and proceeded to wring them out, then began to put my ideas in order for the meeting with Mafia.

I stepped into the hut and waited while Mafia continued to give his full attention to a piece of paper in front of him. Finally

342

he glanced up as if aware of my presence for the first time.

"Sit down." He indicated the same planks I sat on yesterday.

I sat, saying nothing. He turned back to the paper on the desk, ignoring me. I found myself watching his eyes as he looked at the paper. Then I noticed that his eyes weren't moving! He was staring at one point, not reading. I grinned to myself as the stall became evident and chalked up a mental point for my side. He looked up, seeing me for the first time. "And why do you not use your mosquito net? The soldiers have told me you were bitten many times during the night." This came from a mask of bland innocence. He continued, "I see your face is swollen. I will have the guards search for the proper herbs to aid in healing."

Wait a minute here, Mafia. I thought to myself. "The guards took my net and clothing yesterday to wash them, Mr. Hai. The items were not returned last night and I was told that I could sleep without a net like the Liberation Army." I had learned not to mention the name of the guard who had made a particular statement, thus allowing Base to enjoy the false security of anonymity even though we both knew who he was.

Mafia looked concerned, playing his role to the hilt. "Ah, I will see to it that your things are returned when they are dry. Do not worry."

His slip about the things drying gave him away and I chalked up another point. Mafia inquired about the physical distress of such a number of mosquito bites and assured me he had been bitten far worse on numerous occasions. I was greatly cheered by his solace.

After a few inane remarks about how difficult it was to dry clothing during the rainy season, Mafia got down to the business at hand. I had discovered that until Mafia mentioned mosquitoes, I had been unaware of the few that were buzzing around my legs and feet. Once my attention had been focused, my mind took over and it was as if the sound of their wings had been amplified ten times. I imagined phantom stings on my bare feet and felt my skin contracting in anticipation of the onslaught of hundreds of tiny stingers.

Mafia continued, oblivious to my increasing discomfort, expanding slightly on the brief spiel he had given yesterday. There wasn't that much new; only elaboration of details and an air of confidence that he would no longer have to do too much to accomplish what he desired. He reiterated the futility

343

of struggle, useless death, capitalist-imperialist exploitation line and once again dropped the "now you can write for me" bomb.

"Mr. Hai," I answered truthfully, "I'm very tired after last night. I haven't had an opportunity to check my stakeouts or nets and I have no fish for supper. I'm trying to stay alive under very difficult conditions and providing fish for myself is of major importance. Eating rice is very hard and I must have fish. I would like to check my stakeouts and go to sleep. I can't write for you now." I wasn't going to mention what I went through last night. It would give him ideas and the last thing I needed was more mosquito bites.

He paused and appeared to consider for a moment, weighing preselected courses of action against what I had just said.

"The soldiers will give you fish for this evening," he stated. "Do not worry about the fish. The Front guarantees your well-being. We will proceed so that you might see clearly the situation. You must strive to understand the truth and then reflect upon your crimes and how you can correct them."

I was resigned to sitting and listening, hoping I wouldn't go to sleep in front of him or blurt out a bit of my own philosophy. I was pissed about last night and found myself rebelling at having to sit and play this game when we both knew exactly what was going on. The only restraint was that he held all the trumps and I'd have to stay cool until I had a chance to get my points across.

I had long ago subjugated the sense of injustice which in earlier days would have welled up in me at the idea that Mafia had spent the last night in a mosquito net after a comparatively good meal, had rested well, and had spent this morning preparing to dominate our meeting. He was quite confident that he held the upper hand with this physically weakened and mentally exhausted American whose environmental conditions could be arranged to suit the Front's needs and purposes. It was useless to belabor a point over which I had no control. The only avenue open was to make every possible use of what mental faculties I had operating to counter him. I couldn't waste them feeling sorry for myself. The next two hours or so were spent listening to the developments of the revolutionary struggle, the progress of the political struggle, and the certainty of total victory. Mafia spoke without notes, drawing examples from his memory with a phenomenal ability to quote figures down to the last digit. "In the dry season counteroffensive launched by the Imperialist aggressors in 1966 and 1967, they suffered heavy defeats at the hands of the people's armed forces," he said, producing statistics: 28 U.S. battalions were "totally annihilated" and 85,243 "U.S. and satellite soldiers" were wiped out; 1,785 military vehicles were "destroyed."

I mushed through a mental calculation of what that must have done to our manpower base, if it were true. Should the draft-card burners be reading Mafia's script, I could see where they would have some basis for protest about going to Vietnam. I found myself dozing for brief periods, which Mafia ignored or broke into by asking a question. I was becoming extremely tired and had great difficulty maintaining continuity in thought. The snatches of unconsciousness served to interrupt and segment the proceedings with unreal dream scraps far more digestible than Mafia and reality.

Mafia ordered me to stand as he went through yet another reiteration of the futility-uselessness-exploitation line and brought out the paper and ball-point pen. "Now you can write for me what you have learned in our discussion," he declared.

There was no doubt that with all the smoke cleared away from those sessions, he wanted me to write that the effort in Vietnam opposing the revolution was futile, that American deaths were useless, that imperialists exploited the situation and the just cause was represented by the Front. The rest was pure confusion factor. I was tired, so damn tired, and I wanted to go to sleep, but I still had to get fish for the meal, had to clean out the stinking mess that was my cage and had to fix rice for supper.

"Mr. Hai, I'm tired and I can't really think straight." I didn't want to push him and yet I wasn't going to write that crap; I didn't believe it. He anticipated my refusal and leaned back staring at me. "You must not try the patience of the Front!" His voice was soft, but it cut like a knife. "You enjoy the lenient policy of the Front and yet you do not contribute your share toward ending this cruel war. The Front cannot continue to be lenient to those who are not repentant of their crimes. Consider carefully your path." He paused, studying my face, then finished, "Go back to your house!"

I stumbled back to my kitchen with my mind in a frightening slow-motion tumble. Mafia's words were woven in and out of a tumble of thoughts. I was aware that the threat had been made and I knew he didn't bluff.

345

At the kitchen, disregarding all else, I prepared to check the stakeouts and rebait them in hopes of getting fish. My legs had a will of their own and were determined to suspend all further activity. It was a strong temptation to lie down for a moment and drop into beautiful oblivion, but that wouldn't get things done and I had to get food.

"You go now to seek fish?"

I heard the voice behind me and turned. Mafia had paused on his way to the guard hootch where he would spend the next couple of hours taking "*pac* time," the Vietnamese equivalent of a siesta.

"Yes, Mr. Hai. It's difficult to catch them during the day," I replied.

"The soldiers will share with you today their fish, but you must catch many so as to maintain your health." This was spoken in utter seriousness. He added, "In the forest there are many fish." Then, satisfied with his observation, he proceeded to the hootch.

I watched him for a moment, envying the fact that he would shortly be asleep, then turned back to my tasks. I walked to the canal to check the small, patched trap I used to catch bait fish. Often these bait fish became a meal when the larger fish were uncooperative, and I wasn't ruling out that possibility now. I returned to the kitchen to find my two eagles resting on their perch. Ajax was balancing on one foot and industriously scratching the side of his head with the other set of talons. Herc surveyed me as if I were a large morsel of food.

"Hello, idiots," I greeted them.

Ajax continued to scratch, although he did incline his head slightly so as to observe me. Herc was more demonstrative as he let out the piercing cry of the young forest eagle, in a rare show of his former spirit. Ajax almost fell off the perch with shock when Herc screamed, but caught himself and recovered his balance. He assumed a fierce posture, glancing sideways at Herc as if to reassure himself that he was, in fact, correct.

"You great hunters look hungry," I observed. "Too bad the cupboard is bare at the moment. I'm not doing too well myself." Herc continued to glare with his fierce golden-brown eyes, unblinking. He still looked like an eagle and seemed to be trying to set the example for me, clipped wing or not. Ajax maintained his pose for another moment and went back to scratching his head, his eyes rolling back slightly in blissful enjoyment of the sensation. I relaxed for the first time that day, watching my two pets and knowing that at least these two were my friends. Not for long, though, I thought, if I don't come up with some chow. Herc punctuated my thought with another scream. Ajax was ready for this one and only settled both feet on the perch, watching me and making soft sounds in his throat. I glanced at the bait fish in the pan at my feet and decided against using them to feed the eagles. I needed them for the stakeouts. The snake, I thought! I can chop him up and keep them satisfied for a while. I hated to lose the big meal I had planned on, but these two were hungry now.

I took the knife blade from the dish rack and bent over the crock, pulling in the fish line to which the snake was attached. He wrapped around the nearest object and refused to budge, so I had to reach down and grasp behind his head, pulling him free. I laid the head on one of the floor poles and smashed it with the blunt edge of the knife. Both birds were watching me with great interest, and I imagine that if Ajax had a napkin he would have been tying it around his neck at this point in preparation for a feast.

I chopped the head off of the writhing body and dropped it under the floor where the small fish immediately attacked it. The skin peeled back with little difficulty, leaving the nude body twitching and coiling on the poles. Neither bird had moved before, but as soon as I began chopping the snake into sections Herc dropped from the perch, spreading his wings slightly and, compensating for the ragged left wing feathers, broke his descent and landed beside me. Two short hops later, he was standing in reach of one of the sections of fresh snake meat looking up at me and leaving no doubt that he had marked that piece for himself. Any argument on my part would have resulted in a full-scale rumble with a ravenous eagle.

Ajax, as usual, got the word a little late and arrived just after Herc had pounced his prey and hopped over to the log walk to devour it. I held a piece out to Ajax. He hesitated a moment, then delicately plucked it from my fingers with his sharp beak. He tried twice to take it from his beak with his talons, succeeding only in nearly putting out an eye. After that he decided to drop it and then pick it up with his feet. He carefully scrutinized the separations between the poles that formed the floor, selected the spot that would allow him to place it on solid wood, then proceeded to drop it through a crack into the water below. If he could have cried he would. The look of despair was as plain as if he had been human.

I reached under the hootch and fished it out of the water, placing it on a solid portion of the floor. He took no chances this time and proceeded to rip strips of flesh from the bones while holding it down with one set of talons. I chopped up the remainder of the snake and fed it to the birds. Afterward they hopped over to the *nha mam* and Ajax flew to the peak of the roof where he sat and preened his feathers, satisfied at least for the moment.

Somewhat later, as a necessity, I went about cleaning up my cage, washing it as best I could. The sleeping mat went out to dry in hopes it would be ready for that night. I walked back to the kitchen thinking how much I was looking forward to darkness when I'd be able to get some sleep. Just the thought of sleep served to reinforce how tired I was. I felt as if I had been completely drained. The trips to the latrine which had punctuated the day didn't help at all and I could ill afford the increased fluid loss, particularly right now. Again I thought how fortunate it was that early in captivity, while my system was still strong, I had conditioned myself to accept and deal with dysentery. To combat the physical effects and the mental degradation as simultaneous new problems in a weakened state would have been virtually disastrous.

Once again in the kitchen, I swatted a few mosquitoes halfheartedly while sitting on the bench resting. I wondered where I had put my clothes. I had taken the trousers off before going to check for fish and must have forgotten where I put them.

After setting the lamp near the fireplace and splashing a little kerosene on the wood, I put the rice pot on and began cooking. As the afternoon wore on, the mosquitoes reappeared. Soon they were bothering me to the extent that I tried a smoke pot of smoldering coals and bark to try to discourage them, but failed to ease the mind image. I took time out to look for my trousers, failing to find them and growing uneasy with sudden concern. I hadn't lost them, yet I couldn't find them. Could someone have taken them, I wondered? That was a loser of an idea if I ever had one. "Mafia wouldn't..." I began. "Oh yes he would," came the answer. Mafia walked past and peered into the kitchen. "You take supper now?"

"Not yet, Mr. Hai. I'm waiting for the guards to return with the fish."

He stepped into the hootch, standing with his hands clasped behind his back. "You must be careful of the smoke," he said, noticing my smoke pot. "The U.S. aircraft can kill you if they bomb here. It is very dangerous." His observation and comment meant: "Put out that smoke pot," which I reluctantly did.

"It's difficult to sit here with all the mosquitoes, Mr. Hai," I commented. "My trousers seem to have disappeared and these shorts are not that much protection, so I built the smoke pot to keep them away."

For that statement I received a five-minute dissertation on the hardships borne by the soldiers in the "people's army," their sacrifices and unflinching devotion to the revolution, all of which centered around their ability to withstand mosquitoes.

What might have turned into a longer oration was interrupted by Porky's appearance outside the kitchen. He and Mafia exchanged rapid Vietnamese and Porky returned to the guard mess hootch. Mafia indicated the disappearing figure. "Our soldiers have searched far to catch fish for your supper. He reports to me that they could not find the herbs for your condition, but he will go again tomorrow." As he turned to leave he finished, "Prepare now your supper."

Porky came up seconds later with a medium-sized catfish (*ca tre*), its flat skull indented sharply where the knife edge had struck, killing it. He dropped the limp body into the nearest pot and watched me for a moment as I rekindled the dying fire. *"Khoi,"* he observed as the flames caught, sending a puff of smoke upward. *"Them cui,"* he added constructively—Put on more wood (to get a bigger fire and less smoke).

"OK, Porky," I muttered. "I'll take care of the fire. Don't you worry your little head about it."

"Cai gi!" he snapped suddenly, my English having angered him.

"Khong co gi, Anh Giai Phong. Toi chi noi Tieng Ahn." In answer to his question about what I said, I replied that it was nothing. I was only speaking English. Porky was definitely unhappy about my comment, innocent as it was, and he left the kitchen snarling to himself, "American imperialist!"

I filed a reference to refrain from needlessly losing points. There was little to be gained from these nickel-and-dime encounters with the guards and they could serve no more than to put me in worse shape than I was already in. The time to score was in the encounters with the cadre, frustrating their program and throwing off their time schedule. With Mafia tied up here for a couple of days working on me, another American would have a chance to rest. The ultimate score was to escape. Whatever was required to set up a successful break was worth it, because the loss of a POW, alive, was a solid blow to the understructure of this mess. It was the "truth of the situation in South Vietnam" coming to light in pure, unadulterated form, and this the Front didn't want. Only their version of the truth was acceptable. A POW whom the cadre deemed sufficiently aware of "the truth" to present it to the world had a chance to see the world again, but you could forget about those who don't see the VC version of "the light." They are contradictions to the rule and cannot be allowed to exist for they add nothing to the furtherance of the revolutionary cause. My philosophy became: "Don't make a wave unless it is big enough to drown someone." I finished a meal of rice and roasted catfish, soaked in *nuoc mam*. This I topped off with a cup of hot water flavored with leaves from a wild grapevine. By this time I was feeling able to handle the situation, although sleep was high on the list of necessities. I had bathed and gotten myself relatively clean, had two meals of rice and fish, washed my hootch, and fed my eagles; and after checking the stakeouts once more, I could call it a day. The question of my net and clothing was beginning to bother me, but I didn't want to confront that problem until I had to. I was hoping it would resolve itself, in my favor. I was wondering what was next when Base appeared like an evil omen.

"Ah, Anh Giai Phong Te," I smiled at him hoping he'd forget whatever he came down here for. It wasn't going to be of benefit to me.

Base stepped into the kitchen, pausing to savor his undisputed position of authority. "Did you catch many fish?" I continued, referring to his all-day project.

"Nhieu"—Many—he replied, as if it were stupid to assume that he wouldn't catch more than the average VC. He waited another moment as I searched for something else to say, forestalling the event that I now realized was coming. There was a burning sensation in the pit of my stomach and I found it difficult to catch my breath.

"Coi Ao." The words were spoken with the slightest hint of a smile. It wasn't a pleasant smile. Take off your shirt.

My world suddenly tumbled around my shoulders. I felt a prickling sensation over my entire body. I must have given the impression that I didn't hear or I didn't move quickly enough for Base. He repeated the command, adding, *"Hieu, khong?"* — Do you understand?—He was so damn confident, so certain that he was calling the shots and I would respond.

My impulse was to punch him in the face, while I found myself slowly unbuttoning the shirt. There had been a brief conflict but judgment, developed over four years under this type of domination, resolved the issue in my mind. You asshole! I cursed myself as I handed him the shirt without expression.

"Go to your house," Base said. "Prepare to put on the irons." He seemed disappointed I wasn't giving him any trouble.

"I request permission to talk with Mr. Hai," I said. If I could see Mafia I could at least get the satisfaction of breaking his feigned innocence. There was no doubt the mosquitoes were going to have another blood feast tonight, but tomorrow was the real problem when I faced Mafia in the indoctrination.

"Mr. Hai has gone already," Base declared, shutting the door on that idea.

"I request my mosquito net whether it is dry or not. I cannot sleep without it." I tried this line almost in desperation.

It seemed so ridiculous to stand there and carry on a civil conversation when both of us knew exactly what was happening. The façade of civility was sickening. Base was enjoying the little game we were playing. Why shouldn't he? He had nothing to lose.

"Anh Giai Phong doesn't know where your net is," he declared. *"Anh Giai Phong* will go to look for it." With that, he turned and left.

Neat, Base. Very neat, I thought. My chances of your "finding" that net before you get the word to give it back are just about zilch!

Anticipation of pain or irritation is far more devastating than the pain itself. My mind proved that to me in the intervening time between Base's departure and the onslaught of mosquitoes after I had been locked up. I had taken advantage of the advance warning this evening to hide a bottle of kerosene from my lamp in the cage and to gather bark from some of the trees, which

351

I placed under my sleeping mat. The kerosene would serve to ward off the attackers much like an insect repellent. The bark went inside my shorts to plug the tears, thus leaving my towel free for a weapon. My greatest effort went into a smoke pot which I placed in the bottom of the cage, under my sleeping rack. It contained the still-glowing coals from my supper fire, and after dark, when the smoke couldn't be detected from the air, I would add more wood and some of the bark to produce clouds of thick smoke which would effectively cut the mosquito population.

The physical activity and mental involvement in preparing for the night aided in lessening the impact of realization that there would be another night like the last one. The subconscious drew from its files the account of my reaction to the ordeal and began sending signals to the nervous system, re-creating the physical trauma. I could feel the sensations of hundreds of stingers, the welts and itching fungus came to aggravated life, the frustrations of hopeless combat all rolled out of the back of my mind like a wave. When Base came down to lock the irons he was taken off balance by the smoke pot. Not having an immediate comment on it and obviously not having expected an American POW to be this resourceful, he merely locked the irons and informed me that he couldn't find my net, but would ask Porky when he returned. He took a long look at the smoke pot, then deciding not to make any decisions for himself, turned and walked away, singing a revolutionary song in his off-key tenor voice.

Immediately after he turned the corner on the walkway, I grabbed for the bottle of kerosene and spilled about an ounce into my palm. I began smearing the pungent oily fluid over my body, wincing as it ate into the raised areas of fungus. The very act of countering their plan, no matter how meager my efforts, gave me added strength. Determination was already there.

I placed my *nuoc mam* crock on the sleeping rack within reach so I wouldn't be forced to clean out the cage again tomorrow. Thin pads of bark went between the ankle bars and my scrapes from last night's struggles. Not only did they ease the rubbing, they also prevented the mosquitoes from attacking the open flesh. I made a mental check of my activities to ascertain if there was anything I had failed to do. It was a tedious process to force thought through my sleep-oriented mind.

In the midst of this review, I discovered that I had lost sight of the most important factor. I had become so involved in defeating the mosquitoes that I failed to consider getting some sleep! This was the one thing I needed and I was seeking ways to stay awake.

It became a question of less mosquito bites and no sleep or sleep and more mosquito bites. I had the choice, which was made rapidly as the thought of beautiful, soft sleep outweighed any arguments against it. I could feel the haze creeping into my brain.

I awoke with a start. I was covered with mosquitoes! Their stingers seemed to be probing into every pore and those who couldn't reach skin were fighting to get through the masses of them already concentrated and feeding. My dreamless slumber had yet to be completely dispelled. My face was itching and my eyes seemed unwilling to open. It was a combination of sleep and hundreds of bites across my eyelids and face. I shuddered as I crushed a number of the little creatures that had found their way into my ear. There wasn't a place they hadn't attacked.

I groped for the smoke pot, pulling it beside me and scraping among the ashes, looking for the red glow that would indicate a live coal. I found several small ones and blew gently on them, bringing them to life. Next I shredded a piece of bark and placed it on them, blowing again until it flared. After that it took me only a couple of minutes to recreate the dense smoke cloud of before. The mosquitoes thinned immediately and I began to rub more of the precious kerosene over myself.

I was awake now. Sleep had been shattered and the effect of the unhampered assault over whatever period of time it had occurred left me shaking. The edges of my nervous system were in shreds, not so much because of the physical agony, even though it contributed, but because of the mental frustration and the failure to be able to meet the urgent needs transmitted to the brain which, in itself, found no answer for its own frustrations.

I was reliving the previous night. All my preparations could not offset the effect on the mind as it re-created its own torment. "Stop this!" I directed the command to myself, hoping to break the rising panic and frustration. I forced myself to evaluate the number of mosquitoes actually reaching me at that time. Darkness defeated me, preventing a visual count, and for each tiny body I felt, my mind counted ten. I needed light and decided to use the kerosene and smoke pot to get it. I took one of the coals, and after pushing a piece of twisted bark into the bottle for a wick, lit my makeshift lamp. The dull yellowish glow threw odd shadows off the smoky interior, outlining the barred walls. There was miniature carnage on my mat with crushed insects littering it, some of them ground into the woven rice straw, their blood-gorged sacs broken into bright red dots. Only about fifteen or twenty were braving the smoke and kerosene as far as I could see. I crushed them one by one, twisting my finger as I ground them into mash. Each time I killed one was a separate, distinct victory and my mind began to ease its pressure.

After finishing them off, I quickly checked myself before too much kerosene was burned to provide light. My eyes felt as if I had a series of sties along the lids and the smoke was particularly irritating. I ran my hands over my face and touched what seemed to be welts building on welts. The fungus was achieving new heights of irritation with the combination of stings and kerosene. I gave in to a sudden urge and dug into the areas on my arms with a scraper I had carved from a piece of wood. The relief was slow in coming and before I realized the extent of my scratching, I had opened a strip of oozing, sticky fungus and mosquito-bite welts. I knew I'd pay for that in the morning.

Enough! I decided. One more check of the smoke pot and I blew out the lamp. Blackness settled around me and the question was immediate, "What now?" I was unconsciously wiping the fluid off of the drooling fungus as I thought once more of trying to get some sleep. Seconds after the thought registered, I must have gone out again in a stupor.

Several times more during the night I reawoke to find my defenses gone and mosquitoes swarming in for their meal. My efforts to counter them became weaker and less effective as exhaustion rolled over me. There were indistinct periods of consciousness blending with strange dreams and hallucinations, the whole kaleidoscopic mess forming an awful nightmare.

Morning came with its complete unconcern for those below. I was still out when Base unlocked the irons, waking only when he called for me to fix my rice. I heard his voice as part of a bad dream that I wanted to escape and found myself running from it in the great halls of unconsciousness. It followed me until I was dragged back into the realm of reality.

"Let me sleep." I thought I asked it out loud, but it was only in my mind. The task of climbing out of the mire of exhaustion was almost more than I could accomplish, but Base's voice wouldn't let me escape and I finally opened my eyes.

I tried to open my eyes. Tried again, without success. I was fighting the awful weight of my eyelids as well as the new obstructions along the lower eye. The welts were huge and the protective fluid that had poured from my eyes during the night was caked. I reached up and moved the lids gently apart, breaking the crust and admitting the gray light. Fatigue had a viscous blanket wrapped around both my mind and body, preventing immediate action as I lay half asleep, half awake.

There was no desire for anything but the oblivion of slumber. Base called out again, the sound penetrating and activating a portion of my mind. Lying unmoving on the rack, I went through the entire process of getting up and preparing my rice. The automatic sequence that I had performed so many times was as vivid in my mind as if I were actually doing it. Later, when Base came into the cage to get me up, I realized that it had been only another illusion and I had not yet moved.

I managed to sit up and take stock of the situation, trying to induce the desire to move. Some minutes later I had convinced myself that I had to go to the kitchen and prepare rice, the thought of not missing a meal of rice, the requirement for survival, adding impetus to the action. It was difficult to keep my balance as I walked to the kitchen, although I wasn't particularly concerned about falling off. I felt detached from my body.

The preparation of the meal was a nightmare in itself. One of my fish escaped when I failed to grasp him tightly enough prior to smashing his head, the rice was soft and mushy from being overcooked when I fell asleep after putting it on, and the whole thing tasted as if I were eating salty sawdust. Neither this nor the agony of last night could outweigh the need for sleep. I walked back to the cage, I lay down and closed my eyes.

It was midmorning when the urgent need to make a crap run brought me back. I was awake by the time I made the latrine and was already planning on a bath to clear away the cobwebs from my mind and get rid of the mixture of kerosene and crushed mosquitoes that covered my body. The thought of the bath was extremely pleasant for some reason and I felt my spirits begin to lift slightly. I had survived another night.

The effect of a little sleep that morning and the bath now was almost miraculous. I felt logy and somewhat faint when I stood up rapidly, but the overall effects were countered by rising spirits. Bathing in the canal rather than beside it as we had been ordered to do so many times was a small revolt that aided in satisfying my deep craving to strike back. Base would have a shit hemorrhage if he came out and caught me in the middle of the canal, *lac*, diarrhea and all. I almost choked laughing to myself as the thought went through my mind. He wouldn't bathe in this water for a week afterward. I must have been lightheaded because the more I thought about this, the funnier it got until I finally had to climb my small dock and rest before I drowned.

I looked on the roof of the *nha mam* as I passed, wondering where Herc and Ajax were. Ajax had no doubt departed to hunt for food as neither the roof nor their perch was occupied. Herc was in his secret place somewhere, just sitting. I wished they had been around. It would have been relaxing to have played with them for a while. Ajax was the best thing in the world for low spirits because nothing could be more fouled up than my young bird. It was going to break his heart when he discovered he wasn't going to grow up to be a human. He didn't know how fortunate he was to be an animal.

I made a check of the stakeouts although I was unable to rebait the hooks. My bait trap was empty when I checked it and I'd have to wait until afternoon to try for more. The nets produced one small catfish and one *ca ro* which were more than welcome additions to the pantry. After gathering some *rau muong*, a semi-wild green which tastes somewhat like spinach, from the canal bank and putting it in the kitchen for soup that evening, I went back to the hootch for another snooze.

It seemed as if I had just dropped off when I heard Porky's voice calling me. I sat up and was told that Mafia was back and wanted to see me immediately. Porky tossed my shirt and trousers onto the rack beside me, indicating for me to put them on. Suddenly I felt extremely tired again. The pressure was building and I couldn't stop it.

356

Mafia was seated in his usual position. The induced formality used to establish the status of cadre and prisoner was almost ludicrous; however, I couldn't quite bring myself to laugh. I sat on the same planks, looking up at Mafia as he leafed through a sheaf of onionskin paper on the table. He glanced at me as I sat down, his expression unchanging.

"Ah, you look so fatigued," he said solicitously. "Do you have fish for your meals today?"

"Yes, Mr. Hai," I replied; then jumped into the middle of the problem: "I would like to know why I am being forced to stay outside at night without clothing and mosquito net. Am I being punished for something?"

Open confrontation was something Mafia didn't care for. His reaction was to turn my position into a defensive one rather than allowing me the advantage. "You are a criminal!" he chastised me. "You are guilty of bloody crimes against the Vietnamese people. The U.S. aggressors have brought much suffering to our country and they must pay their blood debts. I can kill you, I can torture you because you are my prisoner and must be tried by the laws of my country." He paused for a moment, watching for the effect of his words. He continued, "But no, I do not kill you. Because of the lenient policy of the National Liberation Front you are allowed to live and we make many sacrifices to provide for your welfare. You enjoy the lenient policy of the Mat Trang, but you do not contribute your share to ending this cruel war." His voice was low, without emotion, but carried the confidence he felt in being able to carry out any threat he made. I recalled the Salt Mines and there was little doubt in my mind that Mafia could blow the whistle on me any time he chose. All of a sudden, the mosquitoes seemed very inconsequential. I was sorry I'd opened my dumb mouth and gotten Mafia started.

He read the expression on my face and pressed his attack, realizing that the opening I had given him could be exploited. "And why you do not write for me?" he snapped, his voice suddenly sharp. I jumped when he spat out the question, my nerves quivering like bowstrings. Then he returned to the low pitch: "You must know clearly the situation in South Vietnam and you must realize your duty to the Front because it is the Front that gives you your life. If you recognize your crimes and can know truly the situation"—here he paused, to let the effect build—"the Front can create conditions so you may be

357

released to return to your home in America. And if you do not repent of your crimes"—again he paused—"the Front can no longer allow you to enjoy the lenient policy."

I sat, stunned, wondering how in the hell I'd gotten myself into this and wishing I were back in the middle of the mosquitoes. I could at least take a few of them with me.

Mafia picked up the papers. "I must go today. There are many things I must do. Tomorrow I will return and you can write for me what I have told you." He dismissed me and I forgot to ask if I would get my net and clothes back. Walking back to the kitchen, I was in a semi-daze. The feeling of exhaustion was again strong as Mafia had effectively wiped out my moderately high spirits. As soon as that occurred there was a mercurial drop in my energy level. It was odd how Mafia had shifted my focus. The mosquitoes had been bad until he indicated that things could get worse, and with him running the show that would be a lot worse.

Tomorrow would be the big day, and at the moment I was in no shape, physically or mentally, to match wits with Mafia. The big thing was to get some sleep. The mosquito bites would take care of themselves over a period of time, but the need to get some rest and let the body rebuild was becoming urgent. My mind readily accepted the sleep idea and with equal rapidity violently rejected the idea of more mosquitoes. Once again I experienced the re-creation of the nervous system's response to the last two nights. For at least two minutes I crouched on the kitchen floor, biting my lip and squeezing one of the poles as wave after wave of trembling washed over me. I felt as if I'd barf any second. I've gotta get straight, I kept telling myself. I can't fight this and Mafia at the same time.

Sometime between the beginning of eating rice and getting locked up, I had a visit from Base, who took the clothing as he had done the night before. At this point I really didn't care and after having the leg iron attached, I rolled up in my sleeping mat, wrapped my towel around my face loosely, and went completely out. The mat and towel were of little value as protection since the mosquitoes could enter either end of the mat, and when attacking my face, could penetrate wherever cloth and skin made contact.

That night was one I shall never forget. The moments of cognizance clashed with insensibility in irregular rhythm. The long climb from the depths of exhausted slumber to the brinkof-conscious awareness and the torment of the clouds of mosquitoes taxed my already depleted store of energy. Once the level of being able to sense the stings and react slightly to counter them had been achieved, I could immediately feel myself being dragged back into the depths of unconsciousness. The process was repeated countless times as mind and body fought, each to satisfy the demands of the tortured system. Nightmares accompanying the periods of shallow sleep blended with the agony of reality, giving no rest. I felt like a yo-yo the way I was being pulled up and down, up and down. The only constant was the misery.

During brief periods of rationality the one clear thought was: "I've got to stop this!" Whatever the source, that thought was strong, urgent. The burning pain that accompanied the periodic bursts of diarrhea added its weight to the argument even though the difference from the pain of the mosquitoes was almost a relief. Oddly enough, my moments of relative clarity were during the crock runs.

Sometimes during that endless night I turned the nearly full crock over. This I discovered the next morning when Base appeared, to start another day. I was in a semi-stupor when he arrived and aware of his presence, but not readily associating myself with him. The stench of the crock was the first thing to register in my mind and repulsion brought a portion of my mind awake. A slow-motion evaluation of my situation unfolded before me. The utter futility was so evident. I could see myself, struggling each day to rebuild what Mafia had torn down, yet falling further and further behind. I was so tired and there would be no rest. I felt the frustration building, slowly because my whole system was weakened.

I dozed until the stench of the crock once again aroused me. Base hadn't come back. I imagined he needed more than the camouflage parachute to aid him in facing the wreckage he found in my cage. It was difficult to stand myself. Why get up and fight it? I asked myself. Every time you take a punch and get back up, they just throw another punch. And it'll go on and on and on, added another voice in my head. Then silence as I dropped off into another restless moment of slumber.

It wasn't fully light when the sound of an L–19 shocked my mind into total awareness. The rasping, throaty roar of the engine brought immediate action as past experience pushed me into activity. I unrolled from the mat, rubbing the crusts from my eyes, pushing the lids open. They were swollen almost shut and I saw the green world of trees through slits. I couldn't locate the sound at first since my mind refused to cooperate. Finally, I determined that the "bird dog" was south of us, flying parallel to the river, coming toward us or a little to our east. Just about that time, Base appeared on the log walk, moving rapidly toward the guard hootch to retrieve his pack. *"Chuan bi di! May bay!"* he called to me—Prepare to go! Airplane!

I looked around me rather stupidly, wondering at first what I would use to carry my things and then realizing I had nothing to carry. I picked up my towel and shuffled to the intersection of my log walk and the main one running to the guard hootch. I decided I'd wait there for Base to find out what I was to do. After the initial shock I found my interest and concern dwindling. It might be better to get caught in the strike and get it over with, came that negative voice in my head.

I suppose it must have been the surge of adrenalin through my system, inspired by the L–19, that enabled any thought or action. Were it left up to me, I would still be in the hootch.

Base reappeared, running along the walkway as if it were a sidewalk. He carried his pack as well as two others belonging to the other guards. One Mossin-Nagant carbine was slung, muzzle frontward, under his arm. "Wait in your kitchen," he said as he hurried past. "Don't light the fire."

I complied dumbly, not really caring one way or another. I took mental note of the engine noise, attempting drowsily to estimate the range to the aircraft and how long it would take him to arrive in our area. There had been so many times in the past that it was almost a reflex action and no great problem to determine that we had about three or four minutes before he would begin his circle if we were to be hit. The guards would sit tight until he circled overhead and then we'd move into the trees about three or four hundred meters from camp and squat until he was finished. Then it would be a long walk back— after dark, so there would be no danger of airstrike until the next day.

I sat on the floor of the kitchen with my thoughts, waiting for something to happen, and dropped off to sleep. I was awakened later by Base, nudging my foot with his weapon. The long climb out of my torpor was as tiring as if I had run a mile. I felt short of breath. I became aware of the sound of the engine to the north and the sharp, flat *ka-rump* of H.E. rockets being fired into the forest.

Base informed me that the camp was safe, but I was not to prepare rice since the smoke from the fire would be detected. I didn't particularly care, even though the warning voice cautioned me not to miss a meal. I just had no desire to do anything except sleep. Base went on to say that *Anh Giai Phong* would stand and fight should the aircraft hit here. Some of the guards would take me to safety, but *Anh Giai Phong* Te (Base) would stay to fight.

Oh, what a brave son of a bitch, I thought. Try dueling it out with an F–100 just once, Base, and you'll have a beautiful marker all of your own in the idiots' section of the local VC graveyard. What a contribution you could make . . . by dying!

After assuring himself that I understood what he had said, not so much about the smoke, but how brave he was, he departed. I slumped over in another deep sleep.

The sleep was virtually a coma. No dreams interrupted the body's effort to allow rebuilding of its inner workings, and time was motionless. I don't know how long I slept, but I awoke with Porky standing over me, calling my name. In his hand were my trousers and shirt.

Before he could give my orders, I asked permission to go to the canal and take a bath. There wasn't any doubt that Mafia had returned once the danger of airstrike was past, and I realized it wouldn't do to confront him in my present condition. A cold splash in the canal would help to clear up the drugged sensation that clung to the periphery of my brain. Porky considered for a moment, then, deciding it wouldn't do any harm, nodded and grunted an *"Ua."* "Hurry," he added. *"Ong* Hai must leave soon and can't wait too long."

"OK," I answered as I walked past him, thinking. "Thanks for the tip, Porky. If Mafia's in a hurry then he won't be able to waste time trying to push for a lot of crap." It was damned hard to think straight with my head full of cotton, but the solid points of necessity stood out: I couldn't keep going under these conditions; Mafia could extend this pressure to suit his needs; I required a break to drop back and regroup before something inside went haywire and reduced me to a state of total compliance; I didn't want to face another night like my last few. The overwhelming requirement to sleep, free from attack by the mosquitoes, was primary. Beating my head against the wall now would only mean a bloodier head and less chance to keep going until I could get out of this mess.

The sharp cold of the water cut through my torpor, shocking my system into temporary awareness. I decided that it would be a trade—my giving Mafia something he wanted in exchange for something I needed. There was no doubt what he wanted, and my problem was to give as little as possible in as ambiguous a form as possible, grab my goodies, and run. I prayed that Porky's disclosure was valid. If Mafia was actually in a hurry, I could stall and perhaps come out on top.

"Don't kid yourself," came the inner voice. "Mafia's too competent to lose points and you're ready to give whatever is necessary to get that net back."

"Len nha, Ro a!" Porky's voice broke into my thoughts— Come to the house!

I had no sooner entered the mess hall than Mafia motioned for me to sit on the bench across from him. I did detect impatience in his manner, but his voice gave no indication of anything other than the total assurance that he was master of the situation.

His first comments were ones of concern for the obvious effects of three nights with the mosquitoes. The guards, I was told, had gone to the market to try to buy medication which would ease the irritation of the bites and fungus. I slapped idly at the few mosquitoes on my feet, half-listening to the preamble and dreading the moment when he would launch into the main point. A strong voice in my mind was saying, "Screw him! Don't give him a thing! Take whatever he has to throw at you and if you die trying, you'll be robbing him of a source. At the same time you'll be out of this shit."

Another voice said, "Better go ahead and give him what he wants. It's stupid to put yourself in a worse spot by hard-assing him. Who'll know if you write out what he wants? Who cares? If you do, it'll mean you'll still have a chance to stay alive and go home."

The thoughts clashed and I tried to compromise, realizing I had no intention of dying in this stinking camp. I wasn't going to give Mafia the line he wanted, but I'd have to give him something to get him off of my back. It would be a matter of ambiguity.

"I have taken much patience with you," Mafia began, his

voice suddenly flat and cold, "and you have refused to write for me what you can know of the situation in Vietnam. I speak of the crimes of the U.S. aggressors and their henchmen, the useless death of the young American boys in a land far from their dear family, and of many subjects which you know well. You must see clearly the lenient policy of the National Liberation Front towards you. We do not kill you, we do not torture you. On the contrary, we provide food for you and medication for your maladies, just as the soldiers went out the last day to catch fish for your meal."

"One fish," I thought, "and it gets a starring role in the spiel."

Mafia continued for several minutes with a review of the points I had heard so many times in the last few days. He finished by saying, "I must go, for there is important work I must do. I give you paper and pen for you to write. Think carefully and write what you can know." His tone became almost paternal. "You can write the truth. Act according to your conscience and do not fear what your government might say, because the American people will support your courage to speak out against this cruel war." The paternal note disappeared as he added, "Do not try the patience of the Front, and write what I have told."

"What do I do with it after I finish, Mr. Hai?" I inquired.

"You can give it to Mr. Quan," he replied, referring to Porky. "You can go now," he said as I picked up the paper and pen. He was already putting his papers back into the ammunition can as I walked out of the hootch.

My analysis of the meeting was somewhat foggy, since my mind refused to move faster than a slow walk, but it was apparent that something moderately important had pulled Mafia away from here. He could have been much nastier had he chosen to be. Perhaps the sight of what his "treatment" had accomplished in the last three nights made him feel that the situation was well in hand and didn't require additional effort on his part. After all, he had Base and Porky to carry out any instructions he left. I couldn't disagree that his method was effective and would require little effort to maintain over whatever period of time he chose. The way he talked, I should thank him for the "lenient" treatment I was receiving. He was right, though. I wasn't dead yet.

Again in my kitchen, I laid the paper and pen on the small

table and sat on the floor to rest for a moment. I sat there dozing and enjoying the comfort of the shirt and trousers until Porky came stomping along the walkway. I felt him coming rather than saw him as the floor poles vibrated along with the poles on the walk under his heavy feet.

He entered the kitchen with a broad grin, dumping an armload of mosquito net, clothing and blanket at my feet. *"Lay do, Ro a,"* he said—Take your things, they're dry. He squatted in front of me and asked if the mosquito bites were painful, indicating my swollen eyes. I replied that they were very painful and I was happy to get the net back so I could sleep at night.

"Anh Giai Phong" will seek medicine to help the pain," Porky assured me, his face serious. "Have you written yet?" he asked, making it obvious why my net had been returned and why he had been wearing the smile as he entered.

"Chua, Anh Giai Phong." Not yet.

"Ua," he answered. *"Viet di."* Write.

I told him I was exhausted and would write tomorrow. That seemed to satisfy him, so he arose and informed me that he was returning to the guard kitchen.

Later, I was able to restring my net. Few things could have looked so beautiful to me at that moment as did that mosquito net. I climbed inside, tucking the edges in around the sleeping mat, and was asleep almost before I lay down. Porky woke me up to put on the leg irons, which that night were extremely unnecessary. I was going to get some sleep!

The next day I listed for Mafia's edification the events of the war and political incidents as he had related them and concluded that if these were correct, then the U.S. position in SVN was weaker than I had ever thought possible, and the NLF was on the path to total victory.

After I had written my thoughts for Mafia, the attitude of the guards became almost sickening in the false good-natured camaraderie they displayed. An English-speaking Chinese from Cholon, the Chinese section of Saigon, had accompanied Mafia in on this trip and spent several hours talking with me about Marxism and the "exploitation of the working classes in America." His major points were "Where there is capitalism, there is exploitation" and "Truth is a power." I agreed with the latter, but wondered where he'd ever come in contact with capitalism except in his Marxist textbooks. I was caught in a web of my own making, since I had written Mafia's lessons for him, and had to force myself to sit and listen to the spiels from all the guards as they began to open the doors of the Communist doctrine, repeating the well-memorized political lessons from the pages of their worn copybooks. I was revolted by the condescending attitude and the manner in which each of them tried to convince me of the validity of the doctrine he expounded.

I had reached a point where the war in Vietnam was a total mass of confusion in my mind. It was no longer the war I had known and the American people had obviously rejected it, condemning our government and supporting the demands of the Communists. There were too many conflicting ideas for me to resolve and I couldn't continue to battle on all sides. I had to buy time and try to work out some solution to my problems, but I first had to get my physical condition under control. The *lac* medication had beaten my infection within a couple of weeks, but it was coming back quite strongly. I was so damn happy to get anything to stop the itching, and the medication had done it. I only wished the cure had been permanent. The runs had quieted somewhat, but could break out at any time.

I was given extra gill nets and several stakeouts, which I immediately put to work, and within several days I was catching enough fish to eat and had some days where I caught more than I could eat in a day. It was either feast or famine, however, and I still had periods of several days when none of my nets produced fish. I asked Mafia on one of his vists if I could sell fish as we had been encouraged to do last year. He said yes and instructed the guards to take what fish I had to sell when they went to market and to purchase what I wanted to buy with whatever money I got for the fish. I asked if I could buy food, thinking of the extra nourishment and variety I might get from eggs, vegetables and fruits. This was immediately vetoed: "The Front supplies your needs." I was told that sugar, tea, cofee and cookies were my major items of purchase since the Front provided everything else. That was a shock and I went to other purchases that could be made to get around the refusal. I stored up my fish and over a period of days collected enough *ca ro* to send to market. The slow rate of fish accumulation was going to be my biggest block to adequate finances and I could think of only one solution for that: more nets and stakeouts!

The guards had never encountered capitalism in the raw; therefore, they had no idea of my plan until they brought back

365

my first purchase—new nets and line and hooks for stakeouts. Within a week, I was catching more fish than the guards and they found it necessary to limit my fish-catching expeditions strictly to the forested area to the immediate north.

Mafia was back in late August with the "corrections to my thoughts" and had five lessons to teach me. This took all day and sometimes part of the night, depending on how long it took for me to comprehend or at least signify I understood what he was teaching. Mafia gave the impression he could continue as long as was necessary and I knew that he would do whatever else he felt was required to gain my undivided attention.

The major portion of the lessons were "corrections" to my thoughts, enabling me to "control" my thinking. The lessons covered the same areas he had covered in the past, emphasizing "the duty of the POW, before, during and after release." The Code of Conduct was ridiculed as "a useless piece of paper, opposed by the American people; one which, with many other unpopular laws, will be changed in November by a new government, according to the desires of the people." Mafia made several comments during the presentation which clarified his and my position. "Speak the truth; act according to your conscience, but don't critize the Front." "You are free to speak and ask what you don't understand and don't believe, so the Front can explain to you the correct path. You must decide now your fate and we are to help you choose the correct path." He spoke three times of "upon my release" and caught me leaning to hear the words each time. I noted in my diary, *"I find myself leaning toward the chance to go home—even at this late date—definitely creates a mental receptivity which was absent before—the uncertain status (life-death) here—result of increased air strikes, plain rice, illness, etc. is clashing violently in my mind with the chance to once again be free. The mental pressure which has been building over the past 3–4 months is a definite reality and problem—the band around my brain is under strain although locals will never know how close to popping my cork I have been at times—only the firewood, the trees, the fish nets, the animals know—forced myself to repair nets I tore—slow delicate, tedious work—good therapy."*

The strong conflict in my mind between what I believed to be right and what Mafia was striving to prove to me was right was a complication in the already serious confusion which existed. I knew what was expected of me as an officer; the loyalty and devotion to country and duty that an officer must exemplify, the faith and trust in our government and our cause, the belief in the support of the American people, for whom I believed we were fighting, and the ultimate good which would be wrought by our efforts, no matter how unclear the picture at the present time. I knew the war I had been fighting in 1963, and the errors I had seen in what we were trying to do, the shortcomings that had seemed to be covered up rather than cleared up.

But I also remembered the enemy, the Vietcong and how I had come to despise what they were doing to this country even before they had gotten the opportunity to affect me directly during my captivity. I knew of their dual standard of "justice": anyone who opposed them was an "enemy of the people" and therefore subject to death in any fashion the Vietcong executioner chose; whereas those who supported them—whether they were soldiers, political cadre indoctrinating all those under their control, terrorists bombing and killing innocent people, or just peasants who happened to live in a Vietcong-controlled zone and either willingly or unwillingly aided the revolution—all were "patriots." Any harm to them was considered a "crime against the people." The prostitution of nationalism to secure an objective for the Communist movement had begun with the formation of the Indochinese Communist Party in 1930. Various factions within the country were induced to support a cause which, in the final analysis, would leave them non-voting members when the Communists seized the reins of power. I was aware of all these things and had added to my reservoir of knowledge through my daily contact with my captors. I had developed the ability to reason along their lines of logic, to repeat their rhetoric more comprehensively even than the guards, and also to recognize the blatant hypocrisy with which they dealt with an American prisoner, who was treated not as a human being, but as a propaganda tool, something to be manipulated and exploited. All of these were being contradicted and minimized by the combination of pressures Mafia and the other cadre had succeeded in applying to me.

The war was no longer one I could identify. I could rest my belief in the American soldier, but was unable to state conclusively that we, as soldiers, were supported by the American people. The national leaders I served had been compromised for their stand on the war and the policy I supported was being condemned from within the government itself. The outright pessimism expressed in our news media and the continuing news of widespread defeats created a picture of utter hopelessness in our efforts. The cruelest blow was the open support for the Vietcong and their cause that I saw and heard coming from within my country.

I refused to believe all of the reports that were given me, but there was no way I could deny the existence of an antiwar, anti-Administration movement that hadn't existed in 1963. The most frightening thought was that all it would take would be a new Administration to reverse our stand on Vietnam and I would have spent over four years in this stinking prison for nothing. Three men would have starved to death for nothing and Rocky Versace would have chosen death by execution rather than betray a cause that could be suddenly repudiated by people who had never been here, probably would never come, and knew little or nothing about the true nature of the enemy we opposed.

I had allowed myself to be enticed by the promise of release. Mafia had established the validity of the promise when John, Dan and Jim had regained their freedom. And after the reports of the Tet offensive, my hopes for escape were smashed, even if I had been strong enough to try. Where would I go in a countryside which was no longer spotted with Government outposts? Mafia had neatly trapped me, giving a three-month maximum until the war ended. I had accepted the time frame and set my sights on it as the termination of this confinement. Mafia completely controlled the situation as he first closed off any hope I had for the war ending, then structured the environment to make release by the Front seem so much more acceptable, even desirable in contrast to staying here.

The new aspects of the lesson involved Mafia's urging me to "lean on the antiwar movement" for support, disregarding any threat the government or military might pose. The repetition of Mafia's points drove them deeper into my mind, insuring an almost conditioned response when Mafia would ask certain questions: "What is the just cause and why is the revolution certain to achieve total victory?" "What is the unjust cause and why must the U.S. Imperialists certainly suffer defeat?" "What is the course of the war and what are the victories of the people's armed forces?" "What is the National Liberation Front and why is it the only genuine representative of the fourteen million South Vietnamese people?" "Why does the NLF have a lenient and humane policy toward U.S. and alien captured officers and men?" The sessions ran through the days and into the nights. I knew I'd lie in the mosquitoes at night until Mafia got what he wanted. There was too much to fight at one time. I wrote in my diary later, *"Sessions a mental meat grinder—repeat, repeat, repeat—write. Enough truth to confuse the rest—certain points are unclear in my mind as compared with before—* HAVE *to know* OUR *side!"*

I had been told about a "press conference" that was to be held sometime soon and Major Bay had proclaimed it an "international delegation" which was to see me since I was "a representative of the policy of the Front." I had seen the attempts in the past by these cadre to create a façade of sophistication, respectability and strength in whatever activities were to be viewed by individuals from the activity. It was essential to camouflage the true nature of their functions in order to create the impression of organization, support, dignity and co-ordination. Their attempts to create a false impression were so obvious from the inside, but not so obvious, perhaps, to someone viewing the finished product in the form of photographs or movies. The alterations they accomplished with a few yards of muslin for a wall or the flag-and-slogan-bedecked front of a rundown hut, could make a palace out of a chicken coop. I didn't expect a genuine "international delegation."

My greatest relief was watching "Cyrano II," an exact duplicate of Cyrano from the mangroves in 1964. One of the guards had caught the tree shrew in a rat trap as he attempted to pilfer the bait. I received him as a pet, and he joined my two eagles, five cranes, two pups (since the arrival of a new litter from Miss Fit) and Bounce. I didn't like to see any animal caged and let Cyrano out the second day I had him. The fact that I'd fed him while he sat in the cage atop my wood rack left an impression on him because the day after he regained his freedom, he came back to check out what I was having for supper. I began leaving a portion of my food on top of the wood rack where his cage had been and paid no attention when he approached cautiously along the roof poles, his little legs tensed, ready to flee at my slightest move.

After three or four days, he had become more casual about taking the food on the wood rack and began showing up for both breakfast and supper. I continued to ignore him and soon he was as brash as if the kitchen belonged to him. I took note of him, but made no moves toward him, thus establishing my nonaggressive status. I would feed him an exact portion of what I was eating, and this led him to stop by the small table I had built for myself and check what I had before proceeding to his meal. His tiny nose would twitch as he sniffed the pan of rice and whatever fish or greens I was eating, sometimes placing his forepaws on the edge of the plate and almost burying his nose in the fish for a closer examination. That completed, he would scurry up to his mound of rice and bits of fish and compare the meals. If I had failed to give him a duplicate meal, he was down in front of my plate again in a flash, sitting on his haunches, chattering away in his high-pitched, scolding voice, letting me know I had better put out the proper ration.

Herc and Ajax were in a sharp decline. I had clipped Ajax's wings after the guards threatened to cut it as Mom M had done to Herc. Ajax had refused to leave the camp although I had tried to drive him away, hoping he'd go off on his own before they got to him. My timid eagle wouldn't leave without Herc and the guards were certain to clip him as well, so I did the job myself, cutting as little as possible and still hoping he would be able to fly. There was nothing I could do for my earthbound eagles except watch them slowly die. The guards and cadre had urged me to kill and eat the birds, but I couldn't think of killing the two pets that had given me such relief during times of pressure. They were barely eating and the strength that had been so evident in their wings and breasts was ebbing away. The guards took advantage of the eagles' weakness to tease and torment them, driving the birds to frustration as they were unable to fight back. Not even the cadre would help me in protecting the birds. I finally decided to put Herc out of his misery and took him down to the canal, where we had gone so many times before; with Herc perched in a tree above my head, while I bathed, ready to swoop down beside me as I walked back to the cage after finishing.

This time I took the fish knife and carried Herc on my forearm. He sat quietly all the way to the canal and even when I stood him beside the chopping log, he remained unblinking and still. I never thought it would be so hard to kill something as when I killed Herc. The knife was sharpened to as keen an edge as I could manage, trying to make it quick. He made one cry as the knife took his head from his neck and then lay motionless. That night I got sick trying to eat the stew I made from the eagle.

"Ches," the English-speaker from Cholon, gave me a series of lessons on the "World Revolution" while I waited for Mafia to return with the new "corrections" to my thoughts. I was told, "The American Communist Party is the true representative of the masses of American people and is key to the success of the world revolution. The world revolution will secure world peace and it must succeed because it uses the people of the world to overthrow capitalism. People are a power that cannot be defeated." This concept, no matter how oversimplified by this interpreter, was a basis for the revolutionary movements, people's war. Major Bay had said, "The vital factor in deciding victory or defeat is the man, not the weapon. The spirit of a man can defeat any weapon."

Mafia reappeared with the word that the Central Committee had reviewed my case and decided I had progressed, but my writing was incomplete. He questioned me about the intelligence net at Tan Phu and the agents that had operated in or near the village. The mere fact that he wanted to know was reason enough for me to rely on my cover story and deny knowledge of the intelligence agents who had been operating around our post. He produced the appeal I had written for Sauser. It hadn't passed the censors and Mafia told me specifically what he wanted. I managed to distort it again and was given the damn thing back with Mafia's approved solution. I noted in my diary, *"Early morning session—a revamp of "Appeal"—somehow I managed to screw it up again—now is 95% Mafia's—sounds it."* Mafia's command of the English language was such that he could catch most of the ambiguities and misleading statements that had gotten past less qualified interpreters. His weakness was his absolute confidence in his ability to write English the way an American would. By simply using his wording and phrases, I had as non-American-sounding an appeal as anything I could have composed.

The next day, after Mafia had satisfied his requirements, I was prepared for a "three-day excursion" to see the "reality of the situation in South Vietnam." I was to be taken back to Tan Phu in order that I might see that the post had been overrun and the area had been liberated. In addition, I would visit scenes of American crimes against the people and be shown the people's hatred for Americans.

Major Bay told me to get rid of Ajax before we departed and said if I didn't want to kill him, the guards would take him. The bird never suspected what lay in store for him as he perched on my shoulder, nibbling contentedly on my earlobe with his hooked beak and making little sounds deep in his throat. I took him to the canal as I had done with Herc and tried to think of something I could do with him to avoid having to kill him. He was too helpless, too unable to provide for himself, to survive. If I just let him go, he would come right back to the kitchen and one of the guards would get him.

Ajax stood by the log and must have thought I was playing with him as I had done so many times before. He hopped onto the knife blade, as I honed it on a flat stone, and pecked at my finger gently. It was harder than when I had had to kill Herc. I was going to miss this little idiot.

Ajax was still pulling at my finger when I laid his head over the log and killed him. He'd trusted me as did Herc, and I had no choice but to kill them, the two closest things to friends I had in the camp.

Unraveling the system, after concentrated indoctrination in 1968

Rest there, stranger, and enter not
the green canopied world of progressive decay.
From afar you viewed this land of trees,
standing straight, leafy green,
and thought to yourself in a pleased, human way,
"how tall they stand, how thick the leaves. How
     alive that world of trees must be."
For from afar it so appears. The trees reveal
their gift of Nature, but hide from view the world
     within.
So you approached while the sun was high,
     thinking of the shade and the cool relief
from the sun's burning rays.
I watched you come and knew your thoughts,
for there are those who have entered before.
You think their same thoughts and walk their same
     path.
If you are still and listen for a moment,
you can hear their cries, the voices of the lost.
Their number is many, but their voices are one;
They seek to return, to find the light
and cry for help as they see no path.
For once within the forest land,
the trees are thick, the shade is deep.
One might think, "I'll go not far, just enough to
     find the shade
and thus, when I choose, I can return."

But to enter one step is to lose your way, for the
    spell of the shade
will lure you on
and seek to decay you as the leaves.

Listen, my friend, though I know you not
we are brothers, for we both are men
and as a brother I give this advice:

I have entered and I have returned. If enter you
    must
and enter you will,
then remember these thoughts:

Know who you are and from whence you came;
    Remember the light and the sun's
cleansing warmth;
Mark well the spot at which you entered and mark
    each spot
at which you stop;
Remember your Faith and keep it strong;
Do not expect to find a path and be prepared
to make your own;
When it is day you must travel far, but when it is
    dark, then rest and remember;
Conquer the urge to panic and run,
for they insure you'll never return;
When daylight comes, then rest not long and
    quickly seek your way
or you, like the leaves will also decay.

For night falls early in the forest and darkness
    blinds you,
hides the way.

8

WE DEPARTED THE CAMP ON THE EVENING OF 14 September, with Killer Mouse, "Frank Buck II," and Major Bay accompanying me in the boat. I was placed under my sleeping mat and the guards' equipment, and was ordered to remain still.

After several hours of traveling, I was told to sit up as we came to a hut at the edge of a hamlet. Mom M stood on the bank above the canal and gave directions to Major Bay. I was taken into the hut and immediately placed inside my mosquito net, which had been hastily strung up before I entered. I was apparently not to be seen.

The old man and woman who lived in the hut greeted Major Bay warmly, and the men began talking softly about mutual friends and party functions they'd attended. I gathered that the owner of this hut was the hamlet political cadre for the Front. Shortly after the conversation ended, all of them went to bed.

The next morning I was awake before the cadre, but not before the young daughter of the house. She was up and cooking before the others had stirred. Her mother arose grumbling minutes after the daughter and squatted in the kitchen, supervising the preparation of breakfast. The guards provided fish for our meal, which the young girl cleaned and cooked. I had heard the cadre say so often that all they had to do was travel in the countryside and the people provided food for them, yet for this trip, I had been forced to contribute six *ca loc* for rations. We were not getting anything from the people in this particular hut.

Major Bay told me to take down my net and go into the small partitioned section of the hut where the mother and father slept. Inside the sleeping section, I sat on the edge of the wooden rack, looking at the sparsely furnished room. In addition to the sleeping rack, there was one straight chair, a small rectangular mirror and a makeshift clothing rack made from old wooden ammunition boxes. The cadre and guards squatted just outside the door, waiting until the young girl served them rice and fish on a large round aluminum platter. The mother and daughter stayed in the kitchen, watching while the men ate. According to the cadre, men and women in the revolution were equal, but it didn't seem to apply at mealtime.

Major Bay had F.B. II take my plate and give me a serving of rice and a chunk of fish. I sat back on the sleeping rack and scooped the rice down with my chopsticks, oblivious to everything around me until I sensed someone staring at me. I looked up into the perplexed eyes of the young girl and smiled at her. She disappeared from sight behind the partition and I went back to eating. I felt her scrutiny again and looked up to see two almond eyes peering at me from the edge of the thatch partition. This time she didn't hide when I smiled; instead, she slipped quickly to the edge of the entrance of the room and squatted down, studying me intently as I continued to eat. Major Bay asked what she was doing. "I've never seen an American before and now I'm looking at one very closely," she answered.

She seemed fascinated by my ability to use the chopsticks with the ease of a Vietnamese, hardly the picture of the "American aggressor" she had expected. I continued to shovel rice into my mouth, pausing to smile at her when her examination became so intense I thought her eyes would pop. The old lady squatted beside her and they exchanged rapid comments, obviously about me, with the gray-headed mother turning to Major Bay and chuckling as she told him I was more Vietnamese than American. Major Bay choked on his mouthful of rice and cautioned them that I was to be considered dangerous, even though a captive.

My sun-darkened skin, hardly the "*da trang*" or "white skin" they had expected, coupled with my ability to eat as they did were distinct surprises to the family. I added to their series of discoveries by telling the young girl in Vietnamese that the rice

376

and fish she had prepared were delicious. There was open-mouthed silence when the two females realized I had spoken in their language. When they did speak, it was both of them at once, firing questions at me in unintelligible confusion. Finally the old lady tapped the young girl on the back of the head as a sign to be quiet and then asked me if I liked rice and *nuoc mam*. I lied and told her I enjoyed it very much when I was able to get good *nuoc mam* like she served. She stood up smiling and walked back into the kitchen, clucking to herself. The young girl scooted closer to me and timidly asked if I thought their hut was pretty. I assured her it was the most beautiful hut I had seen in almost five years, which was apparently the right thing to have said as she grinned behind the palm placed in front of her lips, her eyes reflecting sparkling glints of light.

The old lady returned with a brimming bowl of fresh *nuoc mam* and offered it to me for my rice. They both squatted and watched with total absorption as I managed to force the watery rice and *nuoc mam* soup down my protesting throat, slurping with feigned pleasure and appreciation. Major Bay was glaring at me through the open partition and I could imagine his displeasure at this counter-propaganda effort of mine.

Just before noon there was a good deal of activity outside the hut and shortly thereafter Mafia entered the hut and told me to prepare for a trip to visit my old post. They had obtained, with great difficulty, a larger boat with a two-horsepower motor and enough gasoline to take us on the day's journey. Mafia explained the ground rules to me: no talking with the civilians, keep my head lowered and look repentant in the presence of civilians, pay strict attention to the lessons that would be taught me during the trip, and rely on the cadre of the Front to protect me from the wrath of the people, who hated Americans.

Outside were a scrubbed-faced sixteen-year-old girl who was the "official photographer," a wizened old gentleman with snowy hair who was the "district representative of the Central Committee," a middle-aged, sharp-faced individual who was a "journalist for the Western News Agencies," a teenaged boy acting as boatman, and the ever-present Killer Mouse and Frank Buck II. Mafia was quite obviously the honcho on this operation with Major Bay as second in command. We all loaded in the boat and I found myself sandwiched between Mafia and the journalist in the rear of the boat.

I didn't recognize any of the terrain as we putted along the narrow canal, although Mafia assured me we were nearing Tan Phu. As we came to a broad intersection of our canal and a much wider one, Mafia pointed to a reed-covered bank diagonally across the intersection. "There is Tan Phu Post," he declared. I stared in disbelief. There wasn't anything there! In my mind I reconstructed the picture of Tan Phu with its concrete ammunition bunker, walls and tall watchtower, structures which might have remained even though the post had been overrun, but there was no sign that anything had ever existed above ground level. There were only the reeds, swaying gently in the hot breeze. I tried to orient myself, wondering what direction we had approached from. Then I saw the skeletal concrete piers of the bridge which had crossed the Cho Hoi canal rising out of the canal to my front. The bridge had been totally destroyed. The canal we were traveling on was what had been canal number one and where the village had once stood on the banks to my right and left there was now only a wide place in the canal. Not even the banks remained.

The wider canal in front of us, running perpendicular to our path, was the canal Song Trem, running to Thoi Binh, my old district capital. There were the partially shattered piers for the bridge that used to link the camp with the village. I couldn't fit this picture of utter desolation into my memory of the camp we had help build and defend, the faces of the villagers I'd known, the busy marketplace, the village children standing on the arched bridge catching small fish in the evenings. I had prepared myself for seeing the post destroyed, but not the entire area leveled.

I was barely conscious of Mafia as he described the battles which had been fought over this ground, pointing out a large painted tin sign on the bank with a picture of a Vietcong leaping into battle and the words describing the "Great Victory." The young camera girl was snapping pictures as Mafia gestured more for her benefit than mine.

We moved slowly down the Cho Hoi canal, between the slender concrete pillars that had supported the steel bridge we used to dive off of when we swam in the canal. I glanced to the opposite bank, away from camp, searching for the Catholic church that had stood just beyond the bridge. Only a few scarred trees and more waving reeds remained. This was the meaning of their "total destruction": no buildings, no animals, no people.

Tan Phu had ceased to exist, except as a memory.

Cho Hoi was another shock. This village, just like Tan Phu, had ceased to exist. Where the houses had been was bare packed earth, still scorched from the fires. Across the canal, where the post had been, there now stood a Vietcong cemetery with its rows of markers and the brilliantly painted wooden arch declaring this was a "Heroes' Cemetery." I wondered if all the markers were for men killed in the battles for Tan Phu and Cho Hoi; if so, they paid quite a price for the two posts. They'd have to expand if there were any more heroes to go in here.

Mafia took advantage of my barely concealed uneasiness to emphasize the lesson of strength of the NLF as proven by their ability to wipe out the series of posts in the area. I had no reply, since it was obvious that nothing had been spared and the confidence they had shown traveling through this zone seemed justified. I was wondering what had happened to all the people in the villages, but realized I could get no answer from the cadre. No doubt the "enemies of the people" were punished.

We were traveling southwest, toward the hamlet of Dau Nai, when Mafia told me I would now view the crimes of the U.S. imperialists. We stopped against a high bank and got out of the boat. The guards and boatman left with Major Bay and the district representative to find a representative of the Catholic congregation in this hamlet, designated Ho Tan Loc by a large sign on the front of a partially destroyed Catholic church to our front. While we waited for the others to return, Mafia reviewed the lesson I had learned by viewing the destroyed posts and villages. He avoided answering questions about the immediate area as if unwilling to launch into the new script until the entire cast was on stage.

Almost thirty minutes passed before the others returned and notified Mafia that the local churchman would appear presently. Apparently the word had gotten around that an American was in the hamlet, because the youngsters began to appear from all sides. We were followed by a chattering throng as we walked to the church and my two guards were unable to disperse the youngsters. Mafia warned me that the young people in this hamlet had a "fierce hatred before the aggressor" and told me to assume the "repentant" posture. Aside from the occasional touching of my arm and unmistakable request for "gom," I found the children satisfied to watch me through wide, wondering eyes.

Major Bay assumed the role of teacher for this part of my instruction and explained that this church had been built by the people of the hamlet so they "might enjoy the practice of their religious belief," but the structure had been destroyed by U.S. aircraft. I was taken on an inside and outside tour of the building in order to see the wreckage. The corrugated iron church was ornately decorated inside through the efforts of local artisans and carpenters with tin, cut, shaped and painted to form the basic accouterments of a Catholic chapel. The pews, made from locally obtained wood, had survived the airstrike. The statuary near the altar had been shattered by the rocket fragments and machine-gun fire that had torn gaping holes in the roof and walls. The floor was littered with debris and no apparent effort had been made to clean up the wreckage, even though a rapid estimate showed that several hours of concentrated effort could have greatly reduced, if not completely eliminated, the minor rubble lying around. The roofing stringers had been shattered, but could have been replaced. The major damage was to the corrugated iron, which was thoroughly perforated.

The camera girl was at work, taking pictures of me as I was led from point to point by the cadre, insuring that three ingredients were present in each photo, NLF cadre pointing and explaining, U.S. POW looking and listening, and wreckage.

Major Bay informed me that thirty-seven rockets had hit the church and "thousands" of bullets. Mafia took me around the church to show the lack of fortifications in the immediate area and the absence of any troops, not that any of us expected to see any large number of uniformed soldiers standing around. The major lesson to be gained, according to the cadre, was that the United States, a Christian nation, had destroyed a church, thus depriving another Christian group of their ability to worship.

Several incidents caused me to think seriously about the concept these cadre were attempting to impress on me. Major Bay, in the chapel, had stopped by the altar and, in exhibiting the broken statuary, had picked up the severed head of the Christ Child and called the camera girl to take a picture of me standing in front of the altar, holding the head. I was immediately repulsed by the crude effort for propaganda, not only

380

because of the sacrilege in exploiting an already desecrated figure, but because of the use of a religious symbol by an atheist who had no more understanding or feeling for the faith represented by the church, in any form, than he had for what he considered a painted plaster head. I refused to comply and took Mafia by surprise when I commented on Major Bay's obvious lack of understanding of my religious beliefs and disregard for the policy of the Front, which respected my beliefs, as he attempted to force me to be a part of a propaganda ploy using the Christ Child.

The second thought-provoking discovery was provided by one of the villagers, an older woman who commented quietly that over one hundred rockets had been fired into the large rice paddy behind the church without touching the structure. I knew our aircraft wouldn't attack a church without reason and we never fired a load of rockets like that into an empty field. Granted, there were no VC troops in the area now, but how long ago did the incident occur and what were the circumstances then? As usual, the cadre told a person only what they wanted him to know in order for him to draw the required conclusions. Fortunately, I was still able to think for myself.

As a final part of the tour I was given a lecture by the "representative of the Catholic worshippers in the village." He was a tightly drawn, intense younger man who stood on the front portico of the church and delivered an oration on the crimes of the U.S. imperialists and their lackeys in Saigon. The familiar rhetoric sounded like a replay from Radio Hanoi or Radio Liberation and more like a political cadre than a church leader. I asked if he was a priest and learned that he was the local NLF cadre who doubled as both political and religious representative, an unlikely combination but efficient in controlling the people. His "congregation" stood silently in the presence of the higher-ranking cadre with me and seemed preoccupied during his speech. Only Mafia, Major Bay and I were involved in the discourse.

When he finished, I was led back to the boat and the older people in the crowd began to disperse silently. The younger children were making a game of swinging on the bell rope, sending hollow clangings from the single church bell echoing across the vast paddy land.

A visit to a Khmer temple near the Catholic church ended

381

this portion of the trip. The temple had been severely damaged by fragmentation bombs and I was once again given a tour of the wreckage, after which the villagers in the area were gathered together while Major Bay lectured them on the purpose of my visit: to see the proof of U.S. crimes and for the people to see an American POW. He became involved in his own rhetoric and went on for about fifteen or twenty minutes until Mafia finally caught his eye and got him to stop. A Khmer monk, who lived nearby and was responsible for the temple, was called upon to condemn the crimes before the assembled people. The quiet, dignified man in his flowing yellow robe stood in the midst of the seated and squatting circle of people for a moment, his eyes on the ground. Then he looked up at me as I stood, flanked by the two guards and cadre. He spoke slowly, softly in Cambodian while one of the men in the crowd translated from Cambodian into Vietnamese. Mafia translated from Vietnamese into English for me, but it was unnecessary since the speech was brief and clear in the Vietnamese language. Mafia's translation began accurately, but after the first few sentences he began to insert his own words. The speech was not what he intended for me to hear.

After the twenty-minute, hate-filled tirade by Major Bay, the monk spoke for perhaps two minutes and his message was of love and hope. "Death is our brother, and suffering, our sister. These are the relationships forced upon us, not by our choosing, but as our part in life. These we bear, but our teachings are of the greater blessings which await us at the termination of this period. Hatred is of this world and will serve no purpose in the next. To pursue the evils of this world binds us forever to them. What we must bear is difficult, but let us not contribute to the fires which consume us and thus perpetuate them so they also consume our children." He looked levelly at Mafia, turned, and walked slowly away.

I was hustled quickly away from the still-seated people and put back in the boat. Mafia was speaking rapidly as the boat putted noisily down the canal in the late afternoon sun. He reviewed the lessons I should have learned in seeing the "hypocrisy of the Christian U.S. nation destroying the people's ability to worship and denying them their beliefs." I listened, but was beginning to feel a warm sort of glow inside as I heard only the voice of the monk and remembered the actions of the people who were supposed to hate me.

It was dark as we returned along the Cho Hoi canal, traveling back toward Tan Phu. Mafia said there would be one final stop at a village where the people were holding a meeting to discuss the revolution and their contributions in the coming week to insure attainment of final victory. He cautioned me that this would be very dangerous for me since the people in this area had a burning hatred of the Americans and only the presence of the cadre would prevent the people from beating me to death. I was to be exhibited at the meeting and would have to be tied. I would have to maintain the head-down repentant attitude in the presence of the people in order to insure my safety.

When he mentioned the name of the village I was startled. It was near Tan Phu post, and in 1963 we had run medical patrols into the village, bringing in food and clothing, and had developed a reasonably strong rapport with the people. I realized that this was the reason Mafia had questioned me about the intelligence net that had existed in this area. It would have been extremely inopportune if some of the people who had worked with the Government back in 1963 were still present and I could get in the briefest contact with them. I was thankful I had played dumb during the questioning and given him no answer.

As the boat pulled up to the palm-lined bank, I saw and heard a throng of young people from children through teenagers lining the bank and talking among themselves. The word that was repeated over and over was "*My, My*"—American, American. The news was out that an American would be present. It was not an angry shout, but almost a festive air prevailed.

I was dragged from the boat in a display of authority by my two guards and led through a jostling crowd of curious youths. Mafia tried to get them to clear a path, without success, and I began to wonder about my safety in case the crowd was hostile. In the crush of bodies, there would be no way for the guards or cadre to protect me should someone decide to take out his anger on me. I was surprised when only the guards and Mafia were crowded. I was given a small space in which to proceed, always surrounded but not pushed. Hands reached out and touched my arms, stroking the arm hair. In the half-light of a single carbide lamp, faces appeared around me, some openly curious, some smiling.

On the far side of a partially destroyed shed was a cleared, packed-earth circle crowded with people. The carbide lamp hung from a tree branch cast dancing shadows across the faces of elders, middle-aged people, male and female, teenagers, children and babes in arms. The cadre must have turned out every available warm body in the whole area!

As we approached, a cadre was lecturing the crowd on the glorious victories of the Liberation Armed Forces in their march toward final victory. His high-pitched harangue and violent gesturing weren't drawing too much attention and he had to pause several times to call to the chattering group to be quiet in order that he might be heard. I began to wonder about the people's enthusiasm for contributing to the revolution.

My appearance was the signal for total silence as all faces turned toward me. Mafia leaned toward me, pushing down on the back of my head with his hand. "Look repentant!" I stood between Mafia and Major Bay as the cadre completed his spiel and introduced the white-haired district representative who had been traveling with us. He commanded more respect than the cadre and spoke for several minutes to the now-quiet crowd, explaining the importance of unified effort of all the people to accomplish the goals of the revolution and once again bring peace and prosperity to the reunited Fatherland. I was glancing around the rows of faces, searching for anyone who might have been familiar. Mafia once again pushed my head down, cautioning me: "Look repentant and don't anger the people." I could feel the eyes of the crowd focusing on me and there was a curious absence of apprehension on my part. I felt no atmosphere of antagonism or hatred.

To my left rear, at the back of the crowd, I heard several voices talking, audible in the silence of the rest of the crowd. The word *"trung-uy"*—lieutenant—caught my attention and listening more closely, I heard, *"Do la Trung-Uy!"*—That's the Lieutenant! Another voice replied, *"Da, ten gi ca?"*—Yes, what's his name? Yet another voice cut in, *"Quen roi. Phai la Trung-Uy!"*—I've forgotten. But it must be the Lieutenant! There was a surge of elation! I had been recognized!

Mafia was introduced by the district representative and stepped forward into the circle of light to deliver a short speech. As he was explaining the trip I had been taken on and the lessons I had learned, he mentioned that I was the American lieutenant captured at the battle of Tan Phu in October 1963. There was a murmur in the crowd and the voices to my left rear broke out softly, excitedly, verifying their identification.

Mafia continued, explaining the crimes of the U.S. imperialists against the people in this area and saying that the cadre had explained and taught me that the respect the people had for the NLF prevented them from killing me immediately in retaliation for the sufferings my people had brought to the countryside. He pleaded with them to realize that I was a prisoner and was learning of the crimes I had committed in order to repent of them and join in helping the Vietnamese people struggle for their freedom. There was silence from the crowd; only the curious eyes fastened on me.

Suddenly I felt a hand on my shoulder and flinched. The hand remained, gently touching and a voice behind my ear asked, *"Manh khong, Trung-Uy?"* —Are you all right, Lieutenant? The flooding of relief and release of tension was enough to make my knees go weak. I managed to nod, yes. The hand patted me and there was one word, *"Tot"* —Good. The hand was gone, but I had gotten my answer about the people. Mafia could say anything he wanted now! Someone had taken the risk of slipping up behind me among the group of young people and checking to see if I was OK. That gesture in itself was enough to shoot the whole staged production Mafia was carrying out.

I was pushed roughly out beside Mafia by one of the guards and exhibited as a prize of war. Mafia encouraged the people, saying that Americans were not so awesome as the propaganda led some to believe. In my weakened condition, I was the example of the American soldier who would certainly be defeated on all battlefields in Vietnam. He assured the people that he had many more American prisoners he could have brought, but one was enough to convey his idea.

I was studying a beetle crawling laboriously across the packed earth toward the center of light when there was a commotion to my right front and a scrawny, bushy-haired man sprang out of the crowd with his fist upraised, screaming, *"Da dao de quoc my!"* —Down with the American imperialists! I tensed, waiting for the blow to land. Then nothing happened. I glanced up and the man was standing in front of me, quivering, with his face contorted and his fist still clenched. Mafia interjected quickly, "He is crippled by U.S. helicopters." My first thought was that he was quite agile for a cripple. Mafia made no move and the man continued to stand in front of me.

All at once a cadre stepped out of the group of leaders to

my left with his arms outspread and blurted in an imploring voice, "My compatriots, my compatriots, restrain your anger. Do not strike the prisoner. Show compassion." Dan's story of the staged "hate session" he and John had been subjected to, on their trip in 1967, flashed into my mind and I began to smile to myself. It was like a grade-school play and someone had missed his cue.

I looked into the face of the man in front of me. His eyes were on the speaking cadre, his fist still raised to strike but his next action obviously forgotten. When the cadre finished the short speech on the people's loyalty to the Front, the man was even more uncertain what to do. I was watching him with open curiosity. Finally he looked around, managed a sheepish gold-capped grin and shuffled back into the crowd. Someone cackled a crone's laugh back in the midst of the people.

Major Bay stepped into the center of the meeting to give a closing speech after the cadre restored order. He had just begun to speak when an old grandmother, chewing her betelnut, walked up beside me and stood looking at me through half-closed eyes. She reached out and jabbed a bony finger into my ribs. I wondered what was going to happen. Next she felt my forearm and biceps, squeezing what there was left of muscle, until she touched bone. I began to feel like a side of beef being inspected at market. Major Bay was in the midst of his talk, but the crowd was watching the drama involving the old lady, the POW and Mafia. Ignoring Major's Bay voice, she asked Mafia in a sharp voice, "Do you mistreat him?" Mafia was caught off balance and failed to reply. "Do you give him enough to eat?" she demanded. Mafia assured her I was well fed and not mistreated. The grandmother wasn't satisfied. "I remember this boy when he came to our hamlet in 1963. He was a strong boy, very husky, and now he looks weak and sick. You must not be taking care of him."

Mafia was on a spot as the attention of the crowd focused on his answers. There was good-humored chuckling running through the crowd at this little old lady putting a powerful cadre in a tight situation. "The Front provides for the well-being of the POW's," Mafia reiterated. "You must remember the Americans are criminals and deserve only death." He began to slip into the standard line. "But the Front is lenient and spares their lives so they can realize their mistakes."

The old lady wouldn't accept the reasoning. "I know what it is like to be hungry and sick and there is no leniency in inflicting that on another."

Mafia was looking anxiously at Major Bay, whose speech had trailed off to silence. There was no help from the tall cadre. Finally Mafia turned to me in apparent desperation. "Tell her you are well treated!" he ordered sharply. I put my head lower and looked repentant.

The next thing I realized, Frank Buck II and Killer Mouse had my arms and were dragging me into the darkness toward the canal and the boat. Minutes later we were on our way back to the hut we had stopped in the night before, moving rapidly away from the meeting place. All the way to the hut Mafia and Major Bay bombarded me with how fortunate I was to have gotten away from the crowd before they had beaten me. The cadre were careful to outline completely the lessons I had learned during the day, ensuring that I had each major point clearly in my mind. No mention was made of what I had seen, only of what they had wanted me to see.

We stopped only briefly at the hut before setting out on an all-night trip, traveling across narrow, out-of-the-way canals until we reached another hamlet, many kilometers north of the first hut. Several hours before daylight, we approached a cluster of small huts along both sides of the canal. This, Major Bay told me sleepily, was deep in a liberated zone where the Front was strongly supported. I glanced around at the shabbily constructed huts and squalor that was worse than any I'd seen in either Government-protected or even contested zones. This was the "new life" the people were making for themselves under the freedoms imposed in a liberated zone, and what I was seeing hardly matched the glowing descriptions I had received in indoctrinations.

We proceeded down the canal to a preselected hut where Major Bay, the two guards and I would stay. Its owner was the village political cadre and had "volunteered" his hut for our use. Mafia and Mom M left us there while they went in search of quarters for themselves.

As we walked up to the small, one-room thatched hut, the old man and his wife stood in the doorway, silhouetted by a flickering kerosene lamp in the hut. Major Bay greeted the older man, probably in his sixties, and accepted the bowing gesture the old man made to him. The political rank took precedence over respect for elders, I noted, as Major Bay chatted with the couple, asking about the crops and work of the village committee. The old man answered, smiling, but the old lady remained silent. I was watching her as I had watched and listened to the older women the day before. They seemed to be unintimidated by the cadre, as if they had lived their lives and had nothing to fear.

It developed that this old couple was being forced to move out of their hut in order for the four of us to move in. The village cadre had the responsibility for housing us and had to give up his own hut to fulfull the requirement. The man was indebted to the revolution for the lands he now farmed and they could be taken from him as easily as they had been confiscated from one of his unfortunate neighbors who was condemned as an enemy of the people.

The two men finished sipping the tea provided by the village cadre and the couple departed, leaving us to prepare for sleep. Killer Mouse and Frank Buck II immediately strung a single mosquito net for both of them and curled up together. Major Bay indicated a cleared space on the mud floor where I was to sleep and I was soon in a dreamless, exhausted slumber.

The next day was a day of rest while the cadre prepared for some type of function to be held in the village. The guards prepared a few of our remaining fish for a midday meal and spent the rest of the day eating fruit picked from a large *trai oi* tree outside the hut. I was given several at Major Bay's suggestion when he checked on me and found me sitting on the floor, feeding grains of rice to the family rooster while the guards sat on the bed rack stuffing down the fruit. The old lady appeared shortly thereafter and immediately began checking out her hut. The guards had used her rainwater to cook the rice, had burned her firewood, and were throwing the fruit stems on the floor. None of these actions went unnoticed, and she collared Major Bay, much to his embarrassment, and set him straight on the correct behavior for guests in her house. There was no doubt, from her tone of voice and orders, that she expected to be obeyed. After all, she was the grandmother and these were children to her.

Major Bay made amends as best possible, assuring her the guards would cut their own firewood and leave her with more than she had before they came, canal water would be used for the rice instead of the precious rainwater, and her hut would be swept out every morning.

I was ordered to stay inside the hut to avoid being seen, but went out on several occasions to make a crap run and got a chance to look around. The old man had a large plot of land with papayas, pineapples, coconuts and manioc in addition to his rice paddy. With all of this, I noticed the old woman catching small fish from the canal for a meager meal of rice and the tiny fish, cooked in *nuoc mam*. My guards offered her none of our fish. I wondered why they didn't eat some of their produce and asked the old man later that afternoon when he came in to drink some of his tea, depleted by my two guards' constant sipping during the day. I learned that he was required to contribute from two-thirds to three-quarters of what he produced to the revolution, to feed the soldiers, and had little for himself and his wife. That was another point in my diary: given more land than before, but required to contribute most of what he produced to the revolution. Sum total is that he works harder and has less to show for it.

The next morning, Mafia came by and told me I was to attend a "press conference" comprising the journalists from the Liberation News Agency, Progressive Journalists of Vietnam and a representative from the Western press. I was suddenly aware of the purpose behind the long hours of indoctrination, the repetition of questions and the Front's answers, the probing of my thoughts and corrections to my thoughts, his urgent need to "control my thoughts." Mafia stated the reason for me: "You are a prisoner for a long time and you are still alive. You are the living truth of the policy of the Front and must represent to these men what you have learned and what you can know about the unjust war of the U.S. imperialists." I had survived, little thanks to the Front, other than the fact that they hadn't killed me outright, and now I was the "living truth of their policy"! Bullshit, I thought; I'm living proof that an American can be a little tougher and a little more determined than you ever counted on.

Major Bay and several other cadre appeared in the doorway, entering when Mafia motioned to me. All were smiling and quite friendly, shaking my hand and inquiring about my health and my family and asking if I was ready to return home. We chatted for fifteen or twenty minutes, with Mafia interpreting, until my answers began to come before he finished translating the questions and the conversation was conducted strictly in Vietnamese. I found my initial apprehension decreasing as the men joked and made me feel quite at ease. They seemed assured that I was going home soon and this was a last essential part of my preparation, like a final exam. I hated the surge of elation that the talk of release brought. I wasn't going to surrender now, I thought.

Mafia waited until the others left and spoke with me alone. "You must be careful in your answers today. A representative of the Central Committee is here to judge your case and consider your release. You can speak the truth, act according to your conscience, but do not criticize the Liberation Front." Those were the ground rules as I was taken to a dilapidated shed that had been decorated with worn bedspreads covering the open walls and had various slogans painted on signs around the small room. The NLF flag was fastened on the wall behind a raised table at the end of the room. Long, poncho-covered tables ran the length of the walls on both sides of the front table, forming a U-shaped seating arrangement. I was taken into a back room, where the displaced poultry was tied by strings around their legs, and stood waiting among the ducks and chickens until Killer Mouse came in to get me.

As I entered the conference room again there were ten other men besides myself, the two guards and Mafia. The three cadre who had visited with me prior to this were all seated to my left and Mafia sat at my right elbow. Across from me were the press representatives with their pads of paper and tape recorders. Four separate microphones were placed in front of me. Mom M was seated at the end of the press table and Major Bay sat in a lone chair at the far side of the room. With all the cadre I could identify and the representative of the Central Committee sitting behind the front table, I counted only four possible journalists. Not much of a turnout, but par for the course.

The opening statement from the Central Committee representative welcomed the members of the journalistic community to the grand press conference, held by the National Liberation Front to enable them to discuss the conditions of the war first hand with an American prisoner of war who had been a captive for an extended period of time. It was, he said, a unique opportunity for them to have at their disposal such a prisoner who had lived under the lenient policy of the Front and was physical proof of the treatment given by the Front. After that he opened the floor to questions with Mafia translating for me from Vietnamese into English so I would understand the questions completely.

There was no hesitation from the journalists as they plunged into a line of questioning that could have come straight from Mafia's lessons. "What is the course of the war and on what side is the just cause?" "What are the crimes of the U.S. Imperialists in SVN?" "What is your participation in the U.S. effort and can you realize your misdeeds?"

Mafia gave me a sheet of paper and a pen, telling me to arrange my thoughts before answering and to remember that the Front would judge my case by what I said. It was a very neat cul-de-sac in which I had the answers for every question they asked, the exact answers they wanted, and if I gave them those answers, I might be released. If not, I could go back and probably rot before any other chance came up.

Some of the questions demanded an outright condemnation of my government and our army, something I would not do, and I found myself straining for ambiguity, pushing to take up time and space without saying anything. Mafia let it go on the first few questions and then stopped me to reiterate my "duty" to report the facts "accurately as I had learned them." In other words, quit bullshitting and tell the men what he'd pounded into me. I found that as the familiar questions were asked, Mafia's answers that had been repeated so many times, driving them into my mind, came to my lips immediately, without my thinking, and I had to bite them back, lest they slip out.

The questioning turned to the trip I had been taken on to Tan Phu and the church. I was able to comment factually that I had never expected to see the total destruction of not only the post, but the entire village, and to view the apparent physical control exerted by the Front in that area. I commented that the destruction of the church was distressing to me and I hoped that the people would soon be able to rebuild their place of worship. I noticed a few sour faces and downcast eyes when I commented that it takes more than the destruction of a church to destroy faith in God if the believers have a true faith. Mafia again warned me to stick to what I had learned, referring to the lessons I should have learned and not my own philosophy.

There was a break after about two hours and a teenaged girl brought several plates of cookies and some pieces of candy in for refreshments. The cadre and journalists stood around chatting while Mafia gave me a serious talk about responding correctly to the questioning. I realized he was quite angry, but was containing himself. Up to this point his pupil hadn't shown the proper attitude and Mafia was going to answer to his superiors for it. I would have to answer to Mafia, who could be a son of a bitch if he was pissed off. I decided to play it a little looser during the next portion and pull some of the pressure off.

When we began again I was asked about the policy of the Front and my treatment as a POW. I gave the standard "I have not been beaten or physically tortured; I have received sufficient rice for my meals" (I wouldn't mention food); "I have been given items necessary for survival: mosquito net, sleeping mat, clothing; in times of serious illness I have been given medication" (no mention of what kind or how much, no mention of how sick before anything was given at all). Mafia was pleased with that answer. I mentioned that the cadre of the Front had the mission to instruct and correct the attitude of American POW's and in my case they had been very patient over a long period of time, dealing with my incorrect attitude. Mafia interpreted it as a reference to benevolence on the part of the cadre and everyone beamed at me for my understanding.

The session went on with me trading bits of Mafia's lessons for time, wishing the tape would run out. At about four in the afternoon, the Central Committee representative declared the conference at an end and I was taken back to the hut. I felt drained and hoped I hadn't compromised my precarious position.

Back at the hut I sat waiting for the next move. The guards had made no effort to repair the old lady's kitchen floor, nor had they replaced her firewood. Instead, they had eaten most of the fruit from her tree and picked her pepper bush clean, taking the red peppers for their meals later when we were back in the forest. Major Bay had made a minimum effort to sweep the floor, succeeding only in pushing the trash under the sleeping rack. I took mental note of these actions, contrasting them

392

with the glowing accounts the cadre had given me of the love and mutual support shared by the soldiers and people. I wondered why there had been no sharing of our fish with the people and nothing given by the people to us. Where was the open, warm support?

When darkness fell, we prepared to move out. Muoi's last words to the old cadre were to instruct him to be certain that a woman who had refused us a place to sleep was severely criticized in the next hamlet political meeting and an example made of her so that there would not be a recurrence. I considered this in terms of the "democratic processes and liberties" I had heard so much about.

By midnight I was back in my forest cage, not knowing what to expect next, but feeling better equipped to deal with the confusion that had been created in my mind, during the past months, by criticism of the war emanating from my own people. Were I ever to have faltered, were I ever to have been broken, it would have been under the barrage of condemnation of my government and the enthusiastic support for the enemy coming from within my country. The feeling of betrayal and the hopelessness of fighting for a cause that was doomed because of lack of support back home were the enemies I couldn't defeat. The bitter lesson learned by the French forces in their war against the Vietminh proved that war can be lost in the halls of government and on the streets at home rather than on the battlefields. The cadre here had unwittingly provided me with my answers, as I was to learn in the following days. They had carefully staged what they wanted me to see and believe as the "lessons" of reality in a liberated zone, but once again truth had seeped through.

Mafia was in camp the next morning with a tape of the press conference and wanted me to write out what I had said, transcribing from the tape to paper. I listened to the questions, thinking of the party-approved answers and how easy it would be to give them, taking all pressure off myself and perhaps securing the elusive ticket home that had been promised so many times. I thought back to one of Major Bay's comments that had followed a particularly brutal session of quoted condemnation of the U.S. effort from antiwar elements within my government. Major Bay challenged my nonacceptance of the statements, saying, "Soon the people in your country will decide that your coming to Vietnam was a mistake, and at that time those of you who have died here will have died a useless death and those who lead the revolution in your country will be the heroes and the saviors. Why should you perish in this jungle prison supporting an unjust cause which even your own countrymen and leaders condemn to failure?" I had no answer for him because I knew that all it would take would be enough people shouting that we were wrong and we might even be condemned for dying.

Mafia took the transcription when I had finished late that night and left, saying he would review my thoughts and correct them so I might be controlled in presenting only "the truth." There was obviously another editing job to be done on my answers before the Central Committee got a look at them. The system of refinement of answers until they got exactly what they wanted was effective in that they had all the time they needed to obtain the results. My position was weakened by the clawing apprehension in the back of my mind that my government would reverse its stand and leave me clinging to a betrayed loyalty and dedication.

In the following days I resolved the issue in my mind. My major premise that the will of the Vietnamese people should decide the question of just and unjust cause remained firm. It was their country and self-determination belonged to them. Peace, liberty and independence were their aspirations and the issue became one of how they could best achieve those goals. The Communist-controlled revolution was on one side and the recognized government of South Vietnam on the other. My exposure to the rhetoric of Marx and Lenin while observing the indoctrination of the guards left no doubt about the political allegiance of the Vietcong. The leaders, whether they were political or military, were required to be members of the Dang Lao Dong, or Communist Party of North Vietnam. The leadership and indoctrination were Communist. The followers had no voice of their own.

The hypocrisy and deceit I had experienced as a POW was applied equally to the people under the Front's control, giving them the same choice I had: comply or die. Terror and subversion were the VC's chief weapons to secure an area, this I had seen at Tan Phu and had heard from the guards as they described the "punishment of enemies of the people." The basic doctrine included their "three no's": no family, no religion, no nationality. All three were considered means of governing the people and instilling loyalties other than to the party and the state. For that reason they were eliminated. There could be only the party and the state, which, in the revolutionary rhetoric, represented the people. Therefore, to oppose the party was to oppose the people and, conversely, those who supported the party supported the people.

To create their type of state society meant to fragment the home, sowing the seeds of distrust in order to break down opposition and counter the centuries of filial loyalty and obedience which ran counter to the needs of the party. Religion was tolerated, but only until it could be abolished. The entire "lesson" of the destroyed Catholic church shown me on the trip to Ho Tan Loc was shattered by Mafia himself in a later discussion in which he said, "we do not deprive the people of their right to worship because to so deprive them would cause them to resist and we do not desire counterrevolution; but over a period of time, through education and culture, we will show them that there is no God, no life after death, no reason to follow the Church. At that time they will give up their false beliefs freely and follow us." I thought, "What is worse, to destroy the physical structure of a church which can be rebuilt or to destroy the foundations of faith itself and then create an environment in which it can never be reborn?" I realized that Mafia's declaration included not only my faith, but those of the Buddhists, Cao Dai, Hoa Hao and other religious sects. It was a planned total eclipse of religion in a country of deep-seated religious beliefs, dooming future generations to the narrow, materialistic world of atheism. Finally, the spirit of nationalism which had been so tragically prostituted by the Communists in their conquest of power would be stamped out in the rise of proletarian internationalism, world Communism. There would be no vestige of the old culture left if this force were allowed to proceed unchecked.

In North Vietnam after the 1954 Geneva Accords, Ho Chi Minh instituted "Land Reform" programs in which about 100,000 "landlords" were executed by groups of Communist cadre purging the countryside. This was particularly difficult to understand when one considered that approximately 98 per cent of the peasants owned the land they tilled and "landlords" were virtually nonexistent! In most cases, the cadre arrived in a village with a death quota which was to be filled whether anyone qualified or not. Thousands of other innocent peasants were jailed and the suffering and deaths grew to the point that Ho was faced with a revolution in his newly acquired nation. I recalled reading about his famous weeping admission that "mistakes" had been made and his own cadre, who had done his bidding, were purged. I could understand the trepidation of the peasants in South Vietnam, particularly those who had fled from the terror of the North, when they read in the ten-point program of the National Liberation Front those ominous words in point number four, "Land rent reduction and land reform." The hideous specter was again looming before them.

I thought of the Vietnamese people I had known before I was captured and those I had seen on the recent trip. Therein lay my answer! I had been exposed in the prison camp to the cadre's discussions of the utopian promise and of the solid support and love for the revolution, emanating from the people it was supposed to be serving. I was told of the burning hatred of the people for the Americans and the crimes we were committing against the people; yet when I was taken in to the liberated zones, the Communist-controlled zones where support should have been at its strongest, only the prepared script fitted the dreams of the cadre, and even then it served only to accentuate the vast difference between what they wished me to believe and what actually existed. I thought of the quiet dignity of the Khmer monk and his message of love and hope, the concern for my health expressed by the old lady at the meeting, the gentle hand on my shoulder, the curiosity without hatred of the young girl in the first hut, the outspoken old women and their candid comments. Then I thought of the solemn obedience of the groups of people near the church and temple as they gathered in response to the cadre's command to listen to the political speeches by representatives of the Front, the obsequiousness of the old man when he and his wife had to surrender their hut to Major Bay. I chuckled to myself thinking of the cadre's use of the word "puppet" when I recalled the athletic "cripple" who sprang out in front of me at the meeting only to find that someone had apparently cut his strings. I thought of the woman who would be made an example at a political critique because she hadn't given Muoi and Mafia a place to sleep.

They were the people who would live here long after I was gone, long after the last American was gone. From what I had seen, their best chance to achieve the peace, liberty and independence they desired and so richly deserved would be with our help. Self-determination would be dead under Communism, yet with our help, it could live. These people had known nothing but war for two decades and out of the destruction of war they had always rebuilt, but the insidious controlling of their spirit would kill them in a state where they could only comply, without recourse. I had seen, if only in this area, the flame of resistance still burning and asking only to be kindled. If they, in a Communist-controlled zone, were willing to resist, I was now, as I had been in 1963, willing to help. That was my decision.

I concluded that it wasn't those Americans condemning our efforts while they sat ten thousand miles away from Vietnam, most of them never having set foot in the country, who should influence me. I was here and I had seen both sides. I knew the Vietcong and I knew what they promised this country. I knew the Vietnamese people better than the men back in the United States who condemned us for helping them and I disagreed with the opposition to our helping these people. There might be disagreement on how we had gone about our task, but the basic commitment was sound. The Communist dream of "the greatest peace man has ever known, under Communism" was a frightening reality. If they were not stopped by some outside force, their quest for world domination would continue until their goal had been achieved. Their timetable for Indochina, the Pacific and the other countries had been set back, but only in terms of time. I hoped my country would not sacrifice the entire stakes merely because the opponent had raised the betting and the kibitzers were screaming, "Fold!"

My desire to go home was strong, but the repulsion I felt toward their being the ones to grant my freedom was even stronger. I knew Mafia was pushing to get statements which would compromise me in the eyes of my contemporaries and commit me to the support of the revolution. Major Bay had stated that the Front realized "that an American serviceman would be severely punished by his government for violating the Code of Conduct, but he could rely on the support of the

peace- and justice-loving people of America to support him."
The entire undercurrent of their efforts seemed to be based on
the concept that an American soldier, if he could be coerced
or led into violating the Code of Conduct, would be punished
by the government and once punished would be alienated from
the military and the government. He could then be exploited
by groups within the United States which simply opposed our
presence in Vietnam, or which actually supported the Vietcong.
Either way, the individual would become a valuable propaganda tool right within the U.S.

The desire to escape was still simmering. In the back of my
mind. The aircraft overhead would provide me with a greater
chance of reaching friendly forces than at any time in the past
and I began to formulate a plan to beat Mafia to the punch. I
didn't know if he could successfully extract the statements he
wanted from me or edit what he had, but an escape would
invalidate anything he could do. I had bought time by bending
with him where I could without compromising my beliefs and
damaging my country's cause, but the time had been gained
in order for me to take some positive action on my own.

The immediate physical reaction induced by recalling the
correction period in the Salt Mines set in as before, and I spent
two horrible days trying to suppress it. I remembered a quotation from something I had read in the past: "The world is not
interested in the storms you encountered, but did you bring the
ship in." I had gotten this far and I wouldn't bend any more.
I knew after Tan Phu that I was still right in my beliefs, my
course of action was clear and with the Lord's help I would
be able to "bring the ship in."

This thought of escaping had shielded me against the temptation to seek release, but I caught myself slipping into the
trough of acceptance of the idea that I was going home for
certain. On one day when the diarrhea and recurrence of salt
repulsion teamed up to undo what I had thought to be consid-
erable spiritual strength against physical weakness and pain, I
found myself leaning toward the idea of a safe, quick release
and freedom from this environment. I noted in my diary at that
point: "... in case a quick decision is made by the Central
Committee and I move out. I feel it is close, hope it is close,
get it over with and get started on Leavenworth [prison] time—
might be able to get married when I'm 40 or 45—what a way

to spend a life." In this short period of time I slipped from a state of determination and reliance on prayer to an almost frantic struggle to maintain the course I had set. Disease and the gentle coercion of the system were working on me and in my efforts to fulfill my plan, I seemed to bring disaster down around my head. Everything went bad.

Mafia returned with his rewritten version of what I had said at the press conference. He had lifted comments out of context, edited and inserted, and created a perfect example of the line he had worked so long to get me to parrot. I read the statement to myself, shuddering inwardly as I realized that this was not the final version. If he could get me to agree to claim this as my own, then I would be on the merry-go-round and he could refine it further, make its condemnations even more violent, and use the promised release as bait to keep me accepting and repeating anything he brought in. Once committed, I would have to stay committed or lose any hope for release. I cursed the weakness that had made me look to them for my freedom and even consider release. "Your release, sooner or later..." And it could be later, depending on how far he wanted to push me.

After a session that ran from early morning to near midnight with only a short break for me to return to my hut and cook supper rice, I had managed to delete Mafia's additions and unscramble my earlier comments to the point that the statement was no longer recognizable as Mafia's. He had a new National tape recorder and what he finally obtained was a close approximation of my original comments with every conceivable error in grammar and diction I could think to make. There was no doubt in my mind that he was angry, but he didn't show it. I felt like a fish on the end of a line; and he was playing me, reeling me in, but not too fast to break the line. He told me to go back to my hut.

The guards' attitude slipped to neutral, although I was still allowed to go to the canal intersection to catch fish. The mental conflict was building and I sought to eliminate it through what became a disastrous attempt to escape. I was hurling myself at the green wall that surrounded me, trying to break through before it closed in on me.

I was allowed to use the camp boat to check my stakeouts and decided to try to make a bold move, taking the boat as if

399

to pick up fish and continuing on along the canal until I reached canal twenty, the east-west route. Once on canal twenty, I would pole as fast as possible until I either had to abandon the boat or reached the river, which I had identified as the key to getting out of this area. There was a good chance that because of the air activity, there would be no VC on the canals and with free travel I might even be able to wave in an aircraft. Once I was identified as an American, a helicopter would certainly be dispatched to pick me up. If no aircraft appeared, I could travel down the river until I reached Thoi Binh. It was the same basic idea as in 1965, after I got to the river.

I asked permission to check my stakeouts and got a sleepy "*Ua*" from Miss Mouse in the guards' hut. Within minutes I was poling past my stakeouts en route to canal twenty. There was a knot of fear in my stomach as I turned eastward on the wider canal, its banks covered with vegetation despite the fire during dry season. The fast-growing reeds had sprung back and they grew in abundance in scattered patches. The canal was clear as far as I could see and I took a deep breath, thinking of the five or so kilometers I had to cover before I reached the river. I strained to hear or see an aircraft.

I poled for about thirty minutes with my nerves tightening each passing minute, each passing meter. I was passing the point of no return where it would be impossible to turn back or to explain my actions, and I found myself wishing I had taken time to plan this out rather than jumping into it in near desperation. The river seemed to be a thousand miles away and this would be the one day that the L–19's stayed home! I was cursing my luck and stupidy when suddenly my neck tingled in fear! Voices! Another boat on the canal! I looked to both sides of the canal and saw a solid wall of reeds. I couldn't break into them without making noise and leaving a clear trail. The boat floating empty in the canal after I abandoned it would be a sure giveaway. Oh shit! What a stupid son of a bitch! I cursed, my mind whirling as I sought some escape.

I glanced down on the flooring of the boat and my glance fell on a discarded stakeout line and hooks, abandoned by some guard. I jammed the pole into the muddy bottom of the canal, forcing the boat against the bank, and quickly crouched, grabbing the line with trembling fingers, straightening it and reaching to break off a reed just as the other boat came up on me.

There was a startled gasp as I was identified as a POW. I turned my head, trying to appear calm as if there were nothing out of the ordinary in my being there. Cheeta and Porky stood fixed in their boat, their faces unbelieving. *"Ro lam gi day?"* Cheeta snapped out—What are you doing here, Ro? I tried to control my voice, but there was a catch in my throat before I finally managed to blurt out, "I'm putting out stakeouts," holding up the line for them to see. "No!" Cheeta declared emphatically, using one of the few English words he knew. I felt like vomiting, I was so scared.

Cheeta had picked up his submachine gun from the bottom of the boat. "Why are you so far from the camp?" he asked in Vietnamese.

"There are no fish near the camp and I was trying to catch more fish to sell," I answered, constructing an alibi as I went. "There was no one on this canal and I thought I could try to put stakeouts along here."

Cheeta questioned immediately, "Who gave you permission to come here?"

I considered saying that Miss Mouse in his stupor had answered in the affirmative when I had asked, assuming it was just to use the boat. I realized that there had been other guards in the hut and they would have heard me. "No one. I decided to do it after I found my hooks bare at the other place and came out here immediately after."

Porky asked, "How many stakeouts did you put out?"

My mind was racing as I tried to remember how many of the guards' stakeouts I had noticed in passing. "I was using *Anh Giai Phong*'s stakeouts and I don't recall how many." I could see myself rapidly becoming entangled in this impossible story and wished I could have taken a few minutes to cover myself for this eventuality.

Cheeta told me to pole the boat back to camp and I found myself on the way back to the cage with the two guards behind me. They talked in low tones all the way back, but I was unable to make out what was said. I noticed that there were stakeouts all along the canal, some of them in the water, which was lucky for me. I constructed as plausible a story as I could in the time it took to reach camp, hoping I could talk my way out of the mess.

Once at the camp I was taken to my cage and locked inside

401

while Cheeta and Porky conferred with the other guards. It seemed hopeless at this point and I wondered what Mafia would do now.

There was no time lost as the guards decided that I had, at the very least, seriously violated camp regulations and possibly tried to escape. There was enough doubt created by Porky's verification that I had been putting out a stakeout when they found me and other stakeouts were along the canal, but not enough to clear me completely. Killer Mouse left to report to the cadre while Base and Cheeta came down to my cage. That night began a repeat of the correction period I endured in the Mines, with the addition of Base's personal efforts to make the punishment as unbearable as possible. This time there was no way in the world I could find strength enough to smile at him.

Only my denial of attempting to escape and contention that it would be foolish to attempt escape when release was imminent convinced them of my sincerity and the correction period ended. I hadn't tried to hold out this time. There was nothing to prove by enduring and fighting when they controlled the physical conditions. A cadre came in to explain to me why the guards had been forced to punish me and that I should accept it as correction, not punishment. I was assured that the Front would forgive me for my misdeed, since I had recognized it, and that I could still be released if I showed a good attitude from this time on. I knew that Mafia had a bigger lever to use on me now that I had made my attempt and failed. I only hoped I could find the strength and determination and intelligence to make my next attempt successful.

The guards made superficial efforts to erase the memory of the events. I was again allowed to put out stakeouts, but with a guard present at all times. There was justifiable distrust by the guards, but their orders were apparently to keep me clinging to the promise of release, psychologically prepared for Mafia. I took advantage of every freedom and resumed my efforts to build my strength. I would keep myself in condition to react should an opportunity arise which would allow me to escape, even though I couldn't devise a way myself.

The English-speaking Cholon native came into the camp and spent several hours each day talking with me about Marx, Lenin and Mao Tse-tung. I was startled at his open discussion of Communism when the cadre had been so careful to avoid any mention of it with POW's. I was also interested in the praise given to Mao by this member of the NLF and wondered if other ethnic Chinese within the structure of the Vietnamese Communist movement likewise paid allegiance to Mao rather than to Ho Chi Minh. He pursued the "world revolution" theme at great length, saying he looked forward to visiting the United States after the revolution destroyed the base of capitalism and imperialism. I questioned his understanding of capitalism and got a vague reply which indicated only the textbook-supplied answers. As an attempt to perhaps establish a few of the commendable points about capitalism, I showed him a diagram I had used to explain to Chinh and Cheeta, earlier in the year, a simple capitalistic enterprise devoted to producing a better rat trap. The reaction was the same as with the other guards: "There can be nothing good about capitalism. It oppresses the working class." I couldn't explain to him that our "oppressed working class" in America lived better than the working class in any of the Communist countries and he left, unalterably convinced that he was right.

I had been given several baby cranes to feed for the guards and had watched them develop from ungainly, long-legged creatures covered with a bluish down into extremely graceful birds, with their curved necks and beautiful black-tipped gray-blue feathers. Once the cranes were fat enough to eat, the guards began killing them for meals and giving me a small portion of the prepared meat. I hadn't become as attached to these birds as I had with my Herc and Ajax, but the guards' executions aroused a deep sense of remorse and empathy in me. I first heard the pitiful cries of one of the cranes and thought they were killing it before picking and gutting it. As the screeches continued I walked along the poles until I could see Base holding a live, vainly struggling bird, with its feet securely trussed, as he pulled its feathers out, a handful at a time. A delighted audience of younger guards chattered their approval of Base's actions until the bird finally lay exhausted, too weak to protest, making only tiny noises in its throat as the torture continued.

I had seen other senseless cruelty toward animals when the guards had played with one of the pups holding the kicking, squirming little creature underwater until it ceased to struggle, then pulled it out, revived it, and repeated the process. They laughed and joked among themselves as the puppy fought drowning with all its strength, and they repeated the cruel game until the animal was too weak to resist. I wondered again what twisted part of human nature fed itself on the suffering of a dumb animal.

Over a period of days, the attitude of the guards toward me seemed to slip back to the pseudo-congeniality that had existed before my attempt to leave the area with their boat and I began to relax slightly. The relief was short-lived, however. I was called to a meeting in the guards' mess hall one morning just after I had finished my rice. Killer Mouse was unusually antagonistic in ordering me to wear my best set of black pajamas to meet with the cadre of the Front. I anticipated Mafia and was apprehensive enough, but upon entering the hut I saw not only Mafia, but Sauser, Muoi and an older man in his late fifties sitting at the head of the table. All the guards from the immediate area were gathered, and instead of the thought of word of a release, I felt a wall of animosity from the assembled group.

Mafia told me to sit on the floor at the near end of the table, facing the older man and flanked by guards and cadre. My position was below the level of the table and I had to stretch slightly to look up at the cadre, placing him at a psychological as well as physical advantage. There was silence as the older man studied my face. Mafia stared at a sheaf of papers in his hand, his face set, eyes hard and unblinking.

The now-familiar feeling of tension spread through my body as I wildly tried to diagnose the atmosphere. What in the hell were they up to now? What had I done? Could it be a repercussion from the boat incident or from the tape I had fouled up? I could feel the perspiration beginning on my back and the cold prickling fear at the base of my neck.

Finally the old man spoke in a slow, precise voice, enunciating each word and cutting every sound sharply. Mafia translated into English. "I am a representative of the Central Committee, having come to this camp to say a few words to you." His voice was easily identifiable as one accustomed to command. "It is fortunate for us that the peace- and justice-loving friends of the South Vietnam Front for National Liberation in America have provided us with information which leads us to believe you have lied to us."

My throat constricted. There was a violent wrenching in my stomach as the impact of his words slammed into me. He paused, watching me as I fought to keep my face immobile. The eyes of the guards, Muoi's eyes, Sauser's eyes all seemed to be focusing and boring into mine. Mafia handed him the papers, sheets of typed onionskin paper. He put on a pair of metal-framed glasses and began to read.

"According to what we know, you are not an Engineer. You are not assigned to the many universities which you have listed for us. You have much military training which you deny. The location of your family is known. You were an officer of the American Special Forces. Your father's name is Lee and your mother's name is Florence." I felt myself cringing inwardly as my carefully constructed cover story came crashing down around me. The words became a blur of sound. He was picking me to pieces.

"Oh dear, God, I'm scared. God, I'm scared." I fought to control the trembling in my bent knees, fought to mask the effect that piece of paper was having on me. He wasn't guessing. He knew! I tried to remember the points he attacked, so I could try to build some sort of answer, but there was no way to cover all of them.

He handed the paper back to Mafia and removed his glasses. Again he studied my face, watching for some show of emotion. I was biting the inside of my cheek to keep from reflecting the turmoil that rocked back and forth inside of me. "You can realize the seriousness of your misdeed. You have not displayed sincerity toward the Front which has shown you lenient treatment. You must consider the consequences for your actions." I was trying to close my mind to the possibilities of what he could do. There was no light for me anywhere, no path to follow now. I could only sit quietly and listen.

He continued, "Your actions are foolish no matter what you do we will succeed in the final tally. You have provided us with additions to a map of the Huyen Su post in 1964, which were false. Even though we were forced to delay our attack until May 20, 1966, in order to determine the falsehood of the barriers you drew, our attack was victorious and the post was razed to the ground. You can surely realize that no effort of yours will affect our march to final victory." I had a brief surge of relief. My screwed-up additions to the map had done some good, even if they hadn't fouled Charlie up completely.

He turned to Mafia and then back to me. "Mr. Hai has recently reported to the Committee of your visit to the liberated zones to see the reality of the American crimes in our country and the hatred of the people for the aggressor. The Committee took great trouble to allow you to travel among the people and wished for you to see the truth, but your latest crime is of great magnitude and must be considered." There was nothing but the occasional cry of a bird in the forest as the old man paused once more. I waited, wishing he'd go ahead and tell me what they were going to do to me. Don't make me sweat it out!

"Go back to your hut now." Mafia spoke. No one moved as I arose stiffly and walked out of the hut. The poles seemed to waver under my feet and I felt light-headed as I proceeded slowly back to the kitchen. My whole small, miserable world had just collapsed in a mind-crushing heap.

That night there was no word from the guard as he locked my leg irons and the cage door. I lay there, wishing I had someone to talk to, thinking back over the old man's words. Who in the hell would give them the information on me? Where could they have gotten it by themselves? He had to be lying about someone at home sending the biographical data on me! An American wouldn't do that to one of his own people. God only knew, it was tough enough being a POW without someone in the States dumping a load of crap like that on your head. Could anyone be misguided enough to actually help these VC? I thought about the reports I had heard over Radio Hanoi about the "peace- and justice-loving people of America" who were protesting the war.

I could understand opposition to a war and a strong desire for peace. There was nobody who wanted peace more than a soldier because it was his life that was sacrificed in war, his blood that was shed. There couldn't be a protester at home who matched a soldier's sincere desire for peace. Dissent was a part of American life, but to support the enemy at the expense of another American was inconceivable. There was no other place the VC could have gotten some of that information except from the United States and I suddenly felt very sick.

No one spoke to me for several days except for answering my requests to go to the latrine or to check my nets at the camp canal. I was no longer allowed to go to the intersection and my fish supply dropped off rapidly. The diarrhea built up and

I had to begin pushing more rice to maintain the level of strength I had achieved. Beri-beri appeared to be setting in again as I noticed my face and abdomen beginning to swell slightly. The situation was becoming critical and they hadn't even punished me yet.

Mafia visited the camp in early December and I spent several hours with him in the mess hut. He told me that he had interceded for me with the Central Committee and had mentioned the progress I had made over the past few months as evidence of my new attitude. He encouraged me to help myself by helping him prove to the Committee that I was sincere. I naïvely asked what I had to do. He produced the declaration that I had seen so often in the past years with my compromised cover story lined through. "You can tell me the truth of yourself on this paper. It will show your sincerity in correcting your past mistake." I looked at the paper carefully, recalling the items the old man had definitely nailed down and the ones he had hinted at knowing. I asked how much time I would have and Mafia assured me I could write as long as necessary to answer completely. I took the paper, thinking I could figure out something to do. Mafia was pleased and told me to have a cup of tea with him. The relief was almost overwhelming as this first crack appeared in the wall that had confronted me.

In the next few days, the guards' attitudes once again became relatively pleasant and I had a breathing space. I analyzed the activities and saw the pattern emerging through all the smoke. They were working to get the exact statements and declaration from me that were required to fulfill their propaganda requirements. My value as a living POW after five years of captivity must have been quite high and if they could finally get what they wanted it would be a substantial coup. I knew that the U.S. government realized I was alive because Dan, John and Jim had reported it, so there was no way for the VC to deny my presence. They had to get something. I could guess how far they would go to achieve their ends. Mafia obviously felt the year by myself was the answer and was closing the gates on me one by one.

I took advantage of the guards' eating habits to keep myself informed on what was happening. They would spend at least forty minutes together in their mess hut each meal, leaving me alone in the area between their sleeping hut and the mess hut.

I had periodically gone to their sleeping hut during their absence and leafed through the papers they kept in a .30 cal. ammunition box. The papers pertained to camp administration, various orders and travel passes that came to the squad. By scanning the papers, I was able to determine roughly what action of major importance was pending.

Several days after Mafia's visit, I was quickly checking the new papers in the box and found one that immediately caught my eye. My name was on it! I read the heading and saw that it had come from "Phong Chinh Tri Mien," the political office of the zone, and was directed to A5B, T520, this squad. I scanned the words, trying to decipher the meaning of the sentences relating to me. *"Sang chuyen"*—to transfer. *"Ban dan dich van"*—enemy and civilian proselyting section. I was to be transferred from this camp to, or into the reponsibility of, the Enemy and Civilian Proselyting Section at Zone! Transfer to the higher headquarters from this camp at this particular time meant that the resources to deal with me at this level had been exhausted and I was scheduled to move to the Zone where the decision of my living or dying could be made. This order to move me had been given recently, after my confrontation with the old man. I replaced the paper and went back to my hut, wondering what I could possibly do to get myself out of this. At Zone I could expect to give them what they wanted or face execution.

There was no hint of the impending change reflected in the guards' behavior; if anything, they became friendlier and seemingly happier. Had I not spent years watching the mercurial changes in attitude, based primarily on the dictates of the cadre, I would have found myself being lulled into another false sense of security. The ever-present temptation to "cooperate and graduate" might have appeared as a possible course of action, but there was no way for me to rationalize the slightest support to these people.

Killer Mouse was the best indication of the actual feelings of the guards as he came down to fulfill his required minutes of inane chatter. After being mildly ignored he seemed to lose his childish temper and snapped out as he left, *"Ro sau lam! Toi noi rang Mat Trang sap phat. Hieu?"*—Rowe, you are very bad! I tell you that the Front is about to punish you. Do you understand?

I understood all too well and wasn't planning on staying

around for the coming events. In this period of increasing stress, I found myself turning to almost a total dependence on prayer for solace and strength. I had forgotten it for a short while and had found myself floundering as I sought a way out of the maze. Now I was again trusting that "the Lord is my shepherd; I shall not want." With that foundation, I was working to make an escape in early January, prior to a move by the VC. I had selected the trail I had used in my second attempt as an initial route and had gotten away from the camp long enough on two wood carrying details to prepare a "Malayan Gate," the vicious, spike-tipped sapling, tied horizontal to the ground, bent back sharply next to a path, and triggered by a trip string across the path. When an unwary pursuer hit the trip string, the sapling would be released and sweep in a deadly arc across the path, impaling the man on the sharpened stakes tied to the sapling.

This attempt would be an all-out effort and if it required killing guards, I was willing to do it. I had reached the point where I could not afford to be recaptured and the death or serious injury of one or more of the guards would deter the younger ones sufficiently to improve my chances.

I continued to prepare myself physically and to plan in detail for the escape until the night of 14 December, when my ill fortune struck again. The guards told me to pack my belongings for a move to a new camp! There had been indications of construction going on in the area, but I had hoped to escape before the completion of whatever was being built. Had I been able to wait two more weeks, the water would have been low enough for me to undertake my escape plans.

I was blindfolded, tied, and placed in the bottom of a boat for a two-hour ride in circles throughout the area. Porky and Miss Mouse poled the boat into canals and back out of the same canals, backtracked, and generally did their best to disorient me.

Finally we stopped and I was untied and the blindfold was removed. I could see nothing except long tree trunks, cut for construction, floating in the narrow canal. Sparse overhead tree cover and blackened tree trunks indicated that this area had been partially burned off by the fire. Porky led me to a tiny cage, some twenty-five meters from the canal, and told me to prepare for sleep. This was my new home. I could see no other huts in the immediate area although guards' voices were coming from a short distance away. After my irons were locked and the cage door was fastened with wire, I was alone. This had been the worst of the series of bad breaks. My chance to escape, the route I had planned, all the preparations had been compromised. I couldn't even tell where the river was from here. There had to be some reason for this! I prayed for help because I had just about reached the limits of what I could do alone. "He maketh me to lie down in green pastures; He leadeth me beside the still waters."

The next morning I took my first look around and saw that my cage was an isolated hut, freshly built and watched over by a guard hut some twenty-five meters away. Nothing else was visible except trees and scrub brush. The muddy ground showed paths trampled through the patches of reeds where the guards had dragged the construction poles, indicating more huts somewhere near, but unseen. Porky and Killer Mouse came by and told me I would cook and sleep in the same hut. There was enough room for my mosquito net, but not for a fireplace, so I built a small raised log platform just outside the door where I could cook if it wasn't raining. There was no latrine and the canal was shallow and muddy, meaning that sanitation was going to be a problem. All indications were the guards weren't interested in providing anything except security. I wondered if they already had orders to hold me for a specified time before I was to be turned over to the people at Zone. They certainly weren't making any effort to build my strength or health, so the chance that I was to be seen by anyone on the outside was nil. It was a dismal picture of what was coming and I could only pray that the good Lord had something in store for me over which Charlie had no control.

Miss Mouse brought me a white dove in a wire fish trap that had been bent into a sort of cage. "*Anh Giai Phong* gives you this bird to feed. The people contributed it to *Anh Giai Phong* as a gift and you will take care of it." I took the wide-eyed creature and put him inside the hut after discarding the wire basket. I was tired of seeing things in cages. I named my little peace dove "Stokely" and soon had him accustomed to his new home. He was content to sit and eat grains of rice, cooing occasionally, but apparently not geared to anything more strenuous than an infrequent wing stretch and gaping yawn. We became fast friends as he was better company than any of the guards.

410

9

THE MORNING OF 11 DECEMBER WAS LIKE A LOT OF OTHER mornings. The cold mist, left from last evening's rainstorm, clung to the trees. Porky had unlocked my leg irons while it was still quite dark. It had been about an hour or so, before the first rays broke through, gilding the upper leaves. Down below the gray shadows remained much longer. I noticed the guards wearing their new trousers and shirts as they walked along the poles from their sleeping hootch, toward the mess hut. They carried their weapons with them, so evidently there would be no one in the hootch. The younger ones were laughing. I recalled that this would be the day they celebrated the dual birthday of the National Liberation Front and the Liberation Armed Forces, and an air raid drill the day before hadn't dampened the enthusiasm. I squatted idly by the door, slapping mosquitoes and watching the small birds flitting through the reeds, searching for insects. My bare-assed dove had been having a great deal of trouble balancing since the crows had plucked his tail feathers. He was concentrating on the broken rice grains on the bottom of his bamboo palace. Eating was a chore when he had to pick at grains below him.

I could hear the revolutionary songs and scraps of speeches down at the new forum. There must have been a gathering of the whole alphabet from this part of MR III, judging from the noise and singing. New Ba's voice carried, and Mom M's high, sharp tenor reached through the trees clearly enough to make my little dove cringe.

411

I glanced through the trees at my patch of sky. The morning blue was broken by broad streamers of white clouds. It looked as if we would have a good day. The rain clouds had cleared, at least temporarily, and the sun would dry things out. I would take a walk down to the canal in a couple of minutes, I decided. Maybe a destroyer had docked overnight, and I could hitch a ride to San Francisco.

I had turned my attention back to Stokely, taking a few of the grains and holding them up for him to peck comfortably, when my spine turned to ice. There was a brief whistling sound that was all too familiar. As the thunder of bombs rocked the forest, I dropped to the mud below my cage, wondering where they were coming from, and at the same time not really caring. They seemed to be everywhere. The sound was a continuous, growing beat as the bombs walked across the forest. I glanced upward, seeing nothing, but the thought was there: B–52's! Then the sound became more distinct, the concussion slamming into the foliage around me. My cage was shaking and the mud seemed to quiver within itself. By this time my mind was reacting. Grab your stuff and bug! This place is going to get creamed and you'd better be down the canal watching, rather than in this seat!

I had no sooner thrown my few belongings into the pack when Porky came past the cage, his face a study in panic.

"Di, Ro!" He cried. *"*DI, DI!*"* His voice was quivering as he glanced to the east where the bombs were continuing their inescapable march toward us.

I glanced at Stokely huddled in the bottom of his cage and decided to try to carry him. If the camp got hit, it would be a sure death, and even though he'd probably be better off, I didn't want to leave the little fellow. Porky saw me reaching for the bird, and grabbed my wrist.

"Bo no di!" he yelled. Leave him!

The other guards were streaming past, paying no attention to the two of us. Only the equipment they could grab at a run was on their backs, and their intention of getting as far away as possible was not at all influenced by Mr. Sau's commands to get the rest of the equipment and boats. I turned and followed the backs of the guards out of the camp toward the canal just as the bombs ceased. The echoes caromed from horizon to horizon.

As I followed Porky, I looked up through the trees and saw, for a brief second, the sleek sweptback wings of three B–52's as they turned away from the bombing pass. They had been above the clouds; hence we had neither heard nor seen them when the bombs came.

Their first pass had been to the east, moving toward us. The bomb zone appeared to be slightly to the north, and had stopped just short of the camp. The camps to our east had, no doubt, been wiped out under the impersonal pounding of hundreds of 750-pound bombs. The big question in my mind was the second pass. If they continued to bomb along the first strip, extending it to the west, it would be possible for us to be on the fringe of the zone and escape death. However, if they chose to make the second pass south of, and parallel to, the first, widening the bomb zone, there was no place for us to go. The next run would go right over the top of us.

By that time we were one jostling, scrambling mass in the canal. Some of the guards were in one of the boats with sacks of rice, while others pushed the boat, waist-deep in the canal. Still others, like myself, made their way along the bank, sacrificing the open water in the canal for faster travel through the reeds along the slight bank. Mr. Sau was nowhere in sight, although most of the guards were in this confused exodus.

Ri, Porky and Mr. T.D. were in front of me, and Miss Mouse immediately behind. Porky turned as we broke a path through the thick reeds.

"Ro," he gasped, "Anh Giai Phong asks you for information." His pseudo-formality was almost funny.

"Ask, Anh Giai Phong," I replied, equally winded.

"How long before the bombs begin again?" His face was intent and we were equals for a moment. Those were my planes and Anh Giai Phong needed some fast answers to a question the cadre had assured him would never arise.

I answered as we continued to push through the reeds, "They will be back in ten or fifteen minutes. We must move quickly."

"Where will they drop bombs the second time?" he asked.

"They'll extend the first line or they can drop beside it to make a second path. We must get as far to the south as possible before they come back," I replied, trying to get that last idea over to him.

Porky yelled to Ri to move out faster, after which the group with the boat seemed to realize what had been said and exerted additional effort themselves. There was some muttering among them of ditching the boat and coming back for it later, if there was anything left. I could detect the pessimism creeping in. I noticed for the first time an L–19 circling lazily to the south, out of range of the B–52's, but able to observe movement in the area. Then the sound of fighters and choppers became more distinct.

"O Lord, please be with me now." I prayed. "This is going to be nasty. Please get me through it." I began to think of dying, and how simple it would be. The bombs could solve a lot of problems. I hoped my little dove and the dumb cranes wouldn't suffer. As for the humans, it was up to us how we met death, and I promised myself that if I saw it coming, I'd meet it face on. I wouldn't die cringing and hiding. The thought of making it through was little more than a wish at the moment, but with a request in to the good Lord, I felt my chances were better than anyone else's in the group.

The L–19 had a friend behind us to the north. It looked as if they were screening the bomb zone to pick off anyone trying to escape the B–52's. Damn American efficiency, I cursed. How about giving a guy a chance? I thought I saw a flight of F–100's orbiting to the south, but couldn't be certain. If the B–52's didn't get us, those fighters would be all over this area like fur on a bear.

The guards were becoming tired, and wide-eyed glances upward and to the east were more frequent. I caught myself straining to hear the whispered roar of the jet engines.

"Where in the hell are you?" I asked out loud. I could picture the crews of the bombers in their sterile world of instruments and switches, clean and well fed after a full night's sleep, flying this mission as if it were a Pan Am milk run. If you could only see what it's like down here! The thought of death being so impersonal was chilling. They glided thirty thousand feet above the mud, swamp, leeches and mosquitoes, not feeling the devastation their bombs caused. It suddenly was so unfair that death could come from an environment so far removed from that in which the dying occurred.

The days in Tan Phu when I had watched airstrikes going in on the VC flashed through my mind. How I had cheered when I saw the columns of mud and water shooting skyward,

414

knowing that the enemy was dying; yet today I was under the bombs, and the picture was altogether different. The concept of man dying at the hands of another man in combat was something I accepted as part of this hell we humans had created for ourselves. To die at the hands of another man when he and I were matched against one another equally was an inherent risk in the profession of arms, but to be the victim of a computer that I could neither see nor challenge was the ultimate frustration. If machines only killed other machines, the balance would once again be achieved.

I heard the sound, soft, ominous, high to the east, and my stomach knotted. I felt my spine tingle and it was as if my heart froze between beats. "O dear Lord God, please be with me."

The whistle, and then the throbbing blast shattered the calm. It was like being inside a kettledrum and having someone pound on it. The concussion was a series of sharp blows to my chest. My ears pulsated with each shock wave. The guards stood like statues, each face reflecting the terror inside the man.

I strained to see through the trees toward the east. Were the bombs going to get us? I could see the columns of mud and shattered trees climbing skyward, then falling back to earth, meeting other columns as they rose. The bombs continued their inexorable march. The guards were flat on the mud now, some of them digging frantically with their hands, trying to mold themselves into the earth. The young guards' eyes were huge and empty, panic had paralyzed their minds. "Mouse III," a fourteen-year-old, was whimpering deep in his throat, the sound penetrating the roar of the bombs because of its strangeness. Ri and Porky huddled behind two larger trees, their shoulders hunched in resignation. The boat floated empty and forgotten at the edge of the canal.

Watching the guards I found myself suddenly calmer. If I can't do anything else, came the decision, I'll be brave. "Stand, you son of a bitch!" I almost shouted it to myself. "You're going to die standing up!" If it was the last thing those guards saw in their lives, it would be the American standing tall, not cringing and hiding!

God, they were close, I held onto a tree trunk to stay upright. I squinted my eyes against the constant sharp slap of concussions, my ears throbbed, my stomach was knotted inside itself.

415

"Stand, damn it, stand!" I fought the urge to curl up. My bladder felt like it would burst, as if the body was straining to void itself.

I glanced down at Ri and Porky. Ri's eyes were on me, his mouth hanging open. He gestured rapidly for me to get down. A surge of elation went through me. One of them had seen that I was standing! I shook my head at him and managed a smile. "*Khong so*," I yelled to him—No sweat.

The ground, mud, water, trees, the whole world was quivering and recoiling from the battering of tons of explosives. I could feel my knees buckling inward and forced them straight once again. looking back along the canal toward the camp, I watched with horrified fascination as the bombs threw a towering wall of uprooted trees and mud high into the air, obscuring the rest of the canal. They had missed us! They passed north of us and we were safe! O Lord, thank you! Thank you!

I felt suddenly weak and drained. My face was covered with perspiration and the quiver in my legs was almost uncontrollable. I sat down heavily at the base of the tree, drawing my shaking knees up into my chest, and gripping them tightly with my arms. I'm still alive, I thought. I'm still alive! But so what? All this means is I have another chance to die. Why can't I just die and get it over with? No! I'm not going to die!

I found myself staring at a dragon fly that had perched on my elbow. The translucent film of his wings reflected weak sunlight as he flexed them up, and down. "You're lucky, little fellow. You're so damn lucky to be a dragonfly."

The L–19's were circling closer now that the B–52's had finished. I bet they'd have the F–100's to clean up anything the bombers missed. I wondered if the camp had been hit. Where were Sauser and the rest? Can I shake the guards and signal one of our aircraft? The L–19 was out; I'd tried that before, and this would be even riskier since the strike had gone in. Anything they spotted moving down here would get worked over. If only I could get near a chopper.

Minutes later, after I had been placed in the boat, I could hear the jets somewhere to the southeast; it was just a question of when the L–19 found a suitable target. The guards were pushing rapidly, attempting to put distance between us and the camp. Base stumbled and fought his way along in the waist-deep water, refusing offers to put the machine gun in the boat. "*Anh Giai Phong* will not surrender this weapon, even to rest!"

416

Base proclaimed to an unappreciative audience. Ri glanced back at him quizzically, then resumed his pushing.

Suddenly the L–19 cut his engine! Our group froze in place. I could hear the prop windmilling as the plane nosed down. The pilot or observer had spotted something and was lining up to fire a smoke marking round. I searched in the direction I had last heard the plane, but could see nothing through the trees. Base cut quickly to the bank and crouched in a patch of reeds. Porky and Ri sank to their shoulders in the water, their eyes scanning the sky. *Whoosh!* The rocket was on its way. Once again I felt the icy clamp fit around my spine, and the involuntary hunching of neck and shoulders. We waited.

Ka-whump! That son of a bitch! He's using H.E.! The high explosive rocket detonated several hundred meters to our rear, near the camp we had vacated. Immediately after the rocket was fired, the pilot threw the throttle to the firewall, and with the engine roaring, pulled out of the dive and banked to survey the results of his rocket. As he circled the camp I got a close look at the plane between branches of the overhead trees. There couldn't be enough camouflage to prevent him from seeing us, I thought. If he's using H.E., we don't have a chance. I only hope he's found someone back at the camp and clobbers them. Whatever he does, let him leave us alone!

Porky and Ri snapped commands at the young guard, and the boat was secured against the bank. Reeds were broken to cover the boat, and everyone sat unmoving, except for heads and eyes watching the L–19 wheel and turn overhead.

The L–19 cut again, this time in view. The nose dipped slightly. I could picture the pilot lining up the crosshairs on his sight, his gloved thumb poised above the firing button. A little more, just a little more, over those trees in the clearing. There it is! The boat in the canal by that hootch. Line it up. Wait and...Fire! The button is depressed! The ship rocks slightly as the rocket leaves the pod on the starboard wing. Push the throttle forward and pull back on the stick, banking around to watch the round strike. The trail of smoke drifting away from the path of the speeding projectile marks its progress.

Back on the ground the forest echoes with the dulled explosion. The first passes were to rattle the VC loose while he called for the F–100's. I watched as he made a tight circle and dropped his nose once again, the engine cut, the rocket fired.

417

Gunning and pulling out. This time a soft *Pomp!* as the marking round hit. Overhead, the jets circled and broke to make their first pass.

Two F–100's were diving on the patch of rising smoke amid the foliage. The first pass was a dry run as they identified the target. The two jets climbed out, turning sharply and diving back onto the area, their exhausts screaming. The first one pulled out, as a slender cylinder separated from the wing and arced downward toward the trees below. The first bomb had no sooner exploded than the second jet began its dive, released its bomb and pulled out. I watched almost with boredom as the fighters went through the familiar drill: bombs on the first two or three passes, rockets on the next two passes, then machine guns on the final two or three passes. The guards were relaxed after the target had been identified. It was the anticipation, watching the L–19 and wondering if you were going to be in the barrel. Once the jets came in, it was anticlimactic.

We traveled along until dark, passing the same canal twice, several times as Porky and Ri disagreed on turning points. Finally we came upon Sauser's boat, pulled to the side near a thicket of trees and reeds. Porky got out of the boat and, after a short talk with Miss Mouse, came back, telling Ri that I would be staying on the other side of the canal. This was a break, I thought. It would separate me from the guards, and there was no telling what might develop. Ri pushed the bow of the boat until it touched the opposite bank. I grabbed my pack and scrambled over the rice sacks and Mouse III to reach the bank. It was dark enough that I had difficulty seeing, but managed to flatten a small space in which to place my sleeping mat and tie my mosquito net.

It wasn't even near the break of dawn when Porky woke me the next morning as he unlocked my leg irons. I was stiff, cold and wet from the overnight dew that had penetrated the unprotected top of my mosquito net. I realized now how comfortable that cage of mine had been. Again the relativity of it all. Once things got worse, the previous situation seemed so much better.

While it was still dark we got in the boats and moved about two kilometers to a sparsely vegetated area that would have looked bare from an aircraft. There were sufficient reeds to provide camouflage, however, and I was told to prepare a spot for the day. I was not allowed to put up my mosquito net during the day, so sleep was difficult. I cleared a small circular area, bent the reeds back over the top of my spot, and sat down to await sunrise and warmth.

With the first ray of the sun came the drone of an L-19 from the south. There was apparently to be no letup in the air activity. I looked to the southeast and spotted the shape of the tiny observation plane silhouetted against the brilliant sunrise. His flight was unhurried but steady, as if he knew exactly where he was going and exactly what he would find.

The feeling of impotence was increased when I faced death at the hands of my own people, realizing the tremendous power that could be brought to bear. In combat, before my capture, I had had the ability to fight back. As a prisoner, I was greatly limited in how I could fight back against the guards and cadre. But this was a case where I couldn't have fought back, even if I had had a weapon, because those were my people up there. The thought of being killed by Americans was frightening. Frightening beyond the normal sense of the word.

Miss Mouse checked on me periodically during the morning, reminding me to stay out of sight and keep quiet. Once, a boat with an old man, his aged wife and one child came past. Mouse III immediately yelled for them to turn around and go back where they came from. The man replied, in a trembling voice, that there were members of the Liberation Army all around his house and he was afraid that the aircraft would bomb them. He was taking his family to a safer area. Mouse III replied sharply that this zone was closed to civilians because the Liberation Army had camps throughout. "You wise little shit," I thought. "You ought to be saying 'sir' to that old man. Just because someone told you that a black uniform and weapon made you *'Anh Giai Phong'* you think you're king shit! You claim that the people love the Liberation Army. Well, if it's composed of fifteen-year-old assholes like you who let the authority go to their young heads, that love is inspired by fear of that weapon you're carrying, not anything to do with the individual." I wished I could have told the old man to take his family and go wherever he damn well pleased. It was as much his country as theirs. Maybe more so. But I was just a POW and I'd learned to keep my mouth shut.

The old man seemed to ponder for a moment. His wife sat huddled in the bottom of the boat, her most prized possessions piled around her. The child, a little girl, peered fearfully at the guard from under the rag she had tied around her head. Miss Mouse joined Mouse III on the bank and ordered the old man to go back where he had come from. It must have been humiliating to that man to be forced to take his family back into an area of danger at the command of a youngster, forty years his junior, but he hesitatingly reversed his position in the boat and they glided out of sight.

A short time later Ri and Porky returned. I was placed in the bottom of the boat with my pack and covered with my sleeping mat, a poncho and the guards' equipment. It was to be a daylight move to a more remote location. Once under the poncho I discovered that it had been delightfully cool outside in comparison. I had dreaded the thought of being placed under a poncho since that claustrophobia-inspiring ride into this area in 1965. It was a battle to keep from tearing at the suffocating closeness of the imprisoning material. I forced myself to lie motionless, conserving the air and reducing the perspiration that would come if I struggled. The guards were agonizingly slow to move out. The sooner we moved, the sooner I could get out from under this cerecloth.

Finally I felt the boat rock as the guards boarded. Beads of sharply stinging moisture rolled into my eyes, resisting my efforts to blink them away. I tried to turn my head, but the packs wedged on either side prevented the slightest motion. I could feel the panic building as the air became stale and the naked sun beat down, turning my place of imprisonment into an oven. "*Anh Giai Phong,* I can't breathe."

The shock of a blow across my chest sent pain shooting through the top of my head. "*Dung noi!*" The words were almost lost in the roar in my ears—Don't speak! I started to rise, anger boiling over and eliminating caution. The second blow, this time with a blunt object like a rifle butt, slammed me back to the bottom of the boat. Porky was talking rapidly to Miss Mouse. I couldn't understand what he was saying. Someone sat on my chest even though I was unable to move anyway. Ri's voice came sharply through my agony, "Don't hit him again!" One of the Mice must have clobbered me. The second blow had caught me on the shoulder, and now my whole arm was numb. I lay quietly, the heat and closeness forgotten in the pain. Porky said something else and an edge of the poncho was raised slightly, admitting what felt like a breeze straight

420

from a refrigerator. The weight on my chest was removed as whoever it was shifted off of me. Porky's voice came softly by my head. "Don't speak. There are civilians on the canal." I just lay there inhaling the wonderful fresh air, waiting for the pain in my chest to ease up.

The boat stopped and voices called from somewhere to our left. Porky answered, and the sleeping mat was lifted off. The brilliant sunlight made me squint. I felt the air washing over me, refreshing me. Porky grabbed my pack and told me to get out of the boat quickly, indicating the bank next to us. I sat and froze as a sharp pain lanced through my chest, ricocheting off my rib cage. *"Mau di!"* Porky commanded—Move fast! I got to my knees and crawled to the bow, then stepped onto the bank, sinking into the mud and fighting to keep my feet. I grabbed the reeds, pulling myself into the thicker clump Porky had indicated.

My left arm felt as if it were asleep and proved useless as I struggled into a sitting position. The guards had already shoved the boat to the other bank and were piling their gear in the reeds. Sauser's voice encouraged them to hurry.

The days and nights ran together after that. Hiding in the patches of reeds during the day, moving several times between morning and night to avoid civilians, or airstrikes. Watching the increasing activity, both air and ground. There was the new sound of automatic weapons as fire fights erupted in the distance. Artillery was moved into range, bringing harassment and interdiction fire at all hours of the day and night. There were jets and helicopters hitting targets on all sides of us as the pressure was maintained. Another B–52 strike went in to the southeast of us. I cringed inwardly as the sound of the bomb detonations reached me. I wouldn't forget the twenty-second of December for a long time.

The guards and cadre became increasingly tense as the tempo of Allied attacks developed new intensity. Rice was running short and there was apparently no means of resupply, thus creating a severe problem. The importance of rice cannot be understated, for without it the VC cease to function. I gathered from the conversations that this area had been cut off, eliminating the possibility of moving out to another, safer area until the pressure was relieved.

The only bright point was Christmas. I found it difficult to develop any real exuberance, but as I wrote in my diary:

"25/12/68. My spirits today high even in present situation, w/ present AGPs [Anh Giai Phongs], under AGP attitude, primarily because I know that at home the family is together, my Godson is having a fine Christmas & the future is brighter than the present."

The night of 30 December we moved into a small side canal and set up a minuscule area in which to sleep. We were atop a low bank, formed by the mud dug from the canal years before and now covered with the same cattail and bamboo reeds that covered the fields on both sides of the canal. I cleared an area just large enough for my mosquito net and tied the corner strings to upright bunches of bamboo. Miss Mouse came by to lock my irons, after which Porky checked them and I went to sleep, my stomach growling because there had been no supper. The rice was so low that we had one meal a day.

It was a night of disturbed tossing and turning, as much as the leg irons would allow. My mind kept reviewing the deteriorating situation with all the nightmarish possibilities of approaching disaster flooding my subconscious. The guards, who had grudgingly provided for me the absolute necessities for survival during times when they had sufficient supplies and security for themselves, were now faced with the threat of extermination, and my value to them was decreasing as fast as the rice supply.

The order I had seen in their ammo-container file for me to be transferred from Region level to Zone effectively marked me for extinction. The prisoner exploitation organization at that high level would not spare me should I continue to resist as I had with the regional cadre. At Zone there was no pretense of "leniency and humanitarianism." There was a harsh, unyielding process of breaking a man. If the prisoner still refused to comply, it was tantamount to ordering his own execution—probably a politically expedient one at the VC's convenience, following the retaliatory pattern as in the case of Rocky and Ken Roraback. If he complied with requirements, he was of no further use to the Front and yet his release would be of negative propaganda value. He would then be allowed to die at his own speed, but no effort would be expended to help him survive. I was already in the channel after being moved out of the No-K Corral, and now, especially with this situation, there was no reason to hold me for the imminent execution except that the last order they had received was to do just that. I thanked God for their inflexibility. I hoped that there would be no hasty decision to get rid of me before I had a chance to at least try to escape.

It was still dark and cold when Porky unlocked my irons and took my rice cup. I sat shivering for a moment as I wiped my eyes clear and let my mind become oriented. The faint glimmer of a small fire brushed the thick reeds with an orange glow. I could hear the guards talking in low, complaining voices as they squatted around the fire warming themselves.

Miss Mouse pushed through the reeds separating his sleeping area from mine. *"Lay do!"* he spat out, thrusting the barely filled cup at me. *"Khong co do an"*—There is no food. That was obvious as I looked at the small chunks of dirty rock salt lying on top of the steaming rice. It won't be long before there is no rice, I thought. And shortly after that, there will be no Rowe, came the rejoinder from my mind.

The rice was gone almost before I tasted the first mouthful. Even the salt was delicious, although my thirst was increased tenfold. I sat for a moment as my stomach, reacting to the tiny portion of rice, poured its digestive juices into the carbohydrate mass, overwhelming it and then circulating over the stomach lining. The ache of hunger was magnified by the burning stomach acid. What I'd give for a piece of toast.

As daylight came, I saw that Miss Mouse had been sleeping about six feet from me, where he would have been able to detect any movement in my net. Porky and Ri were ten to fifteen feet beyond him, thus establishing a warning and protective setup where one guard would be close enough to my net to monitor my actions, while two more guards, stationed far enough away that I couldn't reach them without first having to go through Miss Mouse, acted as a backup element to reinforce the younger guard should I try anything. Base and Mr. T.D. were beyond Porky, their nets strung in a clump of scrawny young trees. Sauser and the twelve-year-old were on the other side of the impenetrable tangle of dense reeds and dead underbrush at the end of my net.

The older guards were cleaning their weapons after checking the camouflage of the area. Reeds were bent over the top of our sleeping spaces with vines and tree branches added to completely cover the cleared areas. I could hear Sauser giving Little Sau a lecture on the revolution. The familiar phrases, "the just cause of the revolution, *"chinh nghia,"* *"duong loi cua cach mang,"* "the correct path of the revolution," were hollow. They were the assertions and major premises of a movement that employed them to lend stature to what otherwise could be considered a group of revolutionary bandits and terrorists. It was significant to me that Little Sau, who had no background or experience from which to draw his own conclusions, would be strongly influenced by the teachings of a man dedicated to a political god, a man who would sever all basic relationships between family, religion and nationality to serve only his political masters. It seemed so wrong that the cadre had the privilege of warping a mind too young to protect itself against misconception; teaching a child that he had no father, no mother, no God, no loyalties except to the party and the state. The reduction and condemning of this child to the one-dimensional world of dialectic materialism and political servitude was, to me, more hideous than anything they could do to me.

My thoughts were interrupted when Mr. T.D. shouldered his way through the reeds by Miss Mouse's mat and tossed a crumpled grayish form down beside me. *"Anh Giai Phong* gives you back your dove," he said. "Care for it." I picked up the bedraggled little bare-assed dove I had thought dead. It managed a weak cooing sound as if in recognition, then dropped its head. The once gleaming white feathers were dirty and matted, the tiny breast reduced to little more than bone, but the little bird struggled to live, even though he should have been dead. There had probably been no rice for him since I left him on the twenty-second and what nourishment he had been able to obtain for himself was obviously insufficient. I tore open the top of a packet of rice I had saved months ago for emergency, and soaked the contents in water for a few minutes. I opened his beak and pushed rice grains in, one by one. Initially, he lay with his eyes closed, accepting the grains, but refusing to swallow; then he seemed to shudder slightly and began to swallow, slowly at first, increasing to the point that he was eating faster than I could feed him. I wasn't sure that I was accomplishing anything other than prolonging his agony, but if he was willing to try, so was I.

424

Minutes later he was lying on my pack, snuggled into the cloth warmed by a patch of early morning sunlight. I was cleaning my eating cup with a bunch of sword grass, attempting to remove some of the accumulated scum from canal-water washings, when I heard the sound of helicopters approaching. They were low and heading almost straight for us. My throat went dry even though the sound was a common one during the past days. I glanced around, trying to locate the guards. Miss Mouse was standing by his mat, the Mossin-Nagant in his right hand. Porky was shinnying up a low tree to observe the approaching choppers. Base had the machine gun and was fitting a magazine into place while Ri gathered up the packs and equipment. Sauser called for the guards to recheck the camouflage and to stay out of sight. Miss Mouse stepped into my area and rearranged the overhead foliage, making it worse than before, but satisfying the standing rule to alter anything the American had done in order to establish its imperfection. I stood up to check the location of the helicopters and was immediately told to sit down. The sound was louder now; I could distinguish at least two types of choppers from the engines.

Porky pointed and yelled that the ships were only a few kilometers away, apparently searching for targets. Miss Mouse was fidgeting nervously with his weapon as he strained to see through the reeds. He kept unlocking and locking the folding bayonet on the muzzle of the weapon as if it would provide some sort of defense against the threat. Ri and Mr. T. D. had gathered all the equipment and a small sack of remaining rice into a convenient pile at the base of Porky's observation tree, after which they fired questions at Porky about the location of the helicopters. The noise was becoming deafening as the ships circled a short distance to our south.

I could see a Huey circling high above the terrain while the other craft swept low, searching for targets. Porky slid down from the tree, choosing not to observe with the choppers so close. His voice rose in pitch as he excitedly told of the maneuvers executed by the lower-altitude ships. They were apparently "Cobras" and that meant this area was in for a bad day if they decided to work us over.

The piercing, foghorn-like sound of a mini-gun, the electronic multi-barreled machine gun, caused all heads to snap in its direction. The Cobras had found something! A second, short

425

burst was an indication that there was a valid target and the pilots were attacking. I could picture the impact of the hundreds of slugs that poured from the muzzle of the mini-gun in that brief instant of firing, and was glad I wasn't under them. Sauser appeared through the reeds, his khaki trousers rolled to his knees, pistol belt draped over his shoulder and document pouch under his arm. Little Sau splashed along behind him in the calf-deep water like a little puppy, carrying both of their packs and his prized carbine. Sauser glared at me as he passed. The shooting was upsetting him. Little Sau sloshed past, his trousers soaking, but with a proud little smile, apparently because he was allowed to carry Sauser's pack.

A new sound was evident, that of a smaller engine with a high RPM. It was a new one for me, so I stood again to attempt to identify its source. I no sooner stood up than I caught a glimpse of an oval-shaped body, long slender tail section and what looked like huge blades, all in olive-drab color, banking sharply and whizzing off to the south with its landing skids barely above the reeds. I stared in amazement, as the pilot turned the tiny craft on its side in another sharp bank and darted off in another direction. It looked like a rotary-winged hot rod, and the guy flying it either had more guts than anyone else alive or had shit for brains. Another of the little helicopters whizzed into my line of vision performing similar low-level acrobatics. Boy! I thought. You guys get any lower and you might as well get out and walk!

The guards had seen these new ships and were pointing, their comments accompanying the gestures a rapid flow of high-pitched consternation. Sauser studied the strike going in with an outward calm, but his right hand held near the back pocket of his trousers, the fingers twisting nervously in the fabric, betrayed him. He instructed the guards to maintain camouflage discipline, not to move out, and to refrain strictly from firing at the choppers. The last item was the first really sound decision Sauser had made, even though Base disagreed. Miss Mouse and Mr. T.D. were assigned to keep a constant eye on me while the other guards cached some of the equipment and divided the remaining gear into individual carrying loads. Porky was listening to the camp radio, which I hadn't seen or heard since the twenty-second, in an attempt to monitor radio transmissions from the Allied forces.

The choppers were closer now. The Huey must have been the command ship, as it orbited in wide circles above us, observing all of the action below. The smaller choppers were back after a brief absence and their maneuvers were now designed to flush from cover and kill anyone hiding in the reeds. There seemed to be four of them, flying in pairs with one ship slightly lower and in front of the second. They were sweeping back and forth across the huge field of waving reeds with their landing skids almost touching the tops of the reeds. God they were low! The first ship was blowing the reeds apart with the violent downdraft from his rotor blades, and as the reeds parted, the trailing ship would gun down anything that showed below. They performed like an aerial lawn mower and after one murderous burst of fire, I discovered that these helicopters were not only maneuverable and fast, but deadly. They also mounted mini-guns and were using them liberally as targets appeared beneath the speeding Plexiglas canopies.

It was obvious that I, wearing black pajamas, would look like any of the VC to a pilot and my deeply tanned face, even with a beard, would be just another horror-stricken VC face to his combat-conditioned eyes. The split-second hesitation required for him to identify my beard and relate that to the Asian lack of facial hair would be time enough for me to shoot him out of the sky if he were wrong and it wasn't actually a beard he thought he had seen. No, the pilots wouldn't hesitate to shoot first in this situation and I didn't blame them one bit. As low as they were flying, Miss Mouse just might be able to use that bayonet on the bottom of one of their choppers.

I evaluated my chances and came up with a grim picture. The guards had a standing order to kill an American prisoner if they couldn't guarantee his security. It was a case of kill him rather than take the chance of having him get back to the Allies. Signaling a helicopter would be damn risky, at best, and I couldn't possibly do it with all the guards around me. Both sides of the scale were registering negative figures in the analysis of my chances of staying alive.

The Cobras were overhead now. Their sharklike nose and slim, dark-painted airframe made them look fearsome, particularly when you were watching them from the wrong end of those weapons they carried. They roamed arrogantly above the smaller, darting Light Observation Helicopters, as protection against anyone firing on their friends. Once the muzzle blast of a VC weapon was located, or the LOH pilot called for help, the Cobra's nose would dip slightly as the pilot lined up on his target and then the short, brutal burst of firing, the glimmering, fire-hose stream of steel, lancing downward and obliterating everything in the zone of impact. Through the constant whine of the engines and staccato roar of the exhausts, I could hear the rapid shouted commands out amid the reeds where unseen VC dodged and ran for their lives. The sound of submachine-gun fire from the ground echoed weakly against the harsh roar of the American weapons. Base cradled the machine gun, a demented light in his eye as he watched the helicopters. His knees were quaking slightly as he squatted beneath a sheaf of broken reeds. A slight dribble of saliva ran over his chin. Porky's ear was pressed against the radio as he reported anything he heard. His eyes were wide, the whites dominating in sharp contrast to his deeply tanned skin. Little Sau appeared to be the most composed member of the group, but his calm was a result of ignorance. No one had explained the danger to him. He was a twelve-year-old boy, with a twelve-year-old's sense of trust and confidence, but his heroes were betraying that trust.

A LOH made a pass directly over us! I was flat on the ground the instant I heard the high-pitched whine of his engine, my back crawling in anticipation of the rain of steel that would certainly follow. Reeds were battered down all around me by the force of his prop wash, exposing all our black-clad bodies to the trailing gunship. There wasn't time to think as the second ship flashed overhead, again causing a minor tornado on the ground. He didn't fire. They were apparently concentrating on the targets already exposed in the field next to us. A short ripping sound from his weapon indicated he had spotted another group in the reeds. My stomach was spasming and I felt like barfing. Cold sweat covered my face as I curled in the grip of dry heaves, the wave of nausea constricting my throat and cutting off my already short breath. The tingling sensation of abject fear spread throughout my body, robbing me of the ability to move. "O Lord, dear Lord, please don't let me die now. Not now!" It was a plea from the very depths of my being.

I could hear Miss Mouse, his voice soft, sobbing, "*Ma,*

ma." How lost he sounded. How strange that he turned back to the source of love and comfort he had known before joining this revolution. Sauser commanded the guards to replace the camouflage and told them not to fear because we couldn't be seen. His voice lacked conviction and I'm certain I wasn't the only one who detected it.

The others weren't paying too much attention to me now and my mind began to function again. I cleared away some of the tangle still remaining over my head and took off my shirt. The command ship was above us and I might be able to get his attention. Waiting until he banked, I stood and waved the shirt, hoping he'd investigate before calling the gunships in on me. I felt naked standing there, waving the dirty black rag of a shirt, thinking that one of the guards would see me. The chopper continued on his course, giving no indication he had seen me. I sat down, my stomach empty for reasons beyond the lack of food. I had to get out of here!

Porky was talking rapidly, gesturing toward the low-flying helicopters to our southeast. "Troops are being inserted into the area!" Sauser's face went pale under his tan. This was the worst of a terribly bad situation! Vietnamese infantrymen, possibly a Ranger unit, were being landed to finish off the scattered VC units and the pressure would be virtually inescapable. Base stood and declared that he would fight to the death, challenging the others to join him. I began to inch toward the canal behind me. If it came to a shootout, I would be the first KIA in this group, and that wasn't at all what I planned on. Sauser, Lord bless him, declared that their mission was more important than standing and fighting. The unit out in the reeds would take care of the "puppet soldiers," he declared. This was a reprieve, no matter how short-lived.

More instruction followed and the guards hid most of their equipment, shouldering only their packs and weapons. Mr. T.D. shuffled over to my area in a crouch. *"Lay do! Di!"* he snapped—Pick up your gear and go! He pointed, indicating the other guards, slipping into the canal and crossing to the field of reeds behind us, yet unscathed by the blistering attack.

I slipped my pack's rope shoulder straps on. My little dove lay quietly looking up at me, his eyes softly imploring. I couldn't just leave him and I couldn't take him. Quickly I broke a handful of reeds into a small nest and placed him in it with the

429

remaining grains of rice from his meal. "When you die, little bastard, please die quickly." I followed the guards.

All but Porky and Mr. T.D. had already crossed and were pushing their way through the thick reeds. As I stepped down into the canal, those two stepped in behind me.

For the next thirty or so minutes, it was a confused exodus. The dominant idea was to put as much distance between our group and the campsite as possible. Shouting voices could be heard along the canal we had crossed, punctuated by the sharp cracking sound of automatic-weapon fire, this time on the ground. The helicopters continued their hunt, causing us to crouch frequently in the thigh-deep water. I noticed that discipline was disintegrating and it was becoming a case of individual survival. Sauser still maintained a weak grip on the reins of authority, but the muttering behind me from Porky and Mr. T.D. indicated their dissatisfaction with his leadership. Base was proclaiming his willingness to stop and fight and calling on the others to mark well the fact that he was prevented from doing so. Sauser spat out at him in near fury to shut up and do what he was told.

The path we were making was too wide, too obvious. The desire of the guards to escape overrode their caution and they were getting extremely careless. I thought of the target we'd present if one of the choppers should spot our trail and decided that I didn't want to be around when he did. It was stupid to try something with the whole group around me, but there was no indication that they were going to split up.

Sauser called a halt and had Base climb a low tree to try to spot the position of the government troops. Behind me Porky snorted in alarm. Base would be like a beacon to the helicopters in that tree! Porky told Mr. T.D. to get to Base quickly and get him out of the tree before he was spotted, the urgency in his voice adding emphasis. Mr. T.D. shouldered his way past me, slogging rapidly toward the main group. I turned to Porky. "It is dangerous to put him where the helicopters will see him. We will all be killed if they discover where we are."

Porky's face was stoic, his eyes fastened intently on the black silhouette climbing the tree, but his answer gave me an opening I had hoped for. "*Ong* Sau is not a wise soldier." The break in confidence between cadre and guard! If only I could exploit it.

430

"*Ong* Sau has stayed in the camp when *Anh Giai Phong* has gone out to fight. It is logical that *Anh Giai Phong* should know more about combat." I was striving to inflate Porky's estimation of his own capabilities as a leader.

The next part was touchy. "I would feel much safer as a prisoner if *Anh Giai Phong* Quan [Porky] were in command because I know what the helicopters are going to do and I could advise *Anh Giai Phong*, whereas *Ong* Sau refuses to listen to anyone."

Sauser conveniently emphasized what I had said by shouting at Porky to close up the group and not give directions to a cadre. Mr. T.D. was standing helplessly by as Sau directed Base to continue up the tree. I could see Base, smirking as he looked down on the frightened guard below. "Boy, are you in your glory, Base," I thought as Porky and I walked slowly toward the group. "Everyone is a coward except you and Sauser." Porky was muttering to himself about Sauser shouting when the Government forces were within hearing distance. Little Sau was pulling up cattails, stripping the outer covering on the roots, and eating the pulpy tuber. As we approached, he handed me one, indicating that it would help satisfy the hunger we all felt. He was excited, but still unaware of the danger he faced.

Sauser listened intently to Base, who was reporting on what he saw across the waving tops of the reeds. Porky was ignored during the exchange between Sauser and his new ally. This was the breakdown of their system, where a cadre was challenged and sought to polarize the group. I watched the faces of the other guards, trying to determine who would follow Sauser. It was strange to watch the formerly aloof and distant Sauser grope among the guards seeking supporters and followers to side with him against the dissident Porky. Porky and Mr. T.D. were openly questioning Sauser's leadership ability and any chance I had would be with one of them. The tableau was interrupted by Base releasing his grip on one of the limbs and plummeting into the water below the tree. "*Truc-thang!*" he managed to blurt out before the beating sound of the blades and roar of the engine shocked our whole group into activity— Helicopter!

One of the LOH's buzzed past, not fifty meters to the west, scanning the field we were now in. His wingman followed close behind as we stood or crouched behind the clumps of reeds. Fortunately for us, the pilots' attention must have been directed away from us or Base would already have been a mass of bloody pulp, and the rest of us would have had only a short time before we joined him. Sauser gave the word to move out and Base led us off at an angle from the flight line of the choppers. We were moving rapidly, a trace of panic, which had been growing steadily, providing impetus. Mr. T. D. was in front of me and Porky behind me. The rest were drawing away to the front. The sweep pattern had apparently been transferred to this field as LOH's and Cobras were overhead. The command ship still roamed the entire area in huge circles, but the gunships were right on top of us.

I could hear Porky muttering to himself as we slogged through the murky water, concern for his own safety becoming more evident. Taking advantage of his mental state, I frequently pointed out various maneuver patterns I had noticed the choppers using, assuring Porky that Sauser was going to get us all killed through his lack of combat knowledge. Porky at first told me to be quiet, but after a while he began to listen intently as I spoke. He had probably noticed that I was able to predict with some reliability the actions of the feared helicopters. We began to fall further behind the main group. Mr. T. D. was out of sight for brief periods of time as reeds came between him and us. Porky no longer ordered me to hurry and catch up. I watched the choppers as they worked back and forth, occasionally spraying the ground below them with deadly fire. I would have to take a chance soon or I would blow the opportunity to escape, and there was no hope as a prisoner. I said a quick prayer asking the Lord to do what he would, I was going to try my best.

I stopped and turned to Porky, whose face was upturned, watching the gunships. "*Anh Giai Phong*, I'm afraid to follow *Ong* Sau any further because the helicopters will spot him and the others very soon. If we are with him, we will be killed at the same time." I was speaking as rapidly and sincerely as my ability with the Vietnamese language would allow. Porky had to believe me! "I will do all I can to help *Anh Giai Phong Quan* because he has helped me many times in the past years. If we can go by ourselves, making a small trail rather than the large path *Ong* Sau makes, you will be alive and able to fight later while the others will be dead." I paused, studying his face for reaction, while my mind scrambled to assemble another argument in case I needed it.

"Di!" Porky commanded—Go! My whole insides turned over. He was pointing to the left, perpendicular to our line of travel and away from the main group! It had taken only that effort to attain this advantage. One against one, if I could steer him away from the other groups of VC wandering through this area. I began to formulate a plan while breaking a narrow trail for us.

Porky was armed with a burp gun, the Chinese submachine gun used in Korea, with one curved magazine in the weapon and no ammo pouch. The guards had stashed their packs at the last halt and Porky kept only his weapon, the single magazine, and two grenades which were tied to the front of his web belt. This was a real break for me. I began to consider waving in a helicopter and having them pick up both Porky and me. It would mean disarming Porky first, but at this point my determination to escape far exceeded his ability to stop me. I was apparently moving too slowly for Porky, who handed me the camp radio he had been carrying and moved ahead of me, indicating for me to follow at a distance of about three meters. I paused a moment to take my mosquito net out of my pack. It would be wise to wave something white at the helicopters instead of a black shirt and my mosquito net was the biggest, whitest object in my possession. I tucked it under my arm, still folded, and trudged after Porky.

He was breaking the reeds ahead of me, opening only the minimum path that would allow us to pass. His attention was divided between the trail and the helicopters, and I found myself virtually ignored except for the verbal contact we maintained, Porky to ascertain I was still behind him and I to give him advice on direction and avoiding the helicopters. This block of reeds was bordered on four sides by canals like the one we had crossed and it was apparent that Porky was heading for the one farthest to the north in an attempt to move beyond the zone of action. Once we crossed that canal, Porky could travel with relative ease and link up with his comrades. That was not what I intended, so I altered his course several times by telling him that I saw troop-carrying helicopters landing to our north and west which would precede a sweeping operation from those directions.

It wasn't long before Porky was disoriented and wandering

according to my instructions. The faint sun, obscured by clouds, was nearly vertical and of no value for determining direction. It was a matter of keeping him away from the other groups until I had an opportunity to act. My spirits were high and I felt a surge of strength and energy far beyond anything in the realm of physical possibility. I was going to escape and nothing would stop me!

It became a matter of steady slogging through the reeds and water, and waving the now partially unfolded net at helicopters as they came into view. I wasn't having any success, since the reeds, which were over my head, prevented the fast-flying ships from seeing my signal. This didn't dampen my enthusiasm, and as I walked along carrying the radio I thought of the days past that I had listened to Radio Hanoi and Radio Liberation programs pour out their ration of crap over this very radio. I had been prevented from listening to anything else for all those months, and now I had the radio with no one to stop me from listening whatever I chose. I turned it on and quickly dialed across th. band until I heard American music. The sounds were a link with home, bringing me closer to my goal and reassuring me that I was close. Petula Clark was singing "My Happy Heart" and the melody gave me even a greater lift. It seemed so incongruous to be out in the middle of a cattail field, up to my thighs in muddy water, following one of my Vietcong guards while American helicopters swarmed overhead, the threat of death a constant companion, and to listen to the warmly effervescent voice that buoyed my spirits to a new high. I was smiling and really beginning to enjoy the music when Porky stopped and turned. He gestured rapidly for me to turn the radio off. I hadn't realized that it was loud enough for him to hear over the sounds of combat. "Be quiet!" His face was serious. "The helicopters will hear us!" I almost choked when I realized what he had said, but was quick to comply as it was evident that if Porky could hear the music, so could any other VC who might be nearby, but yet unseen.

I continued to wave at the choppers as they passed overhead. Once or twice we had to crouch as the LOH's made firing passes near us. On one pass I thought I heard the sound of a machine gun similar to the one Base had been carrying. The short burst was silenced by a blazing rain from the muzzles of a mini-gun. Then came the screams, the terrified voices, and

434

then quiet from the steel-ravaged killing zone. If the main group hadn't changed direction radically after we left them, that would have been approximately their position. Base might have gotten his wish to die fighting. Little Sau had been afforded the opportunity to die for the revolution. What a waste!

Porky had slung the burp gun across his back to enable him to use both hands in clearing a path. He approached a heavy tangle of reeds and dead brush, deciding to tunnel through rather than break a path which would be visible from the air. I was beginning to feel like a tagalong, since Porky was deeply involved with getting himself out of this mess alive, and not so much with guarding a prisoner. The idea to tunnel through proved to be disastrous for Porky. He became entangled and left me with a view of his back and posterior, while head and shoulders were thrust into the mass of brush. The weapon was temptingly exposed and as I walked up on him, closing the three-meter gap that had existed, I contemplated the various courses of action now open to me. Since the helicopters hadn't sighted us yet and the chances of meeting another group of VC was high, I couldn't afford to try to take his weapon or dump him. I still wanted to bring him out with me. It would have been too high a risk to attempt to disarm him and then try to signal, so the best thing to do would be to neutralize him. The bolt of the submachine gun was closed and I knew from my training that it fired from an open-bolt position; therefore, there was no round in the chamber. All I had to do was get rid of that magazine! I reached forward and tripped the flange release at the rear of the magazine, feeling the click as the catch dropped loose. Porky straightened up seconds later, and as he stepped forward into the tunnel he had made, the magazine of ammunition dropped unnoticed into the water. I stepped on it as I passed, grinding it into the mud. Porky now had an empty weapon on his back, and even though he still had the two grenades, I knew he was afraid for his life and wouldn't take the chance of killing both of us with a grenade.

We must have traveled another hundred meters when, suddenly, Porky stopped and groped for his weapon. He must have felt the difference in weight on his back and was going to check the weapon. Oh shit! I exclaimed. If he finds the magazine gone and begins yelling, there'll be VC all over us in no time. I waited apprehensively, tensing myself to dive at him if he

435

made a sound. I didn't know if I was strong enough to grapple with him, but if I could get one chop at his neck I could equalize the contest. Porky held his weapon in front of his chest, staring at the empty magazine slot. He didn't make a sound, just stared in disbelief at this stroke of ill fortune. He looked up at me, glanced at the ever-present helicopters and then back at me. His lips were twisted in an almost embarrassed, "What do I do now" grin, and the picture that came immediately to my mind was of the poor coyote in the movie cartoon, just before he suffers the consequences of being outsmarted by the Road Runner. I shook my head in sympathy, assuring Porky, when he asked if I had seen it drop, that I had no idea where the magazine was. He glanced around, his discomfort obvious now that the odds had changed so radically. A burst of firing gave me the opportunity to urge him to move out before we were spotted. Without hesitation he plodded off in the direction I indicated. He had yet to question what I was doing with my mosquito net under my arm.

We traveled a little longer and Porky was showing the signs of emotional strain, as well as physical exhaustion. He was more uncertain of the outcome of this day than I, and the lack of food was more noticeable in this guard who was unused to eating meals of rice and salt. For a POW, it was unpleasant, but not unusual. I found my energy level high and although my physical strength was only as much as the sparse diet would allow, the factors of morale and determination gave me a reservoir from which to draw.

The choppers appeared to be making wider circles, skirting the fringes of this field as if preparing to transfer their operation to another area or depart entirely. I couldn't allow that, because Porky was aware of my advantage and probably attributed the loss of his ammunition to me, thus placing me in a situation where failure to make contact with the Americans now would be the last mistake I ever made. The VC wouldn't hesitate to kill me, and the first group Porky linked up with could perform the execution.

I searched the clumps of reeds for one of the numerous short fragments of dead tree branches. The dead wood, exposed to the elements, tended to harden and would serve as a club. I wasn't going to take the chance of wrestling with Porky, since he had a weight advantage as well as a strength advantage. While he walked ahead of me, unaware of what I was doing, I selected a short limb, almost two inches in diameter, and stepped quickly behind Porky. The sharp blow caught him at the base of the skull, just below the back of his floppy brush hat. He sagged and dropped immediately without making a sound. I dropped the club and chopped him twice with the edge of my hand, delivering the blows to the side of his neck below the jawbone. I didn't intend to kill him, but I didn't want him to follow me when I moved out. As I laid him across a thick growth of reeds with his head out of the water, I noticed blood running from his mouth and nostrils. It was too late to worry about it. I picked up his weapon, then retrieved my net and the radio where I had dropped them.

After separating myself from him by about fifty meters, I pushed the useless burp gun, muzzle downward, under the water and into the mud. It wouldn't be too cool to wave at one of our gunships wearing black and carrying a weapon, even if it was empty. I then moved across a narrow ditch and selected a relatively clear area, making it more so by trampling the reeds down. I leveled an area which allowed me to see the helicopters and began to wave my white mosquito net wildly. There was a sense of urgency because of the great possibility that some of the other VC would come across my clearing and, after shooting me, use the white mosquito net and my body for bait to lure the helicopters close enough to be shot down.

After what seemed to be an eternity one of the Cobras passed overhead and banked sharply, circling me. It was joined by the second sleek gunship and my heart was beating so hard I thought my whole body would vibrate. "They've seen me! I'm OK, they've seen me!" I was exuberant and waved even more frantically trying to encourage them to hurry.

Up in the Cobras—I learned later—the radio crackled into life. "There's a VC down there in the open."

From the other ship came the reply, "Gun him!"

The Cobras were preparing to make a firing pass which would have reduced me to another crumpled heap of bloody flesh and tattered rags.

From the command ship which had joined the circling Cobras came the voice of Major Dave Thompson, flight commander

437

of this group of "Dutch Masters," the veteran pilots and crews of B Troop, 7th Armored Regiment, 1st Air Cavalry Division.

"Wait one, I want a VC prisoner. Cover me, I'm going down to get him."

The LOH's and Cobras swept the surrounding terrain, laying a devastating hail of bullets on the hidden VC who were firing at the descending command ship. I watched as the Huey circled wide around me, then lined up for a low pass. I continued to wave my net, fearing they might lose sight of me. The VC were forgotten as I concentrated on the rapidly approaching ship.

In the command ship, the door gunners strained to catch a glimpse of the black-clad figure standing in the clearing waving that white cloth. Their fingers were tense against the triggers of their M–60 machine guns as they waited to foil any trap that might have been set. Suddenly one of them, looking down, spotted the beard.

"Wait one, sir!" The shout went over the microphone with the urgency unique to one soldier as he sees another in need. "That's an American!" The response was immediate.

I saw the helicopter swing into a tight, low turn, braving the automatic-weapons fire directed against it, and completing a rapid traverse, it settled to the edge of the water not more than fifteen meters from me. I ran, dragging my net, stumbling, slipping but staying upright, seeing nothing but the interior of the chopper and the green-sun-visored face of Mike Thompson, the gunner. I dove onto the cool metal flooring and heard myself shouting, "Go! Go!"

438

10

THE CHOPPER LIFTED OFF, ITS NOSE TILTING FORWARD AS it gathered speed. I sprawled on the floor, clutching the leg stanchions of the pilot's seat, and stared over my shoulder as the trees and reeds began to drop away and skim beneath the speeding helicopter. After five years I was out of the "Forest of Darkness." I could see the horizon and the world seemed immense.

The copilot patted me on the shoulder, and as I looked up he smiled broadly, yelling over the sound of the blades. I barely made out "Name?" He leaned toward me as I spelled "R...O...W...E." He repeated the letters into his microphone; then leaned closer. "Are you Nick Rowe?" he shouted. I nodded. "Yes." He pulled his helmet and microphone off, handing them to me. "Get on the horn. A classmate is on the line!" I wasn't even aware of what he was saying, but automatically put the helmet on and heard the familiar sound of static in the earphones. "Nick!" A voice broke through. "Is that you?"

"Yes!" I was still yelling as if trying to talk over the noise of the chopper.

"Welcome home, buddy! Welcome home!" The voice came through the earphones, exuberant. I sat back from the crouch I had assumed, my mind a kaleidoscope of tumbling scenes, faces: Porky, lying crumpled in the mud; Sauser, the cage, No-K Corral; the canals; Ben, Dave, Big Tim; the team at Tan

439

Phu; the unbroken green walls of the forest. I was staring, unseeing, at the canal-crossed landscape far below, framed in the door of the chopper.

I felt a hand on my shoulder and turned sharply, startled. The gunner, with a full-face grin, motioned for me to sit on the nylon seat as he handed me an open C-ration can. I sat back against the olive drab seat, looking incredulously at the can of fruitcake. "Thank you, dear Lord." I prayed. "Thank you for this miracle." I felt the gunner's eyes on me. Specialist Fourth Class Mike Thompson was watching and already had a second can opened and ready for me. On the other side of the ship, Specialist Fourth Class Stevens was also opening cans. I turned my full attention to that beautiful can of C-ration fruitcake, savoring that first bite. The most delicious flavor I had ever tasted.

I gulped down the following cans of pecan nut roll, plum pudding and peaches, pausing only to take long swallows from the canteen of water Stevens handed me. Neither of the men in the aft compartment had an opportunity to do much more, on that flight to Camau, than open cans, hand them to me, and toss the empties out of the chopper.

As I ate, I slowly became aware of the air. It was so clean and cool. I was able to breathe again. I touched the nylon seat, marveling at the interior of the helicopter. The voices, speaking English, were like music. "O Lord, please don't let me wake up and be back in the forest. Please don't let this be a dream."

I looked out over the U Minh, feeling a strange detachment from reality. It had been so long, so long since I had seen the horizon. How many times I had looked up at aircraft, wishing I could be in them, above the mud, mosquitoes and leeches; flying free above the confines of the trees, the green prison.

I looked at my bag of possessions, my mosquito net, the black trousers and shirt I was wearing. How wonderful they had seemed down in the forest. Without them I would not have survived; yet, now, they looked so meager. My earthly belongings, collected, mended, saved during five years; more than the average prisoner had, and now they looked so ragged and out of place. How out of place *I* must look, I thought.

Mike Thompson motioned for me to look out the door. I shifted to my right and saw the outskirts of Camau in the doorway. How it had grown since that last visit I'd made in

1963! Tin roofs reflected sunlight, boats moved down the canals, people went about their business, oblivious to the helicopter passing overhead. I never realized Camau could look beautiful.

We approached the runway to land. I could see a cluster of jeeps and other vehicles parked on the edge of the strip. Various types of aircraft were parked along the ramps. There seemed to be uniforms all over the place and they were our uniforms. The helicopter hovered and settled to the ground. Thompson and Stevens immediately jumped out and hands reached up to help me down.

I recall thinking: "Come on, don't try to help me down. I've been tramping around that damn forest long enough that I should be able to climb out of a chopper by myself." Nevertheless, hands went under my elbows and I was aided in taking that first step onto land, friendly land.

I was greeted first by Colonel Walters, senior adviser to the ARVN 21st Division, and General Nghi, its commanding general. I managed my first salute in five years, wearing black pajamas, unshaven or not. It was so good to hear American voices, to see American uniforms, even though the faces were a blur. People were crowding around, Vietnamese officers were patting me on the back and feeling my arms. Someone asked for my name, rank and serial number.

"Rowe, James N., First Lieutenant . . ." I began.

"That's Major Rowe," came a voice.

I turned slightly, wondering who Major Rowe was. Just then I was handed a jungle fatigue jacket, and gleaming on its collar epaulets was a golden major's leaf, "Oh my gosh!" I thought. "Major!" Things were happening too fast.

I had been carried as Missing in Action for sixty-two months, since no positive determination of death could be established. As a result, I was promoted through the years and passed the rank of captain without ever even wearing the bars. The jacket, I found out, had been commandeered from Lieutenant Ewald and the major's leaf hastily pinned in place over his bar.

Someone helped me to put on the field jacket. A pair of jungle fatigue trousers suddenly appeared and I put them on over the still-wet black pajamas.

"Let's get you over to the Doc and checked out," Colonel Walters said.

A path opened through the crowd and I was escorted to a medical tent where Captain Jim Stinnett, the U.S. doctor at Camau, had me sit on a folding cot as he examined me for any immediate problems. I could have told him that the way I was feeling right then, I could have walked to Saigon or wherever I was to go next. Someone else set a pair of jungle boots beside a cot and handed me a pair of socks. Again a strange feeling: wearing socks and boots after being barefoot.

I still had a curious sense of detachment as if I were standing several feet to the right and slightly above my body and observing the proceedings. It was too rapid a change from the mud, anxiety, fear and impending death of a few hours earlier. Doc was asking me how I felt and the only description I could give was "Great!" which medically speaking, didn't help him a bit.

After the checkup, I was escorted to a waiting jeep for a short ride to another helicopter. Smiling Americans and Vietnamese were everywhere. As I climbed into the back of the jeep and touched the cold steel, I suddenly realized I was free. I was free, alive, and with my own people again. How long I had waited and prayed for this day that so many times had seemed as if it would never come. I had to reach out and touch the cool metal side of the jeep as if to reassure myself that it, in fact, did exist.

At the helicopter I said goodbye to the Camau contingent and boarded for the next leg of my trip home. A young captain was my escort with two warrant officers as pilot and copilot of the Huey. While en route to the 29th Evac Hospital in Can Tho, I stared in amazement at the construction that was going on and that which had already been completed. The picture created by the VC was one of utter desolation and destruction; yet, from the helicopter, I could see large complexes of tin-roofed structures, villages, banana and coconut groves, teeming marketplaces, and boat traffic on the waterways. If only the guards could see this, I thought. If only they could have had the chance to see what really exists outside the forest.

It wasn't long at all before the Huey began its approach to the chopper pad at the Evac Hospital. I was met at the helicopter and escorted into the Quonset-hut hospital, where a slightly perplexed doctor asked me to sit on the edge of a bunk. I hesitated slightly. There were sparkling white sheets and a pillow on the bed and I didn't want to get them dirty.

442

"Do you know what I'm supposed to examine you for?" he asked.

I assured him I hadn't the slightest idea.

"Is there anything in particular wrong with you?" he asked, becoming more perplexed.

"I have a case of dysentery that has been a problem," I offered.

He brightened noticeably. "How long have you had it?"

"About five years," I replied.

He seemed to choke slightly. "Five years?" he asked.

"Right. Off and on since 1963."

Apparently no one had told him the nature of the examination he was to perform other than to examine the individual being brought in by chopper from Camau. I obviously was not what he expected, but it was not really important. I was feeling better with every passing minute of freedom.

Just then a familiar face appeared in the room. An old Special Forces officer from 1963, still in Vietnam, on his third tour. After a warm welcome and a short period of my asking the whereabouts of old friends, we walked into a conference room where the initial debriefing was to be conducted.

I was introduced to the group of men in the room after which there was another short period of recalling old acquaintances. Then the formalities began. I was read my rights under Article 31, UCMJ, which affords an individual the right to remain silent during questioning if he so desires. I was informed that anything I might say could be used against me in a court-martial.

My first reaction was shock. My mind recoiled and the reflex action of this sudden cold pretrial procedure made me curl up within myself. "What's going on?" my mind screamed. "What have I done?" The officer continued to go through the format, informing me of my rights and asking me to sign a form indicating that I understood my rights and that I desired to make a statement, not to remain silent.

The feeling of freedom was gone. Once again I was alone and these were interrogators, just as Mafia had been. I looked around the table at the men. They were all watching me.

Hank spoke up, "Nick, this is just a requirement we have. There's nothing more here than protecting your rights under the Code."

I suppose my repulsion had been evident to them as I stared

443

at the waiver of rights form, not moving to sign it. Five years of developed cynicism washed over me as I viewed the interrogation procedure through the eyes of a prisoner and saw this debriefing as being as dogmatic as my former tormentors'.

It took a moment before I could convince myself that this was a requirement placed on those men and they were only carrying out their orders. "To hell with it," I thought. "If I wind up in Leavenworth prison for violation of the Uniform Code of Military Justice or anything else, I'll at least have three meals a day and a bed to sleep in. Better than that, there'll be indoor latrines." I signed the paper and the debriefing commenced.

Two hours later I was on my way, aboard another chopper heading for Long Binh and the 93rd Evac Hospital. During the flight I tried to relax and watch the countryside below, but the thoughts of what had just happened in Can Tho were like small rocks in one's shoe. They were irritating enough to disturb me.

I did notice the enormous amount of construction that had been carried out here as well. How this part of the country had been built since I last saw it in 1963, and more than likely, rebuilt after the 1968 Tet Offensive. The broad expanse of Long Binh as it came into view was unbelievable. It was difficult to comprehend and associate what I was seeing with the picture of Vietnam I had created in my mind, based on the NLF propaganda. Where was the widespread destruction? The tightly encircled enclaves of starving defenders, vainly resisting the overwhelming might of the Liberation Armed Forces? Where were the flags of the NLF that were said to be flying from masts reaching from the Ben Hai River to the tip of Camau?

No doubt, the Vietcong and NVA were still making their presence felt and had the potential to conduct a protracted struggle which might carry on for years, but the pitiful aspect of distortion of fact through propaganda to encourage their followers was never so clear to me. How I wished Porky, Bud, Chinh, and the others could have seen what I was seeing; perhaps not with the idea of altering their beliefs, but only to allow them to better judge for themselves, to know the truth.

The helicopter settled gently to the ground. As I glanced out of the door I could see an ambulance waiting at the edge of the concrete and medics close by, holding a stretcher upright ready to be rushed to the chopper. "Boy," I thought, "this is really something. Everybody seems to be expecting a basket case. Maybe I ought to lie down and pretend." Even though my spirits had suffered a slight setback, I still could feel myself moving in a sort of trance that was permeated with the sensation of freedom. This would have permitted me to get up and walk even if I had been a basket case.

The door slid open and I stepped down, reaching back to grasp my rice sack of possessions and Porky's radio. I wasn't about to let those out of my sight. The medics were instantly beside me to see if I needed help. I assured them, yelling against the slapping sound of the blades above me, that I was OK. Waving a goodbye to the crew aboard the Huey, I turned toward the ambulance.

The next thing I knew I was swept up in an *abrazo* that would have done credit to a Spanish *patrón* welcoming one of his own back home. The man who had said he was going to stay until he got me out was here to welcome me—John Firth, my B-Detachment executive officer in 1963, now a lieutenant colonel, who had spent the better portion of his four tours in Vietnam looking for me.

I was laughing and talking as if I were trying to make up for the five years of void. The last time I had seen John was in October 1963, at Can Tho, just before I returned to Tan Phu and the last operation. There was so much I wanted to ask, people, old friends, events I had heard about. Where was Ponce? What happened to the team? Did Martin make it OK? What happened at Hiep Hoa? Did Doug and John make it out of that? Where was Ed, that ugly mutha? Words seemed to tumble over one another as we both laughed and created verbal mayhem.

We piled aboard the ambulance for the short ride to the ward where I was to stay. I don't know who was really happier to see whom. John and I fired questions at each other as fast as we could get them in the conversation. By the time we arrived, I had begun to get my second wind and had a hundred new questions to ask him. It was such a relief to actually talk with a friend, even with my tendency to lapse into Vietnamese at crucial times, to communicate with someone who actually gave a damn whether or not you lived or died. The door of the long Quonset hut ward was opened by an orderly and we walked into the cool interior.

I got a glance at rows of white-sheeted bunks, stainless steel partitions with their light-green cloth dividers, a group of faces, before I was ushered into a private room. I remember the bunk was quite high and I had to stretch to sit down on it. Next to the wall was a small bed table and on the other side of the bed was a clothes locker. One straight chair completed the furniture. It looked so luxurious to me. I even had an air conditioner in the window above my bed.

I sat on the edge of the bed, waiting for something to happen, and it wasn't long before a bouncy young nurse appeared in the doorway. I can imagine what an appearance I must have presented with my two-week growth of beard and many days without a bath. She looked at me and her eyes immediately widened, surprise quickly masked as she rose to the occasion and with a smirk said, "Hey, man, all you need is a set of beads and you could be a leader in the movement."

I wasn't even aware of what movement she was talking about. John and the M.I. people in the room got a good chuckle out of my bewilderment and even more of a laugh when this same nurse, looking cuter each time I saw her, reappeared with a Christmas issue of *Playboy* magazine.

"Here," she said, handing me the magazine. "This is the beginning of your therapy!" After a five-year drought, this was too much to take all in one visual gulp. I started to scan the pictures, but found my awakening interest in a subject that had been low on the list for five years now far exceeded my ability to do much about it. I decided to put the magazine away for a while and deal with the next question.

"What would you like to eat?"

I had a menu in mind that I had been building for endless months, yet there was the problem of what to begin with. "This is stupid," I thought. "The people are asking about food and I'm stuck on where to begin." Members of the hospital staff came into the room and introductions were made. "Welcome home." "We're damn glad to have you back." "How would you like to talk with your parents?" The question was like a shot. I hadn't dared ask about Mom and Dad. The years of wondering, hoping, dreaming about them. Praying that they were all right. I hadn't the courage to ask how they were, and now I had the chance to talk to them.

"We have a call going through to them right now," Colonel Firth continued. "How about it?"

"Oh God, yes sir! Thank you." He smiled and indicated for me to follow. We moved to a phone which had been plugged in in the empty room next to mine. A corpsman was talking to the operator. He looked up and grinned as he handed me the receiver. "They're on the line, Major. Welcome back, sir." The men left the room, closing the door as I sat down, holding the receiver as if it were a live hand grenade.

"Hello," I ventured.

"Nick!" Mom's voice came through vibrant. "How are you?"

Her voice, sounding as I had remembered it all these years, was like a stimulant. My already high spirits soared even higher.

"Mom! I'm fine. I'm clean and straight. More important than me, how are you and Dad?"

Her voice was bubbling by this time. "We're just fine, Nick, waiting for you to come home." Then, in the way only my mother can drop a bombshell, she asked casually, "What took you so long?"

I sat stunned for a moment, then almost started laughing with a mixed urge to do something I had almost forgotten, to cry. The long wondering, praying that they would be alive when I finally made it, was finally ended. They were alive and were undoubtedly the same as when I left. No one but my Mom could have asked a question like that at a time like this.

"I tried, Mom, but they just wouldn't let me go. I'll be home soon now, though." The rest of the conversation with Mom and Dad made the moments span years—1963, when I had said goodbye to them; the letters while I was at Tan Phu; then the years of emptiness. But now, all the darkness was wiped away and the whole world looked beautiful.

I hung the receiver up and walked into my room. My smile must have rearranged my face. It couldn't have been bigger.

A corpsman appeared in the doorway with a tray stacked high with golden fried chicken, mashed potatoes and green peas. He barely set it down on the table before I launched into the first real food I had tasted since 1963.

I think the others, watching the delight with which I devoured the chicken down to the bare bones, enjoyed the meal almost as much as I did. The finale was ice cream and I got one cup of each flavor available. I never realized food could taste so exquisitely delicious. There was a nagging thought about too much rich food after five years of rice, but what the

447

hell, this only happens once! I lingered over the ice cream, savoring every spoonful, letting my taste buds reorient themselves.

After the meal, I was escorted to the end of the building for the first of a multitude of physical examinations of various types. Major Clyde Wagner was in charge of this phase and made it as rapid as possible. Before I was aware that all had, in fact, been completed, I was en route back to the room for another surprise. John and my escorts were talking with some of the hospital personnel who had dropped by as I entered the room.

"Major Rowe," they beamed. "Welcome home!" Hands were extended and as I shook them I could think of nothing more profound to reply except "Thank you."

"We're celebrating in the O Club tonight and wanted to make certain you were properly cared for. What's your drink and how much can we get for you?" He paused slightly, then continued, "We just happen to have a couple of double scotch and waters that we brought along in case you're a scotch drinker." With that he brought forth two tall glasses, the pale amber liquid breaching the lip of the glass, ice cubes clinking as he set them down on the table in front of me.

"This looks like a winner to me," I said, concentrating more on the ice cubes than the drink. It was strange how those ice cubes represented civilization. The little aspects of everyday life out here that people take for granted, yet so many other people never have the opportunity to enjoy. When was the last time I had seen ice, I wondered. Was it in 1967 or '68? The guards had made a special trip to the market to buy a little ice for a special celebration and afterward they sat around in the forum crunching away on the frozen delicacy.

With a toast to the New Year, we tossed down the first round of drinks and I found myself on the way to a "wet" evening, for the first drinks had no sooner disappeared than another group appeared with eggnog and, of all treasures, a bottle of champagne!

John and the others were in the midst of the rapidly developing festive gathering as toasts, laughter and a strong feeling of camaraderie filled the room. This was a New Year's Eve to be remembered.

Much later, with John and the others already in their assigned bunks outside the room, I found myself unable to sleep. More than that, I was unwilling to sleep. There was a portion of my subconscious that wouldn't accept the fact that I was free. This was playing out as if it were a portion of a dream and to go to sleep would insure a reawakening back in the forest, the swamp. I wasn't going to take the chance of losing what I felt, and even if it were a dream, I was going to stretch it out as long as possible.

To top it off, the bunk was too soft! After five years on hard pole racks, the mattress was definitely part of the capitalist-imperialist conspiracy I had heard so much about. Such a clever way to make the working masses dependent upon comfort items, thus depriving them of their rugged, self-sustaining power of productivity. The problem was solved by putting the sheets and blanket on the floor, which more closely approximated my beds of the past years. Not even this was satisfactory. The floor was too level! One needs the lumps and ridges of crooked poles in order to achieve authenticity. Nevertheless, I lay down and began reworking in my mind the events of the day.

The rest of the night, what there was of it, was spent making short, hurried trips between my room and the latrine as the food and particularly the rich eggnog slammed into my ill-prepared system, which reacted in the most logical manner. I'm still looking for the guy who brought that eggnog in.

The next morning must have dawned beautifully. I wasn't outside to see it, but my imagination painted it that way. After a fine breakfast (I was appreciated by the mess hall cooks since anything they prepared tasted good to me), I underwent more physical exams, lost blood to the lab, and answered questions for a headshrinker who seemed anxious to know if I identified in any manner with persecuted groups in history. Assuring him I was devoid of any complexes except those normally built up over a period of five years in captivity, we went on to have a most pleasant chat in which I am certain he obtained all the facts he needed to analyze my mental state. The report could have been summarized by me: "Happy, relaxing, hung over."

After returning to the room, I was treated to visits by old friends whom I hadn't seen for years, some of them since graduation from West Point in 1960. It was so damn good to see them, talk with them, find out what had been going on during the intervening years.

A note of sadness crept in with the mention of friends and classmates we had lost in combat. Names immediately became faces in my mind. I remembered the days past we had spent on the football fields at West Point, on weekends in New York City or skiing in Vermont, the multitude of good times we had shared, their plans and dreams for the future, their wonderful families and wives, some of whom I had known as their girls or fiancées. So much had happned in those five years. It was difficult to accept that these men were no longer among us. Then again, this was only a physical passing. Death is a constant companion of those who serve in time of war, and though able to sever the physical tie, it can never break the bonds of spirit. I knew now where the source of additional strength that I had called upon lay. Just as these men stood with us while they lived, they continued to stand with us after their passing. The words, an anthem from the Academy that none of us would forget, never had more meaning than at this moment, "Grip hands with us now though we see not, Grip hands with us, strengthen our hearts; As the long line stiffens and straightens with the thrill that your presence imparts, Grip hands tho' it be from the shadows. . . ."

The mood shifted again as a medic came into the room rocking with laughter. It seemed as if a group of reporters had gathered in the area, seeking a story on my escape and on the release of three other Americans on New Year's Day. They had congregated outside the ward and equipped with that sixth sense and unperturbable persistence common only to members of the free press were homing in on their story source. Efforts to have them desist were futile and it seemed as if their quest would bear fruit; that is, until an ingenious Specialist 5 in civilian clothes took matters into his own hands, deciding to give the security personnel a hand.

Dashing up to the group of reporters, he grabbed the nearest one by the sleeve and dragging him along, dashed off toward a distant ward shouting, "Major Rowe's over here! He's in that ward across the area!" The reporters, seeing two rapidly moving figures and not wanting to be last to capitalize on the story, broke from in front of my ward in a mad dash to follow.

At noontime my special benefactress, a nurse lieutenant colonel, checked by to see if all was going well in the room. The question of food arose and she assured me that she would take care of the situation. A short time later, she reappeared with what looked like a safari of corpsmen behind her carrying trays of food. I hadn't imagined such variety of dishes was available anywhere. There was enough on those trays for five Nick Rowes. All of us had a feast that noon.

That afternoon I was officially reinstated in the 5th Special Forces Group when the group commander, Colonel Aaron, paid a visit. He presented me with a Green Beret and a warm handshake. Then came the real surprise as he awarded me a Bronze Star for my actions while a POW. "This is a token," he said as he pinned the medal on my blue hospital pajamas. "We're glad you're back," he continued, his mouth curving in a slight smile, "and we're proud that you wear the Green Beret."

I think I stood a little straighter as the last words hit me. "They're proud that I wear the beret?" I asked myself. "I'm proud that I wear it," came my answer. There was more to that piece of green felt than the average person can imagine. One has to have been associated with the men, the dedication and the spirit, the sacrifice it represents. The beret is more than a type of headgear, it is a symbol and a challenge to those who wear it. A challenge to meet the standards of those who have worn it before us. "Yes," I thought, "I'm damn proud that I wear the Green Beret!"

We talked for a while as the local Vietnamese barber went to work on my shaggy hair. The haircut was phase three of "operation civilize." I had bathed three or four times already and my beard had met its end the night before. I calculated that with another two weeks of bathing, I might work through most of the accumulated dirt and discover what color my skin actually was. Chunks of a Vietnamese version of "Grandma's Lye Soap" provided by the Vietcong (they used it to wash their packs and web gear) was the first soap I had ever encountered that could penetrate three layers of skin without touching the dirt. Using the hospital soap was pure luxury.

Colonel Aaron departed after our conversation, en route back to Nha Trang and his headquarters. I went immediately into a session with a tape recorder for a tactical debriefing on the area I had come out of. The night before, I had written an appeal to the guards and cadre I had known in MR III, realizing that they were still out in the forest, running and hiding for their lives under the now-increased aerial and ground assault.

I knew that they were disorganized and the younger guards, in particular, were terrified. The message encouraged them to surrender without fear of being tortured and killed. To stay was certain death, but if they surrendered, they would be given clothing and food and their lives would be spared.

I learned later that 160 of them had come out the first day after the leaflet was dropped into the area. Although I have never learned who came out, I hope that some of the "Mice" in my camp were among those who lived. They were too young to be sacrificed for a cause they didn't really understand.

I was told that I would be leaving the next day aboard a Medevac flight for the U.S.A. It didn't really register for a couple of minutes. Those in the room watched me for a re-action, but none was immediately forthcoming. After asking the doctor a few questions about the results of the lab tests, I suddenly realized what he had said!

"Did you say I'll be going home tomorrow?" I asked softly.

"That's right, Nick." He beamed. "You're on a C-141 leaving Tan Son Nhut tomorrow morning and arriving stateside the day after. Can you hang on for that extra day?"

I was definitely grinning when I answered, "Does a bear crap in the woods?" The rest of the day was a relaxed con-versation as all the friends helped to bring me up to date on the events that I had missed. I was issued a pair of low-quarter shoes and a short-sleeved khaki uniform for the trip home. When I tried it on and looked in a mirror, I could recognize the Lieutenant Rowe of 1963, but there was something in the eyes that hadn't been there before. The uniform looked as if it belonged, the beret made the reflection complete. I was ready to go home.

I spent the night down at the nursing station talking with the nurse and corpsman on duty. Another night in which I had no desire to sleep. By now the adrenalin was rushing through my system with such velocity that I couldn't have slept even if I dared. It was a thoroughly enjoyable night spent catching up on the music and dances that had come in since I last remembered. I drew chuckles from both of them when I asked who the Beatles were. It was quite an awakening to learn of the miniskirt, new rock, psychedelic discothèques, and the multitude of other innovations that were only words to me since I had no way of picturing them. Hippies, Yippies, the flower

452

children: I was looking forward to seeing who or what they were.

The following morning, after another monster breakfast, I was ready for the chopper ride to Tan Son Nhut and then home. A final visitor was to arrive shortly and the hospital staff was preparing. This was Lieutenant General Mildren, Deputy Commander of U.S. Forces, Vietnam. I was still not fully convinced that I was a major, or that I had received a decoration, or even that I was actually on the way home; and here was a visit by the Deputy CG of USARV! Boy, would this frost Mafia if he could see it! I chuckled to myself, remembering the days I sat on a pole floor looking up at Mafia perched on a chair behind a poncho-draped stand as he conducted an indoctrination. What he must have thought about the ragged, illness-weakened, fungus-infected POW's in his relative grandeur. In the land of the blind, a one-eyed man is king.

I had checked my khakis for the third time to make sure everything was in order when the ward was called to "at ease." My memory of protocol was shot to hell, never having been too interested in it. I quickly asked John Firth if it was proper to salute while uncovered and indoors. John thought a moment, then advised, "Watch him. If he shakes hands first, forget it."

"What if he doesn't?" I asked.

"Beats me." John replied. He grinned and nodded toward the ward entrance where the General was entering. Staff members and hospital staff were with him. He walked directly over to me and grasped my hand in a crushing grip. "Welcome back, young man. That was a fine job and we're proud of you."

There was no doubt that this man was a general officer. His bearing and manner were clearly indicative of his ability and assurance and his handshake would have done credit to a professional wrestler.

His next questions were related to my health and condition. It was a short, very pleasant reacquaintance with the upper echelon of command. In parting, he said, "If there is anything at all we can do to be of help to you, don't fail to call on us."

It wasn't him or the words he said, because they were spoken with utmost sincerity. The thought was immediately in my mind, "For five years I've called for someone to help me. There's no sweat now, I'm already out." It was a fact. The days that I had watched our aircraft, heard the sound of artillery, hoped and prayed that, perhaps, there would be some help from them. The days of disappointment until, finally, the break did come and freedom was once again mine. What more could I want? What more could there be?

He departed and we began leaving the room for the chopper ride to Tan Son Nhut. John was going along, as my escort from M.I., whom I had just recently identified as the bodyguard type of escort he was. He had joined me in Can Tho, but I hadn't gotten the picture until now. Lou, as I will call him, was a tall, slender, quiet individual. As is the case with most of these people, you'd pass him in a crowd without a second glance. This is their cloak of anonymity, the ability to merge with the crowd, giving no indication of their potential.

After the goodbyes in the ward, we piled into the ambulance for the short trip to the waiting chopper. Then the ride to Tan Son Nhut where the giant C–141 squatted on the runway. Stretchers and walking wounded were being loaded aboard the evac ship as the Huey hovered and landed.

There was a brief goodbye with John Firth. He was never one to make a big thing out of a parting since he had experienced so many of them over the years. A strong grip of the hands, a slap on the shoulder, and he was on his way back to the waiting vehicle on the ramp.

Lou and I were checked on the manifest as we walked up the ramp into the cool interior and moved between racks of stretchers along the bulkheads en route to our seats. We sat down, buckled in, and waited for the ride to begin.

The flight to Tachikawa AFB in Japan was an easy one. Lou and I chatted during most of the flight, and he answered the seemingly endless questions I had about every possible topic. The flight nurses worked quietly and efficiently among the stretcher cases as we traveled, even taking time to exchange wisecracks with the seated passengers. I found myself really enjoying the chance to talk with a female again and was disappointed when she moved to the next row of seats.

We landed at the air base just before dusk and were loaded aboard an Air Force bus for the ride to the hospital where we would stay overnight.

At the hospital, Lou and I were ushered into a private room with a delightful young nurse captain on duty. Not only was she very attractive, but she was also a native of San Antonio, Texas! I had no sooner arrived than I was in an enjoyable conversation about my part of Texas and feeling closer to home with every passing minute. Two members of the hospital staff dropped by to see how we were doing and inquire if there was anything they could provide. I was quite happy the way I was and only inquired about the location of the mess hall so we could get supper. After giving us a rundown on the facilities available, the doctors hinted that they might provide a little something to make the evening more relaxed when we returned.

Lou and I finished supper in the huge mess hall and returned to the room to find several small "prescription" bottles of medicinal Jim Beam sitting on the night table. Packets of toilet articles had been provided and two good bourbon and waters later, I wandered down for a hot shower and shave.

That night was spent in conversation with Lou and his local contact, who had joined us after our arrival. By early morning, Lou was definitely feeling the sleepless hours, but I wasn't even tapping my reserve energy yet. The next morning after breakfast Lou, Jeff and I walked over to the base exchange in order for me to get a look at "the big PX" I had thought about so often.

Before I left Vietnam, the people there assured me that I had sufficient cash to carry me through on the ride home and this was my first opportunity to shop. In exactly forty-seven minutes after entering the exchange, I had covered 90 per cent of the total floor space and purchased a tape recorder, camera, and transoceanic radio; I had gawked at the new stereo sets almost the way one of the guards would have. In the forest, a transistor radio was considered a marvel of science and its inner workings and hidden mechanisms were never really understood.

I was looking around the photography section when my eye caught two individuals down the aisle. "Boy, are those a couple of ugly broads!" came the immediate thought as I scanned their features and shoulder-length hair. Long chains of beads hung from around their necks onto bulky sweaters. As they approached, my next observation was, "Flat-chested, too." They wore tight-fitting trousers, accenting their scrawny legs. Smirks broke out on all faces as Lou and the nurses watched my reactions.

The two hirsute creatures passed beside me, and I asked Lou, "Are they . . . ?"

Lou, grinning, nodded an affirmative. "What do you think

of your first hippies? Genetically speaking, they *are* male."

I could only think of the hairstyles of the medieval age, when it was necessary to cushion the metal helmet on one's head in combat and to provide a degree of warmth about the head during the cold European winters. But that hair was neater. Barbers must be doing a poor business if this was prevalent in the States.

With a grin, one of the nurses spoke up in her official tone of voice, "Conversion reaction through acute trauma producing motor paralysis of speech. In layman's terms, he's in shock."

The young Japanese salesgirl had watched the episode and finally understood that I had thought the two young men were girls. Her peal of tinkling laughter, muffled only slightly by the hand she placed over her lips, brought the other girls at the counter to her side. Once she was able to talk through her laughter, they all joined in and I felt myself beginning to blush. I felt like the country bumpkin on his first visit to the big city. There was a lot that I had to catch up on.

I turned to Lou. "Let's see if we can get out of here without me tripping over my sword again."

We drove back to the hospital with the San Antonio nurse and prepared to leave for the airfield. Several hours later we were on the way to the United States.

It was a quiet flight this time. Lou was sound asleep, catching up on the hours he had lost during the past few nights of conversation. I had yet to feel sleepy and that subconscious block was still there, though growing weaker. I leaned my head back and closed my eyes, letting my mind wander. The thoughts were like pebbles dropping into my mind. I picked each one up, examined it, then tossed it away to make room for the next. What would America be like after five years? Were the changes so radical that I would find myself an alien in my own country? Most important, were there changes in me that I hadn't recognized yet that would come to light when held up to the framework of standards in America? Were the new ideas and new ideals such that I would not be able to accept them?

I thought back to the young hippies I had seen. Was this the new generation and their world or was there still some of the world I had known? The thoughts were a little frightening as my imagination expanded the picture in my mind, adding dimensions of color to an Orwellian fantasy. I glanced around me and found comfort in watching the nurses in their flight uniforms, the khaki-uniformed soldiers, and Lou, slumbering in the next seat, all of them reassuring with their sense of purpose, dedication and direction, tempered with the very human core in each.

What seemed like only minutes later, the copilot came up behind my seat and asked, "Major Rowe?"

I turned, looking up. "Yes?"

"We're almost ready to begin descent into Travis. The base just radioed that you have quite a group waiting to meet you. The press is there and they expect a press conference will be held." Then he added, "Better watch out for those guys, they're a bunch of sharks."

That was all I needed! At that point I was ready to go back to Long Binh where I had established a sanctuary. The thought of dueling verbally with hardened reporters was not pleasant. I wondered if I could remember enough English to express myself correctly and not become entangled with syntax. The only other solution would be to lapse into Vietnamese and let them take it from there.

Lou was awake and ready for the landing. I wondered if there would be any surge of special emotion when I stepped onto the runway and American soil for the first time in over five years. Somehow, that seemed to be important. In all the stories I had ever read about things like this, there was a moment of truth as the main character reestablished contact between his foot and terra firma, usually accompanied by some profound comment. Should I start rehearsing now, I wondered?

The landing was accomplished and before I had an opportunity to speculate further, the door near the cabin swung open and the deputy base commander climbed aboard. "Major Rowe, welcome home and welcome to Travis." He grinned. "We have a press conference arranged if you're ready," he continued, "and one of your classmates, Captain O'Donnell, sent you his ring." He handed me the heavy gold West Point class ring. "Captain O'Donnell thought you might not have yours and asked if you'd wear his."

I was struck dumb. I could only acknowledge my assent by nodding as I slipped the ring on my finger. With it came a surge of confidence as I was able to identify with what it symbolized and reestablished myself with respect to the pending conference. After Mafia, these guys would be no sweat. I smiled to myself.

"Oh yes," he continued, "there's a beautiful young lady with a fine Irish name waiting to see you in the base commander's office. Are you ready to go?"

"Who in the world?" I asked. "What is the fine Irish name, sir?"

"I've completely forgotten, Major Rowe." He grinned, slightly embarrassed.

Stepping down the hatch ladder and onto the runway, I first noticed the California fog and the cold. I shivered in the light khaki uniform as I felt real American cold for the first time in five years. I decided that it was just like the January cold in the U Minh.

We rode to the large headquarters building and dismounted. It was warm as we entered and I was ushered into the office. I saw only one person, although the room was crowded—Mary Grace McInerney, as lovely as I remembered her that last evening at Fort Bragg in 1963, when I had visited her and her husband Dick. It was shortly before my departure for Vietnam that I had seen Dick, a classmate and close friend, at Fort Bragg and had spent a wonderful evening with the two of them, talking about old times and future plans.

Just two days ago, I had learned at Long Binh that Dick had lost his life in combat, and even though one learns to accept the inevitability of death, it was a shock to lose a friend like Dick. The thought that Mary Grace would come here to welcome me home was overwhelming.

I completely forgot the others in the room until a polite cough shattered the spell. I was introduced to the base commander and several members of his staff. The welcome extended by all of the officers was so sincere that I immediately felt a part of the group rather than a stranger in their midst. It was as if I were a member returning after an absence. After explaining the procedures for the press conference and inquiring about my desires on the matter, the others left the room so Mary Grace and I could talk.

The moments I spent with her, laughing, reminiscing, talking about her two fine boys and young daughter, of whom she was justifiably proud, gave me the confidence that I had been trying to establish. After reacting to the calculated and fraud-

458

ulent acceptance and rejection by the guards for so long, I had developed a subconscious barrier to any type of association or real communication. This brief conversation with Mary Grace reestablished a bond that had been suppressed. The friends at Long Binh had laid the groundwork, but this was the key. I knew now that I was not going to reawaken back in the forest.

We walked through the door into the conference room together, still talking and laughing. This press conference had been transformed in my mind from a contest with a group of interrogators into a meeting with a group of friends, even though I didn't know them. They were Americans and that was sufficient for me.

I recall the room was a maze of wires across the floor. TV cables and electrical wiring were like a carpet. The cameras were all focused toward a small podium at the front of the room and the lighting was intense. The room was filled with folding chairs and most of them were occupied. As we entered, I was escorted to the front of the room and after a brief introduction, the newsmen began their questioning. I frankly had no idea what I would say and took their questions one at a time, trying to give as comprehensive an answer as time would allow. The attitude of the gentlemen gathered there immediately dispelled any fears I might have been subconsciously harboring. Their questions were direct, pertinent, and phrased in such a manner that they did not seem to probe or pick. It was a glorious feeling of relief and freedom to be able to react to questions with utter candor. I reveled in the sensations that flowed through me and they lent dimensions to my comments that I never thought impossible. It was truly an experience to realize that I was, in fact, free! The only question which had disturbed me was when one individual asked, "How were you treated?" I sat back in momentary confusion, searching for some sequence of words that would convey, in a matter of seconds, the summation of five years as a POW. There was no means of conveying what those years were like to an audience who had no concept of the constant physical pressures; the filth, disease, hunger; the crushing mental pressure; the frustrations, anxieties, the fears. I couldn't tell him in an hour, or a day even, unless he had been there, and there were only a few who had been and returned. None of them were in this room.

"Were you beaten or tortured?" he prompted me. The ques-

459

tion sounded so familiar. "I have not been beaten or physically tortured." The standard reply was on my lips almost before I could stop it, but I held back, recalling Mafia and Base, the Mines, then dismissing them as unimportant in the context of his question: "Fingernails pulled out, poundings with sticks, the water torture, all the imaginative forms of human mistreatment." Again, it would take too long and there was the consideration of the families of the men still over there who would be watching for what I had to say. Their heartache and anxiety was great enough already without my adding to it. "I was not mistreated severely," I replied. "Because of the men still in captivity and the effect my statements might have on them and their families I would rather not go into this at this time." He seemed to understand and my answer had apparently satisfied him, but he pursued the point one step further: "Were you threatened with death?"

I wanted to answer, "Yes, every day," but told him no overt threats had been made. The questions were too close in this area and I was not going to commit myself to making an allegation about the execution order I couldn't substantiate. The questions shifted to the amount of base pay I'd accumulated and I began to grin again.

At the end of the conference I felt a slight twinge of disappointment. It would have been delightful to have continued the discussion in which I was engaged. The questions were opening areas of my mind that had been shut down for so long. The opportunity to speak English and drag out a few three- and four-syllable words, not concerned about whether or not I would be understood; the joy of speaking at a normal rate rather than slowly to insure being understood—all of these factors contributed to making this my first encounter with the "sharks" one of the most pleasant experiences of my return.

I said goodbye to Mary Grace, wishing I had more time to spend with her, yet feeling an urgent desire to continue my journey toward home. Lou and I reboarded the C-141 and discovered that Captain Pat O'Donnell had taken over the ship and would be flying us to San Antonio. I had never until my return realized the deep tie established between the men who graduate from our Military Academy. From the time I had climbed aboard that chopper in the Mekong Delta until now I had been strengthened by the presence of classmates, whose joyous welcome I can never hope to repay.

The flight to San Antonio seemed to take only minutes. I chatted with Pat during the flight after he had assured himself all was straight on the flight deck.

Pat returned to the flight deck and soon afterward we were on the ground. I said goodbye to Pat and returned his ring, which had been a symbol for me at a time when I needed guidance. There was no way to express my thanks, but I think he knew instinctively.

The first person in the hatch after it had been opened was Tom Matthews, the information officer at Brooke Army Medical Center. Tom, a tall, soft-spoken retired colonel, immediately distinguished himself in my estimation by handing me a field jacket to ward off the unseasonable cold outside. Tom's easygoing manner and complete control of the situation spoke more eloquently than any words of welcome.

Lou, Tom and I proceeded from the aircraft to a small Operations building amid a barrage of flashbulbs and questions from indistinct faces behind outthrust microphones. I do remember one man who broke from the crowd and came up beside me, grasping my shoulder for a moment, "I escaped from the Nazis," he said. "God bless you." Then he was gone.

We entered the building, Tom briefing me, as we went along, about the press conference to be held there. His concise explanation was almost as if he were giving an operation order and I found myself responding, my mind reacting as it had done so many times in the past, before the capture. I felt a rebirth as Tom dealt with me as an equal rather than one who had to be guided every step of the way.

In the conference room I again sat under an arc of dazzling lights, facing the impersonal eyes of the TV cameras and talking with the reporters assembled there. Many of the men here were from my area of Texas and it was refreshing to talk with them of things I remembered of the Valley. Tom was standing to my left rear and I was able to check with him whenever questions bordered on areas that remained sensitive. It was reassuring to think I couldn't go wrong with him standing there.

The conference seemed to end quite rapidly as Tom indicated that I was to be taken into Brooke Medical Center for evaluation and treatment. The members of the press hesitantly broke off the questions, but obviously respected the need expressed by Tom that I get to the hospital. As I stepped down from the platform, another surprise awaited me. D. K. Allen and Les Beavers, two of my close friends and classmates, were there to greet me. We had spent four years together in the same company at West Point and D. K. and I had been roommates. It was old home week right there as the three of us gripped hands, the unspoken words eloquently felt. I learned that General Westmoreland had assigned them as my escort officers to insure a smooth transition for me back into the outside world. As far as I was concerned, he couldn't have picked two better individuals.

All of us went back to the flightline, where we boarded a Huey for the ride to BAMC. We lifted off and I felt a strange sensation creeping over me. The sound of the blades, the vibration of the ship as we sped toward our destination, the nylon seats, all were part of the picture that was dropping in front of my eyes. Only the countryside was out of place. I unconsciously searched for the broad spreading paddies and crisscross canal pattern that I knew should be down there. I felt a touch of panic and loss of the sense of reality as the buildings, expressways and rolling Texas hill country clashed violently with the image my mind was creating. They seemed so out of place.

It required a bit of reorientation to force the images to coincide but with a large Howard Johnson's sign acting to fix my attention on the reality below, I eliminated the mental scenario.

We landed on the chopper pad in front of the main hospital and took a staff car for the short ride to the entrance. I was greeted by staff members of the hospital and representatives of the M. I. detachment who would be conducting my debriefing. Lou left us to file his interim report on the trip and arrange his stay here for a short while to help with the debriefing. The rest of us proceeded to the second floor. The location of the ward was quite convenient since it was just around the corner from the staircase going to the first floor and adjacent to the elevators. The long hall in the ward, freshly scrubbed, was bordered by a series of rooms and offices. The nursing station featured a delightful young blonde nurse.

My room turned out to be a spacious, well-lit miniature auditorium. I felt as if we could have had a basketball game in it if the ceiling wasn't so low. The idea of staying in a room this large by myself was disturbing. I caught myself estimating how many mosquito nets could be strung inside the room and whistled softly at the final count.

As we stood around chatting, the young nurse lieutenant entered. Before I knew what was happening, I was seated on the edge of the bed with a thermometer in my mouth, and my pulse was being taken while questions were being fired at me to satisfy the information requirements on the admission form. I managed to mumble the answers and my heart was still beating, so I passed the entrance exam.

After that, a corpsman appeared with an evil-looking handful of rubber-topped tubes and what I thought were disposable needles. As I examined the disposable needles, he managed to assemble one with vacuum tube and got me from the blind side. I was out 10 cc of blood before I could say "Ouch!" As quickly as it had begun, the processing was completed, leaving me wondering what had happened. After five years of VC "medics" I wasn't accustomed to skill and efficiency.

I met Lieutenant Colonel Jackson, who was in charge of the ward, and received a short explanation of the tests to be conducted in the following days. I would have wagered heavily against any illness escaping detection after he had finished. If I could survive the tests I would be in good shape.

D. K. and Les returned and we prepared to have supper in the room. It seemed that I was in a semi-quarantine until the preliminary tests proved positive or negative on the presence of any disease that could be contagious. There was no indication that any existed, but the precaution was taken. The primary concern was to clear me as soon as possible so that I could return to McAllen and see my parents.

That night I put a call through to Mom and Dad, telling them I was in San Antonio and would be home soon. The joy in their voices carried a physical impact. The Army had offered to fly them to San Antonio to see me, but Mom had stated that they said goodbye to me at home and they would welcome me back at home. It was my wish, also, to first see my parents there. It wouldn't have been right any other way. They were anxious to see me, but were secure in the knowledge that I was safe and receiving the best of care. We had waited for over five years for the moment, we could wait a few more days.

The laboratory test samples had gone in immediately after they were taken, in order to make as rapid a determination of my condition as possible. I was taken completely by surprise the next morning when the doctors told me I was cleared for a trip home. A helicopter had been assigned to fly me to McAllen, and seventy-two hours with my Mom and Dad. D. K. and Les were exchanging broad, conspiratorial grins as they helped me gather the few articles I'd need for the trip. Les brought clothing to outfit me in civilian attire, contributing one of his own sport coats and vests, and within minutes, I was ready to go.

The Huey lifted off from the runway and I experienced the same almost overpowering exultation as I had that day, so long ago it seemed, when a Huey had lifted me out of the darkness and into the light. It was the sharp, clean sensation of freedom, still a unique strangeness and newness that made the day a holiday. I watched the scenery below, searching for landmarks I remembered from years before, finding them and taking instantaneous pleasure from each rediscovery. I was totally absorbed with my thoughts as I watched the towns pass below, bringing me miles closer to my home; it had been such a long, long journey both in time and in space.

The open cattle land became a checkerboard of cultivated green and the rich deep brown of freshly plowed fields. The first citrus groves came into view and I knew we were nearing home; these groves marked the beginning of the Lower Rio Grande Valley. There were still indications of the hurricane, Beulah, which had struck only months before, but the lush citrus groves and tall, stately palm trees stood as I remembered them in 1963.

Within minutes, the Huey banked gently and passed directly over the center of McAllen as it descended toward the International Airport, south of town. The city had expanded and I looked down eagerly, seeing and identifying familiar streets, Lamar Junior High School, the Methodist church, and finally, what I'd been searching for, my home. The house was a dream I'd seen so many times, the green roof and black wrought iron railings on the wide front porch; the emerald-green carpet grass and wild olive trees; it was difficult to accept the reality of what I was seeing as being more than just a creation of my imagination. The times I'd lain in my mosquito net and this image had been there in front of my eyes; this transition was too rapid, the reality too sudden, but I was cognizant of all the surrounding detail and this was actually happening, the dreaming was over.

We landed and the door slid open. I was aware of the cool air blasting in from the prop thrust and stepped out into it, feeling myself entering the world I had, at times, wondered if I'd ever see again. The terminal buildings had been expanded and the airport had grown since I'd seen it last; I could imagine all the changes that must have taken place in five years, how life had gone on in its normal pace back here while I had been held motionless.

D. K., Les and I walked to the terminal building where a small group of friends, only the few who had been told of my special visit, met us. We were in the car and on the way to the house, some ten minutes away, before I fully recovered from the brief warm welcome. I felt a deep calm settling in as the blocks passed and I neared the house and family I'd waited so long to be with again.

The car stopped in front of the two-story white frame house in which I'd grown up. An American flag stood in the front yard, rippling gently in the slight breeze. My eyes swept the entire scene, catching and holding brief images: the wild olive trees, the chimney, the upstairs windows, the front door. I was walking toward the house, my steps quickening as I was drawn to the source of comfort, guidance and strength I had known as a youth and through young manhood. The front door swung open and my Dad stepped out into the light.

There was only one person in the whole world at that time; everything around me faded in a haze and only the slightly built, silvery-haired man on the porch existed: my Dad. The years dropped away and I knew I was home! I was holding him close, afraid if I let him go he wouldn't be there. "Dad, Dad, I'm sorry I didn't get home sooner; they just wouldn't let me go."

We walked through the door into our living room where Mom waited; had waited for five years, never questioning if I would come back, but only when. She waited here, where we had said goodbye, waited to welcome me home. She rose from the couch and I was hugging her, five long years' worth.

The three of us stood for a long moment, touching, communicating without speaking. My world was complete; I had reached out and touched the light.

ABOUT THE AUTHOR

James N. Rowe is now a lecturer, a spokesman on the MIA and POW issues, and a Special Forces LT. Colonel. As Chief of the Survival, Evasion, Resistance and Escape Training Program for the U.S. Army, he is responsible for training personnel in the four SERE disciplines, and in Anti-Terrorism as well. He is currently stationed in North Carolina.

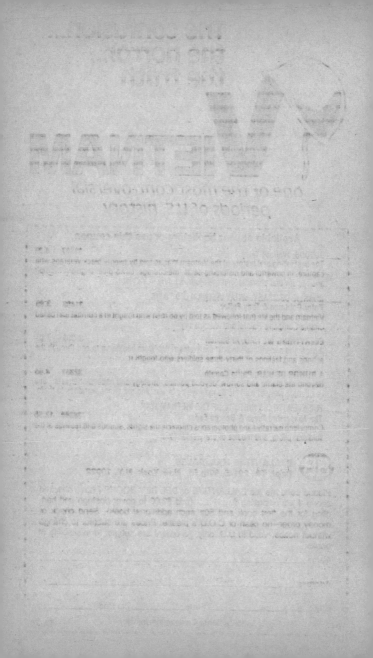